Constructing Realities

Hugh Rosen
Kevin T. Kuehlwein
Editors

Constructing Realities

Meaning-Making Perspectives for Psychotherapists

Jossey-Bass Publishers
San Francisco

The publisher gratefully acknowledges permission received for use of the following: Chapter Two has been adapted from "The Construction of Clinical 'Realities,'" by Paul Watzlawick, in *The Evolution of Psychotherapy: The Second Conference*, edited by Jeffrey K. Zeig, 1992, pp. 55–62, with permission of the author, Brunner/Mazel Inc., and the Milton H. Erikson Foundation.

Chapter Seven: List from "The Politics of Therapy: Putting to Rest the Illusion of Neutrality," an unpublished paper by Michael White, 1995.

Chapter Eight epigraph: Reprinted with the permission of Simon & Schuster Inc. from *The Basic Writings of Bertrand Russell* by Robert E. Egner and Lester E. Danonn. Copyright © 1961 by Allen & Unwin.

Chapter Twelve epigraph: From *Forgotten Truth: The Primordial Tradition* by Huston Smith. Copyright © 1976 by Huston Smith. Reprinted by permission of HarperCollins Publishers, Inc.

Chapter Fourteen epigraph: From "Making Numbers Talk: Language in Therapy," by I. K. Berg and S. de Shazer, in S. Friedman (Ed.), *The New Language of Change: Constructive Collaboration in Psychotherapy*, p. 7. Copyright © 1993 by Guilford Press.

Substantial discounts on bulk quantities of Jossey-Bass books are available to corporations, professional associations, and other organizations. For details and discount information, contact the special sales department at Jossey-Bass Inc., Publishers. (415) 433–1740; Fax (800) 605–2665.

For sales outside the United States, please contact your local Simon & Schuster International Office.

 Manufactured in the United States of America on Lyons Falls Pathfinder Tradebook. This paper is acid-free and 100 percent totally chlorine-free.

Library of Congress Cataloging-in-Publication Data

Constructing realities : meaning-making perspectives for
   psychotherapists / Hugh Rosen and Kevin T. Kuehlwein, editors.
       p.   cm. — (The Jossey-Bass social and behavioral science
   series)
     Includes bibliographical references and index.
     ISBN 0-7879-0195-4
     1. Psychotherapy—Philosophy.   2. Constructivism (Psychology)
   3. Construction (Philosophy)   I. Rosen, Hugh.   II. Kuehlwein, Kevin
   T., [date].   III. Series.
   RC437.5.C646   1996
   616.89'14'01—dc20   95-37811

HB Printing   10 9 8 7 6 5 4 3 2 1   FIRST EDITION

Contents

Preface

The central motif of *Constructing Realities* is meaning-making and its implications for psychotherapy. Yet this is also a book of multiple perspectives, bringing together many diverse voices and viewpoints on its subject. It is based on the premise that human beings, both individually and in concert with one another, actively construct and co-construct meaning out of their life experiences, as opposed to receiving knowledge in pure form directly from the external world. In our view, meaning-making and the reconstruction of meaning is pivotal to the process of psychotherapy, and this book was written with the practicing psychotherapist in mind. However, it is neither a manual nor a cookbook of techniques. It is not designed for a narrow band of therapists working from a single model that purports to be the one true way to do therapy. Similarly, it is not for those therapists who are seeking a secure base of absolutism in the model they ultimately hope to embrace. The views of our contributing authors by no means constitute a consensus, and although all the chapters converge on the meaning-making theme, they nevertheless open up divergent worlds of thought about conceptualizing and practicing psychotherapy. In selecting our contributors, we intentionally sought scholar-practitioners from diverse quarters within the field of psychotherapy, theorists and therapists unified essentially only by their shared meaning-making orientation. The reader will encounter themes of narrative, constructivism, social constructionism, postmodernism, epistemology, developmental constructivism, language, and social discourse—all contributing to the contemporary dialogue on the nexus between meaning-making and psychotherapy.

Further, because the ideas presented here are metatheoretical, they are applicable across the entire range of therapeutic schools. They have the potential to enrich the work of any practicing psychotherapist and to infuse new vitality, meaning, and direction into preexisting models, be they psychodynamic, cognitive-behavioral, humanistic-existential, or some other variation of therapeutic practice. In the same fashion, the theoretical and case-based stories told in this book will hold interest and meaning for therapists ranging across the mental health disciplines within psychology, social work, psychiatry, and nursing and also those therapists who have entered the field through alternate routes. This is a book that will also be of significance and use to students, trainees, teachers, supervisors, and experienced clinicians alike. Individual members of each group will find that they will proactively make meaning out of the chapters of *Constructing Realities*, based upon their own personal and professional knowledge paradigms, which they will bring along with them as they journey through this book.

This book's ideas and perspectives have the potential and the power to enrich and transform the way therapists construe their work and their clients as well as their own selves. Indeed, such enrichment may have already occurred for some chapter contributors. It is remarkable how many of them have conveyed to us that to their surprise, writing their chapter turned out to be one of the hardest writing assignments of their careers; yet upon completion, they felt as if they had gone beyond themselves to reach new creative heights.

Overview of the Contents

Part I and Chapter One present an orienting framework as Hugh Rosen surveys critical ideas, perspectives, and movements that char-

acterize meaning-making. The organizing themes are constructivism, social constructionism, narrative theory, developmental constructivism, and postmodernism, and the chapter serves as a window
through which the reader may more clearly glimpse the multiple
meanings of the stories and narratives that follow.

Part II examines constructivist and social constructionist epistemology and praxis and contains Chapters Two, Three, and Four.
Chapter Two, the only reprinted chapter in this collection, is a significant paper by Paul Watzlawick, presented at the second Evolution of Psychotherapy Conference, in 1990. Watzlawick disavows
that people ever come to know any absolute reality. Even clinical
"realities" are actually socially constructed phenomena. Psychotherapy, for Watzlawick, consists of taking an old fictional version of reality that is not working and reframing it into a new
fictional version that does work.

In Chapter Three, Jay S. Efran and Mitchell A. Greene advocate that psychotherapists use Maturana's epistemological model of
structure determinism as a compass to find their way through the
complex maze of therapeutic theory and practice. In what may well
be one of the clearest expositions of Maturana's work available, they
describe its implications for therapy as conversation within the
social domain. Their radical constructivist view clearly depicts what
they believe therapy is about—and what it need not be about.

Sheila McNamee, in Chapter Four, reflexively examines the
practice of psychotherapy itself through the lens of social constructionism. In the process, she deconstructs psychotherapy within the
context of its modernist roots and then reconstructs it; the resulting transformed psychotherapy is a phenomenon of postmodernism.
The shift is from an essentialist and individualist orientation to psychotherapy, characterizing the modern era, to a constructionist and
relational orientation, the postmodern emphasis.

Part III, encompassing Chapters Five, Six, and Seven, views the
social context of construing. In Chapter Five, Carolyn Saari, writing
from a psychodynamic perspective, presents a view of identity as a

meaning system that derives from an ongoing dialogical process within a social matrix. Identity is viewed not as a fixed essence but as that which evolves over time through interpersonal transactions. Psychotherapy itself is conceived of as an interpersonal interaction leading to the creation of new meanings.

In Chapter Six, Nancy Rule Goldberger presents theories and research findings on ways of knowing as meaning-making frameworks. The emphasis is on women's epistemological styles and development. "Separate knowing," more commonly found among men, is contrasted to "connected knowing," more commonly found among women. The metaphors of "silence" and "voice" as they relate to women's often marginalized status are explored within the psychotherapeutic context.

In Chapter Seven, William D. Lax bridges East and West as he compares the ancient Buddhist tradition of insight meditation to the postmodern take on cultural stories. In his view, just as meditation liberates the individual from identifying with and becoming entrapped in his or her own thoughts, so might psychotherapy liberate the client (and the therapist) from reifying and becoming embedded in his or her privileged cultural stories (or theories).

Part IV, comprising Chapters Eight and Nine, analyzes the construction of affect. In Chapter Eight, Elma P. Nunley and James R. Averill delineate a social constructionist view of emotion, discussing rules and myths about emotions and considering the nature of emotional creativity. They explore the implications of these facets of emotion for the kinds of couples workshops that they conduct and for individual psychotherapy. While a social constructionist approach is applicable to all emotions in clinical treatment, what is highlighted in this chapter is the emotion of love.

In Chapter Nine, Jeanne C. Watson and Leslie S. Greenberg depict a dialectical constructivist model that is the foundation for their views on emotion theory and experiential therapy. From this perspective, therapy is construed as the creation of meaning through a complex dialectical synthesis involving both emotion and cognition. The implications of this meaning-making approach to emotion for the practice of experiential therapy are developed as the chapter proceeds.

Part V, ranging across Chapters Ten, Eleven, and Twelve, discusses constructivist metatheory in psychotherapy integration. In Chapter Ten, Stephen Soldz discusses the interface between constructivism and psychoanalysis. He explores constructivist trends surfacing in psychoanalytic thought and highlights the potential for cross-fertilization between the two orientations. Soldz examines the meaning-making tradition primarily in terms of Kelly's personal construct theory. He sees constructivism as providing a metatheoretical framework for understanding psychotherapy and a metalanguage for discourse across therapeutic models.

Robert L. Russell and Mary L. Wandrei, in Chapter Eleven, discuss the use of narrative as a distinguishing characteristic of human beings and a major way through which individuals structure their experiences. After locating narrative within the context of broader intellectual currents, they discuss narrative constructivism in the psychopathology and clinical treatment of both children and adults. They also emphasize the significance of both personal narrative constructions and societal and cultural narratives.

In Chapter Twelve, Mary Baird Carlsen discusses the creative role of metaphor in the process of psychotherapy. Metaphor is presented as a heuristic device for meaning-making in individuals' lives and as a reflection of how clients in psychotherapy may undergo a process of metamorphosis. Throughout the chapter, Carlsen's own literary style evokes the meaning-making power of metaphor.

Part VI, containing Chapters Thirteen, Fourteen, and Fifteen, presents examples of the personal implications of constructivist and social constructionist psychotherapy. In Chapter Thirteen, Robert A. Neimeyer first discusses how Kelly's personal construct theory has served as a home base for him, providing a metatheoretical lens for organizing seemingly disparate approaches of different therapeutic models. He then introduces a taxonomy of conversational process interventions for the constructivist psychotherapist, derived from a self-reflective examination of his own evolving practice over the years. Neimeyer's work serves as an exemplar of an eminent scholar-practitioner's willingness to expose his fledgling ideas to his colleagues in the hope of creating new meaning through the process.

Steven Friedman, in Chapter Fourteen, presents therapeutic conversations through which the therapist facilitates the process of couples' finding and creating new meanings in their relationships. Deemphasizing problem talk, his work is solution focused and competency based and is predicated upon what he views as postmodern implications for the therapeutic relationship and process. He sees the work he presents here as a therapy of "possibilities."

Robert L. Selman, Steven Brion-Meisels, and Gregory G. Wilkins, in Chapter Fifteen, offer a detailed exposition of their application of a developmental constructivist approach to treating conduct-disordered adolescents in a residential treatment center. They focus on enhancing the adolescents' interpersonal negotiating strategies through promoting the youths' developmental progression. The progression is expected to lead adolescents to use more adaptive ways of making meaning out of interpersonal relationships.

Part VII, consisting of Chapter Sixteen, closes the book with an integrating framework for all the chapters, as Kevin T. Kuehlwein, applying the metaphor of a quilt, brings together the diverse patterns and threads from the various chapter authors. He notes both creative tensions and harmonies throughout their themes, foci, and images; and he draws out larger meanings from their various realities.

Acknowledgments

We would like to acknowledge all our contributors for their dedication and commitment to making this book a success. We thank Becky McGovern, our acquisitions editor, for her faith in our abilities as well as her support and counsel along the way. Our thanks also go to Katie Levine for facilitating the movement of our manuscript through the process at critical junctures. We are fully appreciative of and grateful for the careful attention given by Michele Hubinger, our project editor, to our manuscript. Our thanks also go to all of the many people at Jossey-Bass whose efforts behind the scenes helped bring this work to fruition. We were blessed with two very thoughtful and thorough prepublication reviewers, William J. Lyddon and Stephanie Harter, to whom we are indebted. Lastly, we thank Tonya Meadows, whose secretarial competence and patience proved invaluable to us.

Hugh Rosen's Acknowledgments

I would like to acknowledge my friends and colleagues Pam Buccelli and Carol Jacques for their loyalty and encouragement over the years. My thanks also go to Will Green, dean of the School of Health Sciences and Humanities at the Medical College of Pennsylvania and Hahnemann University, for maintaining an ambiance of congeniality and collegiality in which creativity can flourish. To my brother and sister (in order of appearance), I owe a debt for their emotional support and love over a lifetime. To the memory of my parents, I pay tribute, knowing that they would have been pleased to see the publication of this book. I would also like to thank John and Linda Gist, as well as their son Evan, for their enduring and loving friendship and for the interest they continue to display in my professional projects. Last but not least, I would like to acknowledge my best friend and coeditor, Kevin Kuehlwein, for co-constructing with me wonderfully new and vital meanings over the last thirteen years.

Kevin T. Kuehlwein's Acknowledgments

I would like to thank the many people who have helped me construct my visions of the world, including pointing out these visions' functional inadequacies from time to time. First, my parents, Robert and Teresa Kuehlwein; my brother, Michael; and my sister, Shannon, for their lifelong support and confidence in me. Next, my clients, who have at times inspired, puzzled, and/or challenged me to create new bridges for crossing over into better mutual understandings. Third, my friends Jim Hess, Brad Carey, Dennis Sharkey, Guillaume Lovelle, Lamar Freed, and Susan Moyer, who have all nurtured me in important ways over the years. Lastly, I owe an incalculable debt of gratitude to my two-time coeditor and all-time wonderful friend, Hugh Rosen. He has seen and helped me evolve over the past thirteen years into an inquiring student of the world. He has helped me most of all to glimpse and utilize a playful, creative spirit in making meaning out of this puzzle we call life.

Philadelphia, Pennsylvania   Hugh Rosen
November 1995   Kevin T. Kuehlwein

The Editors

. . . .

Hugh Rosen is professor and interim chairperson of the Department of Mental Health Sciences, School of Health Sciences and Humanities, at the Medical College of Pennsylvania and Hahnemann University. He is also associate dean for graduate education in the School of Health Sciences and Humanities. He was the first faculty member to receive the Distinguished Faculty Award of the school and is also a recipient of the Lindback Award for teaching excellence. Rosen received his B.S. degree (1958) from St. Joseph's University in Philadelphia, with a double major in English and philosophy. He was awarded his M.S.W. degree (1962) from the University of Pennsylvania and his D.S.W. degree (1979) from the Columbia University School of Social Work. He has written three books, including *Piagetian Dimensions of Clinical Relevance* (1985). He is coeditor of *Constructivist Perspectives on Developmental Psychopathology and Atypical Development* (with D. P. Keating, 1991) and *Cognitive Therapies in Action: Evolving Innovative Practice* (with K. T. Kuehlwein, 1993). He is also a member of the editorial board of the *Journal of Constructivist Psychology*. Rosen received training in cognitive therapy through an extramural program conducted under the leadership of Aaron T. Beck at the Center for Cognitive Therapy at the University of Pennsylvania, and he has also completed a three year gestalt therapy training program at the Gestalt Therapy Institute of Philadelphia. He has had lifelong interests in moral issues, clear thinking, personal transformation, creativity, and epistemology.

Kevin T. Kuehlwein served as the first clinical coordinator of the Beck Institute for Cognitive Therapy and Research, in suburban Philadelphia. He is currently a staff psychologist and clinical associate at the Center for Cognitive Therapy at the University of Pennsylvania, where he completed a postdoctoral fellowship in 1991. He received his B.A. degree (1983) from Swarthmore College, in psychology, and his Psy.D. degree (1989) from the Clinical Psychology Program at Hahnemann University (now the Medical College of Pennsylvania and Hahnemann University). He taught cognitive-behavioral therapy at Hahnemann University for several years and is currently adjunct assistant professor at the Medical College of Pennsylvania and Hahnemann University. He has trained numerous therapists in the cognitive therapy model and also lectured internationally on this topic. He authored a chapter on the use of cognitive therapy in fostering positive self-identity in gay men for the *Comprehensive Casebook of Cognitive Therapy* (edited by Freeman and Dattilio, 1993). Kuehlwein is also the coeditor of *Cognitive Therapies in Action: Evolving Innovative Practice* (with H. Rosen, 1993). His early interest in meaning-making approaches was reflected in his dissertation topic, the social construction of adulthood. In 1990, with Hugh Rosen, he co-led a series of cognitive-experiential therapy groups to assist HIV-positive men to cope more effectively with stress. His interests include the use of metaphor and bibliotherapy and the use of cognitive therapy with minority groups to promote empowerment and improved self-image. He maintains a part-time private practice.

The Contributors

James R. Averill is professor of psychology in the Personality and Social Psychology Program at the University of Massachusetts, Amherst. He received his Ph.D. degree (1966) in physiological psychology from the University of California at Los Angeles. Averill has published four books, including *Voyages of the Heart: Living an Emotionally Creative Life* (with E. P. Nunley, 1992). He has authored numerous journal articles and book chapters and is a consulting editor for three journals, including *Cognition and Emotion*. His current research focuses on emotional creativity and aesthetics of the natural environment.

Steven Brion-Meisels received his Ph.D. degree (1976) from the University of Utah, in educational psychology. He has been adjunct faculty member at the Harvard Graduate School of Education, Lesley College, the University of Reyjkavík (Iceland), and the University of Utah. His professional work has involved linking theory with practice in the service of social change. His publications have focused on the integration of academic and social literacy through means of the curriculum within a classroom context.

Mary Baird Carlsen is a clinical psychologist in Walla Walla, Washington. She received her Ph.D. degree (1973) in adult development at the University of Washington. After spending sixteen years in private practice, she currently serves as teacher/consultant in the areas of life transitions and creative aging. Carlsen is the author of two books: *Meaning-Making: Therapeutic Processes in Adult Development* (1988) and *Creative Aging: A Meaning-Making Perspective* (1991), and she has crossed interdisciplinary lines to do research and writing in adult development, constructivist psychology, creativity and aging, meaning-making, psychotherapy, and career development.

Jay S. Efran is professor of psychology and director of the Psychological Services Center at Temple University, in Philadelphia, where he has also served as director of clinical training. He is the coauthor of *Language, Structure and Change: Frameworks of Meaning in Psychotherapy* (with M. D. Lukens and R. J. Lukens, 1990), and he has written extensively on issues of contextualism and constructivism. Efran received his Ph.D. degree (1963) in clinical psychology from Ohio State University.

Steven Friedman is a psychologist and family therapist at the Braintree Massachusetts Center of Harvard Community Health Plan, a health organization based in New England. He received his Ph.D. degree (1971) from Boston University, in psychology. Friedman coauthored *Expanding Therapeutic Possibilities: Getting Results in Brief Psychotherapy* (with M. T. Fanger, 1991) and is the editor of *The New Language of Change: Constructive Collaboration in Psychotherapy* (1993) and *The Reflecting Team in Action: Innovations in Family Therapy* (1995).

Nancy Rule Goldberger is a member of the clinical psychology faculty of the Fielding Institute, an innovative doctoral distance-learning institution for midcareer professionals. She received her Ph.D. degree (1966) in clinical psychology from New York University. She is coauthor of *Women's Ways of Knowing* (with F. Belenky, B. M. Clinchy, and J. M. Tarule, 1986) and coeditor of *The*

Culture and Psychology Reader (with J. Veroff, 1995). Goldberger has published widely on the topics of women's development and epistemology, innovative education, adolescence, and intellectual and ethical development.

Leslie S. Greenberg is professor of psychology at York University, in Ontario, and director of the Psychotherapy Research Centre. He received his Ph.D. degree (1975) in clinical psychology from York University. A past president of the Society for Psychotherapy Research, Greenberg is in private practice in Toronto and also trains therapists in emotionally focused approaches to treatment. He has written a number of books with colleagues on psychotherapy research and emotion in psychotherapy, the most recent of which is *Facilitating Emotional Change* (with L. Rice and R. Elliot, 1993). His forthcoming books include *Working with Emotion* and two edited texts: *The Therapeutic Alliance* and *Emotion in Marriage and Marital Therapy*. He has published extensively in the area of research on individual and couples therapy and is on the editorial board of a number of journals. He is currently conducting a National Institute of Mental Health–funded research project on experiential change processes in depression.

Mitchell A. Greene is head clinic assistant of the Psychological Services Center at Temple University, in Philadelphia, where he is also completing his doctoral studies in clinical psychology. He received an M.A. degree (1994) in clinical psychology from Temple University. Greene has previously conducted research on the residential instability patterns of homeless substance abusers and is now studying issues of acculturation in Hispanic American families.

William D. Lax is associate chairperson of the Department of Clinical Psychology at Antioch New England Graduate School, in Keene, New Hampshire, and a staff psychologist at Brattleboro Family Institute, in Vermont. He received his Ph.D. degree (1983) in clinical psychology from the Fielding Institute. Lax's publications include articles on the reflecting process and postmodern thinking in clinical practice. His current interests, exemplified by his chapter in this book, include the narrative approach of Michael White, postmodernism, and Buddhist thought and practice.

Sheila McNamee is chair and associate professor of communication at the University of New Hampshire. She received her Ph.D. degree (1982) from the University of Massachusetts at Amherst, in interpersonal communication and communication theory. McNamee has also trained and practiced as a family therapist. She lectures internationally and has published extensively. She is coeditor of *Therapy as Social Construction* (with K. J. Gergen, 1992) and currently is writing a book (also with Kenneth Gergen) on the concept of relational responsibility.

Robert A. Neimeyer is a professor in the Department of Psychology, University of Memphis, in Memphis, Tennessee, where he also maintains an active private practice. He received his Ph.D. degree (1982) in psychology from the University of Nebraska. Neimeyer has published twelve books, including *The Development of Personal Construct Psychology* (1985), *Personal Construct Therapy Casebook* (coedited with G. J. Neimeyer, 1987), and *Constructivism in Psychotherapy* (coedited with M. J. Mahoney, 1995). He is coeditor of the *Journal of Constructivist Psychology* (with G. J. Neimeyer) and serves on the editorial boards of a number of other journals. He is the author of over one hundred articles and book chapters.

Elma P. Nunley is a clinician whose extensive counseling practice includes adults and adolescents. She received her Ed.D. degree (1985) in counseling psychology from the International Graduate School, a division of the World University System. She is coauthor of *Voyages of the Heart: Living an Emotionally Creative Life* (with J. R. Averill, 1992).

Robert L. Russell is currently professor of psychology at Loyola University of Chicago. His main areas of interest are psychotherapy process and outcome research, developmental psychopathology, pragmatic development, philosophy of science, and postmodernism. He has edited two books on psychotherapy research—*Language in Psychotherapy: Strategies of Discovery* (1987) and *Reassessing Psychotherapy Research* (1994)—and has written two books soon to be published—*Essentials of Child Psychotherapy* (with S. Shirk) and *Narrative Discourse in Psychotherapy*. In 1989, he received the early career contribution award of the Society for Psychotherapy Research.

Carolyn Saari is a professor in the School of Social Work at Loyola University of Chicago and has also taught at the Smith College School for Social Work and the Institute for Clinical Social Work, in Chicago. She received her Ph.D. degree (1973) in social work from Smith College. Saari is the author of two books—*Clinical Social Work Treatment: How Does It Work?* (1986) and *The Creation of Meaning in Clinical Social Work* (1991)—and the editor of the *Clinical Social Work Journal*. She maintains a private practice in Chicago.

Robert L. Selman is professor of education at the Harvard Graduate School of Education and professor of psychology in the Department of Psychiatry at the Harvard Medical School. At the Harvard Medical School, he is also cochair of the steering committee of the Manville School of the Judge Baker Children's Center. Selman received his Ph.D. degree (1969) from Boston University, in counseling, clinical, and community psychology. He is the author of *The Growth of Interpersonal Understanding* (1980) and coauthor of *Making a Friend in Youth* (with L. Schultz, 1990). In addition, he has written scores of articles on social development.

Stephen Soldz is director of evaluation for Associates for Human Potential, in Boston. He is also assistant clinical professor of psychology at Harvard Medical School at the Beth Israel Hospital, where he is involved with the Harvard Center for Psychotherapy Research. Soldz is also director of research at the Boston Institute for Psychotherapy and a faculty member at the Boston Center for Modern Psychoanalytic Studies. He is on the editorial board of the *International Journal of Constructivist Psychology*. He received his Ph.D. degree (1986) from Boston University, in clinical psychology. Soldz maintains a private practice of psychotherapy in Brookline, Massachusetts.

Mary L. Wandrei is lecturer and psychotherapy extern at Loyola University of Chicago. She received her M.A. degree (1993) in psychology from Loyola University of Chicago, where she is currently a doctoral candidate. Her theoretical and empirical work is in linguistic representations of subjectivity in psychotherapy, postmodern and feminist epistemologies, and women's career decision making.

Jeanne C. Watson is an assistant professor at the University of Windsor, in Ontario, where she teaches, conducts research, and provides clinical supervision. She is a proponent of the experiential approach to psychotherapy. She received her Ph.D. degree (1993) in clinical psychology at York University, in Ontario. She is actively involved at York University in a National Institute of Mental Health research project (with L. Greenberg), investigating the efficacy of experiential psychotherapy in the treatment of depression.

Paul Watzlawick received his Ph.D. degree (1949) in philosophy and modern languages from the University of Vienna. He has been a research associate at the Mental Research Institute, in Palo Alto, California, since 1961. He is also clinical professor in the Department of Psychiatry and Behavioral Sciences, Stanford University Medical Center. Watzlawick is the author, coauthor, or editor of twelve books and scores of articles and book chapters. His books include *Change: Principles of Problem Formation and Problem Resolution* (with J. Weakland and R. Fisch, 1974), *How Real Is Real* (1976), and *The Invented Reality: How Do We Know What We Believe We Know? Contributions to Constructivism* (edited collection, 1984). He has lectured widely in the United States and abroad and has worked as a consultant to international corporations.

Gregory G. Wilkins received his Ph.D. degree (1977) in clinical psychology from the University of Florida. He has held a number of clinical, administrative, and research positions. Currently, as director of research and clinical training at the Brandywine Treatment Center of the Devereux Foundation, his primary research and clinical training interests include disruptive behavioral disorders, developmental psychopathology, psychometrics, and the use of pair therapy and animal-facilitated therapy in residential treatment settings. During the last several years, he has been investigating the influence of social relationships with animals and contact with nature on human behavior and health.

Part I

An Orienting Framework

Meaning-Making Narratives

Foundations for Constructivist and Social Constructionist Psychotherapies

Hugh Rosen

*Why would anyone in his or her right mind not want
to use what's left? And why would anyone in his or
her left mind not want to do what's right? Indeed, it is
only when both sides of the embodied mind are integrally collaborating that the whole person is making
meaning and is interacting meaningfully with others.
When two such embodied minds enter into dialogue,
there is the further potential for a synergistic co-
construction of new and novel meanings emerging
between them.*

Co-constructed by Hugh Rosen and Kevin T. Kuehlwein

This is a book about meaning-making and its implications for
psychotherapy. Although this opening chapter is organized,
inescapably, in a visually linear fashion, I have designed it so that
conceptual matters are overlapping and interlocking. The meaning-making motif confers coherence upon the multiple voices whose
sounds and stories travel through the labyrinths of the chapter.
Human beings are meaning-making creatures, and they will spin
their webs of meaning throughout all of time, much as they have
been doing ever since the dawn of awareness. As for psychotherapy,
there are many ways of construing it, but a view of it as a dialogical
process between two or more persons, leading to the reconstruction

of old meanings and the creation of new meanings, is congenial to the present context. Taking a similar construal of therapy to a second-order level, Gergen (1994a) has suggested that it is a "transformative dialogue," which "is a progression from learning new meanings to developing new categories of meaning to transforming one's premises about the nature of meaning itself" (p. 250).

The purpose of this chapter is to provide a broad survey of the ideas, perspectives, and movements that have the human construction of reality as a central theme. The major headings covered are constructivism, social constructionism, narrative theory, developmental constructivism (largely a view of the Piagetian paradigm), and postmodernism. In addition to outlining key tenets of each perspective and movement, I cite selected literature for further reference, and I offer some thoughts on the relation of major perspectives to psychoanalysis.

The Meaning of Constructivism

In the foreword to his novel *The Magus*, John Fowles tells us that he despairs of ever convincing contemporary students to cease expecting that he can or will reveal this novel's meaning to them. In fact, he contends that the novel is like the Rorschach test; it requires that the reader determine the significance of the work for himself or herself: "Its meaning is whatever reaction it provokes in the reader, and so far as I am concerned there is no given 'right' reaction" (Fowles, 1965, p. 10). This is a view that would seem to be shared by Bruner (1986), who writes, "In the end, it is the reader who must write for himself what *he* intends to do with the actual text" (p. 24). And what if all the world is a text, written, perhaps, by an unknown author? Be it literary fiction or natural world, the "reader" of it is not the passive recipient of received knowledge but must take the stance of an active agent who constructs and organizes meanings out of life's encounters. No one ventures into the world without a text of his or her own in mind, and thus each person's interpretations of the natural and social worlds are based, in large measure, upon a reading of the pages of that interior text.

While there are a variety of constructivist models, they all hold in common the epistemological belief that a totally objective reality, one that stands apart from the knowing subject, can never be fully known. They reject the correspondence theory of truth, which postulates that our mental representations mirror an objective reality, "out there," as it truly is. Rather, knowledge, and the meaning we imbue it with, is a construction of the human mind. The way we represent what we know to ourselves does not bear a one-to-one correspondence with a given external reality existing independently of our knowledge of it (Rorty, 1979). Bruner (1986) expresses the hope that we will teach young people "an appreciation of the fact that many worlds are possible, that meaning and reality are created and not discovered" (p. 149). It is our own personal truth, with its inner coherence and internal logic, that we construct (Guidano, 1987), and the constructions that constitute this personal truth cannot not be evaluated by a standard of comparison that posits an objective reality. Therefore, constructivism is concerned with the adaptive utility of these personal constructions for the individual or social unit embracing them. It is concerned with the fit of any one construction within the total ecology of the individual's construct system or the social group into which that system is integrated (Neimeyer, 1993b). As Mahoney (1988a) states, "The key issue in therapy is the pragmatic utility, rather than the bedrock validity, of the client's system of understanding" (p. 5).

(Recent books that pursue the implications of constructivism for psychotherapy include Duncan, Solovey, and Rusk, 1992; Mahoney, 1995; and Neimeyer and Mahoney, 1995.)

A Constructivist Epistemological Spectrum

There is a tendency in the literature on constructivism to conflate ontology and epistemology. As might be expected, this is a source of confusion at times. *Ontology* is a study of the nature of being, whereas *epistemology* is concerned with the nature of knowledge. The two areas of study are related, of course. For example, if one were to posit the commonsense ontological notion that a material world exists independently of our perceptions or mental representations of it (that is, a metaphysical realism), that idea would lead to a series of epistemological questions regarding whether we can ever know anything of the world as it really is and what the means are through which we come to know whatever it is that we do know. To illustrate, David Kelley (1986) believes that we perceive reality exactly as it is. There are no inferences, representations, or constitutive activities necessary for this accomplishment. Furthermore, what we see has independent ontological status apart from our perception, and what we perceive imparts immediate knowledge to us of things as they are. This view is a radical form of realism, which does not even posit that a mental representation must correspond to an independent object in order to have truth value.

Radical Constructivism

Mahoney (1991) has suggested that *radical constructivists* tend to fall into the ontological camp of idealism. While I believe that some radical constructivist writings imply a metaphysical reality, particularly in the case of Watzlawick (1990), for all practical purposes radical constructivists have banished metaphysical reality from their epistemological worldview: there is no reality that extends beyond the individual's own experience. They take an extreme position on the absolute unknowability of a world beyond our own mental system of knowing. All that we know is determined by the psychological structure of our minds, rooted in a complex neuropsychological network. What we know does not mirror a reality out there. Our minds constitute autonomous knowing systems that are closed systems with respect to input from any outside world. The following discussion of three of the major figures generally regarded as radical constructivists expands upon these ideas.

Humberto R. Maturana

I find the antithesis of Kelley's radical realism to be exemplified in the work of Humberto R. Maturana (Efran, Lukens, & Lukens, 1990; Maturana, 1988; Maturana & Varela, 1987). In Maturana's epistemology, no independent reality to speak of exists. Each person has his or her own worldview, but it would be misleading to think of this worldview as a personal map of reality, for there is no independent terrain from which to draw such a map (Elkaim, 1990). Maturana should not be mistaken to mean that an objectively existing independent reality may be interpreted by each person in different ways, as if there existed one universe that is then diversely construed. This distinction is particularly salient from a therapeutic standpoint: Maturana asserts that each member of a family does not simply have his or her own view of a single objective family system but rather that each member has an equally valid construal of the family system, constituted by that member's own experience. There is no independent objective family system that exists in addition to, or outside of, the varied personal construals (Simon, 1985). To reinforce his view, Maturana (1988, p. 30) typically writes "objectivity" in parentheses to give recognition to its subjectivist, that is, its personally constructed, nature. What do exist are *multiverses*, all the individual worldviews of existing people; what does not exist is a single universe about which each person has a viewpoint. For Maturana, "Outside language nothing (no thing) exists because existence is bound to our distinctions in language" (1988, p. 80). As we use language to make distinctions, therefore, it is our selves that we are illuminating and not an objective world. It is perhaps since Maturana is himself a biologist that his radical constructivism is biologically rooted, emphasizing the structures and functions of both the brain and the nervous system as the source of meaning-making. This is a very different emphasis than that of the social constructionists, whom we shall turn to later in this chapter, with their strong focus on dialogue and culture. (However, see Chapter

Three for a discussion from a radical constructivist perspective of language as socially contextualized.)

Ernst von Glaserfeld

Ernst von Glaserfeld (1981, 1984) is by self-definition also a radical constructivist. While he does accord ontological status to a world independent of the observer, he denies any possibility that the observer might ever acquire an accurate or true knowledge of that world. He considers a correspondence theory of reality untenable since the observer can never transcend his or her own representation of reality in order to match it against the true picture of reality, to which the personal representation must correspond to be objectively accurate. Hence, since we never have direct access to any objective reality, there can be no way for us to verify our mentally constructed representations as true to reality.

Thus, in his theoretical writing, von Glaserfeld chooses to replace the commonly used word "adaptation" with the word "viability" because adaptation suggests an internal change in an organism to *match* a structural modification in the environment. To employ adaptation would be to talk knowingly about features of an independently existing world; a world that we can know nothing about, according to radical constructivism. Further, it is not the environment, as suggested by the word adaptation, that produces structural changes in the organism that correspond to the environment. Instead, the changes in the organism derive from its own "inherent variability" (von Glaserfeld, 1981, p. 90). Put another way, for von Glaserfeld, adaptation means nothing more than to be viable, or in a state of fit, in relation to our experience. As he states: "The fact that some construct has for some time survived experience—or experiments for that matter—means that up to that point it was viable in that it bypassed constraints that were inherent in the range of experience within which we were operating. But viability does not imply uniqueness, because there may be innumerable other constructs that would have been as viable as the one we created" (1981, p. 93).

The environment does impose constraints that could lead to the extinction of ideas or organisms, but even given those constraints, various solutions that sustain survival may be possible. The question is not whether our knowledge is true but whether it promotes the achievement of our purposes. Even at those times when the constraints of the world confront us, we do not know them as such, for we can know only our own constructions and experience of those constraints. Thus, the constraints we are subject to derive not only from our environment but from within ourselves as well. For as Mahoney (1991) has so succinctly put it, "Our private assumptions and ingrained beliefs constitute everpresent anticipations and constraints on what and how we experience" (p. 25).

Paul Watzlawick

Paul Watzlawick (1984) has played a major role in bringing to prominence such significant radical constructivists as von Glaserfeld (1984) and von Foerster (1984) and even includes himself in this category (see Chapter Two). Nevertheless, in my own understanding of his work, he has taken a more moderate position on constructivism. He refers freely to enabling the client to reframe situations while in the therapeutic context (Watzlawick, 1990; Watzlawick, Weakland, & Fisch, 1974), thereby seeming to give credence to the objectivity of the client's problematic situation in its raw form while highlighting the client's capacity for shifting his or her subjective perspective on any particular situation or event. Watzlawick (1990) explicitly refers to objects as having properties and characterizes these properties as constituting "reality of the first order." This first-order reality is the "universe of 'facts' which can be established objectively in as much as the repetition of the same experiment yields the same result independently of by whom, when, and where the experiment is being carried out" (p. 243). (That is hardly a description of ontological idealism as attributed to radical constructivists.) Watzlawick contends that a serious limitation in this conception is that reality of the first order contains no basis for imparting meaning to its facts. The construction of meaning and the attribution of value does not reside in the external world of objects and facts but in the mental activity of the knowing subject. From this mental activity arises reality of the second order. One reframing, or alternative perspective, in second-order reality is neither more right nor wrong than another. The essential criterion for assessment is again the pragmatic one that takes into account which fiction produces the desired practical results.

I am reminded, on a grander scale, of the classic novel *Of Human Bondage*, by Somerset Maugham (1915/1963), in which the protagonist, Philip, sees life as meaningless. In a dialogue on the subject of life's meaning, Philip is told by his companion, Cronshaw, to visit a particular museum in order to observe Persian carpets, with their exquisite colors and intricately beautiful patterns. He is told that if he does this, then eventually he will come to understand the meaning of life. Philip's only response at the moment is to find Cronshaw's remarks puzzling. In my construal of Cronshaw's cryptic comments, he is saying that the threads of our life, some of which are given at birth and others of which we acquire along the way, do indeed have no meaning in themselves (they are first-order facts). However, like the artist who weaves a Persian carpet, we are free to weave and reweave these threads of our lives into beautiful and meaningful designs to suit our purposes (the meaning we give to the designs are second-order reality). What Maugham writes of Philip at the end of the story is in keeping with this interpretation: "He thought of his desire to make a design, intricate and beautiful, out of the myriad, meaningless facts of life" (p. 606). We find a more intense reflection of the same idea in those Holocaust survivors who could cultivate the will to live in order to bear witness afterward and even find meaning in their suffering (Frankl, 1985). Their example should bring hope to those who despair of weaving lives for themselves that embody purpose and meaning.

Critical Constructivism

As Mahoney (1991) makes clear, constructivism does not necessarily preclude openly embracing a position of hypothetical realism.

Critical constructivists subscribe explicitly to the notion that a physical world continues to exist independently of human minds, while they also question what we can actually know about that world and how we arrive at such knowledge. Thus, despite acknowledging a hypothetical reality, critical constructivists believe that we do not acquire direct or objective knowledge of things as they "really" are. However, even though for critical constructivists it is also the case that we construct our own personal realities, they believe that we do so through a process of interaction with the environment. The personal paradigms we construct are more or less adaptive, depending upon the context and constraints of the real environment with which we interact. As described by Mahoney (1991), critical constructivists are more likely to construe the acquisition of knowledge as based upon a co-construction between self and other rather than as produced by a solitary thinker. It is acknowledged that the world out there does have an influence upon us even though we can never acquire objective knowledge of it.

In addition to himself, Mahoney cites Guidano, Kelly, and Piaget, among others, as critical constructivists. Interestingly, radical constructivists invoke the name of Piaget to bolster their epistemological position as well. More will be said about Piaget in a later section of this chapter. The comments below briefly examine the work of Kelly and Guidano.

George A. Kelly

The personal construct system devised by Kelly (1955) constitutes a comprehensive constructivist model of meaning-making (see Chapter Thirteen). It is an amusing testimony in support of the constructivists' argument that Kelly's theory has been variously labeled as cognitive, emotional, phenomenological, existential, behaviorist, zen buddhist, and psychoanalytic. Further, he was also told that it is exactly what is meant by dialectical materialism (Kelly, 1969). For the most part, Kelly eschewed these labels. While there is a strong phenomenological component in personal construct theory, Kelly's work does posit the existence of a real world within which we navigate our way through life. What is important is what we make of the world. Not only can what exists be personally construed but the construals themselves can be revised and reconstructed as well.

For Kelly, constructs are bipolar (for example, good/bad, right/wrong) and organized into a complex hierarchy containing both superordinate and subordinate constructs. Constructs also have a predictive character to them: if, for example, you were to call someone reliable, you would be predicting that he or she would meet his or her obligations and fulfill any promises made. The accuracy of a prediction, however, is viewed by Kelly as an indicator not of any absolute truth about external reality but of the temporal utility of the construct that gave rise to the prediction. Constructs that are repeatedly disconfirmed lead ideally to revision and reconstruction. Each individual's construct system is therefore private, idiographic, and personal in the way it makes meaning out of the world and the individual's experience in it. As idiographic as personal constructs are, however, Neimeyer and Feixas (1990) point out overlapping commonalities among them, derived from shared familial and cultural membership. And the social implications of Kelly's earlier formulations continue to be expanded upon by contemporary advocates of his work (Alexander & Neimeyer, 1989; Loos & Epstein, 1989; Neimeyer, 1993a; Neimeyer & Neimeyer, 1987).

Vittorio F. Guidano

Vittorio F. Guidano's systems/process-oriented paradigm offers the most comprehensive and systematic contemporary constructivist approach to psychopathology and psychotherapy available. Drawing heavily upon Piaget's cognitive-developmental theory and Bowlby's attachment theory, he articulates a view of self-organizing processes throughout the life-span. Both the construction of identity and the evolutionary and ontogenetic role of emotion play a central part in Guidano's model. Rationality is defined as subjective, as that which provides internal coherence and reliability within the framework of the individual's cognitive organization. The epistemological emphasis is not upon validity (that is, correspondence of an individual's beliefs to objective truth) but upon viability (that is, the pragmatic adaptability of the individual's beliefs, so that he or she can navigate successfully within the world). It follows from this view that Guidano's therapeutic goal is not to correct false or distorted patient views of the world but to assist the patient to become aware of, examine, and modify tacit core self-structures and definitions of identity that may once have been adaptive but are no longer so. As Guidano states, "Maintaining an adaptive adequacy essentially means preserving one's sense of self by continuously transforming the perceived world rather than merely corresponding to it" (1991, p. 9). For Guidano, this transformational process involves the ongoing reorganization of internal coherence, leading to "the discontinuous emergence of more inclusive levels of the knowledge of self and of the world" (p. 9).

Guidano (1991) maintains that an essential defining characteristic of any individual is his or her continuous quest for and construction of personal meaning. This search takes place within a social matrix, however, entailing reciprocal and co-constructive activities. Guidano advocates that the therapist not cling to the stance of "objective observer" but recognize "that any knowledge is 'participatory' and based on the reciprocal negotiation of a mutual agreement rather than on a mere transmission of data" (pp. 206–207).

Developmental Constructivism

A strong developmental emphasis in constructivist psychotherapy can be found in the work of Carlsen (1988), Guidano (1987), Guidano and Liotti (1983), Lyddon (1992, 1993), Mahoney (1991), Rosen (1985, 1991, 1993), and Selman (1980). Although the work involved is vast and complex, a major point of emphasis in *developmental constructivism* is that an individual creates alternative and more adaptive ways of meaning-making and thus meanings when that individual's self-organization is thrown into a state of disequilibrium. Confronted with environmental demands and constraints that render the present self-organization less than adequate, the individual experiences perturbation as his or her psychological system is thrown off balance. Yet while threat to the current self-organization may be entailed, disequilibrium also presents an opportunity for the self to evolve to a more highly differentiated and complexly organized stage of meaning-making (Kegan, 1982).

In Kegan's self-object relations theory (1982), each newly developed stage is characterized by a self that has transcended its former embeddedness in one way of knowing-in-the-world (that is, meaning-making) to construct another way, which can now take the old self as an object of knowledge. For example, at stage 2 the self is embedded in and defined by its needs. Not having its needs met is a threat to the very existence of the self at that stage. However, upon evolving to stage 3, the self is no longer defined by its needs, but by relationships. The self is no longer equated with or *subject* to its needs, and these needs shift to being an *object* of knowledge upon which the individual can reflect. The person has gone from being someone who *is* his or her needs to being someone who *has* needs. At this stage, not getting its needs met no longer poses a threat to the very existence of the self. Then, at stage 3, the self is defined by its relationships, and the disruption or termination of relationships now poses the greatest threat to the self's existence.

Kegan's model of self-object relations has spawned significant findings on the relationship between psychiatric diagnoses and meaning-making. Rogers and Kegan (1991) have reported that psychiatric patients in different traditional diagnostic categories have more in common with each other when they are at the same stage of meaning-making than they do when they share the same diagnostic category but are at different meaning-making stages. Further, in terms of possessing a self-structured way of making meaning, even a severely disturbed patient, such as one who suffers from schizophrenia, can be developmentally more advanced than a nonpsychotic and much less disturbed patient (see Chapter Fifteen, for related findings).

Social Constructivism

The term *social constructivist* is rarely used by those to whom it is often applied, as they prefer to be known as *social constructionists* (Hoffman, 1990; Gergen, 1994a). Gergen (1994a), after acknowledging some similarities between constructivism and social constructionism, proceeds to drive a sharp wedge between the two meaning-making orientations. He distances himself as a proponent of social constructionism from what he construes as the "Western individualism" of constructivism, while rejecting conceptualizations of separate minds and an independent world. Neither mind nor world has, in his words, "ontological status." For Gergen, "social constructionism traces the sources of human action to relationships and the very understanding of 'individual functioning' to communal interchange" (p. 68).

Gergen does identify a group he calls social constructivists. However, although members of this group (for example, Mead and Vygotsky) emphasize social processes in the acquisition of knowledge, Gergen disaffiliates himself from them because their work is also characterized by explanations of mental processes. Hence, he maintains the purity of social constructionism. For these reasons, I have devoted a separate section of this chapter to the construction of social realities, following my comments on constructivism and psychotherapy.

Constructivism and Psychotherapy

Mahoney (1988b), citing the increasing convergence of the hundreds of extant therapeutic models, suggests that constructivism, as well as some of the cognitively oriented therapies, may provide "a metatheoretical home for diverse approaches to psychotherapy" (p. 307). In a similar vein, Neimeyer and Feixas (1990) point out that constructivist trends have been emerging across a broad band of therapies, and they go on to develop the position that these trends hold promise for integrating the various psychotherapies under the umbrella of a constructivist metatheory. Neimeyer (Chapter Thirteen) has forged a range of dialogical therapeutic interventions that put his constructivist orientation into practice. For Neimeyer (1993b), contemporary constructivism itself may exist within the broader context of postmodernism.

Waters (1994) has suggested that constructivism can be put into action in what he refers to as "dialogic" therapies (Friedman, 1993; Gilligan & Price, 1993). Rather than seek historical roots for problems in the client's present life, dialogic therapies emphasize the current meanings attached to past events. The past lends itself to multiple interpretations, just as persons in the present are capable of a diversity of ways of being-in-the-world at various times. According to Waters (1994), "Instead of pursuing some central 'reality,' dialogic [constructivist] therapists reconstruct events to emphasize the best and most productive aspects of a person's current functioning, and to create the likelihood of more positive future functioning" (p. 73).

Constructing Social Realities

The *social constructionist* movement (Berger & Luckman, 1966; Gergen, 1985, 1991, 1994a; Harré, 1986; Searle, 1995; Shotter, 1993a, 1993b; Watzlawick, Weakland, & Fisch, 1974) has been gaining momentum in recent years. McNamee and Gergen (1992) have coedited a book that brings to light the implications of this form of meaning-making for psychotherapy.

A basic tenet of social constructionism is reflected in the work of Watzlawick, Weakland, and Fisch (1974). They suggest that when a sufficient number of people reach a consensual definition on something, that thing is then viewed as an objective reality. The construction process and the accompanying social agreement recede into the background, and a sense emerges that what has been constructed by consensual definition exists out there, in the foreground of the real world.

Gergen on Meaning as Socially Constructed

Kenneth J. Gergen (1985, 1991, 1994b) emphasizes that the generation of knowledge and our concepts of reality are sparked by a social process, with the use of language being critical to the process. He states: "Words are not mirrorlike reflections of reality, but expressions of group convention. Various social groups possess preferred vocabularies, or ways of putting things, and these vocabularies reflect or defend their values, politics, and ways of life. For participants in such groups, these forms of talking (or writing) take on a local reality. They seem totally convincing. Yet their very 'reality' is their danger, for each renders the believer heroic and the nonbeliever a fool" (1991, p. 119).

In the social constructionist view, therefore, the interactive relationship between people is central to the construction of knowledge, while the notion that the ahistorical, decontextualized individual constructs and possesses knowledge independently in his or her own head is rejected. For Gergen (1990, 1994a), meaning does not reside in the minds of individuals but is located in and is the product of interaction within the context of continuing relationships. Gergen would have us focus on how, within the matrix of the social collective and historically over time and in specific contexts, our concepts and understanding of reality in various domains have changed. His thesis is demonstrated in a vast range of literature encompassing such concepts as childhood, health, alcoholism, emotions, homosexuality, gender, morality, mental disorder, and romantic love, to name only a few.

One somewhat amusing example of how our concepts of reality evolve over time appeared in a health newsletter, which informed the reader that at one time, "Lovesickness, a palpitating heart, racing pulse, and the absorbed preoccupation with one individual, was considered a 'real' and widespread physical malady. . . . The cures included having sex, vomiting, long baths, long walks, and drinking wine (preferably in excess)" (Saracino, 1991, p. 3). Today, romantic love is no longer considered an illness in need of a cure.

Emotion and Society

A less whimsical and quite profound illustration of how the social construction of reality can greatly influence the life of an individual whose emotions and behavior do not conform to that construction can be found in Camus's (1942/1988) novel *The Stranger*. Meursault, the protagonist, living in Algiers, is accused of having murdered an Arab while strolling on the beach. Although there are mitigating circumstances, Meursault did, in fact, shoot the gun that killed the Arab. Yet at his trial, little attention is paid to the circumstances of the crime. What the prosecution hammers away at and what thoroughly absorbs the jurors is Meursault's apparent indifference and detachment toward his mother's recent death. At the trial, he is described as having been calm and without tears upon learning of her death and as a generally unfeeling man. It is brought out that on the day following his mother's burial, Meursault had gone swimming, met a woman, gone with her to see a comic movie, and afterwards made love with her. He is a simple man, lacking conventional emotional reactions, who enjoys common physical pleasures. At the end of the trial, however, he is found guilty and sentenced to death, and Camus leaves the reader with the uneasy feeling that the jurors found Meursault guilty *not* because he had shot and killed someone but because they were repelled by his failure to experience life and its emotions in accord with the jurors' own collective construction of life and feelings. In effect, Meursault lived a life that was true to him but strange to his contemporaries when they viewed it through their socially constructed reality (Carey, 1990).

Wood (1986), commenting on the social construction of emotion, states: "In learning that we ought to experience a particular emotion, we also learn what to do and think. Emotion involves the internalization of social representations of broad scope, including a range of attitudes and desires" (p. 196). Referring to a person's not experiencing emotion "appropriately," or as others expect, she observes that "failure to meet these expectations is not simply surprising: it is seen as 'wrong'" (p. 186). Averill (1986), while not discounting a biological substratum to emotions, emphasizes that "emotional schemas are the internal representation of social norms or rules" (p. 100). As social constructions, they are subject to change throughout each person's development during the life-span and when each person shifts from one context to another. Implied in Averill's social constructionist view of emotions is the social regulation of emotional experience and expression. That is, depending on the circumstances, the individual who violates societal expectations and departs from convention may either be admired for his creative freedom of emotional expression or condemned as an outcast, as in Meursault's dramatic case.

(See Chapters Eight and Nine for contrasting views on emotion and meaning-making. Also, Harré (1986) has edited a collection of chapters that are particularly germane to the social construction of emotions.)

Essentialism Rejected

The social constructionist rejects essentialism. He or she adopts a view of knowledge generation that is not predicated on an ontology of existing essences that the human mind strives to discover and comprehend. In ancient Greek philosophy, Plato posited essences as "forms," or "ideas," that existed in a transcendent sphere, which the mind strove to enter upon freeing itself from earthly illusions and constraints. For Aristotle, essences were to be found within the things of this world, and it was the function of the intellect to pierce through the materiality of things to apprehend their immutable essences. In the view of social constructionists, by contrast, no such static, universal essences exist. Further, social constructionists place no emphasis upon the intentions, thoughts, feelings, or wishes of the individual human mind in isolation, be they conscious or unconscious (Gergen, 1985, 1991). It is on the everyday playing field of social exchange and in the relationships between individuals that understanding, knowledge, and meaning are generated. The particularized historical and sociocultural contexts are paramount in this interactive, collaborative, evolutionary view of knowledge construction.

Knowledge and meaning are constructed and reconstructed over time within the social matrix. They do not constitute universal and immutable essences or objective truths existing for all times and cultures. As social constructionism is formulated by Shotter (1993b), "It is the dialectical emphasis upon both the contingency *and* the creativity of human interaction—on our making of, and being made by, our social realities—that is . . . common to social constructionism in all its versions" (p. 13). In this vigorous conceptualization, Shotter maintains that not only is knowledge a social construction but so is the world of our everyday experience. Shotter accords a central role to the ways we communicate, or dialogue, with one another and to our reciprocal attempts at understanding and responding to each other. It is through this dialogical process that our social relations are formed, and it is this process that leads us to what we are to become.

Psychoanalysis as Socially Constructed

In a popular textbook on comparative psychotherapy, the prominent and influential psychoanalyst Jacob A. Arlow (1989) had this to say about psychoanalytic theory: "Although there are many ways to treat neuroses, there is but one way to understand them—psychoanalysis. . . . Psychoanalysis is the only approach that makes clear what is going on in neurosis; it is the one theory that gives a scientific explanation to the effectiveness of all psychotherapies" (p. 21). I cite this comment as an example of the antithesis to the social constructionist zeitgeist (and the postmodern zeitgeist as well, as discussed later in this chapter). It illustrates what might be called theoretical supremacy or theoretical fundamentalism. It exhibits no recognition of the possible existence or credibility of other interpretations of the facts of psychological disturbance. It shows no awareness that the viewing of a particular class of human problems as "neuroses" is itself a human construction with a historical origin, a construction kept alive over the years by like-minded persons as they communicated through textbooks, journals, conferences, study groups, and training institutes. All these methods of communicating constitute avenues for social discourse within a community of people sharing a common language and its accompanying norms, practices, and ethics. Indeed, in the psychoanalytic community, dissenters have been subject to coercion to comply or, at the more extreme end, to expulsion from the community upon failure to comply. Concepts such as the id, the ego, the superego, defenses, drives, the unconscious, and the Oedipal complex—all the basic constructions endlessly discussed among Freud and his contemporaneous followers as well as their descendants—have been reified and projected into the outer world, where they are intended to be accepted as objective realities or universally immutable truths about human nature and its disorders. Hence, what is symbolic and metaphoric is often taken as literal independent truth (Spence, 1987). It is this practice that has led Bruner (1990) to personify psychoanalysis as an "essentialist sinner." (The reader interested in pursuing the social construction of early psychoanalysis as revealed through its case studies may wish to consult Sulloway, 1992.)

It should not go unnoticed that in Arlow's comment, psychoanalysis lays claim to the scientific respectability of explaining not only its own successes but those of *all other* therapies as well. Asserting this requires no small feat of the imagination, but I shall not address it further except to say that it neglects to take into account the extent to which science itself is a process of social construction (Purkhardt, 1993). It would be helpful for all therapists and theorists to keep in mind Gergen's counsel that "any given theoretical view simultaneously serves to sensitize and to constrain; one sees more sharply but remains blind to that which falls outside the realm of focus. Thus it may be argued that any theory that commands widespread belief, that serves as the univocal view of reality within a given culture poses a threat to the culture" (1994b, p. 168). It would seem that even if it had done so at one time, psychoanalysis no longer poses a threat to the culture, as indicated by its waning command over "truth" in the realm of the theory and practice of therapy. Indeed, a wide diversity of psychoanalytic models have evolved over the years, and they now compete with one another. This psychoanalytic pluralism may be regarded as having been inevitable and predictable from a constructivist perspective.

(See Chapter Ten for a metaview of constructivist trends in psychoanalysis; see Chapter Four for an exposition of the socially constructed nature of psychotherapy.)

Story or Narrative as Metaphor

Narrative theory is yet another aspect of constructivism and it holds considerable promise for enlarging our understanding of individuals as meaning-makers in social contexts. Bruner (1986) posits two thought modes through which reality is constructed and organized: the *paradigmatic* mode and the *narrative* mode. The paradigmatic mode is defined in terms of logic and science; it seeks truth in the form of empirical verification. The narrative mode is less abstract; it emphasizes the construction of good stories played out temporally in particular contexts. A good story seeks to offer coherence, to be compelling, to impart meaning, and to move the listener. (See Chapter Eleven for a discussion of narrative constructivism and therapeutic process.)

Recently, the power of metaphor has been gaining substantial recognition in the field of psychotherapy (see Chapter Twelve). In keeping with this trend, narrative has been singled out by Sarbin (1986) as a root metaphor for psychology to adopt because it is "a fruitful metaphor for examining and interpreting human action" (p. 19). It provides an equally fruitful means for understanding and for imparting meaning and coherence to human feelings, intentions, and aspirations. Increasingly, the psychotherapeutic literature has been reflecting the usefulness of the narrative metaphor in thinking about individual and family therapy (Forster, 1994; Gonçalves, 1994; Neimeyer & Mahoney, 1995; Russell, 1991, 1995; Schafer, 1992; Spence, 1982; White & Epston, 1990). Gonçalves advances the idea that the therapeutic process entails working with each individual's "prototype narrative," the overall system through which the individual engages in constructing personal meanings: "The objective of every therapy should be to orient the client into new life narratives, bringing with it a sense of acting and authorship. . . . The venture into the unknown, the world of possibility, is indeed the final objective of therapy" (1994, p. 119).

Embeddedness in Stories

We are born into stories: the stories of our parents, our families, and our culture. These made meanings, which predate us and envelop us upon our arrival into the world, can be constraining, even imprisoning, or they can be freeing and liberating. The personal narrative prototype that we develop over time is not constructed in a vacuum but instead incorporates much that is derived from the cultural stories and myths we are born into (Bruner, 1990; Howard, 1991). All too often, however, we take these tales to be universal and objective realities, and the story that might have been merely a prism of the mind becomes a prison of the mind. The stories of other groups and cultures are then viewed as false while our own are believed to be true. As we develop reflective or metacognitive ability, however, the opportunity to understand these stories as relative to our own culture presents itself. There is no guarantee that we will take this opportunity to reposition our stories in relation to those of other cultures. Nevertheless, the capacity to review and revise our familial and cultural narratives is a developmental acquisition and provides us with a potential key to the prison, enabling us to walk out through its doors and into new stories.

Born into the cradle of familial and cultural stories, we begin to construct personal narratives not long afterward, with all the idiosyncratic features that this may entail. However adaptive these stories may have been at one time, they may no longer be adaptive as we move on to new phases, relationships, and places in our lives. Yet, as Freud has taught us, we all too often repetitively live and relive the same story, long after it has any adaptive function. It is the task of therapy to assist clients in revising their old stories and in constructing new ones that have more relevance and meaning for their current and future lives. As Freeman (1993) in his treatise on "rewriting the self," states, "We must be receptive and respectful enough of the texts we encounter to remain open to the possibility of entirely new forms of interpretations: if the old plots don't do, then it might be time to explore something different" (p. 165).

Dominating Power of Stories

It is not only our own stories that can imprison us, however, for we also find ourselves to be characters in the stories written and lived by others. At times, we may change our own story to accommodate a role assigned to us by another. Indeed, sometimes we may feel as if we have no story of our own but are condemned merely to playing a role in somebody else's story. At such times, we experience no sense of creativity, autonomy, or agency, only a sense that we are caught up in another person's plot and speaking lines being fed to us. Being a character in others' stories is inevitable, due to the social nature of our lives. The issue is one of dominance. It is not uncommon for clients to enter therapy at just that point when they realize that they are feeling no sense of self-authorship but, instead, are living roles in others' stories. The task of therapy, then, is to help these clients escape such subjugation by authoring dominant plots that endow them with the feeling that they can invent their own characters and script their own actions. (See Gonçalves, 1994, for a detailed version of how this may be accomplished.) Narrative revision, therefore, involves the reconstruction of meaning as the client alters both plot structure and character delineation.

Just as one client may feel dominated by another's story, a second client may be attempting to dominate others by subsuming them within his or her story. This attempt often leads to frustration and failure in human relationships. While it will always be the case that we are destined to play roles in each other's narratives, we sometimes must struggle to learn that we cannot seize total authorship of another's character and story. Just as we must maintain self-authorship despite having roles in stories being lived by others, so must we allow others that same privilege of self-authorship, despite their having roles in our personal narratives. Ultimately, the solution to the dilemma of dominance within intersecting stories resides in the process of dialogue. It is in genuine dialogue that each participant is free to craft his or her own lines and through which new and novel meanings emerge. Such dialogue requires not only the freedom to create one's own character and speak one's own lines but also a commitment from each participant to listen with respect and concern for what the other is saying (Holquist, 1990). Often, dialogue is a process of volitional coauthoring.

The theme of domination by another's narrative and of liberation through the dialogical remaking of meaning is beautifully illustrated in the play *Into the Woods* (Sondheim & Lapine, 1987). Throughout the first half of this work, one character stands on the edge of the stage narrating the actions of the other characters, who then enact that narration, being subject to the story as told by the narrator. However, as the play unfolds, the characters in the narrated plot are threatened by a hungry giant. No one of them wanting to be a sacrifice to the giant, they at last break out of the plot in which the narrator has placed them and then seize the narrator in order to feed him to the giant. Having accomplished this, they are no longer governed by an outside force or "author." (We must, of course, suspend our disbelief here, forgetting that this is a play within a play and that Sondheim and Lapine are still dictating the action.) But once the characters have freed themselves from living within another's story, the initial price of that liberation is fear and confusion. The task of writing their own scripts now lies before them. The dialogue among them is elevated to a new plane, as each must now rewrite his or her own story.

It is much like this in therapy. As I mentioned earlier, when clients first seek help, they often feel as if they are living a life narrated by someone else. They do not experience a sense of agency or volition. As personal, familial, and cultural scripts, or narratives, are reviewed during the course of a client's therapy, they are replaced with new and revised narratives that impart a sense of intentionality and renewed meaning to the client's life. In this process, the therapist assumes the role of secure base, helping clients, through dialogue, to construct their own compasses so that once "out of the woods," they will no longer need the therapist. Acquiring their own senses of direction, the clients are liberated to create their own meanings, to narrate stories of their own making.

Hermeneutics and Interpretation

Hermeneutics is the art of interpretation and understanding. Its origins lie in the disputes around the interpretation of the Bible that arose during the Reformation. In recent times, much attention has been devoted to the interpretation of the Constitution of the United States and to the interpretation of historical events. Literary criticism, also, is permeated with various approaches to establishing a philosophical basis for the interpretation of literature. The traditional position on interpretation can be found in the work of Hirsch (1967), who argues for searching out the intended meaning of the author in order to understand objectively the meaning of the literary piece the author has produced. In Hirsch's view, the meaning is determinate and fixed, waiting to be found by the reader who works hard at discovering it. As Hirsch somewhat paradoxically states, "Objectivity in textual interpretation requires explicit reference to the speaker's subjectivity" (p. 237). At the other end of this spectrum of literary criticism, we have the radical view of Fowles (1965) that I quoted earlier, which places emphasis upon the reader's views and likens interpretation of a work of literature to a Rorschach test. From this perspective, meaning is completely subjective and indeterminate, residing in the interpreter. It is a viewpoint that raises the specter of solipsism and relativism; however, Fish (1980) has a response to this concern. Although he would agree that the meaning of a text does not inhere in its language, he does contend that interpretations are constrained by the "interpretive community" to which one belongs. No one exists independently, having no adherence to the norms and values of such a community. These norms and values are context bound, and while individuals can transfer their allegiance from one interpretive community to another, they cannot successfully transcend all their embeddedness in a social matrix. If we substitute persons for texts (Gergen, 1990), we see these constraints played out repeatedly in the field of psychotherapy, as therapists from one school argue dogmatically for the correctness of their interpretations and explanations, derived from their school's assumptions, over the "incorrect" interpretations of therapists from other schools.

In the hermeneutic philosophy of Gadamer (1975), we find an attempt to transcend the subject-object dichotomy. As Outhwaite informs us, for Gadamer, "Understanding is not a matter of forgetting our own horizon of meanings and putting ourselves within that of the alien texts or the alien society, it means merging our own horizons with theirs" (Outhwaite, 1985, p. 25). In its broadest sense, an understanding of art, science, and the social sciences must take into account the historical and social context of both the knower and the known. In a review of Gadamer's work, Strenger (1991) asserts that this hermeneutic philosopher views interpretation as the interpreter entering into a dialogue with the text. Drawing upon the philosophy of Heidegger, Gadamer sees the whole world as text to be interpreted: "To be a human being is to be constantly structuring [one's] world in terms of meaning" (Strenger, 1991, p. 31).

For Gadamer, while there may not be a single correct interpretation, some interpretations are, nevertheless, better than others. Criteria of internal consistency and comprehensiveness are brought to bear to support this position (Hollinger, 1994).

Narrative, Interpretation, and Psychoanalysis

Contemporary psychoanalysis has taken up the question whether achieving objective truth in interpretation is necessary or even possible (Schafer, 1992; Spence, 1982; Strenger, 1991). If theoretical supremacy is regarded as characteristic of psychoanalysis as a general psychology and a theory of psychopathology, then regardless of what material arises from the analysand, that material will always be assimilated by the analyst to fit the preexisting objective truth that the theory posits. Arlow (1989) and Brenner (1982) are two psychoanalysts who exemplify the position that the theory constitutes valid and objective truth and who regard other theories as insufficient and false in explaining human motivation and behavior. In contrast to this position of theoretical supremacy, the hermeneutic endeavor seeks to forge meaning and understanding out of the practical activities and contextualized lives of individuals, without benefit of preestablished theoretical assumptions (Packer, 1985).

The question of truth and objectivity in psychoanalysis concerns not only the truth value of the theory out of which the analyst operates but also whether the analyst can expect to uncover historical truths from the patient's free associations and remembrances of things past (as Proust put it). The view that one can expect to uncover such truths is rooted in Freud's archeological metaphor that suggested the analyst is on an expedition to dig up fragments of the patient's actual life that lie buried in the unconscious. Yet Spence (1982), in a radical departure from this view, maintains that "the associations of a patient have no one-to-one correspondence with his memories and dreams, much less his unconscious thoughts" (p. 28). Rather than emphasize historical truth, Spence (1982) adopts the premise that "narrative truth has a special significance in its own right and that making contact with the actual past may be of far less significance than creating a coherent and consistent account of a particular set of events" (p. 28). The idea here is not that historical truth does not exist but that to the extent that it emerges, it has been selected out of many other factual events from the patient's past and ascribed particular meanings that will vary with the circumstances that brought it to mind. Further, it must be constructed into a narrative truth: a good story that is plausible, coherent, and compelling. In Spence's account, the construction of a good story out of the material that issues from the patient becomes as crucial a "truth" for the patient as historical accuracy and translates into a vital component of the cure in psychoanalysis.

The Power of Telling One's Story

Everyone has a story to tell. Most stories are a mixture of pain, suffering, frustration, and shame on the one hand and pleasure, joy, satisfaction, and pride on the other hand. Many stories contain secrets that people seek to conceal for fear of rejection or humiliation or both. Yet often, people who risk revealing their stories to others find relief and sometimes even release. They have been trapped in their respective stories and the simple act of telling these stories to others brings new meaning and perspective to people's lives.

Mikal Gilmore is the younger brother of Gary Gilmore, the notorious convicted U.S. murderer who refused to seek an appeal to save his life and who was subsequently executed by the state. For fifteen years after that, Mikal refused to discuss the facts of his family's tragic history that were still not publicly known. He sought escape from that history, but in the end, he concluded that escape was impossible without his facing the facts of his family's past by formulating his story in his own words and communicating it to others. So he wrote *Shot in the Heart* (1994) telling us in the beginning of the book: "I have a story to tell. It is a story of murders; murders of the flesh, and of the spirit. . . . I know this story well, because I have been stuck inside it. I have lived with its causes and effects, its details and indelible lessons, my entire life. . . . And if I ever hope to leave this place, I must tell what I know" (pp. x–xi; reprinted with permission).

While not everyone has the inclination, resources, or ability to write a book, many people have turned to psychotherapy for the opportunity to tell their stories. For some few, the telling alone has a healing effect; for most, it at least offers a soothing benefit; and for many, it constitutes the necessary prelude to doing the work of therapy. The latter circumstance is depicted at the end of Phillip Roth's novel *Portnoy's Complaint* (1969), when Alexander Portnoy's analyst suggests, after Alexander has gone on repetitively telling his stories at some length, that perhaps *now* they can begin the work of therapy (Pape, 1994).

Pessimism and Optimism About Narrative

Recent books by Friedman (1993), Gilligan and Price (1993), and Hoyt (1994) illustrate therapists' attempts to engage clients through conversation in a coauthoring process that aims to rewrite client narratives. To maintain our theoretical balance here, however, it is wise to keep in mind that not everyone looks sanguinely upon individuals' potential for rewriting their own stories. In his poignant novel *Scar Tissue*, Ignatieff (1993) writes: "We are addicted to a vision of life as narrative, which we compose as we go along. In fact we didn't have anything to do with the beginning of the story; we are merely allowed to dabble with the middle; and the end is mostly not up to us at all, but to genetics, biological fate and chance" (p. 68). Perhaps the fact that the novel tells of a son experiencing the decline of his mother through Alzheimer's disease explains the pessimism of these words. Nevertheless, even if we were to accept this pessimism, it is precisely the ability to "dabble with the middle" that imparts dignity and autonomy to our lives and that offers some grounds for the hope that we can lead more meaningful lives.

Developmental-Constructivist Perspectives

We can examine developmental-constructivist perspectives largely through the contributions and elaborations of the Piagetian developmental-constructivist paradigm. Mahoney (1991) refers to Jean Piaget as "the most visible and influential twentieth-century constructivist" (p. 99), and the differentiating and distinguishing characteristic of Piaget's approach to constructivism is its developmental component. His entire work can be construed as a view of the human organism as a developmental meaning-making system (Overton & Palermo, 1994).

The Developing Constructivist Mind

Working within a Piagetian framework, Chandler (1988) advances the position that the constructivist mind is itself a developmental phenomenon. Preschool children are said to subscribe to a theory of mind that holds that an individual's sensory apparatus produces absolute and certain knowledge derived from the environment. They believe that mental structures mirror reality exactly as it is. (This is, of course, an implicit theory, not one of which children are metacognitively self-aware.) By the time of middle childhood, youngsters' theory of mind has developed toward a recognition that there are multiple perspectives on reality and even contradictory perspectives. However, their bedrock belief continues to be that there is only one *right* view of reality and that any other view is subject to correction. In middle childhood, therefore, youngsters' epistemology continues to embrace a correspondence theory of truth, despite these changes in their theory of mind. It is only during adolescence that the constructivist theory of mind emerges. The adolescent realizes the existence of a plurality of viewpoints and the nonexistence of an objective standard for achieving absolute certainty about the world. Doubt, ambiguity, and uncertainty are the result, often plunging the adolescent into what Chandler calls "epistemological loneliness." The further developmental progression to adulthood brings the individual's acceptance of a multiperspectival world without certain knowledge, accompanied by the individual's capacity to make a personal commitment to one viewpoint over another (Perry, 1970).

(King and Kitchener, 1994, and Baxter Magolda, 1992, have presented further research on epistemological development in young adults. Belenky, Clinchy, Goldberger, and Tarule, 1986, have focused specifically upon the epistemological orientations of adult women in their research; see Chapter Six.)

Social Aspects of Piaget's Work

Piaget focused mainly, but by no means exclusively, on the young person's evolving forms of knowledge about the physical world (Piaget, 1970; Piaget & Inhelder, 1966/1969). The social aspects of his work, however, have been greatly underestimated and overlooked by many. Much of his work with a sociological orientation had never been published in English and therefore has been unfamiliar to the majority of those interested in his theories and research (Chapman, 1988). However, the recent publication of *Sociological Studies* (Piaget, 1995) in English will finally make readily available some of his most substantive work in this area. A picture of the child constructing knowledge in splendid isolation, while not totally unwarranted by many of Piaget's writings, is incomplete. In fact, Piaget's first book (1923/1955) was devoted to a study of children communicating with one another. As children's age progressed, Piaget observed the gradual decline of egocentric speech and the corresponding ascendancy of sociocentric speech, in which the speaker increasingly takes into account the listener's needs. In his fifth book (1932/1965), Piaget repeatedly emphasized that "the need to speak the truth and even to seek it for oneself is only conceivable insofar as the individual thinks and acts as one of a society, not of any society . . . but of a society founded on reciprocity and mutual respect, and therefore on cooperation" (p. 164). Youniss and Damon (1992) have highlighted what they view as essential co-constructive activities between children and their peers and also between children and adults. They maintain that co-construction is central to a comprehensive understanding of Piaget's epistemology.

Others working in the tradition of Piaget's developmental-constructivist paradigm, have put forth well-researched theories on moral meaning-making (Kohlberg, 1981, 1984), interpersonal understanding (Selman, 1980), self-object relations (Kegan, 1982), and the cosmic quest for meaning based on stages of faith (Fowler, 1981).

The Piagetian Paradigm

Although Piaget is recognized as having possessed the *mind* of a genius, his theory and research were generated within a highly diverse *social* context. This process is, of course, very much in keeping with the co-constructed nature of knowledge depicted earlier. Piaget's approach to his work was interdisciplinary, and he attracted thinkers and doers from many fields, including philosophy, psychology, biology, cybernetics, mathematics, physics, and education, to study and conduct research at the International Center for Genetic Epistemology in Geneva, Switzerland. The range of themes he addressed throughout his lifetime was extensive, bearing on such subjects as language, imagery, perception, number, space, causality, memory, time, movement and speed, chance and probability, possibility and necessity, and, in general, the growth of rationality and knowledge from infancy through adolescence.

The Epistemic Subject

While Piaget's vast work has profound ramifications for understanding persons as individuals, paradoxically, he was not interested in the individual as such but rather in the epistemic subject. In other words, his interest lay in the developmental construction of generic and universal forms of knowledge and not in idiographic or cultural constructs. Piaget's research goal was to trace the development of *necessary* knowledge and the elimination of *pseudo-necessity*. Pseudo-necessity is taking as necessary knowledge that which is only historically contingent and is not causally or logically related in any essential way. An example from the realm of statistics is that empirically, the mean and the median scores may be the same in a given instance. However, the median score will necessarily be the middle number of a range of numbers, because that is its defining characteristic, whereas the mean will not necessarily be the middle number, because its meaning resides elsewhere. Pseudo-necessity, in this case, would be the assumption that the mean will always be in the middle of a set of numbers because it has been empirically found to be so on some occasions (Smith, 1993). And what is necessary knowledge? We have just seen one example: the concept of a median in statistics. Smith puts it succinctly: "Necessary knowledge is *necessary*, where this property [of necessity] is not due to the contingent fact that a specific person has acquired such knowledge in the actual world. Necessary knowledge is the knowledge of a necessary truth, which—by definition—is true in *all possible worlds*" (1993, pp. 50–51). Thus, for example, if $A = B$ and $B = C$, then $A = C$. This transitive statement is contingent on neither context nor social consensus but is universally true and would be so in any conceivable world. This concept differentiates Piaget's work from George Kelly's personal construct psychology and the work of the social constructionists, although to my mind, the latter are potentially complementary and integrative models as opposed to mutually exclusive and divisive models. Evolving knowledge structures, in Piagetian terms, impart qualitatively different *forms* of understanding self, others, environment, and any subject or concept. The *content*, however, of what an individual constructs on a personal or idiosyncratic level is shaped by each individual's unique history, experience, family, culture, and choice. Piaget's field of study was that of deep universal structures, which are constructed over time by the auto-regulative activity of each developing individual. These structures are not innate; nor do they appear maturationally at periodic times as if a biological clock were ticking away. Based on ecological opportunities and social stimulation, the pace at which these endogenously constructed structures emerge will vary from culture to culture and from individual to individual.

Increasing Integration and Adaptiveness

Development progresses from the simple to the complex, as put forth by Werner (1948) in his orthogenetic principle. Over time, there occurs a process of integration of structures into increasingly organized and hierarchical knowledge components. Note, moreover, that the progression of development is not from something absent to something present. As Smith (1993) makes manifest, "the claim is that all of the central notions and principles (conservation, identity, transitivity, number, causality, and the rest) are present in some form at every level of development. . . . In Piaget's account, development occurs not as a transition from absence to presence but rather as serial differentiation and integration over time" (p. 49).

From a Piagetian viewpoint, some ways of knowing-in-the-world are more adaptive than others. Higher stages facilitate a simultaneous widening and coordination of the individual's perspectives. Each higher stage offers more efficient strategies for reasoning and problem solving. Each higher stage provides the necessary condition for more adaptive social and moral reasoning. Higher stages promote increasingly greater self-awareness, emotional stability, and an enhanced sense of coherence within the individual and in his or her understanding of the world. Though its progression is admittedly an ideal, development follows a personal evolutionary process from the individual's emerging out of embeddedness in his or her earlier impulses and needs to the individual's establishing the ultimate evolutionary balance of intimacy, community, and interdependence— a process eloquently articulated by Kegan (1982) in his synergistic synthesis of Piaget's and Kohlberg's theories. Piaget himself identifies four stages of development: sensorimotor, preoperational, concrete operational, and formal operational.

Postformal Thought

Integrating models of postformal thought (Basseches, 1984; Commons & Richards, 1984) with Piaget's four stages of development, Stevens-Long (1990) observes: "If we adapt the notion that development proceeds from embeddedness to objectification, from differentiation to integration, from absolute to relative, middle-aged people are at the relative end of the spectrum. Thought in middle age is contextual and probabilistic. All truth is seen as the product of a particular system. There are no great, universal truths, only socially adequate solutions. . . . Perhaps an appreciation of the interrelatedness of systems, rather than their differences, occurs among the most mature of us" (p. 159).

Carlsen (1988) has explored the developmental-constructivist implications of a therapy of meaning-making that takes into account postformal thought, going beyond the final stage of formal thought in the Piagetian paradigm. Formal thought marks the attainment of scientific reasoning and enables the thinker to take a view of the world in which reality is seen as only a subset of the range of possibilities (Inhelder & Piaget, 1958). Postformal thought is said to be dialectical, relativistic, metasystemic, and based on problem finding rather than problem solving. Nevertheless, it is not regarded as having the formal properties of a structured stage, as described by Piaget, and there appear to be a variety of suggested models for it rather than a single agreed-upon one (Alexander & Langer, 1990; Commons, Richards, & Armon, 1984; Kegan, 1994).

Disembedding from Egocentrism

Egocentrism is the inability to differentiate between the knower as subject and the known as object. Each stage of development in Piaget's theory is characterized by a particular type of egocentrism. For example, the concrete operational thinker cannot differentiate between that which is known and familiar to him or her and that which is hypothetically possible but outside his or her realm of experience. Interpersonally, egocentrism results in an individual's inability to take the perspective of another, especially when the other's perspective differs from the individual's own. As development proceeds, the individual's capacity for taking on multiple and wider perspectives increases, as does the ability to coordinate them simultaneously.

At any given stage, the individual is said to be embedded in the limitations that typify that stage. Upon developing to the next stage, the individual becomes disembedded from the constraints of the previous stage but embedded in the limitations of the newly acquired stage. As Kegan (1982) puts it, each new stage becomes a theory of the prior stage. That is to say, the developing person can now take the former stage as an object of knowledge; a feat that the person could not accomplish while embedded in, or subject to, that stage. What is of greatest importance in the development and reorganization of knowledge at each new stage is *how* one knows rather than *what* one knows (Kegan, 1982).

Meaning as Relational

It is a superordinate postulate of Piaget's paradigm that meaning inheres neither in the knowing subject nor in the known object but, instead, is a relationship between knower and known. Therefore, whenever a therapist discusses a concept with a client, he or she must keep in mind that the meaning of that concept to the client will always be commensurate with the client's stage of meaning-making. For example, in an early stage of the child's evolving concept of friendship, friendship is construed in external and material terms. A friend so conceived is one who does things for you, who will give you things. He or she is someone close at hand with whom you may physically interact at the moment. You can have only one friend at a time. As the concept evolves through cognitive-structural advances, however, the growing youngster ultimately conceives of friendship in terms of loyalty, trust, intimacy, and mutuality, and widens his or her scope to include the possibility of multiple simultaneous friendships, and autonomous interdependence (Selman,

1980). What a vast difference from the early stage! Clearly, therefore, therapist and client may ostensibly be speaking *about* the same subject in their sessions, but the *meanings* of what is being spoken about may differ so greatly that genuine communication never takes place. It is therefore incumbent upon the therapist to be familiar with the range of developmental-constructivist possibilities of meaning-making and to take these into account in work with the client. These observations apply to any subject, of course, not just to the concept of friendship that I used for the purpose of illustration. As Kegan (1994) has observed, the way that we hear a communication (that is, the meaning we make of it) is limited by the way of knowing that we have constructed at any point in time during our developmental journey.

(For amplified accounts on the application of the developmental-constructivist paradigm to therapy, see Rosen, 1980, 1985, 1989, 1991, 1993.)

The Postmodern Connection

Anyone who thinks he or she knows exactly what postmodernism is and offers a clear, precise, and coherent definition to demonstrate that knowledge is probably mistaken. Postmodernism is anything but clear, precise, and coherent. It is instead fragmented, diverse, paradoxical, ironic, and contradictory. I mean this not as a criticism but as a characterization. Postmodern theorists are self-consciously and self-reflexively aware of this same characterization of their field and make no apology for it. The question, "What is postmodernism?" evokes a plurality of responses, and that pluralism itself emphasizes a defining feature of the postmodern movement.

Perhaps the one unifying theme that draws the many diverse perspectives on postmodernism together is that there does not exist a set of immutable objective truths in the "real" world to serve as the bedrock, or grounding, upon which knowledge can be built (Rorty, 1979). Somewhat paradoxically, this position is held to be universally true. Starting with this antifoundational premise opens the door to an exploration of the notion of multiple realities and even multiple worlds (Goodman, 1978).

It is not even clear that postmodernism has a sharply demarcated historical origin and duration, for while some believe it does, others view it as a cluster of attitudes and beliefs that can be found across various historical eras (Readings & Schaber, 1993). Just as the post-modern zeitgeist may not be time-bound, it is also not confined to any one field but has surfaced within such wide-ranging areas as architecture, art, photography, fiction, literary criticism, film, history, geography, economics, sociology, anthropology, religion, communi-cation media, psychology, philosophy, and psychotherapy.

Against Modernism

In general, postmodernism is antimodernist and sees the Enlight-enment, with its emphasis that reason and science lead us along a linear path toward unerring progress, as a failed project. Grand nar-ratives, such as those of Hegel, Marx, and Kant, with their totalizing and universalizing structure, are rejected (Lyotard, 1984). They are seen as suppressing or silencing other voices while privileging their own, and this, of course, has political implications. Other major fig-ures, in addition to Lyotard, who are concerned with the marginal-ization of deviant, dissident, and minority voices are Foucault (Rainbow, 1984) and Derrida (Kamuf, 1991).

Postmodernism questions authority and challenges the status quo. Attempts are made to dismantle, to deconstruct, the apparent stable and finite meanings of language in texts, broadly construed, in order to reveal their masked contradictions as well as to bring into sharp relief submerged and suppressed voices previously silenced. What appear to be determinate and final meanings shim-mering on the surface prove subject to an infinite variety of inter-pretations (Derrida, 1967/1976). The process of deconstruction is as applicable to the theories of therapists and the words of clients as it is to literal texts.

Among postmodernists, the role of language in constructing meaning, influencing our conceptions of reality, and even exerting tyranny over us is a theme of central importance. As Marshall (1992) states: "Postmodernism is about language. About how it controls, how it determines meaning, and how we try to control through language. About how language restricts, closes down, insists that it stands for some *thing*. Postmodernism is about how 'we' are defined within that language and within specific historical, social, cultural matrices" (p. 4).

The work of both Anderson and Goolishian (1988) and Hare-Mustin (1994) offers excellent examples of the roles of language and discourse in family therapy: how they can entrap us, and how they can liberate us (when properly understood and used).

Restoring Reason Within Postmodernism

Postmodernism is not without its critics, of course (Callinicos, 1989; Norris, 1990, 1992; see especially Held, 1995, for a critical analysis of postmodern theory in psychotherapy), and the wise practitioner will avoid totally and uncritically embracing it without reflection, despite its many merits. It offers no standards for making value judgments or guiding ethical principles that apply beyond one's immediate local community. While it decries reason and science for producing Auschwitz and Hiroshima, it is difficult to see on what basis it can transcend its own profound relativistic epistemology to condemn these horrible events. The condemnation itself seems to confuse scientific reasoning and methodology with the moral arena within which the human decisions leading to these tragic events were made. Postmodernism itself seems, paradoxically, to amount to a metanarrative whose very nature is rendered untenable by its leaving no criteria by which it can be evaluated on its own terms.

Much of postmodern thought appears to go beyond recognizing the limitations of reason to being blatantly anti-reason. It is as though postmodernists have concluded that if there are no grounds for absolute certitude about knowledge and reality, then there is no special value to rationality or reasonable grounds for thoughtful argumentation and conclusions. There is no apparent recognition given to the distinction that a belief need not be true to be rational. It seems not to be considered that the rationality of a belief is determined by the criteria for embracing it and by the grounds upon which it would be relinquished, rather than its truth value. Rationality is simply the enemy for a large segment of postmodernists. My own leanings are more in line with Nozick (1993), a contemporary philosopher who states: "Our principles fix what our life stands for, our aims create the light our life is bathed in, and our rationality, both individual and coordinate, defines and symbolizes the distance we have come from mere animality. It is by these means that our lives can come to mean more than what they instrumentally yield. And by meaning more, our lives yield more" (p. 181).

Be that as it may, rationality spoken of as a singular and static faculty cannot tell the whole story, for as the developmental-constructivist paradigm conveys, rationality and the evolving self undergo a series of transformative stages, each succeeding one being more complex and qualitatively more adaptive than its predecessor (Kegan, 1982). In his most recent work, Kegan (1994) has formulated five levels of consciousness, of which postmodernism is the fifth. The fourth level embodies the modernist mind, characterized by embeddedness in a system or ideology. At this level, the individual takes his or her own system of thought to be whole, complete, and absolute. Alternative systems are viewed as not only in conflict with the individual's own but as separate and wrong. It is not until the attainment of the fifth level of consciousness that the individual is no longer subject to his or her own system or ideology, for it has become relative, becoming an object of knowledge. The individual's epistemological organization is now not simply systemic but trans-systemic or cross-theoretical. The individual becomes conscious of and can reflect, therefore, upon his or her own system. Further, the individual's own system is partialized, rather than absolutized, and its connectedness to other systems with which it may be in conflict is recognized. At this stage of consciousness, the dominance of any one system or ideology is diminished. Alternative systems are not repudiated but seen to be in a prior relationship with the individual's own. At the same time, the deficiencies in the individual's own system are recognized. To illustrate the relationship, Kegan uses the analogy of a cylinder with two openings, one at each end, openings that we can equate with systems or ideologies. These openings do not first exist independently and then come together but rather are constituted by their relationship to the cylinder of which they are a part.

Kegan (1994) also distinguishes between a deconstructive and a reconstructive form of postmodernism. Deconstructive postmodernism is "antimodern," and while it deconstructs and rejects the logocentrism (the view that knowledge is immutable and absolute) of the fourth level of consciousness with its belief that the individual's system is separate from other systems, it offers no grounds for judgment or attempts at improvement of that system. Reconstructive postmodernism goes beyond the differentiation of the antimodernist stance toward the reintegration of modernism into a transformative way of knowing. This new way of knowing is characterized not by absolutism or theoretical supremacy but by advocacy of "a theory that was really a theory about theory-making, a theory that was mindful of the tendency of any intellectual system to reify itself, to identify internal consistency with validity, to call its fourth brand of subjectivity 'objectivity.' The expression of such a theory's 'maturity' would not be the modernist capacity to defend itself against all challenges, to demonstrate how all data gathered to it can find a place within it, but to assume its incompleteness and seek out contradiction by which to nourish the ongoing process of its reconstruction" (Kegan, 1994, pp. 329–330). Thus, Kegan reasons that his own meaning-making theory of subject-object relations is one that can be generalized and universalized without running counter to the postmodern repudiation of absolutism. Thus, as we have seen, his model of epistemological development posits reconstructive postmodernism to be the result of a developmental-constructivist progression of differentiation and integration. Deconstructive postmodernism constitutes the first phase of the fifth level of consciousness, and reconstructive postmodernism the second phase.

Conclusion

I conclude with a brief vignette, a true story from the Second World War, relayed in Oliner and Oliner's *The Altruistic Personality* (1988). It has implications for the theme of meaning-making that winds its way through this chapter and the remainder of this book. A woman tells the story of her husband, who as a civilian in Nazi-occupied territory during the war rescued a German soldier after a bombing in which the soldier was badly wounded. Later, her husband was accused by the couple's friends of being a traitor for having helped the enemy soldier, and the husband replied, "No, the moment the man was badly wounded, he was not an enemy anymore but simply a human being in need" (Oliner & Oliner, 1988, p. 228). To my way of making meaning, this is a simple but profound and poignant story that exemplifies the dialectical interplay between implicit universal principles of compassionate solidarity and respect for life and the actualization of those principles in a historically contextualized situation. Yet, in the spirit of Fowles's comments cited in the beginning of this chapter, each reader still has the task of making his or her own meaning out of this story, for while I can share my interpretation, I cannot instruct another on how the story ought to be construed.

References

Alexander, C. N., & Langer, E. J. (1990). *Higher stages of human development.* New York: Oxford University Press.

Alexander, P. C., & Neimeyer, G. J. (1989). Constructivism and family therapy. *International Journal of Personal Construct Psychology, 2,* 111–121.

Anderson, H., & Goolishian, H. A. (1988). Human systems as linguistic systems: Preliminary and evolving ideas about the implications for clinical theory. *Family Process, 27,* 371–393.

Arlow, J. A. (1989). Psychoanalysis. In R. J. Corsini & D. Wedding (Eds.), *Current psychotherapies* (4th ed., pp. 1–16). Itasca, IL: Peacock.

Averill, J. R. (1986). The acquisition of emotions during adulthood. In R. Harré (Ed.), *The social construction of emotions* (pp. 98–118). New York: Basil Blackwell.

Basseches, M. (1984). *Dialectical thinking and adult development.* Norwood, NJ: Ablex.

Baxter Magolda, M. B. (1992). *Knowing and reasoning in college: Gender-related patterns in students' intellectual development.* San Francisco: Jossey-Bass.

Belenky, M. F., Clinchy, B. M., Goldberger, N. R., & Tarule, J. M. (1986). *Women's ways of knowing: The development of self, voice, and mind.* New York: Basic Books.

Berger, P. L., & Luckman, T. (1966). *The social construction of reality.* New York: Bantam Doubleday Dell.

Brenner, C. (1982). *The mind in conflict.* Madison, CT: International Universities Press.

Bruner, J. (1986). *Actual minds, possible worlds.* Cambridge, MA: Harvard University Press.

Bruner, J. (1990). *Acts of meaning.* Cambridge, MA: Harvard University Press.

Callinicos, A. (1989). *Against postmodernism.* Cambridge, MA: Polity Press.

Camus, A. (1988). *The stranger* (M. Ward, Trans.). New York: Vintage Books. (Original work published 1942)

Carey, G. (1990). *Cliff notes on Camus' The Stranger.* Lincoln, NE: Cliff Notes.

Carlsen, M. B. (1988). *Meaning-making: Therapeutic processes in adult development.* New York: W.W. Norton.

Chandler, M. (1988). Doubt and developing theories of mind. In J. W. Astington, P. L. Harris, & D. R. Olson (Eds.), *Developing theories of mind* (pp. 387–413). New York: Cambridge University Press.

Chapman, M. (1988). *Constructive evolution: Origins and development of Piaget's thought.* New York: Cambridge University Press.

Commons, M. L., & Richards, F. A. (1984). A general model of stage theory. In M. L. Commons, F. A. Richards, & S. Armon (Eds.), *Beyond formal operations: Late adolescent and adult cognitive development* (pp. 120–140). New York: Praeger.

Commons, M. L., Richards, F. A., & Armon, S. (Eds.). (1984). *Beyond formal operations: Late adolescent and adult cognitive development.* New York: Praeger.

Derrida, J. (1976). *Of grammatology* (G. C. Spivack, Trans.). Baltimore, MD: Johns Hopkins University Press. (Original work published 1967)

Duncan, B. L., Solovey, A. D., & Rusk, G. S. (1992). *Changing the rules*. New York: Guilford Press.

Efran, J. S., Lukens, M. D., & Lukens, R. J. (1990). *Language, structure, and change: Frameworks of meaning in psychotherapy*. New York: W.W. Norton.

Elkaim, M. (1990). *If you love me, don't leave me: Constructions of reality and change in family therapy*. New York: Basic Books.

Fish, S. (1980). *Is there a text in this class?* Cambridge, MA: Harvard University Press.

Forster, J. (Ed.). (1994). Special section on narrative theory and therapy. *Journal of Constructivist Psychology, 7*, 219–261.

Fowler, J. W. (1981). *Stages of faith: The psychology of human development and the quest for meaning*. San Francisco: HarperSanFrancisco.

Fowles, J. (1965). *The magus*. New York: Bantam Doubleday Dell.

Frankl, V. E. (1985). *Man's search for meaning*. New York: Washington Square Press.

Freeman, M. (1993). *Rewriting the self: History, memory, narrative*. New York: Routledge & Kegan Paul.

Friedman, S. (Ed.). (1993). *The new language of change: Constructive collaboration in psychotherapy*. New York: Guilford Press.

Gadamer, H. G. (1975). *Truth and method* (G. Burden & J. Cumming, Trans.). New York: Seabury Press.

Gergen, K. J. (1985). The social constructionist movement in modern psychology. *American Psychologist, 40*, 266–275.

Gergen, K. J. (1990). If persons are texts. In S. B. Messer, L. A. Saas, & R. L. Woolfolk (Eds.), *Hermeneutics and psychological theory* (pp. 28–51). New Brunswick, NJ: Rutgers University Press.

Gergen, K. J. (1991). *The saturated self: Dilemmas of identity in contemporary life*. New York: Basic Books.

Gergen, K. J. (1994a). *Realities and relationship*. Cambridge, MA: Harvard University Press.

Gergen, K. J. (1994b). *Toward transformation in social knowledge* (2nd ed.). Newbury Park, CA: Sage.

Gilligan, S., & Price, R. (Eds.). (1993). *Therapeutic conversations*. New York: W.W. Norton.

Gilmore, M. (1994). *Shot in the heart*. New York: Doubleday.

Gonçalves, O. F. (1994). Cognitive narrative psychotherapy: The hermeneutic construction of alternative meanings. *Journal of Cognitive Psychotherapy: An International Quarterly, 8,* 105–125.

Goodman, N. (1978). *Ways of world-making.* Indianapolis, IN: Hackett.

Guidano, V. F. (1987). *Complexity of the self: A developmental approach to psychopathology and therapy.* New York: Guilford Press.

Guidano, V. F. (1991). *The self in process: Toward a post-rationalist psychotherapy.* New York: Guilford Press.

Guidano, V. F., & Liotti, G. (1983). *Cognitive processes and emotional disorders: A structural approach to psychotherapy.* New York: Guilford Press.

Hare-Mustin, R. T. (1994). Discourses in the mirrored room: A postmodern analysis of therapy. *Family Process, 33,* 19–35.

Harré, R. (Ed.). (1986). *The social construction of emotions.* New York: Basil Blackwell.

Held, B. S. (1995). *Back to reality: A critique of postmodern theory in psychotherapy.* New York: Guilford Press.

Hirsch, E. D. (1967). *Validity in interpretation.* New Haven, CT: Yale University Press.

Hoffman, L. (1990). Constructing realities: An art of lenses. *Family Process, 29,* 1–12.

Hollinger, R. (1994). *Postmodernism and the social sciences: A thematic approach.* Newbury Park, CA: Sage.

Holquist, M. (1990). *Dialogism.* New York: Routledge & Kegan Paul.

Howard, G. S. (1991). Culture tales: A narrative approach to thinking, cross-cultural psychology, and psychotherapy. *American Psychologist, 46,* 187–197.

Hoyt, M. F. (1994). *Constructive therapies.* New York: Guilford Press.

Ignatieff, M. (1993). *Scar tissue.* London: Chatto & Windus.

Inhelder, B., & Piaget, J. (1958). *The growth of logical thinking from childhood to adolescence* (A. Parsons & S. Milgram, Trans.). New York: Basic Books. (Original work published 1955)

Kamuf, P. (Ed.). (1991). *A Derrida reader: Between the lines.* New York: Columbia University Press.

Kegan, R. (1982). *The evolving self.* Cambridge, MA: Harvard University Press.

Kegan, R. (1994). *In over our heads: The mental demands of modern life.* Cambridge, MA: Harvard University Press.

Kelley, D. (1986). *The evidence of the senses: A realist theory of perception.* Baton Rouge: Louisiana State University Press.

Kelly, G. A. (1955). *The psychology of personal constructs* (2 vols.). New York: W.W. Norton.

Kelly, G. A. (1969). The psychotherapeutic relationship. In B. Maher (Ed.),

Clinical psychology and personality: The selected papers of George Kelly (pp. 216–223). New York: Wiley.

King, P. M., & Kitchener, K. S. (1994). *Developing reflective judgment: Understanding and promoting intellectual growth and critical thinking in adolescents and adults.* San Francisco: Jossey-Bass.

Kohlberg, L. (1981). *Essays on moral development: Vol. 1. The philosophy of moral development.* New York: HarperCollins.

Kohlberg, L. (1984). *Essays on moral development: Vol 2. The psychology of moral development.* New York: HarperCollins.

Loos, V. E., & Epstein, E. S. (1989). Conversational construction of meaning in family therapy: Some evolving thoughts on Kelly's sociality corollary. *International Journal of Personal Construct Psychology, 2,* 149–167.

Lyddon, W. J. (1992). Cognitive science and psychotherapy: An epistemic framework. In D. J. Stein & J. E. Young (Eds.), *Cognitive science and clinical disorders* (pp. 171–184). San Diego, CA: Academic Press.

Lyddon, W. J. (1993). Developmental constructivism: An integrative framework for psychotherapy practice. *Journal of Cognitive Therapy, 7,* 217–224.

Lyotard, J. (1984). *The postmodern condition: A report on knowledge.* Minneapolis: University of Minnesota Press.

McNamee, S., & Gergen, K. J. (Eds.). (1992). *Therapy as social construction.* Newbury Park, CA: Sage.

Mahoney, M. J. (1988a). Constructive metatheory: I. Basic features and historical foundations. *International Journal of Personal Construct Psychology, 1,* 1–35.

Mahoney, M. J. (1988b). Constructive metatheory: II. Implications for psychotherapy. *International Journal of Personal Construct Psychology, 1,* 299–315.

Mahoney, M. J. (1991). *Human change processes: The scientific foundations of psychotherapy.* New York: Basic Books.

Mahoney, M. J. (Ed.). (1995). *Cognitive and constructive psychotherapies.* New York: Springer.

Marshall, B. K. (1992). *Teaching the postmodern: Fiction and theory.* New York: Routledge & Kegan Paul.

Maturana, H. R. (1988). Reality: The search for objectivity or the quest for a compelling argument. *Irish Journal of Psychology, 9,* 25–82.

Maturana, H. R., & Varela, F. J. (1987). *The tree of knowledge: The biological roots of human understanding.* Boston: New Science Library.

Maugham, W. S. (1963). *Of human bondage.* New York: Viking Penguin. (Original work published 1915; U.S. publisher, Bantam Doubleday Dell)

Neimeyer, R. A. (1993a). An appraisal of constructivist therapies. *Journal of Consulting and Clinical Psychology, 61,* 221–234.

Neimeyer, R. A. (1993b). Constructivist psychotherapy. In K. T. Kuehlwein &
H. Rosen (Eds.), *Cognitive therapies in action: Evolving innovative practice*
(pp. 268–300). San Francisco: Jossey-Bass.

Neimeyer, R. A., & Feixas, G. (1990). Constructivist contributions to psychotherapy integration. *Journal of Integrative and Eclectic Psychotherapy, 9*, 4–20.

Neimeyer, R. A., & Mahoney, M. J. (Eds.). (1995). *Constructivism in psychotherapy*. Washington, DC: American Psychological Association.

Neimeyer, R. A., & Neimeyer, G. J. (Eds.). (1987). *Personal construct therapy
casebook*. New York: Springer.

Norris, C. (1990). *What's wrong with postmodernism: Critical theory and the ends of
philosophy*. Baltimore, MD: Johns Hopkins University Press.

Norris, C. (1992). *Uncritical theory: Postmodernism, intellectuals, and the Gulf
War*. Amherst: University of Massachusetts Press.

Nozick, R. (1993). *The nature of rationality*. Princeton, NJ: Princeton University
Press.

Oliner, S. P., & Oliner, P. M. (1988). *The altruistic personality: Rescuers of Jews in
Nazi Europe*. New York: Free Press.

Outhwaite, W. (1985). Hans-Georg Gadamer. In Q. Skinner (Ed.), *The return of
grand theory in the human sciences* (pp. 23–39). New York: Cambridge University Press.

Overton, W. F., & Palermo, D. S. (Eds.). (1994). *The nature and ontogenesis of
meaning*. Hillsdale, NJ: Erlbaum.

Packer, M. J. (1985). Hermeneutic inquiry in the study of human conduct.
American Psychologist, 40, 1081–1093.

Pape, G. J. (1994). Lacanian perspective: A Lacanian analysis of *Portnoy's Complaint*. In P. Buirski (Ed.), *Comparing schools of analytic therapy* (pp. 63–79).
Northvale, NJ: Aronson.

Perry, W. G. (1970). *Forms of intellectual and ethical development in the college
years*. New York: Academic Press.

Piaget, J. (1955). *The language and thought of the child* (M. Gabain, Trans.).
Cleveland: Meridian Books. (Original work published 1923)

Piaget, J. (1965). *The moral judgment of the child* (M. Gabain, Trans.). New York:
Free Press. (Original work published 1932)

Piaget, J. (1970). Piaget's theory. In P. H. Mussen (Ed.), *Carmichael's manual of
child psychology* (pp. 703–732). New York: Wiley.

Piaget, J. (1995). *Sociological studies* (L. Smith, Ed.). New York: Routledge &
Kegan Paul.

Piaget, J., & Inhelder, B. (1969). *The psychology of the child* (H. Weaver, Trans.).
New York: Basic Books. (Original work published 1966)

Purkhardt, S. C. (1993). *Transforming social representations: A social psychology of common sense and science*. New York: Routledge & Kegan Paul.

Rainbow, P. (1984). *The Foucault reader*. New York: Pantheon Books.

Readings, B., & Schaber, B. (Eds.). (1993). *Postmodernism across the ages*. Syracuse, NY: Syracuse University Press.

Rogers, L., & Kegan, R. (1991). Mental growth and mental health as distinct concepts in the study of developmental psychopathology: Theory, research, and clinical implications. In D. P. Keating & H. Rosen (Eds.), *Constructivist perspectives on developmental psychopathology and atypical development* (pp. 103–147). Hillsdale, NJ: Erlbaum.

Rorty, R. (1979). *Philosophy and the mirror of nature*. Princeton, NJ: Princeton University Press.

Rosen, H. (1980). *The development of sociomoral knowledge: A cognitive-structural approach*. New York: Columbia University Press.

Rosen, H. (1985). *Piagetian dimensions of clinical relevance*. New York: Columbia University Press.

Rosen, H. (1989). Piagetian theory and cognitive therapy. In A. Freeman, K. M. Simon, L. Beutler, & H. Arkowitz (Eds.), *Comprehensive handbook of cognitive therapy* (pp. 189–212). New York: Plenum.

Rosen, H. (1991). Constructivism: Personality, psychopathology and psychotherapy. In D. Keating & H. Rosen (Eds.), *Constructivist perspectives on developmental psychopathology and atypical development* (pp. 149–171). Hillsdale, NJ: Erlbaum.

Rosen, H. (1993). Developing themes in the field of cognitive therapy. In K. T. Kuehlwein & H. Rosen (Eds.), *Cognitive therapies in action: Evolving innovative practice* (pp. 403–434). San Francisco: Jossey-Bass.

Roth, P. (1969). *Portnoy's complaint*. New York: Random House.

Russell, R. L. (Ed.). (1991). Narrative. *Journal of Cognitive Psychotherapy, 5* [Special issue], 239–324.

Russell, R. L. (Ed.). (1995). *Discourse narrative in psychotherapy*. Washington, DC: American Psychological Association.

Saracino, M. (1991). Lovesickness: A disease in medieval disguise. *Health Lines, 7*(1), p. 3.

Sarbin, L. R. (1986). The narrative as a root metaphor for psychology. In T. R. Sarbin (Ed.), *Narrative psychology: The storied nature of human conduct* (pp. 3–21). New York: Praeger.

Schafer, R. (1992). *Retelling a life: Narration and dialogue in psychoanalysis*. New York: Basic Books.

Searle, J. R. (1995). *The construction of social reality*. New York: Free Press.

Selman, R. L. (1980). *The growth of interpersonal understanding: Developmental and clinical analyses*. San Diego, CA: Academic Press.

Shotter, J. (1993a). *Conversational realities: Constructing life through language*. Newbury Park, CA: Sage.

Shotter, J. (1993b). *Cultural politics of everyday life: Social constructionism, rhetoric and knowing of the third kind*. Toronto: University of Toronto Press.

Simon, R. (1985). Structure is destiny: An interview with Humberto Maturana. *The Family Therapy Networker, 9*, 32–37, 41–43.

Smith, L. (1993). *Necessary knowledge: Piagetian perspectives on constructivism*. Hillsdale, NJ: Erlbaum.

Sondheim, S., & Lapine, J. (1987). *Into the woods*. New York: Theatre Communications Group.

Spence, D. P. (1982). *Narrative truth and historical truth: Meaning and interpretation in psychoanalysis*. New York: W.W. Norton.

Spence, D. P. (1987). *The Freudian metaphor: Toward paradigm change in psychoanalysis*. New York: W.W. Norton.

Stevens-Long, J. (1990). Adult development: Theories past and future. In R. A. Nemiroff & C. A. Colarusso (Eds.), *New dimensions in adult development* (pp. 125–169). New York: Basic Books.

Strenger, C. (1991). *Between hermeneutics and science: An essay on the epistemology of psychoanalysis*. Madison, CT: International Universities Press.

Sulloway, F. J. (1992). Reassessing Freud's case histories: The social construction of psychoanalysis. In T. Gelfand & J. Kerr (Eds.), *Freud and the history of psychoanalysis* (pp. 153–192). Hillsdale, NJ: Analytic Press.

von Foerster, H. (1984). On constructing reality. In P. Watzlawick (Ed.), *The invented reality: How do we know what we believe we know? Contributions to constructivism* (pp. 41–61). New York: W.W. Norton.

von Glaserfeld, E. (1981). The concepts of adaptation and viability in a radical constructivist theory of knowledge. In I. E. Segal, D. M. Brodzinsky, & R. M. Golinkoff (Eds.), *New directions in Piagetian theory and practice* (pp. 87–95). Hillsdale, NJ: Erlbaum.

von Glaserfeld, E. (1984). An introduction to radical constructivism. In P. Watzlawick (Ed.), *The invented reality: How do we know what we believe we know? Contributions to constructivism* (pp. 17–40). New York: W.W. Norton.

Waters, D. (1994, November/December). Prisoners of our metaphors: Do dialogic therapies make other methods obsolete? *The Family Therapy Networker*, pp. 73–75.

Watzlawick, P. (Ed.). (1984). *The invented reality: How do we know what we believe we know? Contributions to constructivism*. New York: W.W. Norton.

Watzlawick, P. (1990). *Münchhausen's pigtail or psychotherapy and "reality"*. New York: W.W. Norton.

Watzlawick, P., Weakland, J. H., & Fisch, R. (1974). *Change: Principles of problem formation and problem resolution*. New York: W.W. Norton.

Werner, H. (1948). *Comparative psychology of mental development* (rev. ed.). Madison, CT: International Universities Press.

White, M., & Epston, D. (1990). *Narrative means to therapeutic ends*. New York: W.W. Norton.

Wood, L. A. (1986). Loneliness. In R. Harré (Ed.), *The social construction of emotions* (pp. 184–208). New York: Basil Blackwell.

Youniss, J., & Damon, W. (1992). Social construction in Piaget's theory. In H. Beilin & P. B. Pufall (Eds.), *Piaget's theory* (pp. 267–286). Hillsdale, NJ: Erlbaum.

Part II

. . . .

Constructivist and Social
Constructionist Epistemology and Praxis

The Construction of Clinical "Realities"

Paul Watzlawick

As clinicians, we are not usually also epistemologists, that is, we have no training in that branch of science that studies the origin and nature of knowledge. The implications and consequences of this are far-reaching and certainly go well beyond my own meager training in philosophy. However, I believe that at least some basic epistemological considerations determine the direction our field is taking, and they thus do enter into the subject matter that clinicians must consider.

Defining Normalcy

Let me begin with one such consideration that may be trivially obvious to some and almost scandalous to others: in contrast to the medical sciences, our field does not have a generally accepted, final definition of normalcy. Physicians are in the fortunate position of possessing a fairly clear, objectively verifiable idea of what may be called the normal functioning of the human body. This enables them to identify deviations from the norm and allows them to consider them pathologies. It goes without saying that this knowledge does not also enable them to treat every such deviation. But it definitely means that they presumably can make distinctions between most manifestations of health or of illness.

The question of the emotional or mental health of an individual is a totally different matter. It is not a scientific, but a philosophical, a metaphysical, or even a plainly superstitious assumption. For us to become aware of what or who we "really" are would require us to step outside ourselves and look at ourselves objectively, a feat coming close to what so far only Baron von Münchhausen was able to accomplish when he saved himself and his horse from drowning in a quagmire by pulling himself out by his own pigtail.

Any attempt by the human mind to study itself leads to the problems of recursiveness or self-reference, which have the same structure as certain jokes, such as the question, What is intelligence? and the answer, Intelligence is that mental capacity that is measured by intelligence tests.

Throughout the ages, insanity was considered the deviation from a norm that itself was considered to be the final, ultimate truth. So "final" was that truth, that to question it was itself a symptom of madness or badness. The age of enlightenment was no exception, except that instead of reason being some divine revelation, the human mind itself now had divine properties and was referred to as *déesse raison*. According to the pronouncement of this Goddess Reason, the universe was governed by logical principles, the human mind was capable of grasping these principles, and the human will was capable of acting according to them. Let me mention only as an aside that the enthronement of the Goddess Reason led to the killing of about 40,000 people by means of Dr. Guillotin's enlightened invention and eventually, feeding back upon itself, to the establishment of yet another traditional monarchy.

Over one hundred years later, a far more pragmatic and humane definition of normalcy was introduced by Freud, who defined it as "the ability to work and to love." For many people, this definition seemed to serve its purpose and thus found wide acceptance. Unfortunately, however, according to this definition, Hitler would have been sort of normal because, as we all know, he worked very hard and he loved at least his dog if not also his mistress, Eva Braun. In addition, Freud's definition is found lacking when we are faced with the proverbial eccentricities of particularly outstanding people.

These problems may have contributed to the general acceptance of yet another definition of normalcy, namely, that of *reality adaptation*. According to this criterion, normal people (and especially therapists) see reality as it really is, while people suffering from emotional or mental problems see it in a distorted way. This definition unquestioningly assumes that there is a real reality that is accessible to the human mind, an assumption that has been philosophically untenable for at least two hundred years. Hume, Kant, Schopenhauer, and many others have insisted that of the real reality we can only have an opinion, a subjective image, an arbitrary interpretation. According to Kant, for instance, every error consists in taking the way *we* determine, divide, or deduce concepts for qualities of the *things* in and of themselves. And Schopenhauer, in *The Will in Nature* (1912), wrote: "This is the meaning of Kant's great doctrine, that teleology [the study of evidences of design and purpose in nature] is brought into nature by the intellect, which thus marvels at a miracle that it has created itself in the first place" (p. 346, my translation).

It is quite easy to dismiss such views scornfully as merely "philosophical" and therefore devoid of practical usefulness. But similar statements can be found in the works of representatives of what is generally considered to be natural science at its best: theoretical physics. In 1926, during a conversation with Heisenberg on theory building, Einstein is said to have asserted that it is quite wrong to try founding a theory only on objective observation. The very opposite is true: it is the theory that decides what we can observe.

In a similar vein, Schrödinger (1958), in his book *Mind and Matter*, asserts, "Everyman's world picture is and always remains a construct of his mind and cannot be proved to have any other existence" (p. 52).

And Heisenberg (1958) states on the same subject:

> The reality that we can talk about is never the "a priori"
> reality, but a known reality shaped by us. If with regard
> to this latter formulation it is objected that, after all,

there is an objective world, independent from us and our thinking, which functions, or can function, without our doing, and which is that which we actually mean when doing research, this objection, so convincing at first blush, must be countered by pointing out that even the expression "there is" originates in human language and cannot, therefore, mean something that is unrelated to our comprehension. For us "there is" only the world in which the expression "there is" has meaning [p. 236].

The self-referential circularity of the mind when it subjects itself to a "scientific study" was well described by the famous biocybernetician Heinz von Foerster (1974).

We are now in the possession of the truism that a description (of the universe) implies one who describes (observes) it. What we need now is the description of the "describer" or, in other words, we need a theory of the observer. Since it is only living organisms which would qualify as being observers, it appears that this task falls to the biologist. But he himself is a living being, which means that in his theory he has not only to account for himself, but also for his writing the theory. This is a new state of affairs in scientific discourse for, in line with the traditional viewpoint which separates the observer from his observations, reference to this discourse was to be carefully avoided. This separation was done by no means because of eccentricity or folly, for under certain circumstances inclusion of the observer in his descriptions may lead to paradoxes, to wit the utterance "I am a liar" [p. 401, my translation].

And perhaps even more radical (in the original sense of "going to the roots") is the statement of the Chilean biologist Francisco Varela (1975) in his *Calculus for Self-Reference*.

The starting point of this calculus . . . is the act of indication. In this primordial act we separate forms which
appear to us as the world itself. From this starting point,
we thus assert the primacy of the role of the observer
who draws distinctions wherever he pleases. Thus the
distinctions made which engender our world reveal precisely that: the distinctions we make—and these distinctions pertain more to a revelation of where the
observer stands than to an intrinsic constitution of the
world which appears, by this very mechanism of separation between observer and observed, always elusive. In
finding the world as we do, we forget all we did to find
it as such, and when we are reminded of it in retracing
our steps back to indication, we find little more than a
mirror-to-mirror image of ourselves and the world. In
contrast with what is commonly assumed, a description,
when carefully inspected, reveals the properties of the
observer. We, observers, distinguish ourselves precisely
by distinguishing what we apparently are not, the world
[p. 24].

All right, we may say, but what has all of this to do with our profession, in which we are up against the stark realities of behavior
whose insanity not even a philosopher could deny?

In reply, let me cite that strange incident that took place more
than two years ago in the Italian city of Grosseto. A woman from
Naples, on a visit to Grosseto, had to be admitted to the local hospital in a state of acute schizophrenic excitement. Since the psychiatric ward was unable to admit her, it was decided to send her
back to Naples for proper treatment. When the ambulance attendants arrived and asked where the patient was, they were told in
what room she was waiting. Upon entering, they found the patient
sitting on a bed, fully dressed and her handbag ready. When they
invited her to come downstairs to the waiting ambulance, she again

became quite psychotic, physically resisting the attendants, refusing to move, and above all, depersonalizing. She had to be forcibly tranquilized and carried down into the ambulance, and off they went to Naples.

On the *autostrada* outside Rome, the ambulance was stopped by a police car and sent back to Grosseto: there had been a mistake; the woman in the ambulance was not the patient but an inhabitant of Grosseto who had gone to the hospital to pay a visit to a relative who had undergone minor surgery.

Would it be exaggerated to say that the mistake had created (or as we radical constructivists would say, "constructed") a clinical reality in which precisely the "reality-adapted" behavior of that woman was clear evidence of her "insanity"? She became aggressive, accused the staff of evil intentions, began to depersonalize, and so on.

Whoever is familiar with the work of the psychologist David Rosenhan did not have to wait until the Grosseto incident for examples of these matters. Fifteen years earlier, Rosenhan published the results of an elegant study, "On Being Sane in Insane Places" (1984), in which he and his team proved that normal people are not detectably sane and that psychiatric hospitals create realities of their own.

An essentially analogous example was reported by the news media about a year ago from the Brazilian city of São Paulo. According to this report, it had been found necessary to raise the (very low) railing of the terrace of the Riding Club, since a number of visitors had fallen backward over the railing and severely hurt themselves. Since apparently not all these accidents could be simply explained away by drunkenness, another explanation was suggested, presumably by an anthropologist: different cultures have different rules regarding the "correct" distance to assume and maintain while engaged in a face-to-face conversation with another person. In Western European and North American cultures, this distance is the proverbial arm's length; in Mediterranean and Latin-American cultures, it is considerably shorter. Thus, if a North American and a Brazilian began a conversation, the North American presumably would establish that distance that to him was the "correct, normal" one. The Brazilian would feel uncomfortably distant from the other and would move closer, in order to establish the distance that to the Brazilian was the "right" one; the North American would move back, the other would move closer, and so on, until the North American would fall backward over the railing. Thus, two different realities had created an event for which, in the classical monadic view of human behavior, the diagnosis of accident proneness or even of the manifestation of a "death instinct" would not be too far-fetched and would thus construct a clinical reality.

The reality-creating power of such cultural rules is the subject of Walter Cannon's classic paper "Voodoo Death" (1942), a fascinating collection of anthropological case material demonstrating how a person's firm belief in the power of a curse or evil spell may lead to the death of that person in a matter of hours. In one instance, moreover, when some members of an Australian bush tribe forced a medicine man to withdraw his curse, the victim, who had already sunk into lethargy, recovered in a very short time.

As far as I know, nobody has studied the construction of such clinical realities in greater detail than Thomas Szasz. Of his many books, *The Manufacture of Madness: A Comparative Study of the Inquisition and the Mental Health Movement* (1970) is of particular relevance to my subject. And of the many historical sources utilized by Szasz, let me refer to the one with which I am most familiar. It is the book *Cautio Criminalis*, dealing with trials of witches, written by the Jesuit Friedrich von Spee in 1631 (reprinted in Ritter, 1977). In his capacity as father confessor of many people accused of witchcraft, von Spee witnessed the most atrocious torture scenes, and he wrote the book in order to make the court authorities aware of the fact that under their rules of trial procedure, no suspect could ever be found innocent. In our terminology, the rules constructed a reality in which any behavior of the accused was evidence of guilt. Here are some of the court's "proofs":

- God would protect the innocent from the beginning; "therefore," not being saved by God is in and of itself already proof of guilt.

- A suspect's life is either righteous or not. If it is not, that is additional proof. If it is, that gives rise to additional suspicion, for it is well-known that witches are capable of creating righteous impressions.

- Once in jail, the witch will be either fearful or not. If fearful, this is obvious proof of a guilty conscience. If without fear, this confirms the probability of guilt, for it is well known that the most dangerous witches are capable of appearing innocent and calm.

- The suspect either tries to flee or not. Any attempt to flee is obvious and additional proof of guilt, while not attempting to flee means that the devil wants the suspect's death.

As we can see again, the *meaning* attributed to a set of circumstances within a given frame of assumptions, ideologies, or beliefs constructs a reality all of its own and reveals that "truth," so to speak. In Gregory Bateson's terms, these are double-bind situations, logical impasses, of which he gave countless clinical examples—in particular, in his book *Perceval's Narrative: A Patient's Account of His Psychosis* (1961).

John Perceval, son of the British prime minister Spencer Perceval, became psychotic in 1830 and remained hospitalized until 1834. In the years following his release, he wrote two biographical accounts, entitled *Narrative*, detailing his experiences as a mental patient. Here is just one of Bateson's observations about the interaction between the patient and his family: "[The parents] cannot perceive their own perfidy except as justified by the patient's behavior, and the patient will not let them perceive how his behavior is related to his view of what they have done and are now doing. The tyranny of 'good intentions' must endlessly be served while the patient achieves an ironic sainthood, sacrificing himself in foolish or self-destructive actions until at least he is justified in quoting the Saviour's prayer: 'Father, forgive them, they know not what they do. Amen'" (p. xviii).

However, the ancient wisdom *similia similibus curantur* (likes are cured by likes) also applies to these situations. The most ancient example known to me of the construction of a positive clinical reality is reported by Plutarch in his *Morals* (Goodwin, 1898) and deals with the extraordinary success of the "mental health authorities" of the ancient city of Milesia in Asia Minor.

> A certain dreadful and monstrous distemper did seize the Milesian maids, arising from some hidden cause. It is most likely the air had acquired some infatuating and venomous quality, that did influence them to this change and alienation of mind; for all on a sudden an earnest longing for death, with furious attempts to hang themselves, did attack them, and many did privily accomplish it. The arguments and tears of parents and the persuasion of friends availed nothing, but they circumvented their keepers in all their contrivances and industry to prevent them, still murdering themselves. And the calamity seemed to be an extraordinary divine stroke and beyond human help, until by the counsel of a wise man a decree of the senate was passed, enacting that those maids who hanged themselves should be carried naked through the market-place. The passage of this law not only inhibited but quashed their desire of slaying themselves. Note what a great argument of good nature and virtue this fear of disgrace is; for they who had no dread upon them of the most terrible things in the world, death and pain, could not abide the imagination of dishonor and exposure to shame even after death [p. 354].

Maybe that wise man was aware of the equally ancient wisdom of Epictetus, who said that it is not the things that bother us, but the opinions that we have of things.

But these examples are exceptions. By and large, our field has never stopped assuming that the existence of a name is proof of the real existence of the thing named, Alfred Korzybski (1933) and his warning—namely, that *the name is not the thing, the map is not the territory*—notwithstanding. The most monumental example of this kind of reality construction, at least in our days, is the *Diagnostic and Statistical Manual of Mental Disorders* (DSM), now in its fourth edition (American Psychiatric Association, 1994). Its creators must be credited with what is probably the greatest therapeutic success of all times. Reacting to growing social pressure, they no longer included in the third edition (DSM-III) homosexuality as a psychiatric condition, thereby curing millions of people of their "disease" by the stroke of a pen. But leaving facetiousness aside, the practical, clinical consequences of the use of diagnostic terms are being studied seriously by Karl Tomm and his team in the Family Therapy Program, Department of Psychiatry, University of Calgary.

What practical, useful conclusions may be drawn from all of this?

If it is accepted that mental normalcy cannot be defined objectively, then, of necessity, the concept of mental illness is just as undefinable. But then, what about therapy?

Implications for Therapy

It is at this point that we should turn our attention to a phenomenon that has been known for a long time, albeit almost exclusively as a negative, undesirable set of circumstances: the self-fulfilling prophecy. The first, detailed study goes back to the research of Russell A. Jones (1974) (and here I quote the subtitle of his book) into the "social, psychological, and physiological effects of expectancies."

As is by now generally known, a self-fulfilling prophecy is an assumption or prediction that, precisely because it has been made, causes the expected or predicted event to occur and, thus, recursively, confirms its own "accuracy." The study of interpersonal relations offers numerous examples. For instance, if a man assumes, for whatever reason, that people do not like him, he will, because of this assumption, behave in such a hostile, overly sensitive, suspicious manner as to produce in his human environment that very dislike that he expected, and that "proves" to him how right he was from the beginning.

A self-fulfilling prophecy on a statewide scale occurred in March 1979, when the California mass media reported an imminent severe gasoline shortage as a result of the Arab oil embargo. As a result, California motorists did what, under the circumstances, was the only reasonable thing; they stormed the gas stations to fill up their tanks and to keep the tanks as full as possible. This filling up of 12 million gas tanks (which up to that point had probably been about 70 percent empty) depleted the enormous fuel reserves and brought about the predicted shortage, literally within a day. Endless lines formed at the gas stations, but about three weeks later, the chaos came to an end when it was officially announced that the allotment of gasoline to the state of California had been reduced only minimally.

Other by now classical studies are the highly interesting investigations of Robert Rosenthal, in particular, his book *Pygmalion in the Classroom* (Rosenthal & Jacobson, 1968), to say nothing of a plethora of investigations into the effects of placebos, those chemically inert substances that the patient assumes are newly developed powerful medications. Although known since ancient times and used by all sorts of "spiritual" healers, *curanderos*, and the like, the placebo effect did not receive much scientific attention until about the middle of our century. According to Shapiro (1960), more research reports on this subject were published between 1954 and 1957 alone than during the fifty preceding years.

To what extent mere assumptions or attributions of meaning to perceptions can have a powerful effect on a person's physical state is well borne out by an example I have already reported elsewhere (Watzlawick, 1990).

A hypnotist, highly respected for his skills and clinical successes, was invited to give a workshop for a group of doctors in the home of one of them. Upon entering the house, he noticed that, as he put it, "every horizontal surface was filled with flower bouquets." Because he was afflicted with a strong allergy to freshly cut flowers, almost immediately the well-known burning sensations made themselves felt in his eyes and nose. He turned to the host and mentioned his problem and his fear that under these circumstances he would be unable to give his talk. The host expressed surprise and asked him to examine the flowers, which turned out to be artificial. Upon his making this discovery, his allergic reaction subsided almost as quickly as it had come on.

This example seems to provide clear evidence that the criterion of reality adaptation is, after all, fully valid. The man *thought* that the flowers were real, but as soon as he discovered that they were only nylon and plastic, this confrontation with reality resolved his problem and he returned to normalcy.

First- (and Second-) Order Realities

At this point, it becomes necessary to draw a distinction between two levels of reality perceptions that are usually thrown into one pot. We need to distinguish between the image of reality that we receive through our senses and the meaning we attribute to these perceptions. For instance, a neurologically healthy person can see, touch, and smell a bunch of flowers. (For simplicity's sake, we shall disregard the fact that these perceptions also are the result of fantastically complex constructions carried out by our central nervous system. Let us further disregard the fact that the phrase "bunch of flowers" has meaning only for English-speaking people. It is meaningless noise or a series of letter symbols for anybody else.) Let us call this the *reality of the first order*.

However, matters rarely rest at this point. Almost invariably, we attribute a sense, meaning, and/or value to the objects of our perception. And it is at this level, the level of the *second-order reality*, that problems arise. The crucial difference between these two levels of reality perception is well illustrated by the old joke, what is the difference between an optimist and a pessimist? The answer: an optimist says of a bottle of wine that it is half full; a pessimist says that it is half empty. The first-order reality is the same for both of them (a bottle with some wine in it); their second-order realities are different, and it would be totally useless to try to establish who is right and who is wrong.

In the case of the hypnotist with the allergy, then, his allergy can be considered a phenomenon that usually takes place on the level of his first-order reality, that is, his system reacts in typical, objectively verifiable ways to the presence of pollen in the air. But as the example demonstrates, the mere assumption of the presence of flowers (in other words, the construction of a second-order reality) produced the same result.

As I have already mentioned, the medical sciences do have a reasonably reliable definition of such first-order-reality events and processes. In the realm of psychotherapy, however, we are in a universe of mere assumptions, convictions, and beliefs that are part of our second-order reality and, therefore, are constructions of our minds. The processes whereby we construct our personal, social, scientific and ideological realities and then consider them "objectively real" are the subject matter of that modern epistemological discipline called *radical constructivism*.

Reality and Psychotherapy

Probably one of the most shocking tenets of this school of thought is that of the real reality we can at best know what it is *not*. In other words, only when our reality construction breaks down do we realize that reality is not the way we thought it was. In his "Introduction to Radical Constructivism," Ernst von Glaserfeld (1984) defines knowledge as

> Something the organism builds up in the attempt to order the as such amorphous flow of experience by establishing repeatable experiences and relatively reliable relations between them. The possibilities of constructing such an order are determined and perpetually constrained by the preceding steps in the construction. This means that the "real" world manifests itself exclusively there where our constructions break down. But since we can describe and explain these breakdowns only in the very concepts that we have used to build the failing structures, this process can never yield a picture of a world which we could hold responsible for their failure [p. 39]).

But it is these failures, these breakdowns, that we are faced with in our work, these states of anxiety, despair, and madness that befall us when we find ourselves in a world that gradually or suddenly has become meaningless. And if we can accept the possibility that of the real world we can only know for certain what it is not, then psychotherapy becomes the art of replacing a reality construction that no longer "fits" with another, better-fitting one. This new construction is just as fictitious as the former except that it permits us the comfortable illusion, called "mental health," that we now see things the way they "really" are and that we are thus in tune with the meaning of life.

Seen in this perspective, psychotherapy is concerned with *reframing* the client's worldview, of constructing another clinical reality, of bringing about deliberately those chance events that Franz Alexander (1956) called corrective emotional experiences. Constructivist psychotherapy is under no illusion of making the client see the world as it really is. Rather, constructivism is fully aware that the new worldview is, and can only be, another construction, another fiction—but a useful, less painful one.

At the end of a brief therapy (of nine sessions), one client, a young woman, had this to say: "The way I saw the situation, it was a problem. Now I see it differently, and it is no problem any more."

To me, these words are the quintessence of successful therapy: the reality of the first order has, of necessity, remained unchanged, but the client's second-order reality now is different and bearable.

And these words bring us back to Epictetus: it is not the things that bother us, but the opinions that we have of things.

References

Alexander, F. (1956). *Psychoanalysis and psychotherapy.* New York: W.W. Norton.

American Psychiatric Association. (1994). *Diagnostic and statistical manual of mental disorders* (4th ed.). Washington, DC: Author.

Bateson, G. (1961). *Perceval's narrative: A patient's account of his psychosis.* Stanford, CA: Stanford University Press.

Cannon, W. B. (1942). Voodoo death. *American Anthropologist,* 44, pp. 169–181.

Goodwin, W. W. (Ed.). (1898). *Plutarch's miscellanies and essays* (Vol. 1). Boston: Little, Brown.

Heisenberg, W. (1958). *Physics and philosophy.* New York: HarperCollins.

Jones, R. A. (1974). *Self-fulfilling prophecies.* New York: Halsted.

Korzybski, A. (1933). *Science and sanity.* New York: International Non-Aristotelian Library.

Ritter, J. F. (1977). *Friedrich von Spee.* Trier: Springer-Verlag.

Rosenhan, D. L. (1984). On being sane in insane places. In P. Watzlawick (Ed.), *The invented reality: How do we know what we believe we know? Contributions to constructivism* (pp. 17–44). New York: W.W. Norton.

Rosenthal, R., & Jacobson, L. (1968). *Pygmalion in the classroom.* Troy, MO: Holt, Rinehart & Winston.

Schopenhauer, A. (1912). *Über den Willen in der Natur.* Munich: Piper.

Schrödinger, E. (1958). *Mind and matter.* Cambridge, England: Cambridge University Press.

Shapiro, A. K. (1960). A contribution to the history of the placebo effects. *Behavioral Science,* 5, 109–135.

Szasz, T. (1970). *The manufacture of madness: A comparative study of the Inquisition and the mental health movement.* New York: Bantam Doubleday Dell.

Varela, F. J. (1975). A calculus for self-reference. *International Journal of General Systems, 2*, 5–24.

von Foerster, H. (1974). Notes pour une épistemologie des objets vivants. In E. Morin & M. Piatelli-Palmarini (Eds.), *L'unite de l'homme* (pp. 401–417). Paris: LeSeuil.

von Glaserfeld, E. (1984). An introduction to radical constructivism. In P. Watzlawick (Ed.), *The invented reality: How do we know what we believe we know? Contributions to constructivism* (pp. 17–40). New York: W.W. Norton.

Watzlawick, P. (1990). Therapy is what you say it is. In J. K. Zeig & S. G. Gilligan (Eds.), *Brief therapy: Myths, methods, and metaphors* (pp. 55–61). New York: Brunner/Mazel.

3

Psychotherapeutic Theory and Practice

Contributions from Maturana's Structure Determinism

Jay S. Efran and Mitchell A. Greene

Neophyte therapists often express confusion about their role—should they be empathic listeners, reflecting mirrors, conflict mediators, social advocates, political reformers, conversational hosts, junior physicians, psychological coaches, religious guides, or New Age gurus? Lacking role clarity, novices frequently find themselves at the mercy of clients' demands and expectations, and they may become defensive when asked direct questions about how therapy works. Because of their insecurity, they are also apt to oscillate between therapeutic models—sometimes mixing several therapy styles in a single session.

Unfortunately, such issues are not limited to beginners. Even some experienced therapists waffle when asked to describe succinctly what they do or to explain why some of their cases turn out more successfully than others (Omer & London, 1988). To gain clarity, therapists have borrowed models from a variety of neighboring fields, including medicine, religion, social engineering, and labor relations. However, these role appropriations are often as confusing as they are helpful in specifying the therapist's task. For example, jargon derived from medicine—such as the familiar concepts of "treatment," "cure," "patient," "case," "symptom," "pathology," "illness," "health," "placebo," "disease," and "prognosis"—loses its precise meaning when transmuted to the mental health field. It was George Kelly (1955), the early constructivist thinker, who frequently argued that the word patient inappropriately implies that a person having problems should wait *patiently* on the sidelines for the good doctor to perform his or her ministrations. Other medical terms can be equally misleading. For instance, the term treatment suggests the existence of specialized mental health techniques, analogous to the interventions of physical medicine. However, therapists have no ointments or tourniquets to apply, no antibiotics to administer, and no surgical procedures to perform.

There are, of course, special conversational formats for therapeutic interaction—for example, psychoanalytic free association, rational-emotive disputations, cognitive-behavioral restructuring, client-centered reflecting, solution-oriented reframing, and so on. However, the magic of therapy is not contained in any specific formula. In the final analysis, therapy is basically just *talk*—ordinary conversation. Although it has often been made to sound complex and mysterious, it is actually one of the most straightforward operations imaginable.

To find a way through the maze of apparent therapeutic complexities, we recommend using a framework derived from Humberto Maturana's theory of *structure determinism* (Maturana & Varela, 1980, 1987; Zeleny, 1981). In our view, this modern biological perspective, with its broad scope and high degree of internal consistency, offers a solid theoretical grounding for mental health professionals in search of clarity about their profession.

Maturana's Emerging Epistemology

Humberto Maturana is a Chilean biologist who, along with his former student and colleague, Francesco Varela, has formulated a radically new epistemology of living systems. Maturana's early research investigated the visual system of the frog (Maturana & Varela, 1987). His findings in that domain ultimately caused him to question the existing views of perceptual and cognitive functioning, leading him to an almost complete revamping of biology's basic assumptions. Perhaps most significantly, his investigations forced him to conclude that an organism's nervous system is *closed* rather than open to outside information. In other words, it does not absorb "data" from the outside, as people have so long believed, nor does it store internal representations of external stimuli. Basically, the nervous system is a closed network of neuronal connections that operates in accordance with its own structure. Outside events may *trigger* nervous system operations, but they never determine or circumscribe the exact nature of the resulting neuronal activity. This is a point to which we will return later.

Defining Life

At about the same time that Maturana was coming to these far-reaching conclusions, an innocent inquiry from a medical student about how living systems are to be defined prompted him to further question biology's fundamental postulates. When the student posed the question, Maturana realized that neither he nor other biologists could adequately define the boundary between living and nonliving systems. Such lack of clarity about basic definitions occurs often in scientific enterprises because workers tend to take so much for granted in their daily conversations with each other. Biologists trying to define life found themselves in a position not unlike Supreme Court Justice Potter Stewart's predicament concerning pornography: after several attempts to formally delineate the boundaries of pornography, Stewart reputedly stated, "Perhaps I can't define it, but I know it when I see it" (Hall, 1992, p. 837). Similarly, biologists studying organisms had not been able to arrive at an all-encompassing definition of their subject matter. Older biological viewpoints—for example, that only living things "grow"—had long since been rendered obsolete by advancements in theory and research.

Having promised the medical student that he would return with a better answer, Maturana set out to work with Varela on two closely related problems that initially appeared to Maturana and Varela to be quite separate. First, what does it mean to be alive, and second, how do living organisms come to know what they seem to know? Although Maturana and Varela originally studied nonhuman species—notably frogs and pigeons—they developed a model that turned out to have direct applicability to human functioning. As a side benefit, this framework can be of enormous practical significance to mental health practitioners (Dell, 1982a, 1982b; Efran & Lukens, 1985; Efran, Lukens, & Lukens, 1990; Varela, 1989). In particular, Maturana and Varela proposed a useful and inclusive definition of language as a biological phenomenon and explicated its central role in shaping human cognition.

Redefining Science

As Maturana continued pondering about the human condition, he soon realized that earlier descriptions of science were also deeply flawed. Scientific inquiry has traditionally been portrayed as opening a privileged window on reality. However, this conceptualization does not fit with Maturana and Varela's interpretation of how human beings generate knowledge or how their nervous systems operate. Maturana (1990) demonstrated that even when the canons of scientific research are scrupulously followed, the structure of an organism and the manner in which it is *coupled* with its environment *must* become part of the knowledge equation. In other words, *observer* and *observed* can never fully be separated. Thus, it is impossible to draw a totally unbiased conclusion or produce a fully objective observation. As Varela (1979) has stated, "Everything said is said from a tradition" (p. 268). Therefore, this tradition colors meaning. And therefore, although science can yield useful insights about living, it cannot fulfill its original mission of providing a context-free purview of an external reality.

Constructivists had previously espoused a similar position on the basis of philosophical speculation, logical deduction, and practical experience (Anderson, 1990; Efran, Lukens, & Lukens, 1988; Gergen, 1982, 1985; Mahoney, 1991; Watzlawick, 1984). However, Maturana and Varela gave the viewpoint added cogency by arriving at an identical conclusion on the basis of their neurological investigation.

Before anyone too hastily concludes that the new definitions Maturana and Varela proposed bring scientific investigation and clinical work to a standstill, note that neither the everyday craft of science nor the daily operations of a therapist actually hinge on the assumption that there is an independently knowable universe. Although both activities are presumed to be grounded in facts about an external world, both scientific and clinical practice have generally been about human beings, about all of *us*, and about minimizing the hazards of communal living.

The Vocabulary of Structure Determinism

A complete understanding of Maturana's theory requires tackling some difficult concepts—at a minimum, the terms *autopoiesis, structural coupling, purposeless drift, orthogonal interaction, instructive interaction*, and *emotional contradiction*. His unfamiliar vocabulary will strike some readers as arcane and cumbersome; the way he defines language will startle some. However, as the theory of structure determinism itself implies, new and initially odd phrasings constitute the tools needed for breaking out of traditional thinking patterns. New conceptualizations require new words—or old ones "retrofitted" for the purpose.

The Importance of Being in Language

Maturana attributes to language processes all those qualities considered most human about people. For instance, language makes possible a sense of self and the phenomenon of self-awareness. It permits all of us to distinguish a world of separate *things* and *events* (including ourselves and our activities). As human beings operating in language, we are able to become observers of our own evolving circumstances and can engage in the sorts of self-examination processes that characterize psychotherapy (Efran & Fauber, 1995). Explanatory schemes, comparisons, meanings, and future plans are all constructed in language, along with the perspective of time and the lineal concept of cause and effect. Without language, there is only the silent here and now of our immediate experience.

Language as Social Action

Although most of us tend to think of language functions, such as thinking and reasoning, as located in the cortical regions of the brain, Maturana argues compellingly that these higher functions actually exist in the social domain. Surely, a cortex is needed for a person to enter into conversation, but words are communal actions, not individual performances. In order for people to operate in language, they need a certain degree of nervous system plasticity as well as a history of collective action in closely knit social groups. In that sense, "languaging" is for humans what grooming is for chimps—a crucial factor in establishing and maintaining the social order.

For Maturana, language consists of both words and symbols. It also includes the kinesic (Birdwhistell, 1970) elements that help establish and convey meanings. Although older definitions of language have separated language and action, Maturana insists that language is a *form* of action. Biologically speaking, it is the second-order coordination of activity in a social domain—a coordination of coordinations.

It is not unusual for members of other animal species to play, hunt, feed, and procreate together in choreographed sequences. However, language makes possible additional layers of complexity in the group choreography. Animals establish a pecking order through their immediate performances, but human beings go several steps further, *discussing* each other's status and emblazoning symbols of hierarchy on office doors, desk signs, and organizational charts. Moreover, the recursive property of language makes possible a practically endless nesting of linguistic layers, creating self-referential loops of mind-boggling complexity. For example, a client can drink to excess, talk about abstaining, admit to being a hypocrite when he talks that way, resolve to stop being so hypocritical, and finally, indicate (in disgust) that all his previous chatter should be taken with a grain of salt. Therapeutic dialogue, in particular, contains a dizzying array of explanations, excuses, disavowals, and reinterpretations. Clients have insights about their insights, and insights about those insights. To make matters worse, this language spiral is not simply epiphenomenal. In other words, an unfolding pattern can be changed by how an individual chooses to describe it. Thus, if the drinker in our example listens to his own rhetoric long enough, he may soon convince himself to attend an Alcoholics Anonymous meeting. At that meeting, his earlier hypocrisies may then serve as the starting point for his latest attempt at recovery.

Because talking is acting, anything said colors whatever is next said or done, in an unending series of reciprocal loops. As many clients have noted, even an offhand remark or chance occurrence can spark a major shift in their lives' ongoing conversational drift.

A Useful Accident

Not long ago, an anxious young girl being seen in our clinic witnessed her therapist accidentally trip over a wastebasket in the hallway. According to her later report (and confirming observations from parents and teachers), this fortuitous event created more therapeutic movement than a number of lengthy therapy discussions. The girl was impressed at how unconcerned the therapist was about "appearing foolish" when she tripped. The girl was also intrigued that onlookers seemed more interested in checking on the therapist's physical welfare than in ridiculing her "mistake." The therapist's casual handling of the entire incident contrasted with the girl's own perfectionist predilections, and she soon found herself judging her own behavior less harshly. Although neither she nor her therapist could have planned it that way, the hallway mishap provided just the right conversational perturbation to alter the drift of the client's internal dialogue.

Trivial and Nontrivial Systems

As the previous example illustrates, we can never be certain what a nervous system will do with a particular external trigger. The nervous system continuously creates its own meanings using the raw material the medium provides. In cybernetic terms, living systems are *nontrivial* machines. By contrast, computers—even those of great complexity—are *trivial* machines, meaning that output is entirely contingent on input. With living systems, there are always surprises. Knowing the starting conditions does not allow us to predict the outcome. An intervention that works wonderfully with one client falls flat with the next, even though the two clients' situations seem virtually identical. A client who has failed to make progress with many therapists suddenly improves even though nothing new appears to have been added to the equation. Because therapy deals with nontrivial machines, it is, and will likely remain, an inexact science, regardless of how much hard-nosed manual-driven research is conducted. The best a therapist can do is make educated guesses based on past experience, basic principles, thoughtful research findings, and the cues the client provides. Only modest levels of predictability and control are possible. However, if clinicians come to accept the inherent uncertainty of their work as ordinary and inevitable, then they might view the therapeutic venture as more challenging and less frustrating.

Words and Actions

Because language is activity, words and symbols are as important as physical circumstances in determining the outcome of events. For instance, when two people agree to call their get-together a "date," expectations are generated that partly determine how the evening will unfold and how satisfied each participant will be with the resulting interaction. The label date is not an abstraction or an inert classification. It is a major factor in shaping the interaction that is to follow, cuing the participants about appropriate ways to behave. The same activities cannot be performed identically under other rubrics. Thus, an important aspect of dating—or for that matter, any other human activity—is coordinating behavior by invoking the expected linguistic symbols. Labels matter. Calling a waltz a tango is tough on one's toes. In our therapeutic work, we are primarily interested in having clients say what they mean and mean what they say.

Clients and therapists sometimes have difficulty recognizing how strongly life is affected by language classifications because Western culture trivializes words and overemphasizes the power of concrete circumstances. Few people fail to appreciate the force of machine-gun bullets, childhood disease, and poverty, for example. However, words and symbols are traditionally relegated to secondary status. People forget that guns are usually fired in the service of linguistically negotiated territorial disputes, that flags and fences have symbolic value, and that both war and peace are, in fact, language *declarations*. Maturana has argued that words are like cudgels—system perturbations that can hurt. In therapy and elsewhere, it is virtually impossible to exaggerate their importance.

Everyday Linguistic Paradoxes

The recursive property of language makes linguistic paradoxes likely, as when people pay homage to social customs while simultaneously disavowing them. For example, two individuals meeting at a singles bar may bond by stressing how much they both detest "pickup joints." Each offers an excuse for being there: "I just wanted to satisfy my curiosity," or, "My friend needed company." (Of course, at the other end of the bar, the friend may be using the same excuse.) Thus, paradoxically, a pickup is facilitated as it is derogated.

It is not unusual for client statements to contain multiple paradoxes. Clients show up voluntarily for a session, saying, "I didn't really want to come." They claim, "The situation is *hopeless*," while actively contemplating solutions. The statement "I'm certainly willing to try it" is used to communicate an expectation of failure. Each of these pronouncements simultaneously reveals a truth and a falsehood. Because people have been raised to expect either/or logic, in which statements are either true or not true, they are frequently baffled by the paradoxical elements in human conversation. Yet the more one is attuned to them, the more one discovers them everywhere: a person wants to quit smoking but keeps right on buying cigarettes; a client favors change without any intention of acting differently; another client complains constantly about not fitting in at work but is shocked when fired.

Linguistic paradoxes are not pathologies. As we stated earlier, they stem from the recursive loops of language. They are surmounted when both sides of a duality are incorporated into an individual's appreciation of the situation. Life is serious and humorous, therapy is simple and complex, and genuine change is ubiquitous *and* rare.

Cummings (1979) had great success with addicts by insisting that they precede treatment by doing the impossible—remaining abstinent for a specified time period. After they accomplished that task, he was then willing to treat their addiction! Similarly, Milton Erickson, a master of therapeutic paradox, instructed a woman who was "unable" to lose weight to call for an appointment only after first gaining and then losing an agreed-upon number of pounds (Rosen, 1982). Again, the prelude to treatment consisted of the very task the person presumably needed help accomplishing.

It is not so much that therapeutic interventions are purposely paradoxical, as some have argued. It is *life*, lived in the multiple recursions of language, that is paradoxical. Therapy simply needs to acknowledge this and "get with the program." People's descriptions of their goals and actions usually contain self-fulfilling prophecies and other linguistic *strange loops* (Hofstadter, 1979). To be effective, the therapeutic intervention must encompass the dialectic. An example of how a duality is spanned is the "you have to do it yourself, but you will need my help" formulation with which many clinicians are already familiar. Similarly, Alcoholics Anonymous members typically espouse the position that alcoholism is an uncontrollable disease that the alcoholic will have to control on a day-to-day basis, partly by acknowledging that the condition is uncontrollable (Efran, Heffner, & Lukens, 1987).

Language acts also become paradoxically intertwined with all other forms of human activity, from international banking to athletic performance. It is not by accident that popular sports manuals—for example, Gallwey's *The Inner Game of Tennis* (1974)—address the issue of taming the recursive influence of language on motor performance. As Gallwey notes, positive self-talk can interfere with performance as easily as self-criticism can. Tennis players may double fault because they are kicking themselves for having just hit the ball out of bounds, but they may also double fault because they are busy complimenting themselves on a previous volley. They may also lose points while telling themselves to stop talking to themselves. In all three instances, words and symbols have become thoroughly woven into the fabric of action pursuits.

The Language of Therapy

Language is both friend and foe. On the one hand, it extends the range of plasticity in human behavior: books are written, plans formulated, hypotheses tested, and mistakes corrected. On the other hand, once human beings are "in language," they are never again free of the incessant dialogue of appraisals and self-doubts that make trips to a therapist both possible and likely (Efran, 1994). Hence, therapy must take place in the same realm as these other evaluative activities. It is a matter of fighting fire with fire. Therapy sometimes includes homework assignments, free association, experiential exercises, relaxation training, and in vivo desensitization, but these activities are all aspects of a fundamentally linguistic interchange.

The Dangers of Using Words Loosely

In granting words their due, it is useful to note that there are no true synonyms—every word contains a unique slant on the way life is experienced. Two or more words may have overlapping zones of meaning, but when their functions *totally* coincide, one is eventually discarded in favor of the other. In the clinic, therapists must be particularly wary of translations—both from clients and themselves—because something is always lost or changed when wordings are modified. When a therapist allows sloppy phrasings to slip by unnoticed or too readily accepts the substitution of one term for another, the fuzzy-thinking monster rears its ugly head and does damage to the entire therapeutic enterprise. Conversely, careful attention to the subtleties of language yields big payoffs in the consulting room.

For example, therapists frequently ask depressed clients, "What made you feel sad?" From the point of view presented in this chapter, that familiar phrasing is doubly mischievous. First, it implies that an external circumstance has the power to change a client's internal state—that the person is essentially *at the command* of his or her environment. That belief is not empowering, and it inhibits flexible thinking. It also flies in the face of the definition of the nervous system as an autonomously functioning network. As pointed out, the nervous system operates *in connection with* outside events, not at their behest. The authors of this chapter, therefore, train clients to use careful wording in describing their circumstances. It is suggested, for instance, that they describe themselves as being "sad in connection with" a given event rather than because of it. Although a little unusual sounding, this locution reminds everyone listening (including the client) that reactions are not fully specified by their triggers.

A person may have angry thoughts *in connection with* a friend's being late for a lunch meeting. However, to assume that the anger is due to the friend's lateness goes beyond the available facts and reinforces simpleminded cause-effect thinking. As has been indicated, thought patterns and other reaction elements are never solely determined by circumstances. Lateness is bothersome only in certain contexts and in conjunction with a particular history of expectations and meanings. On some occasions, lateness goes completely unnoticed or is laughed off as inconsequential. In the instance just cited, the friend's late arrival may have occurred at the same time that the person was having doubts about his own importance, had just accidentally erased a crucial computer file, was up against a job deadline, and had developed a worsening headache. These factors (and their historically determined meanings) cannot be attributed to the friend's lateness, per se. The tardy individual has *something* to do with the upset, and the resulting adverse reaction will surely be aimed in the friend's direction, but a one-to-one causal relationship between event and reaction cannot be inferred. The anger says more about the system of the person experiencing it then it does about the instigating event.

Actually, there is no event to discuss until someone, using language, dissects the ongoing flux of life into discrete units and assigns them meanings. Someone else, slicing the flow differently, would create a very different set of stimuli to which to respond. "Lateness," then, exists only when it has been generated as a series of distinctions in one's automatic and semiautomatic conversations with oneself and others. If the perception of lateness is shared by the two friends in our example, it is because they have similar nervous systems and come from similar social backgrounds. Through the mechanism of social consensus, they carve up the terrain in comparable (but not identical) ways and thus hear related cultural melodies. That enables them to play out coordinated roles in a familiar scenario—an unfolding, jointly produced social drama.

Socially Negotiated Truths

The dramas that individuals bring to the attention of therapists are essentially socially created playlets. However, to the participants, they appear to be composed of harsher stuff—immutable, universal givens. That is because they carry the authority of longstanding social agreements.

Moreover, because individuals are lifelong members of a social community, they are not always clear about when and where they gave their *personal* assent to the agreements and meanings their developing narratives contain. Yet despite the ambiguity surrounding the origins of these constructions, they hold sway and produce palpable effects until or unless modified by social renegotiation (Sarbin, 1986; Shotter, 1993).

People's lives are, at root, a series of social pacts and commitments (White, 1993). Conditions such as low self-esteem, anxiety, and depression, which in other schools of therapy are taken to indicate behavioral deficits or personal pathologies, are more likely to be construed by structure determinists as the fallout from unfulfilled promises and other contractual loose ends. As one author puts it, "depression" consists of a person's inability to envision how he or she will be able to satisfactorily handle an accumulation of personal and societal debts and obligations (Bergner, 1988).

Promises that are kept contribute to psychological order. Commitments that are broken or ignored place strain on both the psyche and the social system. People trust individuals who fulfill their communal obligations; they become angry or impatient with those who do not. Even betrayals of commitment that are known only to the person himself or herself can have profound mental health consequences. Because life is lived in language, a person's word is a precious commodity that should not be allowed to fall into a state of disrepair.

The therapy room is one of several places where the status of contracts with self and others can be reviewed. Both the obvious and hidden expense of neglecting obligations can be assessed, and plans to renegotiate stale agreements can be formulated. Out of such discussions, a gay person may decide to come out of the closet, a daughter may elect to move in with a roommate, a couple may decide to separate, and an office worker may find the courage to decline preparing everyone's morning coffee. These changes, large and small, produce identifiable shifts in a person's "mental health," which we take to be a summary statement about the individual's relationship to self and others.

Thoughts Versus Feelings

The query, "What made you feel sad?" has still other disadvantages. The question creates the subtle implication that feelings are more central than thoughts in capturing the essence of an event. Similarly, it perpetuates the Aristotelian split between thoughts and feelings and implies that action belongs in a separate category altogether. These legacies of older cathartic and experiential approaches reveal an outmoded model of human system operations. Such naïve physiologizing makes for bad clinical practice (Efran & Blumberg, 1994).

The structure determinist understands that all language is action and that thoughts have important consequences. Within this viewpoint, emotional states are defined as bodily settings that underlie and accompany behavioral acts, both trivial and profound. Even routine activities, such as eating, reading a book, or daydreaming, require particular body postures and calibrations. As activity in the system changes, emotional states also shift in a recursive flow of "emotioning and languaging" (Maturana, 1988). Feelings, then, are nothing special—they are not "stored," do not require "release," and are simply the ordinary accompaniments of action patterns.

People colloquially identify feelings with states of high drama, such as passionate sex, angry tantrums, or hopeless depressions. However, all activities enjoy the support of bodily settings. In fact, one of the feeling contexts of greatest importance—understanding—is usually not even classified as an emotion. Yet it is the basis for logical deduction, reasoned debate, and calm deliberation—crucial human activities.

With changes in mood, entire classes of action become more probable or less probable because behaviors require particular bodily supports to be enacted. It is, for example, virtually impossible to continue to make logical points in the midst of a temper tantrum, and sexual arousal may diminish to the vanishing point if the telephone rings every five minutes. Many a child learns to escape a parent's wrath by being cute at just the right moment or by sidling up for a hug, actions calculated to induce an affiliative mood in the parent. Conversely, the parent may forcibly spurn the child's approach, in an attempt to sustain the body postures that allow annoyance and displeasure to be expressed. Arguing and affiliating require opposite settings of the *bodihood*. Therefore, they cannot occur simultaneously. In the interaction between parent and child, one mood will prevail over the other. However, at the juncture of these pathways, there is apt to be a moment or two of *emotional contradiction*, where the discord in mood settings is keenly experienced.

A person usually risks indigestion when grabbing something to eat while running to catch a train. Rushing and eating require different physical calibrations. The organism still operates as a single unit, not as a series of warring mind entities or organismic subsystems. The turmoil exists in the conflicting goals to which the system is attempting to accommodate. When there is a directional conflict, shifting visceral sensations are apt to become the focus of conscious awareness, at least temporarily. When the system is operating smoothly, there is little in the way of feelings to report; the internal state is in sync with the outward activity patterns.

We should also note that plans formulated in one emotional context are apt to be rendered inoperative in the next. A client's resolve to confront his or her boss may evaporate when the boss enters the room. An airplane phobic's determination to board the plane may dissolve at the boarding gate. Ordinary logic goes out the window when an outraged driver becomes determined to get revenge for having been cut off on the highway. These represent shifts in one's emotional framework, not the operation of insidious unconscious motives or deficiencies in logic, memory, or willpower. One reason people do not always appear to be rational beings is that their sensible plans may become null and void when the emotional setting shifts.

Cognitive-behavioral therapists, forgetting the impact of shifting moods, inappropriately attribute inconsistent or self-defeating behavior to maladaptive cognitions. Often the client does possess the appropriate cognitions but cannot make good use of them at the time. Several years ago, a man in the authors' town who was exasperated about people who were taking advantage of him got out his rifle and shot at some teenagers who had been throwing snowballs in his direction. In the domain of logic, he presumably understood the absurdity of battling snowballs with gunfire. However, rage has its own logic, and at the moment of the incident, he was undoubtedly savoring the sweet taste of retribution, not pondering the ethics of vigilante justice or weighing the hardships of a lengthy prison sentence.

Attempting to talk logic to an angry individual or a panicked flight phobic is not a very productive treatment strategy, nor is there any point in bothering to teach such people cognitions they already possess. It *is* useful for therapists to help individuals gain an appreciation of the profound effects mood shifts can have on their outlook and behavior and to urge them to plan accordingly. Moods come and go. They are not indications of personal weakness, hidden motives, or defective reasoning. Self-recriminations for undesirable moods simply exacerbate the problem, as do direct attempts to argue with or control moods that have already arisen.

Paradoxically, accepting a mood as a given can diminish its effects and decrease its longevity. For instance, both of the chapter authors now personally recognize that whenever it comes time to give a talk, they will experience jitters, wonder whatever possessed them to agree to give another presentation, rue not having spent more time preparing, and so on. There will be the conflicting desire to appear calm while simultaneously seeking a socially acceptable excuse to flee. The cure for all these indications of emotional contradiction is to leave them alone, noting that they are the ordinary manifestations of system perturbation. When the talk starts, it will all sort itself out (or it won't). In the meantime, there is material that they have agreed, by social contract, to communicate somehow to the waiting audience.

As will be discussed later, it is also useful for individuals such as the gentleman in the snowball example to have adequate avenues for self-expression and personal fulfillment. Otherwise, small incidents are likely to escalate into major catastrophes. Suicide, for example, has sometimes been construed as a large and final no from an individual who has had difficulty expressing many smaller noes along the way.

Thoughts and feelings should not be talked about as if they were separate subsystems competing for system dominance. The presumed battle between the intellect and the gut is really a warfare of opposing motives and conflicting societal demands—one's supervisor wants the assignment finished by morning, one's child won't go to sleep without hearing another bedtime story, one's ailing mother is insisting on quiet in the house so that she can get some rest, and one's favorite television show is about to come on (Akillas & Efran, 1989).

Myths of Rational and Irrational Supremacy

In the realm of emotion, many therapists, as well as other members of this culture, have been misled by the so-called myths of rational and irrational supremacy (Mahoney, 1991). The first myth is the erroneous assumption that human beings are ordinarily rational creatures who are occasionally overrun by powerful and irrational emotional forces rising up from below. In this view, mental illness is frequently construed as emotions run amok. The second myth, equally fallacious, is the assumption that feelings are the core of our existence and that pathology occurs when emotions are blocked. The villains in this scenario are the intellect and the so-called conditions of worth imposed by civilization (Rogers, 1951).

From the perspective presented here, both these constructions are misleading. Emotions are not heroes or villains, and they are neither rational nor irrational. If a person's physiology is intact, it can be generally assumed that the emotions will take care of themselves. Being neither broken nor out of control, they do not need fixing.

Re-creations of Experience

It was Jackins (1965), the originator of reevaluation counseling, who first noticed that focusing directly on reports of feelings can be *less* useful than asking clients to retell their stories or to fix their attention on specific images embedded in past events. For example, instead of asking a grieving husband what he is feeling, it would be better to ask him to recall a pleasant time he and his spouse spent together, perhaps when the two of them were sitting side-by-side under a tree. When the details of such an experience are recalled in a safe environment, associated mood states—sadness, anger, fear, joy, loneliness, and so on—are automatically reactivated.

Not only is this a more effective strategy for putting a person back in touch with his or her experience, it also avoids the intrusiveness and self-consciousness of direct questions about feelings. A person in the midst of grieving is not apt to react kindly to being asked, "How do you feel?" when the answer should be obvious. When necessary, clinicians can almost always *infer* emotional contexts by carefully attending to the content (and intent) of client declarations, as the next example illustrates.

A Communication Problem

Consider a couple who come to therapy complaining about their problem communicating with each other. Initial inquiries reveal that they actually do communicate quite well. For instance, they easily mimic each other's responses in a typical argument. Thus, their characterization of their situation as a communication breakdown is not fully accurate. Like many other couples, they do a fair amount of talking but are frustrated when these discussions do not produce more immediate agreement.

Living in Emotional Contradiction

Although the couple continue to share a basic passion for living together—what Maturana (1985), speaking as a biologist, calls love—they are also living in emotional contradiction, attempting to pursue divergent goals and aspirations. If they were not sharing finances and living quarters, the "rub" would not be so pronounced. However, being together in a small space amplifies the annoyance of differing styles and aims. Also, both individuals were raised with the ethic that happily married folks should spend most of their time together and should see eye to eye on most matters. Therefore, they rarely give themselves permission to be apart or to indulge their separate interests. Instead, they squabble over large and small issues. One of them thrives in clutter that the other cannot tolerate. One likes loud parties; the other is uncomfortable around strangers. One is ambitious, but the other has little interest in further career advancement. One enjoys close family ties, but the other regards even the semiannual family get-together as an imposition. They have somewhat different sexual proclivities and rhythms at this stage of their lives, and although they began with very similar political beliefs, over the years, one has grown more conservative while the other remains passionately dedicated to liberal causes.

Contrary to certain theories of couples therapy, the more they air their preferences the less they enjoy each other's company. Friday night has become an occasion for bickering rather than an opportunity to take in a movie, visit the shopping mall, watch television, or curl up with a good mystery. The couple frequently engage in what Maturana has called "conversations of characterization, accusation and recrimination" (Mendez, Coddou, & Maturana, 1988, p. 158). Each partner complains about the other and recites his or her litany of entitlements. In those conversations, basic differences are exacerbated by a series of logical justifications and moral imperatives. In such contexts, one partner may temporarily succeed in proving that his or her position is right and that the other partner is wrong, but it is impossible to achieve marital tranquility while playing the right/wrong game. Again, it is not that either participant lacks communication skills—in fact, the two usually make their *points* quite effectively. However, they are unable to escape the emotional contradiction of being closely coupled while also attempting to enact partly incompatible agendas.

Reconceiving Stereotypical Expectations

Ironically, once a couple's preferences are fully acknowledged in an appropriate emotional context, conflicting goals may not be that difficult to reconcile. This is especially true if *both* partners are willing to give up stereotypical notions about how marital roles should be played out. Particularly destructive to many such relationships is the cultural belief that a good marital partner will be able to meet most of his or her partner's interpersonal needs. The perpetuation of this myth burdens many people with unrealistic demands and expectations. Once freed from these restrictive rules and customs, more creative problem solving can occur.

It is not absolutely necessary for a couple to vacation together, to converse intensely on long car trips, to be especially well-matched in sexual habits, to enjoy all the same friends, to be interested in each other's workday, or to be on the same meal schedule. The apportionment of household chores and responsibilities need not follow traditional gender assignments but can instead take into account each partner's particular skills and preferences. When stereotypical requirements are loosened, alternatives that were originally invisible or inconceivable can be brought into focus and used to resolve conflicts. Moreover, each spouse can be encouraged to develop outside subgroups to support the values, points of view, and pursuits not well represented within the marriage. There are some couples who get along better when more of the outside world is brought into the marriage. They can, for instance, invite guests over on a regular basis, adopt a child to raise, or share their living quarters with boarders—perhaps another couple. In the family of one of the authors, it became a common practice to send the children off to have dinner at a neighboring aunt's house. There, the kids seemed on their best behavior and were less fussy about experimenting with new foods. Even the same meal, served over there, somehow seemed to taste better. This rearrangement in the usual dinner pattern turned out to have mental health benefits for everyone concerned.

In order for nontraditional solutions to be initiated, the right/wrong framework must be put aside. Because it is notoriously easy for either partner to slip back into the language of justification and psychological intimidation, forceful attention to language specifics is paramount. Both parties must be helped to maintain a nondefensive context. Active intercession—not therapeutic "neutrality"—is required. The therapist must be especially alert to either partner's using the *language* of openness and acceptance as a means to gain competitive advantage in the right/wrong game.

Going Beyond Duplicity

For the structure determinist, language does not consist of disembodied words floating through the ether but of contextualized language acts that advance particular causes and claims. Therefore, it is possible for the words typically associated with one domain—such as acceptance and cooperation—to be used hypocritically as part of an alternative strategy. Such hypocrisy is neither rare nor illegitimate. As Maturana often points out, people save their lives many times over through hypocrisy. In fact, given our multiple group affiliations and conflicting obligations, it is amazing that there is *ever* consistency between rhetoric and other forms of action. Nevertheless, the therapist in this situation must nip duplicity in the bud if the conversation is to be kept on a problem-solving track.

Obviously, a therapist can only intervene this actively within the guidelines of a well-constructed therapeutic contract through which the participants have agreed temporarily to eschew conversations of accusation, recrimination, and characterization. Other-

wise, the multiple interruptions required might seem rude and intrusive. In this situation, rather than focusing on individuals, the therapist directs interventions at maintaining an open framework for
discussion and at giving everyone the maximum opportunity to
adhere to the contract.

Working with a Therapy Contract

The therapeutic contract provides the authority for the necessary
linguistic surgery. The contracts we ourselves usually arrange with
clients prepare them for a considerable amount of active experimentation with words and tasks. Therapy is an uncertain enterprise even in the best of hands, and clients need to understand at
the outset that the process is apt to involve some trial-and-error
linguistic tinkering.

Part of the purpose of a contract is to sustain momentum when
the going gets rough, as it almost surely will. It is *threatening* to be
faced with the prospect of becoming something which, by definition, one does not yet fully comprehend. It is far easier to stay in
familiar territory. As Kelly (1969) observed, "Almost everything
new starts in some moment of confusion" (p. 151). Moreover,
when an individual realizes that turning the next corner is apt
to mean being "profoundly affected" (p. 152), he or she is likely to
want to beat a hasty retreat, postponing the mission or abandon-
ing it altogether. At similar moments, a good coach might remind
team members of the old weight-lifting adage, "No pain, no gain."
The therapist does the same—reminding clients about the goals of
the project and the terms of the therapeutic contract they all
helped create.

Maturana points out that all systems are by nature conservative. They easily repeat what they have already done. People talk
a good game about "welcoming change," "thriving on challenge,"
and so on. However, they do not visit a therapist in order to "grow."
They are not there for adventure. They enter therapy in an attempt
to regain lost stability and forestall any further erosion in their

quality of life (Marris, 1974). Moreover, they venture into the unknown only when shoved from behind. Therefore, the therapist must do more than just commiserate with the client's predicament, endorse existing cultural suppositions, or examine past events for evidence of similarities to current happenings. Therapy requires the use of a clear contract to generate orthogonal interaction.

Orthogonal Interaction

By definition, an *orthogonal interaction* involves a change in a system component that subsequently modifies that component's interaction with other system components. To take a simple example, an auto mechanic removes a spark plug and adjusts it. When it is replaced, the car runs differently. Three points are worth noting. First, the mechanic's interaction is orthogonal to the usual functioning of the automobile—spark plugs must be removed to be readjusted. Second, the interaction results in a spark plug change that later affects how the entire system operates. Third, the mechanic "relates" to the spark plug in a way that its structure permits—otherwise, readjustment would not be possible. Something similar to spark plug adjustment characterizes the psychotherapy conversation. The client and therapist get together to do something that cannot readily be accomplished elsewhere and that will change the client's structure. When completed, that change will automatically affect the other social organizations in which the client holds membership.

People are members of a variety of formal and informal social "clubs." Each one promotes its own unique reality and uses distinct sets of rules and rituals to enforce club values. Group affiliations are, of course, a necessary aspect of life, and no one can get by without them. As the advertisement says, "Membership has its privileges." However, despite the best of intentions, all groups impose blinders on their members, limiting their vision to the restricted set of options permitted within club boundaries. Certain cognitive and perceptual distinctions are encouraged whereas others are disallowed or invalidated. Furthermore, realities supported in one club often conflict with those endorsed in another. For instance, a treatise on the big-bang theory of the universe's origin may earn an A from one's physics instructor, a reprimand from one's pastor, and puzzled stares from one's parents.

As a member of multiple groups, each of which demands allegiance to its particular worldview, a person experiences the stress of emotional contradiction. Moreover, certain aspects of an individual's identity may cause tension because they cannot be adequately expressed within the confines of currently available club structures.

For example, a female client who was an accomplished musician recounted tearfully how her dream of becoming an orchestra conductor was repeatedly ridiculed by family and friends in her small town. Even her music teacher regarded it as an absurd aspiration for a young girl. He insisted that she forget such nonsense and focus her attention on "more practical" goals. Therapy was a place where these preferences that were disparaged elsewhere could be given voice. The consulting room is truly, as Hillman and Ventura (1992) have noted, "a cell of revolution" (p. 46), where the seeds of individual rebellions are planted and nourished.

Client and therapist profit when their discussions can be based on distinctions that are not easily drawn in other settings. Of course, if the therapeutic association merely replicates the rules of a person's other affiliations, little will have been accomplished. Furthermore, there is little point on insisting that people make distinctions that are beyond their structural capabilities—for example, an average six-year-old can have only a rudimentary appreciation of the big-bang theory. However, a client and therapist might together create many distinctions that are outside the realm of constructions ordinarily elicited in the person's environment.

An Endorsement of Pessimism

For a simple example of orthogonal interaction, consider a client who enters therapy complaining that his situation is hopeless. As a clinician, the therapist knows that friends and relatives have already attempted to talk the client out of his pessimistic stance, perhaps by pointing to his past accomplishments, by suggesting alternatives that he has not yet explored, or by reminding him that others whose circumstances were even worse nevertheless "made it." However, it is also apparent that none of these all-too-familiar strategies has been effective. After all, the client is still depressed and complaining. Therefore, something different must be tried, something orthogonal to the tactics of the client's friends.

In our own work in such situations, we have found it useful to further legitimize the person's pessimism rather than attempt to argue against it. Remember, a mood *resisted* tends to linger longer, having more material to feed on. It is easy for us to accept the person's gloomy outlook, partly because we understand emotional contexts and partly because we embrace—as a deep philosophical premise—the proposition that people have the right to give up their life struggles any time they want. To our way of thinking, people are fully responsible for their acts, including the decision to give up or end it all. We agree with Szasz's (1990) point that "he who does not accept and respect the choice to reject life does not truly accept and respect life itself" (p. 251).

Our stance, although not devised for strategic purposes, has the benefit of putting the discussion with the client on a new footing. Moreover, because conversation is dialogical, when one conversant changes themes, the other must also hum a different tune. In the context we provide, there is little motivation for the client to continue arguing that life is unfair, that circumstances are miserable, and that little can be done to change matters. We already accept all that. In fact, we may point out some dismal aspects of the situation that the client forgot to include in his own catalogue of horrors. In other words, the situation is even *worse* than he imagined!

We also have no objection to starting a therapeutic project at rock bottom. In fact, we rather prefer it. As people in Alcoholics Anonymous noticed long ago, hitting bottom provides an excellent motivational opportunity. There is nowhere for the person to go but up, and there is pain enough to impel his or her exploration of a new alternative. It is the sort of fortuitous shove for which we are always on the lookout. Frankly, we sometimes suspect that our more comfortable clients would do better if they were a little more desperate for change. In any event, we welcome the client's pessimism rather than being frightened or put off by it.

Clinicians sometimes get into unnecessary trouble by interpreting clients' statements too literally, as if static, unchanging facts were being disclosed, when, on the contrary, all presentations are devised to create a particular impression, to steer the conversation toward certain conclusions and away from others. Furthermore, as we have already suggested, pieces of a conversation fit together hand in glove. Thus, when the therapist positions himself or herself differently, new "facts" and perspectives are apt to emerge, and old concerns may vanish without fanfare even though never formally addressed.

To Whom It May Concern

The work of Murray Bowen, the well-known family systems thinker, provides another example of orthogonal interaction (Kerr & Bowen, 1988). Bowen recognized that parents often present a united front to their children—their individual points of view are, for all intents and purposes, fused into a single team position. Oftentimes, one parent becomes the spokesperson for the team, with the other passively giving assent. To help break this fusion, which Bowen considered detrimental to family operation, he would urge the client to compose separate letters to his or her mother and father and to include different content in each. He objected to the client writing joint letters home, particularly those that began with the ambiguous greeting, "Hi"—a phrase not much more personal than "To whom it may concern." Along similar lines, he also suggested that when clients called home, they should first speak with one parent and then ask to speak, independently, to the other. This simple change in phone protocol causes quite a stir in families where one parent is used to controlling the flow of information back and forth. It is a good example of how a small change, based on an orthogonal interaction between Bowen and his client, can generate distinctions that rearrange family boundaries and produce potentially beneficial reverberations throughout the system.

A Rule of Thumb

An implication of the principle of orthogonal interaction is that a clinician in doubt might at least try something different from what others might have been doing (de Shazer, 1991). Recently, one of the workers in our clinic was asked to assist a woman with a long history of agoraphobia. She had not ventured out of her house in months, but now had an important doctor's appointment. She did not see how she could bring herself to get to his office, even though it was only a few blocks away.

The clinician specifically refused to become involved in the usual persuading and cajoling conversations that friends had tried. Nor did he attempt to boost the woman's confidence, to reiterate the importance of the visit, or even to assure her that she would be safe if she decided to make the trip. He did offer to make himself available to accompany her to the doctor's office, should she elect to go. The final decision was to be hers. Because all this had been made clear in advance, there was an absence of high drama on the day of the appointment. The client simply got into the car and was driven matter-of-factly to her appointment. The trip was a success, but the therapist was quite prepared for her to change her mind at the last minute and stay at home.

Orthogonal interaction can take many forms, including various homework assignments and thought exercises. For instance, we have requested that a client experiment with a solo family visit, rent and watch a specific videotape, walk home instead of taking the bus, or have coffee with an acquaintance that he or she dislikes. We have asked clients to move out of their houses (for a set period), to drop the role of "good child" (in their next family phone conversation), to use the phrase "I want to" in place of "I have to" (when talking about household chores), to telephone an old high school buddy (who has not been heard from in years), and to give a gift to a colleague (without waiting for a special occasion). We have urged people to pick up trash in a nearby park (without seeking special credit), to cook themselves an elegant breakfast (complete with a flower on the table), to purchase a new outfit (even though the budget is tight), to allow themselves an evening off (although they do not deserve it), and to write to an estranged daughter (who will probably not write back). In the domain of *thought questions*, we have asked parents to ponder how their children might describe them to others, and clients to recall how and when they became convinced they could not be playwrights (or attorneys), to devise a plan for cleaning up the mess created by breaking a promise, and to list the conditions necessary to reexperience a current job as a choice rather than a burden. Such assignments have the potential of generating provocative dialogue both inside and outside the consulting room.

The Explanatory Domain

In other therapeutic approaches, it is frequently assumed that problems can be solved mainly or wholly through the mechanism of explanation. Insight, for example, is an explanatory scheme that has traditionally been expected to play a major role in the remediation of problems. Similarly, therapists regularly feel obliged to trace the history of problematic reaction patterns back to childhood events. Yet, gaining insight or understanding historical precursors may or may not have any real impact on current client problems. The confounding of explanation and client change in certain types of therapy is what gave rise to Woody Allen's well-known quip that he could neither imagine completing his psychoanalysis nor imagine being changed by it.

For the structure determinist, an explanation is simply the *reformulation* of a phenomenon in an alternative linguistic domain.

Whether any particular reformulation will bring about desired changes is an empirical issue. Clients can change in the absence of any explanation whatsoever. Conversely, explanations, even when correct, do not necessarily lead to favorable client outcomes. Lightning is frequently described as a discharge of electrons. In the realm of physics, that constitutes an acceptable explanation. However, it does little to render lightning any less impressive or dangerous on a stormy night.

Technically speaking, the domain in which a phenomenon occurs is entirely separate from the domain in which an explanation is proposed. Therefore, there is no a priori reason to expect that an explanation will prove an effective tool for change. Moreover, orthogonal interventions—the major weaponry in the structure determinist's therapeutic arsenal—can be devised and incorporated into treatment strategies with only a modicum of detective work into either past events or the characteristics of the current social network.

In our view, therapists who operate as if change follows from explanation waste too much time taking histories and plumbing the depths of childhood memories. As Hillman and Ventura (1992) note, the typical therapeutic "rituals of evoking . . . and reconstructing childhood" (p. 6) celebrate romanticized images of defenseless children that actually get in the way of therapy's major objective—empowering adults to be responsible and productive members of their community. Similarly, Dawes (1994) challenges the scientific basis for the mainstream therapy notion that childhood events are intimately connected to adult behaviors, symptoms, and pathologies. He considers this widespread belief a contemporary cultural fable, as primitive and pseudoscientific as a "belief in a mountain god" (p. 223). For our current purposes, it is sufficient to recognize that explaining and changing are activities that take place in different phenomenal domains—they have no necessary connection.

Autopoiesis and Purposeless Drift

According to Maturana (Maturana & Varela, 1980, 1987), life is an autopoietic process. *Autopoiesis* literally means "self-producing." Maturana invented the term to describe the defining feature of all living systems. An autopoietic entity recreates itself on many levels. Cells reproduce, as do individuals, families, and—some would say—cultures and political systems. Autopoiesis is neither a mysterious life force nor a "will to live"; it is a circular organization of processes that happens to result in system sustenance and self-creation.

Therefore, life is neither a promise nor an entitlement. It has no overarching purpose. As long as the autopoietic organization remains intact, life continues as a *structural drift* through a medium. Whenever any of the critical elements in the organismic circularity break down, perhaps because of an inhospitable element in the internal or external environment, there is a destructive interaction, and the system loses its self-creative properties. In common parlance, it dies. It ceases to be distinguished by an observer as belonging to the class of living entities.

The notion of *drift* implies that the organism is not headed anywhere in particular. It drifts continuously along like a boat without a motor, sails, oars, or a rudder. How that boat travels and where it ends up depends entirely on the interaction between its structure and the characteristics of the surrounding medium—the wind and the waves. These continuously shifting structural couplings determine its ultimate end.

Although the boat has all along been in a purposeless drift, someone watching its trajectory from above might very well infer motives, including a determination to stay afloat, to keep moving east, to outlast the night, and so on. All these would be observer inferences that made use of the same explanatory mechanisms people use to attribute meanings to their own purposeless drifts. In a structural drift, there is no free will. Choices, plans, hypotheticals, alternatives, and goals all arise in the ontology of observers—in our conversations with each other.

It is always an observer speaking to another observer (who might, in fact, be himself or herself) who draws distinctions and thereby brings entities, living or otherwise, into existence. In structure determinism, these observer distinctions are the necessary reference points for any discussion. The observer decides what is good or bad, wholesome or pathological. Nature, itself, does not choose sides, make mistakes, or host pathologies.

It is also in the domain of the observer that the illusion of self-control is created. A basic principle of cybernetics is that a system cannot be controlled by a component of that same system (McCulloch, 1965). This principle applies to human systems as well as to machines. Although people egocentrically like to believe they determine their own destinies, they are actually unable to control their thoughts, their moods, or their exact bedtimes (Ornstein, 1991). People's basic "desires" are discovered—not chosen—and they change from time to time without giving advance warning.

Although individuals do not have unilateral control over themselves, they can and do participate in social conversations that influence the directions of their lives, including those we classify as therapy. For a number of reasons, the term *conversation* is ideally suited for describing such interactions. In a conversation, it is impossible to tease apart the exact contributions of any one of the participants, and the influences that arise are never simply unidirectional. A therapeutic conversation is a co-drift that changes both client and therapist simultaneously. Even though therapists may think of themselves as team leaders, there is a circular exchange of ideas, as there would be in any effective teaching or coaching context.

Therefore, those who argue that clients essentially cure themselves have a good point but so do those who insist that the success of therapy is in the hands of the clinician. In a conversation, such arguments are formally undecidable. As Varela (1979) points out,

"If we consider a conversation as a totality, there cannot be distinction about what is contributed by whom" (p. 269). Ultimately, the punctuation of the sequence is arbitrary—it is the structural coupling that matters (Watzlawick, Beavin, & Jackson, 1967). In that coupling, therapist interventions and client responses are inextricably linked and reciprocally defined.

In structure determinism, all changes of an organism are structural changes, including those that observers may dismiss as transient, inconsequential, reversible, or "merely mental." In a structure-determined world, life never doubles back on itself, and every coupling leaves its distinct mark on the organism's makeup. Moreover, because people are nontrivial systems, it is impossible to predict which interaction will later seem, to an observer, to have significantly altered a person's drift. After all, it takes only one final bend to break a piece of fatigued metal, and it is difficult to know in advance which twist will do it. As in the example of the therapist who tripped in the hallway, an accidental occurrence may prove the key to a longstanding puzzle or dilemma.

Nervous System Closure and the Myth of Instructive Interaction

Maturana's writings about the closure of the nervous system have turned ordinary neuroscience on its head. The traditional research strategy was to attempt to correlate internal neural activity with externally defined stimuli. In fact, this is precisely what Maturana and Varela (1987) first attempted to do in their work on the visual system of the frog and in studying color vision in the pigeon. But the outcomes were not as they had predicted, and after many failed attempts to make the traditional model work, they concluded that their lack of results could simply not be explained on the basis of experimenter error. Instead, they realized that there is no one-to-one correspondence between what goes on inside the nervous system and what goes on outside. To be a bit anthropomorphic about it, the nervous system does not give a hoot about the outside world. It "hears" and responds only to its own neuronal music.

One of the authors was recently stuck for several hours on an Amtrak train that had lost power, leaving the passengers at a standstill and in almost complete darkness. Reactions to this event were interesting to observe. In one car, a rather festive atmosphere developed. Passengers were enjoying milling around and trading Amtrak war stories. In another car, the tone of the group was entirely different and was characterized by an irate passenger's fight with a crew member about the lack of information available to the riders. All the people in that car seemed to be angry and frustrated, preoccupied with how late they would be arriving at their destinations. Different nervous systems were responding very differently to largely comparable external triggers. (Of course, the author was neither upset nor joyous—characteristically, he was moving between the cars, gauging people's reactions.)

There are parallel events in the clinic: some people always seem ready to complain while others usually seem willing to make the best of a situation. An individual in the first group might be colloquially described as "a fight waiting to happen," whereas a person in the second group seems to be heeding the poster that reads, "When life hands you lemons, make lemonade."

Sometimes it is difficult to apprehend, from the outside, why the events that prevent one person from enjoying life are largely invisible to another. People's objectivist upbringing leads them to expect more commonality than truly exists. In families, this presents special difficulties because one family member almost invariably has trouble appreciating why another insists on making commotions over seemingly inconsequential events. Yet, to the person involved, nothing could be more self-evident. Matters are made worse by attributing ugly motives to those whose reactions are hard to fathom: is he or she just trying to be difficult or cause trouble?

Cognitively, no one lives in a single predefined universe—each person lives in a *multiverse* of his or her own neural creation. In this connection, Maturana has argued that there is more than one family living under any single roof. Each family member creates a unique family, using the other individuals in the household as characters in his or her unfolding drama. Thus, when family members compare notes about presumably identical events, they are often astonished to discover the disparity in their experiences. A joyous holiday celebration for one member of the family is a dreaded ritual for another. We recall a client who reported suffering through years of backyard football games that his father had instigated. The father evidently believed his son was enjoying the interaction as much as he was. However, the son not only disliked playing but hated having to pretend to be enthusiastic about it.

Perception and Illusion

A closed nervous system cannot distinguish between perception and illusion. Until a person is awake, the nightmare monster chasing him or her across the room is as "real" as an actual assailant pursuing the person down a dark alleyway. Dreams and reality are made of the same neural stuff. It is only by comparing notes with other observers in the community that people can tell them apart. As people grow up in a culture, this operation becomes so commonplace that they can afford to take it for granted until something goes wrong and they are thrown back into confusion about what is real and what is not. Reality, as the term is generally used, is a language-based social consensus (Maturana, 1988). Because they fall outside the consensus, delusions and hallucinations are labeled pathological and illusory even though, biologically speaking, they are as solid and legitimate as any other neurological creations.

Co-Drift in the World of Art

An artist's painting provides a good example of how autopoietic entities with closed nervous systems operate. The canvas an artist produces is an *opportunity* for viewers to create art. It is not, in itself, the artistic experience. Artists wishing to be well-received have to hope they will run into just the right sort of audience, made up of individuals who will be appropriately perturbed by the artists' creations but not totally perplexed. The likelihood of this happening is reasonably good because the patron and the artist generally have similar biological structures and similar cultural backgrounds. Therefore, in painting for themselves, artists are also painting for others.

However, artists often position themselves at the outposts of mainstream culture. This provides a good vantage point from which to introduce a bit of orthogonality into the viewer's world. Recognizing how much the viewer contributes to the art, many artists refuse to explain their work, and some even refrain from using descriptive titles. Perfunctory names such as "Work #1" or "Watercolor on Parchment" clearly place the lion's share of responsibility for creating meaning on the shoulders of the observer. As in other conversations, there is a necessary coupling between the artist and the viewer and also between the artist and the creative medium. Oils, pastels, and acrylics all lend themselves to different kinds of conversations.

Therapists, too, prod and poke their clientele, triggering system reactions. They, too, are more effective if they are not too thoroughly enmeshed in the dominant culture. For that reason, the therapist's role has been compared to that of court jester (Szasz, 1973). A jester is given license to disobey the rules of court etiquette, provided he does not go too far. If he exceeds the bounds of propriety, he is apt to lose his job and possibly his head. In the meantime, he brings important issues to the attention of the king—issues that others in the court, obliged to comply with stricter boundaries, are unable to pose. He does so as a loyal employee and with as much tact and humor as skill allows. However, make no mistake about it, the jester's barbs and the therapist's prods address serious matters, and both allow their employer (the king or the client) access to more options in responding to threats than would otherwise be possible.

Conclusion

Maturana's work has been slow to be appreciated by clinicians. His writing is highly technical—extraordinarily precise but too dense for the casual reader to penetrate. Furthermore, because he is not himself a clinician, it has been left largely to others to extrapolate the implications of his theory for the clinical enterprise. It is in the realm of family therapy that his ideas were first introduced to members of the mental health professions. Family therapists were primed for these ideas by their familiarity with Bateson's influential writings (1972, 1979) on cybernetics and systems. Dell (1982a, 1982b), writing in *Family Process,* provided an initial exposition of Maturana's theory. Later, he elaborated on the similarities and differences between structure determinism and the Batesonian legacy (Dell, 1985, 1987).

In a way, it has been useful that Maturana is a biologist and cyberneticist rather than a clinician. Being outside the mental health field, he can afford to let the chips fall where they may, having no investment in either defending or attacking any particular school of psychotherapy. What he has done instead is to present a crisp, coherent, logically sound and internally consistent picture of how living systems function and how they create and utilize knowledge. Moreover, he has described, in a way many find compelling, how language, viewed as a biological phenomenon, affects communal organization and the practice of science. His perspective resolves many old problems—for example, the role of explanation in producing change—but it also creates new vexations. For example, it challenges clinicians to accept that people operate in a multiverse of possibilities, where they are forced to decide for themselves what life means. In structure determinism, there is no certitude outside self.

Like a work of art, the therapeutic conversation is a creative endeavor that is invented anew with each client and in every moment of every session. It is a co-drift, not a mechanical formulaic procedure. Therefore, on the one hand, although this therapy is at root a simple process, it is apt to appear hopelessly complex to those who insist on having surefire recipes. On the other hand, although the approach requires that clinicians make peace with a certain degree of creative uncertainty, the theory is not devoid of useful guidelines. We have attempted to explicate some of these throughout the chapter, and we will close with a review of the most important.

First, therapy and orthogonal interaction go hand in hand. The coupling of client and therapist is best described as a *revolutionary* activity. The alternatives entertained go beyond those sanctioned in other settings. Questions are posed that are difficult or impossible to raise elsewhere, and options come to light that were invisible under the dim light available in other clubhouses. Because orthogonal interaction is crucial, the therapist who is unsure which direction to take might at least experiment with conversational tacks that differ from those friends and relatives have pursued. In other words, when in doubt, try something different.

Systems are conservative. They easily repeat what they have already done. Consequently, the process of psychotherapy necessitates perturbing the system. As British essayist and novelist Aldous Huxley once noted, learning the truth can be illuminating, but it is also disconcerting. In other settings, conflicts between opposing realities are likely to be covered over by euphemisms and hypocrisies— fables that aim to keep everyone happy. Here, such convenient fictions are reexamined. The therapist focuses on arenas of emotional contradiction, where conflicting allegiances need to be sorted out. Serving as a kind of linguistic detective, he or she brings to the client's attention broken or ignored promises and other forms of unfinished business. These are realms in which unanswered questions need to be addressed. Kelly (1969) went so far as to define symptoms—the manifestations of emotional contradiction—as "urgent questions, behaviorally expressed, which had somehow lost the threads that lead either to answers or to better questions" (p. 19).

Emotional contradiction, as we have defined it, is not an illness. It is the price individuals pay for living in multiple social domains and being pressed to pay homage to conflicting realities. An individual, like it or not, is stationed at the interface between clashing social forces (Rabkin, 1970). In that war zone, it will not be sufficient for the therapist simply to provide empathy and support. Nor will it suffice to endorse preexisting social agreements or endlessly review past injustices. Once the past has been acknowledged, the person needs to explore, in conversation, how social pacts can be renegotiated to make existence at the interface more liveable.

In the conversational coupling that is therapy, it is neither necessary nor possible to fully sort out influences. A client's responses inspire a therapist's suggestions, and vice versa. Moreover, structure determinists are not interested in drawing fine lines between verbal discussions and what some others consider more active forms of engagement. Before the Wright brothers did much backyard tinkering, they had to assert, in conversation with themselves and others, that man could fly. Some would argue that this was the hardest part of their job, especially since that declaration faced stiff opposition from a large contingent of doubters. Similarly, effective therapy often takes the form of a simple but clear discussion about which distinctions are to be upheld and which will be disintegrated. It matters less whether a host of fancy techniques are used.

Emotions are not irrational forces that need taming, nor is so-called emotional discharge an end in itself. The settings of the bodihood shift automatically as action and language states flow into one another. Most of the mental states clients complain about are not irrational feelings per se but the stresses of emotional contradiction. Furthermore, thoughts and feelings are not in opposition to one another. Thoughts, even if they are only daydreams, are significant forms of action, and emotions are bodily calibrations and supports that enable various classes of activity to be enacted. Experience is best recreated by reviewing images and thoughts—by storytelling—not by focusing self-consciously on internal states.

The structure deterministic therapist is relatively uninterested in applying objective-sounding disease names to what are essentially social dilemmas. Many therapists talk as if they are healing deficient organisms. This is presumably a legacy of the field's pseudomedical inheritance. As clinicians, we find ourselves working mainly with biologically intact organisms making legitimate responses to inconvenient circumstances.

Good therapy requires a well-formed therapy contract. The contract establishes each participant's rights, privileges, obligations, and expectations. It also contains criteria for determining when the therapy project has reached a satisfactory conclusion. Such contracts do not need to be formal or presented in written form. However, an ambiguous contract will almost invariably create role confusions along the way. Contracts may have to be renegotiated as circumstances warrant, but it is never advisable to set out on an important journey without some sort of road map. The therapy contract not only sets the agenda, it serves as a working example of the value of linguistic clarity.

In therapy, as in life, it is not surprising to find that statements contain paradoxes. Bohr, the Nobel laureate physicist, argued that "the opposite of a great truth is also true" (cited in Overbye, 1981, p. 62). The same idea might be stated in the language of therapy. The client both does and does not want to change, therapy is both serious and whimsical, the therapist is both leader and follower, and so on. Life itself is profoundly meaningful and, at the same time, a colossal joke. Paradoxes need to be surmounted, not solved. Dualities are to be embraced, not discounted.

Finally, therapy is about change, not explanation. Change can occur in the absence of explanation, and vice versa. The therapist's focus needs to be on triggering orthogonality, not simply trading explanatory fictions.

Maturana regards life as a purposeless structural drift with no objectively set destination or mission. In living, people generate their own meanings and values. Paradoxically, although people do not control their own systems, they have ultimate responsibility for the actions that result from their participation in communal conversations, including those called psychotherapy.

References

Akillas, E., & Efran, J. S. (1989). Internal conflict, language and metaphor: Implications for psychotherapy. *Journal of Contemporary Psychotherapy, 19,* 149–159.

Anderson, W. T. (1990). *Reality isn't what it used to be.* San Francisco: HarperSanFrancisco.

Bateson, G. (1972). *Steps to an ecology of mind.* New York: Ballantine Books.

Bateson, G. (1979). *Mind and nature.* New York: Dutton.

Bergner, R. M. (1988). Status dynamic psychotherapy with depressed individuals. *Psychotherapy, 25,* 266–272.

Birdwhistell, R. L. (1970). *Kinesics and context: Essays on body motion communication.* Philadelphia: University of Pennsylvania Press.

Cummings, N. A. (1979). Turning bread into stones: Our modern antimiracle. *American Psychologist, 34,* 1119–1129.

Dawes, R. M. (1994). *House of cards: Psychology and psychotherapy built on myth.* New York: Free Press.

de Shazer, S. (1991). *Putting difference to work.* New York: W.W. Norton.

Dell, P. F. (1982a). Beyond homeostasis: Toward a concept of coherence. *Family Process, 21,* 21–41.

Dell, P. F. (1982b). In search of truth: On the way to clinical epistemology. *Family Process, 21,* 407–414.

Dell, P. F. (1985). Understanding Bateson and Maturana: Toward a biological foundation for the social sciences. *Journal of Marital and Family Therapy, 11,* 1–20.

Dell, P. F. (1987). Maturana's constitutive ontology of the observer. *Psychotherapy, 24,* 462–466.

Efran, J. S. (1994). Mystery, abstraction, and narrative psychology. *Journal of Constructivist Psychology, 7,* 219–227.

Efran, J. S., & Blumberg, M. J. (1994). Emotion and family living: The perspective of structure determinism. In S. M. Johnson-Douglas & L. S. Greenberg (Eds.), *The heart of the matter: Perspectives in marital therapy* (pp. 172–204). New York: Brunner/Mazel.

Efran, J. S., & Fauber, R. L. (1995). Constructivism: Questions and answers. In R. A. Neimeyer & M. J. Mahoney (Eds.), *Constructivism in psychotherapy* (pp. 275–304). Washington, DC: American Psychological Association Press.

Efran, J. S., Heffner, K. P., & Lukens, R. J. (1987). Alcoholism as an opinion: Structure determinism applied to drinking. *Alcoholism Treatment Quarterly, 4*, 67–85.

Efran, J. S., & Lukens, M. D. (1985). The world according to Humberto Maturana. *The Family Therapy Networker, 9*, 23–25, 27–28, 72–75.

Efran, J. S., Lukens, M. D., & Lukens, R. J. (1990). *Language, structure, and change: Frameworks of meaning in psychotherapy.* New York: W.W. Norton.

Efran, J. S., Lukens, R. J., & Lukens, M. D. (1988). Constructivism: What's in it for you? *The Family Therapy Networker, 12*, 27–35.

Gallwey, W. T. (1974). *The inner game of tennis.* New York: Random House.

Gergen, K. J. (1982). *Toward transformation in social knowledge.* New York: Springer-Verlag.

Gergen, K. J. (1985). The social constructionist movement in modern psychology. *American Psychologist, 40*, 266–275.

Hall, K. L. (Ed.) (1992). *Oxford companion to the Supreme Court of the United States.* New York: Oxford University Press.

Hillman, J., & Ventura, M. (1992). *We've had a hundred years of psychotherapy: And the world's getting worse.* San Francisco: HarperSanFrancisco.

Hofstadter, D. R. (1979). *Gödel, Escher, Bach: An eternal golden braid.* New York: Basic Books.

Jackins, H. (1965). *The human side of human beings.* Seattle, WA: Rational Island.

Kelly, G. A. (1955). *The psychology of personal constructs* (2 Vols.). New York: W.W. Norton.

Kelly, G. A. (1969). *Clinical psychology and personality: The selected papers of George Kelly* (B. Maher, Ed.). New York: Wiley.

Kerr, M. E., & Bowen, M. (1988). *Family evaluation: An approach based on Bowen theory.* New York: W.W. Norton.

McCulloch, W. S. (1965). *Embodiments of mind.* Cambridge, MA: MIT Press.

Mahoney, M. J. (1991). *Human change processes: The scientific foundations of psychotherapy.* New York: Basic Books.

Marris, P. (1974). *Loss and change.* New York: Random House, Pantheon Books.

Maturana, H. R. (1985). Reflexionen uber Liebe [Reflections on love]. *Zeitschrift fur systemiche Therapie, 3*, 129–131.

Maturana, H. R. (1988). Reality: The search for objectivity or the quest for a compelling argument. *Irish Journal of Psychology, 9*, 25–82.

Maturana, H. R. (1990). Science and daily life: The ontology of scientific explanations. In W. Krohn, G. Kuppers, & H. Nowotny (Eds.), *Self-Organization: Portrait of a scientific revolution* (pp. 12–35). Boston: Kluwer Academic.

Maturana, H. R., & Varela, F. J. (Eds.). (1980). *Autopoiesis and cognition: The realization of the living*. Boston: Reidel.

Maturana, H. R., & Varela, F. G. (1987). *The tree of knowledge: The biological roots of human understanding*. Boston: New Science Library.

Mendez, C. L., Coddou, F., & Maturana, H. (1988). The bringing forth of pathology. *Irish Journal of Psychology, 9*, 144–172.

Omer, H., & London, P. (1988). Metamorphosis in psychotherapy: End of the systems era. *Psychotherapy, 25*, 171–180.

Ornstein, R. E. (1991). *The evolution of consciousness: Of Darwin, Freud, and cranial fire: The origins of the way we think*. New York: Prentice Hall.

Overbye, D. (1981, June). Messenger at the gates of time. *Science*, pp. 61–67.

Rabkin, R. (1970). *Inner & outer space: Introduction to a theory of social psychiatry*. New York: W.W. Norton.

Rogers, C. R. (1951). *Client-centered therapy*. Boston: Houghton Mifflin.

Rosen, S. (Ed.). (1982). *My voice will go with you: The teaching tales of Milton H. Erickson*. New York: W.W. Norton.

Sarbin, T. R. (Ed.). (1986). *Narrative psychology: The storied nature of human conduct*. New York: Praeger.

Shotter, J. (1993). *Cultural politics of everyday life: Social constructionism, rhetoric and knowing of the third kind*. Toronto: University of Toronto Press.

Szasz, T. (1973). *The second sin*. New York: Doubleday, Anchor Press.

Szasz, T. (1990). *The untamed tongue: A dissenting dictionary*. LaSalle, IL: Open Court.

Varela, F. J. (1979). *Principles of biological autonomy*. New York: Elsevier North-Holland.

Varela, F. J. (1989). Reflections on the circulation of concepts between a biology of cognition and systemic family therapy. *Family Process, 28*, 15–24.

Watzlawick, P. (Ed.). (1984). *The invented reality: How do we know what we believe we know? Contributions to constructivism*. New York: W.W. Norton.

Watzlawick, P., Beavin, J., & Jackson, D. D. (1967). *The pragmatics of human communication*. New York: W.W. Norton.

White, M. (1993). Commentary: The histories of the present. In S. Gilligan & R. E. Price (Eds.), *Therapeutic conversations* (pp. 121–135). New York: W.W. Norton.

Zeleny, M. (Ed.). (1981). *Autopoiesis: A theory of living organization*. New York: Elsevier North-Holland.

························

4

Psychotherapy as a Social Construction

Sheila McNamee

Psychotherapy, by its very name, draws our attention to a person's inner life. In fact, the term *psychotherapy* is derived from the Greek *psyche* ("soul") and *therapeuein* ("to nurse" or "to nourish"), thus suggesting that the purpose of psychotherapy is to nourish the soul. The use of a term meaning soul implies a romanticist orientation to therapeutic process, one that places emphasis on those aspects of a person that are essentially intangible yet ever present. Phrases such as "moral fiber," "emotional sensibility," "creativity," and "passion" come to mind when we think in romanticist terms. Typically, we locate these "qualities" within the person, and therapy is the profession designed to help us get at them.

To many, Freud's psychoanalysis provided a quasi-scientific technique for examining this mysterious soul, or psyche. Freud provided a link between the romanticism of the early nineteenth century and the rise of modernism in the early twentieth century. In fact, Freud has been identified by many as responsible for making psychology in general and psychotherapy in particular "scientific."

The efforts that have followed Freud's contributions at the frontier of psychology have maintained a sort of schizophrenia between rational scientific method and our respect and awe for our mysterious inner passions. We see it in any history of the therapeutic profession: the constant attempts to develop a method or technique that will allow us to say something about a person's inner life. In most therapeutic models, the attempt is to externalize the internal. This may take the form of paper-and-pencil tests or stories and descriptions of specified materials. A person's psychic life is eventually measured and evaluated by his or her performance on these preestablished exercises. As Gergen (1985) has argued, the quest to chart internal (what he calls "endogenic") processes ultimately relies on external ("exogenic") methods.

What is most interesting about the strange marriage between romanticist notions of the psyche and modernist attempts to explain, predict, and control it is the continued focus on individuals. Additionally, the intriguing question that surfaces asks *how* the transition into modernist discourse opened the possibility for psychotherapy's acceptance as a viable and sustainable profession. Once the romanticized inner life of the individual was cast as a likely candidate for scientific examination, psychotherapy became a popular cultural resource for those identified as having problems, because the modernist focus on progress ensured movement toward cultural standards.

My first aim in this chapter is to examine how the psychotherapeutic process has been socially constructed. The rise of the profession can be associated with a continued concern about the self-contained individual (Sampson, 1993), and in that regard, the social construction of psychotherapy as we know it is strong testimony to the prominence of modernist discourse. I begin by describing the pervasive construction of therapy as individually and (in most cases) internally focused. In so doing, I wish to establish the dominant construction of psychotherapeutic practice as a candidate for deconstruction. A deconstruction of this privileged view will locate its significance and scope within its historical and cultural context. It will illustrate that what we take to be the unquestionable contours of the profession are by-products of relational interplay. More directly, to deconstruct psychotherapy is to see it as a *social construction* emerging within a particular cultural discourse. My second aim in this chapter is to entertain burgeoning reconstructions of psychotherapeutic practice in a postmodern world, where relational engagement is privileged over staunch individualism.

Modernism and Psychotherapy

Freud's success in delivering psychotherapy to the modern world was not divorced from critical historical and social influences. The rise of modernism at the turn of the twentieth century was in large part due to the growing capacity of persons to expand their communities via increased options in transportation and communication. With such expansion, people depended less on family and close friends in times of difficulty. The expansion of relational networks also increased venues for comparison. The integrity of an individual's way of being in the world was now open for comparison and evaluation within a broader arena. A man might be quite like his family and close friends and less like his successful and socially graceful business associate. But to which relationship should he turn for advice? Which one should serve as his self-evaluative measure? It is not so far-reaching to suggest that psychotherapy at this time was appealing to people not only for its newfound linkage with science but also for its ability to substitute for family and friends in the role of confidant. If we are to explore the impact of these changes, it will be useful for us first to understand the scope of modernism.

In the following section, I provide a summary of modernism. For more extensive treatment of this topic, there are several excellent sources (see Berman, 1982; Levenson, 1984; Turner, 1990). My main objective here is to connect the rise of modernism at the beginning of the twentieth century with the rise of psychotherapy as a profession: how it is that psychotherapeutic practice becomes, at this historical moment, broadly accepted in the culture.

Rationality, Individualism, and Scattered Communities

Twentieth-century modernism is a continuation of the turn to reason associated with the Enlightenment of the late eighteenth century. Within this discourse, rationality is featured and reasoning abilities are viewed as an individual possession (Macpherson, 1962; Sampson, 1993).

Modernism, as a cultural discourse, champions the individual. Sampson (1993) has identified this individual as *self-contained*. A world of self-contained individuals suggests a world populated with autonomous, intentional persons who possess the means to reason properly within the social arena. Communities do not reason. Cultures do not reason. Groups do not reason. All reasoning abilities are assigned to active agents whose rationality can be measured against culturally defined standards.

The focus on the self-contained individual continues the romanticist theme of inherent qualities but adds to that theme the modernist emphasis on progress. With science as a central metaphor, attention is directed toward the powers of explanation, prediction, and control. Explanation of human beings' reasoning abilities initiates the possibility of altering these abilities when needed. If we assume some standard rationality, then we can develop techniques to foster it in individuals. A common rationality will be followed by predictable and controllable actions that, in turn, will ensure a coherent and well-coordinated social structure.

A coordinated social structure was in great demand during the rise of industrialization and urbanization in the twentieth century. Psychotherapy offered an important social service in this historical moment: a technique by which the internal self could be kept in check amid the ever growing complexities of daily life. In short, as possibilities for communication and transportation expanded, individuals were given more and more opportunities to move beyond the confines of their local communities. But with access to numerous and differing communities, the individual's previously secure identity was under threat of change.

Urbanization and industrialization introduced yet another significant change for individuals. Whereas, previously, a person could discuss difficulties, problems, and questions of identity with family members, close friends, and community and religious leaders—all of whom lived within the same small community—the vast changes in transportation and communication technologies made such "therapeutic" conversations less likely. When confronted with a different rationality, value system, or ethical code, individuals did not find it always conceivable to discuss their intrigue, disapproval, or even endorsement of those differences with others in their local network who might not share an exposure to more expansive communities. In these conditions spawned by twentieth-century modernism, psychotherapy offered the means by which both local communities and broader cultures could protect the integrity of the individual.

Psychological Health

Being a good, or a psychologically healthy, person, then, takes on a very specific meaning in modernist discourse. First, there is the embedded assumption that a psychologically healthy person possesses reasoning abilities. Equipped with the proper reasoning abilities, that person will behave in an expected and appropriate manner. Thus, we can expect to identify good or psychologically healthy individuals by virtue of their behaviors (what they do and say), which are actually reflections of their inner reasoning abilities. Furthermore, if we know what constitutes a good person, we can manipulate both environment and person to ensure *production* of a good individual.

This latter feature of modernism can be seen in this century's spawning of educational, medical, and business institutions that are reminiscent of the factory assembly line. These institutions have flourished with the rise of modernism, in large part because they are seen to serve as conduits for the ultimate construction of good citizens. With such institutions in place, a common rationality becomes a conceivable cultural achievement.

The self that was necessary for successful production in the modern world could also be continually reconstructed through the therapeutic process. As Cushman (1992) notes, "The state had to develop ways to control a new kind of subject: more mobile, less constrained by tradition and religion, less confined by role, and less predictable" (p. 25). Psychotherapy became prominent as a means for controlling this new kind of subject and therefore became an essential aspect of contemporary life. Thus, psychotherapy's position within modernist scientific discourse can be credited with the profession's cultural acceptance.

Science, Diagnosis, and Multiple Voices

At the turn of the twentieth century, science was viewed as the most sensible way for humanity to progress—after all, science and technology could deliver cures for disease, broader economic bases, widespread educational and business opportunities, and an entire host of promising social advantages—and the model science provided featured rationality and, with that, individuality. The resulting cultural emphasis on taking the rational and individual view—that is, the privileging of science as our way of moving into the future—gave a particular form to social life.

Yet at the same time that modernism was reinforcing a vision of uniform rationality, it was setting the stage for a very rich alternative. Along with the increasing demand for coordinated efforts beyond the boundaries of the individual's protected community and the increased capacity to achieve that coordination, there were burgeoning possibilities for a rich relational life that was populated with conflicting and incommensurate rationalities. Modern institutions such as psychotherapy and public education (to name only two) are illustrations of large-scale efforts to ensure uniformity amid the growing eclecticism. Yet in the past two decades, as these relational possibilities have increasingly emerged as possibilities not only for the elite and educated but for the broader population, the profusion of voices, values, moralities, and ethics has become more and more difficult to ignore.

Indeed, in the psychotherapeutic profession, the expansion of relatedness has had dramatic impact on the listing of recognized diagnoses in the *Diagnostic and Statistical Manual of Mental Disorders*. Earlier in this century, there was no difficulty in gaining agreement that homosexuality was pathological. Today, this diagnosis of homosexuality is nowhere to be found in DSM-IV (American Psychiatric Association, 1994). Today, premenstrual syndrome figures as a legitimate diagnosis; there is no trace of this psychological problem in earlier manuals. These two examples provide us with interesting data. Is it the case that science has helped us *discover* the true nature of these facets of psychological life, or is it the case that as homosexuals and women have been recognized as having legitimate voices—through expanded communication technologies—we have *expanded our understanding of and tolerance for* alternative rationalities? In sum, science originally generated a preferred discourse that ensured protection of the individual's autonomy and freedom. But as more and more facets of the culture have been invited into the conversation, our sense of what makes a good or healthy person and what is rational has been questioned.

In the quest to understand psychotherapy as a social construction, it is useful to discuss modernism as more than technological or scientific advancement. In the next section, I turn my attention more directly to the *selection* of science as the metaphor that is the hallmark of this century. In highlighting science as a *metaphor*, I connect the modernist way of life with *language*.

Modernism as a Discursive Option

Modernism is a way of talking, a discursive option, and to consider individualism as conversational resource rather than reality is to shift the terrain of our discussion. Rather than simply reflecting reality, the modernist way of talking has created a particular kind of reality. This reality includes all the features I have outlined: objectivity, individuality, uniform rationality, and progress. To put it this way is to say that modernism provides a distinctive discursive repertoire.

Submerged in Modernism

We often do not recognize the mark of modernism because it has inscribed itself on our way of living. In psychotherapy, where attention is directed to our inner processes, we do not question whether or not we have internal feelings, emotions, thoughts, and so forth. We seldom find ourselves pondering whether intentionality is central to our own or others' actions. We are not likely to wonder if the attention we give to outcomes, products, and goals is well placed. And clearly, when challenged, we do not hesitate to offer facts or evidence to support the rationale behind our actions. In fact, it is commonplace to expect that our conversational partners will (or at least should) be able to offer good reasons for their actions and that these reasons will (or should) meet some objective criteria for evaluation.

The discourse of reason is so commonplace to us that the concerns I raise in the previous paragraph are most likely to be viewed as curious rather than coherent. We simply *expect* others to be able to provide rational and objective evidence supporting their claims. We *expect* people to be individually responsible for their actions and to lay claim to their intentions. It is difficult to disrupt this way we have of relating to each other and worth questioning why we would want to change it in the first place.

Yet to see these views as by-products of a particular approach to language rather than as descriptions of the essential nature of reality provides us with a means for employing alternative resources. For when we understand that our words are not necessarily reflections of our interiors, we can recognize that seeing our words as interior reflections is a discursive tradition. It is a tradition identified as representational and having strong roots in modernism and science.

Representational Language

In accordance with the traditional view of language, we generally treat words and gestures as if they pictured an independent world. This tradition fosters a belief that there could be a correct way to put things, a better method for reaching truth, or a more accurate representation of what is *really* there. And if language pictures reality and if individual speakers utter words, then accurate representation of reality must be accomplished by *individuals* whose words reflect the inner workings of their minds. With this view in place, it is not difficult for us to describe how we have come to focus on individuals and their words or actions as a way of understanding the internal, mysterious mind or psyche. Additionally, it is not difficult for us to appreciate *how* psychotherapy has secured such a dominant cultural position. In this reasoning, psychotherapy gains significance as a profession necessary to cultural progress.

It is also not difficult for us to recognize the connection between the representational view of language and the scientific method. In both, the belief is that we can know with certainty. A representational view of language positions language as a conveyor of what is really there. Thus, a speaker's words and gestures are taken to be accurate reflections of his or her knowledge and, therefore, a reflection of reasoning abilities. In science, we can have knowledge via proper methods—which are, of course, born of individuals' abilities to reason.

Steeped as we are in the representational view of language, it is not difficult to understand the current and popular vision of psychotherapy that says language represents reality and that when a person speaks or acts, she or he is depicting reality either accurately or inaccurately. Our veracity check, in this view, is to compare the supposed inner representations of the individual with the established and presumably univocal social criteria. Once the nexus of meaning is located inside the individual, we are then prompted to explore any need for change or adjustment on an individual basis.

Not only is change directed toward individuals, but the language of individualism that emerges from the representational view invites a vast array of pathologies. These pathologies can be framed as possible limitations of individualist discourse.

Most obvious of the pathologizing possibilities offered by individualist discourse is the construction of a sense of personal deficit. Discussing the sense of deficit, Gergen (1990) explains that when meaning and action are seen as originating within the individual, it is ultimately the individual who is seen as flawed, deficient, and in need of remedy when a problem in meaning or action is thought to exist. Clearly, psychotherapy becomes the natural context within which individuals may do this reformatory work.

Again, most of us would be surprised at any attempts to call these internal aspects of human life into question. Yet by linking these taken-for-granted aspects of personhood to a particular discursive tradition, we are able to examine them by way of the social life forms they invite. Individual discourse, while enduring and valuable, is only one way of talking and, thus, only one way of being. It is the discourse that emerges within a modernist sensibility. Fully armed with the discourse of individualism, we have been able to locate a broad array of qualities within persons, ranging from intellect to leadership to sociability to agency. It is individuals who reason, who lead, who relate, and who act intentionally. Thus, it has been only reasonable to conclude that it is individuals who should become the focus of treatment when actions or meanings do not fit with culturally preferred norms.

Limits to Modernist Discourse

Several theoretical threads have been developed that weave a backdrop for a critique of modernist discourse. My treatment of these significant movements will be brief as my aim is simply to set the stage for today's disenchantment with modernism.

Ideological Critique

The first significant body of work that concerns us here is known as *ideological critique* (Althusser, 1971; Marx & Engels, 1970; Gramsci, 1971). This work is important for its emphasis on the value-laden nature of any theory. In other words, all perspectives are ideological. Thus, our ability to objectively examine the social world is called into question. Any person's attempt at or claim to objectivity is, itself, suggestive of that person's values. To ignore the ways in which ideology shapes our theories of the social world is to engage in what has come to be known in the field of cultural criticism as false consciousness. (This term, originally attributed to Marx, is believed by current Marxist scholars to have actually derived from Engels. See Barrett, 1991, p. 5.)

Literary Criticism

The second critique of modernism was introduced via literary criticism. Derrida (1978) and Fish (1980), among others, argue that such terms as *objectivity, rationality,* and *individuality* are simply linguistic conventions, ways of talking and nothing more. This critique questions the notion that what we are really examining when we engage in psychotherapeutic practice is a person's inner self. When we question what that psychic interior is, the literary critics suggest that our answer is simply a referral to yet another linguistic convention. There is never a point at which we can actually get to the *thing* we are talking about, to its essential nature. To put it another way, our knowledge of anything is not knowledge of the thing-in-itself but is already circumscribed by the text or discourse in which we are immersed. Terms gain their meaning in relation to other terms. Thus, we "know" a healthy psyche only by its comparison to an unhealthy one. Further, the very terms *healthy, unhealthy,* and *psyche* are themselves terms that gain significance within a particular text. If this is the case, then, the literary critics argue, we can never realize the modernist notion that we can, with proper methods, know the essential features of the world.

Social Critique

The final challenge to modernist discourse is best known as *social critique*. Here, the emphasis is on how knowledge is constructed in a social world. Kuhn (1970) presented this perspective when he introduced his critique of science. To Kuhn, we view the world from within a perspective, and that perspective is created and nurtured in social contexts. Once we are fully immersed in a perspective, it is difficult if not impossible for us to see the world in any other way.

Thus, my perspective tells me what counts as data. In the psychotherapeutic world, we could say that if the therapist's perspective is cognitivism, he or she will see a client's problems as, for example, the product of improper information processing or a dysfunctional cognitive scheme. It is, says Kuhn, difficult to move beyond the boundaries of our perspectives.

From Discontentment to Postmodernism

These three critiques have proved rich soil; upon them the seeds of discontent have grown. Each challenge to modernism has proposed its own antidote to modernist views. For those engaged in ideological critique, the antidote has been recognition of their ideological commitments. Yet this solution presents its own problem. How do we adjudicate among ideologies? Which theory is better? Are the feminists correct (and if so, which version of feminism)? Or is it the Marxists who offer a more compelling social theory?

Literary criticism also presents constraints. If we cannot escape the confines of our language, if each term we use is simply a deferral to other terms, what can we say about the social world? Can we say anything at all? Why should we bother with professions like psychotherapy if there is nothing substantial to be said or done?

The critiques offered by these two traditions are significant in the deconstruction of modernism. Yet it is the social critique that offers the most promising antidote to modernism. Social critique privileges relationships. And rather than describe language as a conveyor of essences, social critique describes language as performance. Language is something that we do together in social interplay, and thus, it is the way in which we create our worlds.

As I have described, it has been the very workings of modernist logic that have propelled us into a more relationally sensitive postmodern world (which has then given rise to the critiques of modernism). In the postmodern world, "individuals" continually confront rationalities whose contours are markedly different from the shape of the individuals' own rationalities. Television, film, video, and print media; telephone transmission, satellite communication, and jet transportation propel us into the world of the "other." Does our rapid immersion in this world foreshadow the demise of psychotherapy? Up to this point, psychotherapy has served the modernist world as an institution that maintains cultural standards for individuals' emotional and reasoning abilities. Does movement into a relationally complex world with shifting rationalities signify the death of psychotherapy, or can psychotherapy be reconstructed within this relational world?

The Construction of Psychotherapy in a Relational World

By deconstructing the modernist discourse from which the psychotherapeutic profession emerged, we free ourselves to consider alternative constructions of both psychotherapy and social life. To deconstruct modernist discourse requires that we describe our prominent way of talking as just that, a way of talking. Modernist discourse, rooted as it is in the scientific metaphor, directs our attention to the possible explanation and articulation of the essential aspects of whatever phenomenon we are examining. Thus, in therapy, the modernist goal of preserving and adjusting one's selfhood begins with the therapist's and client's explorations of the reaches of the client's true self. The essential features of this true self will vary from one psychotherapeutic model to another. Yet all the models strive to treat basic enduring features of the individual.

But in a world where access to multiple rationalities and forms of living is easily available through advances in transportation and communication media and technologies, what form might psychotherapy take? Gergen (1991) has argued that technological advances have created a sort of "social saturation" (p. 3) in which each of us becomes populated with others. It is no longer meaningful to talk about a core identity when identity shifts by virtue of the relational context in which a person is presently immersed. If I am a successful professional, does that negate the possibility of my being a good mother? Does motherhood require constant presence and attention that full immersion in my profession would prohibit? Beyond my identities as professional and mother, who am I in my community, to my friends from foreign countries, to others enrolled as I am in Latin dance classes? How can I manage all these identities and more without slumping into anxiety over which one is "real"? (And if I do choose one as real, do I thereby pathologize all the others?) Can psychotherapy in this relationally complex world be something other than a context for fine-tuning or reinstating a unified sense of self?

Two possibilities are available. One would have us create psychotherapeutic practice that is focused on relational engagement—instead of treating individuals, the psychotherapist would treat relationships. The second would identify psychotherapy as a profession charged with attending to the processes of construction themselves. As we know, the first option has been explored in great depth. The second option, I believe, offers more longevity and promise for psychotherapy as a cultural resource.

Relational Psychotherapy

Theorists and clinicians have made a variety of attempts to introduce the relational element into an understanding of psychotherapeutic process. The work of Harry Stack Sullivan (1953) and the object relations theorists (Fairbairn, 1952), as well as the efforts of people engaged in variations of humanistic psychology and cognitive psychology, introduced the relation between self and other as a significant source of identity. Speaking of these early relationally focused attempts, Cushman (1992) states: "They had to adjust psychoanalytic theory to the broad historical trend of personal relatedness while staying within the limitations of the masterful, bounded self. Because the individual . . . obviously is not a completely self-contained entity, interactional activity, nourishment, guidance, and a cultural frame of reference had to be brought from the outside to the inside" (p. 54).

These efforts were followed by the family therapy movement. Clearly, the pioneering work of the early family systems therapies, illustrated in the works of Bateson (1972), Watzlawick, Beavin, & Jackson (1967), Minuchin (1974), Haley (1971), and Jackson (1968), was radical in its time for its shift of focus from individuals to integrated systems. Examining social behavior as a by-product of interrelated parts working in concert provided many years of rich research and creativity in the therapeutic profession.

Ironically, however, these early attempts to introduce a relational element maintained the essentialist argument of modernism. These models, which were based on General Systems Theory (Bertalanffy, 1968; Laszlo, 1973), can be cast as a simple shift from examining the objective observations of individuals to examining the objective observations of systems such as families or groups. Recognition of the dynamic interplay among participants edged psychotherapy beyond the limits of the psyche and into the world of communication. However, the grip of the modernist proclivity toward universal rationality, objectification, evaluation, and control was still strong.

The therapeutic models developed in those early years illustrated the modernist allegiance in a variety of ways. Some touted a "preferred" or "normal" family structure achieved through communication that created and maintained appropriate boundaries, hierarchies, and subsystems (Minuchin, 1974). Others maintained the modernist focus on objective observation by attempting to examine behavioral sequences surrounding or associated with an identified problem and then offering a new frame for making sense out of those very sequences (Watzlawick, Weakland, & Fisch, 1974). There were many variations on these particular methods, but the genre was the same: problems were no longer located within individuals; now they were located within systems or relationships. The well-trained therapist could closely examine and observe these systems and intervene to eliminate unwanted problems.

While the relationships among participants or among behaviors was acknowledged in this early work, the relational sensibility that erases objectivity, univocal rationality, and active agency was not yet achieved. Therapists were still beholden to preferred family structures and preferred interactional patterns. Clients who did not change as a result of these therapies were still labeled "resistant" and thereby pathologized for not accommodating to the normalized routine.

The early systems therapies evolved into second-order, or constructivist, therapeutic models where attempts were made to incorporate not only the relationships among those in the system being observed (the family system) or the relationships among their actions but also the relationship of the observer (therapist) to the observed (family, couple, and so forth). Maturana (1988) captures the thrust of this new move when he says, "everything said is said by an observer to another observer that could be him- or herself" (p. 27).

The focus of the second-order systems models was the self-reflexive process of the observer. In an attempt to incorporate the relational terrain of observer and observed, theorists and practitioners denied the observer's objectivity. This view clearly is consistent with the relational sensibility of a constructionist orientation, yet in taking it, the constructivists essentialized the observer's cognitive and perceptual processes. They reasoned that no observer is free of biases, and thus, any observation made of another system must, through the self-reflexive nature of language, be more a statement about the observer than the other system.

Clearly, the focus of this wave of relational therapy was on the *internal* processes of the observer (the therapist). Again, we recognize that there is an essential object offered for our attention. We remain within a representational view of language because we must rely on the therapist's words and actions to tell us of his or her perceptual and cognitive processes.

This is only a small sampling of the relational efforts in psychotherapy. However, attempts over the past twenty to thirty years to move psychotherapy into the relational domain have not positioned it much beyond the challenges offered by modernism and its individualist-centered models. These challenges include the simple acceptance of dysfunctions or diseases as actual states of being rather than ways of talking, the positioning of the therapist as one who can "know" disease and dysfunction when he or she sees it rather than one who sees problems as discursive constructions that are jointly achieved, and the notion that therapy will (or should) cure psychological and social distress as opposed to the idea of therapy as a conversational arena within which new relational realities can be constructed. In sum, the social construction of the individualist and relational models of therapeutic practice maintains the discourse of modernism, thereby privileging objectivity, individualism, and a univocal rationality. Thus, psychotherapy remains a profession charged with helping individuals (and now families and groups) fit into idealized social structures.

The problem with this view of psychotherapy is that as our abilities to explore new and different relational realities grow, the psychotherapy that is credited with helping us fit in to reality may become obsolete. Psychotherapy as currently constructed must be reconstructed if it is to endure in this multivocal postmodern world. Psychotherapy's longstanding focus on individuals (or individual units such as groups and families) and a common rationality is at cross-purposes with the multiplicities in our lives today. Instead of *adjusting* identities to some cultural standards, the demands presented require *construction* of various and often competing *relational* possibilities. Is it possible for us to reconsider what psychotherapy is? Can it be reconstructed as a context we turn to for conversational engagement about various ways of juggling multiplicity, moving beyond consistency across contexts and relationships as well as beyond rationality in harmony toward the polyphony of multiple rationalities?

Relational Engagement Psychotherapy

An alternative construction of psychotherapeutic practice has emerged within a more fully relational sensibility. Here the relational component is not offered as an addendum to the well-established individual focus, as it was in the early systems and second-order work. It is not simply another element to be examined objectively or to be understood via words and actions that are meant to represent aspects of essentialized relationships or of the perceptive/cognitive abilities of those in relationships.

Instead, the relational sensibility put forward in more recent constructions of psychotherapeutic practice (see McNamee & Gergen, 1992) draws from a very different set of orienting premises. These premises position relational engagement as central, rather than as a by-product of individuals' coming together. In other words, any sense of individuality is described as a by-product of relatedness. This option centralizes the *processes* by which people come to create particular modes of interpretation and action.

Bringing processes rather than products of relational engagement to the foreground represents a significant shift. Psychotherapy from this orientation has little to do with delivering well-adjusted individuals, families, or groups to the broader culture. Now psychotherapy takes as its purpose the creation of conversational opportunities—both within the therapeutic context and beyond. In other words, psychotherapeutic practice becomes a dialogical relationship where multiple rationalities are discussed. Not all will be treated equally. But none will be demonized out of context. The task of therapy is to bring significant conversations into the therapeutic conversation, just as the therapeutic conversation should be brought to pertinent relationships. Rather than serving as judge to competing identities, moralities, and values, psychotherapy serves as a conversational arena for participants to explore the discursive traditions within which disparate views have evolved.

For example, a therapeutic conversation could invite an array of variously connected relationships into the discussion, never fully terminating with one story or one voice but temporarily crafting a rationale that grants significance to participants' relational networks. The work of Tom Andersen (1991) approaches this to the extent that he encourages therapist and client to continually shift from listening to reflecting positions and back again. The constant movement centralizes the process of relational engagement rather than allowing the dominance of any one voice.

Similarly, the work of Penn and Frankfurt (1994) constructs a dialogical relationship where multiple rationalities are entertained. They believe that different voices can be invited into the therapeutic conversation through writing. Specifically, writing letters or journal entries to relational partners not immediately engaged in the current problem invites clients to consider typically silent voices as possible resources with something to contribute to the current situation. As clients review and rescript their writing inside and outside of therapy, they find themselves fully engaged in the process of constructing relational realities.

To fashion psychotherapeutic practice in this way is to sanction the contingency of relational life. It is to normalize (not pathologize) the indeterminacy of the worlds we construct. It is to give voice to the multiple meanings that emerge within varying social communities. To that end, the reconstruction of psychotherapy in a relationally complex world embraces the relativity of meaning but stops short of the nihilism spawned by what some call rampant relativism. It is important to explore ways of acting and making sense of the world in relation to the setting within which such constructions emerge. However, one is not ever free to construct the world alone. The emphasis on *social* construction underscores the relational engagement that is necessary for the viability and sustainability of any rationality.

Conclusion

This chapter could have easily been about applications of social constructionism in therapeutic practice. However, many have already contributed creative and compelling descriptions of such applications (see McNamee & Gergen, 1992). The less frequently considered territory is the construction of psychotherapy itself. My examination of this construction in this chapter is not far removed from the challenges social construction introduces to psychotherapeutic practice itself. Theorists and practitioners have translated in unique ways the indeterminacy, multiplicity, and relativity of meanings, values, and forms of action in therapeutic practice. They have generated methods that centralize participants' relational enmeshment over the modernist notion of self as agent. These creative applications speak to the shift from psychotherapy's construction in the past to what its reconstruction should be. Additionally, the ways in which psychotherapists have expanded the reach of their professional work to include heated political and public issues (see Chasin, Chasin, Herzig, Roth, & Becker, 1991; Roth, Chasin, Chasin, Becker, & Herzig, 1992), organizational contexts (Lang & Little, 1992), and broader social concerns such as poverty (Pakman, 1994) do more than simply foreshadow the significant role psychotherapy can (and does) play in a relationally complex world.

This discussion of the therapeutic process suggests that this process gains its significance as a cultural resource available for exploration of relational possibilities. It is the context within which people can survey a wide range of rationalities—problematizing some while privileging others, but only temporarily. The constant shifting of contexts, relationships, and resources means that today's "problem" may be tomorrow's "exemplary performance." Because the immediate demands of any social context require adjudication, the choices we make are genuine choices in the particular interactive moment but may nevertheless have to be discarded in the future.

The demands on us to coordinate our activities in so many differing domains suggest that psychotherapy needs to be less about the continual construction of a unified, self-contained individual and more about the expansion of identities in the ever-changing sea of relatedness. Psychotherapy in this multivocal world becomes a profession we turn to for an exploration of possibilities. No longer are there clear answers about how psychotherapy can move individuals, families, and groups toward productive participation in their communities. The form and content of productive participation is in continual flux. Therapy becomes a venue one seeks to engage in, in "interested inquiry" (Gergen & Kaye, 1992, p. 182) of the various stories that could become real. Our history and culture have provided us with a limited range of conversational repertoires about psychotherapy. Now we may consider expansion of these repertoires. Rather than replacing healing conversations with family and close friends, does psychotherapy supplement such conversations? How does it supplement, in addition, our disembodied electronic conversations? What resources for social life do all these avenues for construction offer and how do they work in concert? These are the questions that face a psychotherapy reconstructed as a relational, not an individual, phenomenon.

References

Althusser, L. (1971). *Lenin and philosophy and other essays* (B. Brewster, Ed. & Trans.). London: New Left Books.

American Psychiatric Association. (1994). *Diagnostic and statistical manual of mental disorders* (4th ed.). Washington, DC: Author.

Andersen, T. (Ed.) (1991). *The reflecting team: Dialogues and dialogues about the dialogues*. New York: W.W. Norton.

Barrett, M. (1991). *The politics of truth: From Marx to Foucault*. Stanford, CA: Stanford University Press.

Bateson, G. (1972). *Steps to an ecology of mind*. New York: Ballantine Books.

Berman, M. (1982). *All that's solid melts into air: The experience of modernity*. New York: Simon & Schuster.

Bertalanffy, L. von (1968). *General systems theory*. New York: Braziller.

Chasin, L., Chasin, R., Herzig, M., Roth, S., & Becker, C. (1991, Winter). The citizen clinician: The family therapist in the public forum. *American Family Therapy Association Newsletter*, pp. 36–42.

Cushman, P. (1992). Psychotherapy to 1992: A historically situated interpretation. In D. K. Freedheim (Ed.), *History of psychotherapy* (pp. 21–64). Washington, DC: American Psychological Association.

Derrida, J. (1978). *Writing and difference* (A. Bass, Trans.). Chicago: University of Chicago Press.

Fairbairn, W.R.D. (1952). *An object-relations theory of the personality*. New York: Basic Books.

Fish, S. (1980). *Is there a text in this class?* Cambridge, MA: Harvard University Press.

Gergen, K. J. (1985). The social constructionist movement in modern psychology. *American Psychologist, 40,* 266–275.

Gergen, K. J. (1990). Therapeutic professions and the diffusion of deficit. *The Journal of Mind and Behavior, 11,* 353–367.

Gergen, K. J. (1991). *The saturated self: Dilemmas of identity in contemporary life.* New York: Basic Books.

Gergen, K. J., & Kaye, J. (1992). Beyond narrative in the negotiation of therapeutic meaning. In S. McNamee & K. J. Gergen (Eds.), *Therapy as social construction* (pp. 166–185). Newbury Park, CA: Sage.

Gramsci, A. (1971). *Selections from the prison notebooks* (Q. Hoare & G. Nowell Smith, Eds. & Trans.). New York: International Publishers.

Haley, J. (1971). *Changing families.* Philadelphia: Grune & Stratton.

Jackson, D. D. (Ed.). (1968). *Communication, family, and marriage.* Palo Alto, CA: Science and Behavior Books.

Kuhn, T. S. (1970). *The structure of scientific revolutions* (2nd ed.). Chicago: University of Chicago Press.

Lang, P., & Little, M. (1992, May). Centre for systemic management. *Kensington Consultation Centre Newsletter.*

Laszlo, E. (1973). *Introduction to systems philosophy.* New York: HarperCollins, Torchbooks.

Levenson, M. (1984). *A genealogy of modernism.* New York: Cambridge University Press.

McNamee, S., & Gergen, K. J. (Eds.). (1992). *Therapy as social construction.* Newbury Park, CA: Sage.

Macpherson, C. B. (1962). *The political theory of possessive individualism.* New York: Oxford University Press.

Marx, K., & Engels, F. (1970). *The German ideology.* New York: International Publishers.

Maturana, H. (1988). Reality: The search for objectivity or the quest for a compelling argument. *Irish Journal of Psychology, 9,* 25–82.

Minuchin, S. (1974). *Families and family therapy.* Cambridge, MA: Harvard University Press.

Pakman, M. (1994, October). *Therapy in contexts of poverty and ethnic dissonance: Constructivism and social constructionism as methodologies for action.* Paper presented at the conference New Voices in Human Systems, Northampton, MA.

Penn, P., & Frankfurt, M. (1994). Creating a participant text: Writing, multiple voices, narrative multiplicity. *Family Process, 33,* 217–232.

Roth, S., Chasin, L., Chasin, R., Becker, C., & Herzig, M. (1992). From debate to dialogue. *Dulwich Centre Newsletter,* No. 2, pp. 41–48.

Sampson, E. E. (1993). *Celebrating the other.* Boulder, CO: Westview Press.

Sullivan, H. S. (1953). *The interpersonal theory of psychiatry.* New York: W.W. Norton.

Turner, B. S. (1990). *Theories of modernity and postmodernity.* Newbury Park, CA: Sage.

Watzlawick, P., Beavin, J., & Jackson, D. D. (1967). *The pragmatics of human communication.* New York: W.W. Norton.

Watzlawick, P., Weakland, J. H., & Fisch, R. (1974). *Change: Principles of problem formation and problem resolution.* New York: W.W. Norton.

Part III

. . . .

The Social Context of Construing

5

Relationship Factors in the Creation of Identity
A Psychodynamic Perspective

Carolyn Saari

The lack of a clear and acceptable way of defining psychological health has frequently forced conceptions of therapeutic action in psychotherapy to focus on the elimination of pathology rather than on the promotion of health. Clinical experience, however, has demonstrated that too exclusive a focus on pathology in the treatment hour is often experienced by the patient as critical, demeaning, and/or unhelpful (Wachtel, 1993). Fortunately, recent theoretical advances in the understanding of meaning and its creation in treatment now make possible approaches to psychotherapy that both focus on the promotion of health and have a conception of how that health is fostered through the therapeutic relationship. This chapter outlines one such approach.

Previous Conceptualizations of Psychological Health

There have been serious problems with most previously articulated formulations of psychological health. Freud's ideas about the need for individuals to resolve the Oedipal complex are now generally recognized as sexist. Much psychological thinking has operated on an adaptation model of health—and continues to do so, in spite of an awareness that neither Hartmann (1958) nor others since have truly been able to answer the question, adaptation to what? Moreover, such psychological thinking persists even though social systems are often oppressive and a focus on adaptation, in many instances, can be seen as simply furthering this oppression. Cognitive approaches, for their part, have also had difficulty accommodating to the postmodern understanding (Bruner, 1986; Gergen, 1991) that ultimate truth and a distortion-free perception are not possible.

Diagnostic and Statistical Manual formulations, pretending to be theory free, have operated by defining pathology rather than health, basing the definition on a highly elaborated symptom list (American Psychiatric Association, 1994). While such formulations may provide a basis for operational definitions in research, experienced psychotherapists ordinarily find that a focus on pathology with the patient in treatment is likely to increase pathology, whereas a focus on the possibility of health is likely to increase the patient's possibility of health. Recognizing that labeling (Goffman, 1961) can create problems in the application of a theory of human functioning, many social constructionist theorists have been reluctant to propose a theory of pathology. Yet it is clear that although the recognized symptomatology and the treatment procedures employed may vary from culture to culture, mental illness *does* exist in all societies (Kleinman, 1988).

Psychological Health in a Social Context

The perspective I present in this chapter attempts to solve the problems I have described by viewing psychological health as the achievement of a complex identity (Guidano, 1987; Saari, 1991), capable of serving as a basis from which the individual can perceive a range of possible behaviors and make choices among them. If we view culture as shared meaning (Becker, 1986), mental illness may be understood as an inability to participate or share in the meaning system of the culture and the relevant social structure or as a serious limitation on the ability to envision potentially available behavioral choices and their likely consequences within a given society.

Note that there is a fundamental difference between an *inability* to comprehend or share in a meaning system and *disagreement* with the tenets of that system. For example, the individual who knowingly flaunts nonconforming behavior, either to protest or to rebel against social norms, may be psychologically healthy, whereas the person who is unable to comprehend those norms would not be. While in practice this distinction may be difficult to make, in theory it is a crucial one.

Participation in a cultural meaning system as a criterion of psychological health strongly implies a social component to the achievement of that health. The perspective presented here assumes that human beings are fundamentally social animals and that not only is the cultural meaning system transmitted through social interaction but also the human capacity to create meaning. The meaning-making capacity is dependent upon interpersonal transactions for both its development and its maintenance throughout life. Thus, any judgment about an individual's psychological health must be made in the context of the culture to which that person has had an opportunity to be socialized.

One advantage of this approach for a theory of psychotherapy is that it recognizes that while coherence (that is, interconnectedness and unity of content) in an individual's identity or meaning system is important for that person to be able to function well, there is no ultimate "truth" upon which that person's identity rests. Additionally, in this approach, pathology may be envisioned as a limitation in the individual's capacity to create meaning, with that capacity based in the ability to participate in human relationships. In this manner, the theory can elucidate the reasons for the significance of the human relationship in therapy and can provide a basis for understanding the professional use of that relationship. Also, within this definition of mental health, treatment can be assumed to work through helping the individual, not to alter directly behavior that may be maladaptive in particular context(s), but rather to develop an identity capable of encompassing the meanings found in a variety of contexts and cultures.

Identity as a Personal Meaning System

Identity is defined here as a personal meaning system that is created over the course of the individual's experience with the world and is organized primarily in narrative form (Bruner, 1990). In other words, identity is the content of the autobiographical stories told to self and others. This understanding of identity can be seen to have some differences from Erikson's ideas (1963), in which there is an underlying, though probably unintentional, implication that a healthy identity assumes a unitary form through consolidation in adolescence (Saari, 1993; Searles, 1979). An understanding of identity as unitary is more consonant with a belief in an objective reality and a correspondence theory of truth than with a social constructionist perspective. From my perspective, identity may also be seen as an individual's personal theory about himself or herself, about the world, and about his or her relationship with the world and vice versa. It is through this personal theory that the individual organizes past experiences and plans future actions (Epstein, 1973).

In the course of everyday life, an individual ordinarily encounters not a singular or static environment but a wide variety of contexts that make differential demands for adaptive behavior. In order to function maximally, therefore, an individual needs to be capable of accommodating to, or comprehending his or her relationship to, that contextual variety. Assuming that identity is the personal meaning system upon which the individual bases his or her comprehension of the environment, it follows that a healthy identity, capable of dealing with a range of situations, would be complex in the sense of being highly articulated, differentiated, and integrated (Werner, 1948).

The narrative form is an expression of a high order of meaning-making, one that reveals and integrates seemingly disparate aspects of a person's life into a unified whole (Polkinghorne, 1988). Further, narrative through which human identity emerges and is progressively constructed and reconstructed over time (Bruner, 1987; Polkinghorne, 1988) is ideally suited to achieving the articulation, differentiation, and integration necessary for generating complexity within a coherent whole and for enabling the revisions that life experience makes perpetually necessary. Plots and subplots can readily be woven together in patterns implying multiple causation, in spite of the basically linear temporal form of this medium. Additionally, since narratives involve not only the inner life of an individual but also delineate the relationship of the characters to each other and to the place or setting, narrative form also captures a picture of the human being not as an isolated and independent being but rather as an active participant in a social context. From the perspective of the efficacy of psychotherapy, it may be that treatment works at least partially through assisting the client in the creation of a narrative identity that has a potential to achieve a satisfying ending to the autobiographical story.

Interpersonal Development of Identity

Among current theorists of psychoanalytic development is a growing consensus (Bretherton, 1994; Emde, 1994; Fonagy, 1994; Stern, 1994) that the preverbal experiences underlying identity and the capacity to create meaning are interpersonal and interactive. While not discounting a biological base for human functioning, Daniel Stern (1985), for example, sees the roots of an inner life as fundamentally interpersonal. Stern pictures the very young infant as becoming quite used to having caretakers act in the role of the self-regulating other, the person who calms the agitated infant by holding her warmly and securely in his arms. Thus, Stern's theory posits a fundamental relatedness between interpersonal interaction and intrapsychic experience that is not possible in older psychoanalytic theory.

Affect Attunement as Interaction

In addition to the self-regulating other, Stern discusses the importance of affect attunement, which involves not only the traditionally understood categorical affects such as mad, sad, glad, and scared but also the cross-modal matching of vitality affects such as rhythm, tone, intensity, or shape. A mother might, for example, say, "Whee, whee," with a timing and tone that is in precise conjunction with the pace of her small son's activity in pushing a toy car with vigorous enjoyment. The child understands from his mother's vocalization that she knows of the inner pleasure he gains from this play. Affect attunement is normally carried out without conscious awareness.

In an elaboration upon his ideas about attunement, Stern specifically indicates that affects not attuned by others in the caretaking environment cannot be shared with others. It would seem reasonable to assume, although Stern does not make this point, that experiences that cannot be shared with others would not be sharable with the self either. In fact, the intersubjective theorists Stolorow and Atwood (1992) have suggested that consciousness consists of that which has been affectively attuned. According to this theory, all of an individual's conscious inner experience has its origin in interpersonal interaction.

Meaning-Making as Interpersonal Negotiation

Stern and others, however, have also viewed meaning as created in the interaction between at least two people. "Meaning results from interpersonal negotiations involving what can be agreed upon as shared. And such mutually negotiated meanings (the relation of thought to word) grow, change, develop and are struggled over by two people and thus ultimately owned by *us*" (Stern, 1985, p. 170). The assumption that meaning is owned by more than one person requires a revision of our comprehension of the fundamental nature of communication. In previous conceptualizations, the myth of the isolated mind (Stolorow & Atwood, 1992) has usually been perpetuated in part by the accompanying use of a transmission model of communication, expressing the accepted belief that interpersonal communication involved a message fully formulated in advance by the sender and transmitted intact to the receiver. Yet the idea that communication is the intact transmission of a preformulated message is highly questionable. The simple childhood game of "gossip," for example, illustrates the extent to which a single statement regularly becomes distorted when transmitted secretly and sequentially, from one person to another, through a number of individuals.

The Russian psychologist Bakhtin (Holquist, 1981; Wertsch, 1991) has pointed out that since all communication, even a monologue, has an audience, the content of all communication minimally involves contributions from two persons. There are at least three reasons for his argument:

1. Even simple statements can be interpreted in more than one way by the listener, given that a potential multiplicity of meanings can be attributed to any one statement.

2. The influence of context on meaning causes any statement or text to be interpreted according to its context, and the contexts of any two communicative partners will invariably be different. Thus, each will interpret the content from the individualized perspective of his or her experience prior to the communication.

3. It follows, from the fact that a multiplicity of meanings can be attributed to any one statement and from the contextual influences of interpretation and response on meaning, that the topic of communication is essentially negotiated. Each communicative partner will make adjustments in the content of the message sent in order to conform to the perceived interest and understanding of the other. Bakhtin also notes that communicative partners interact so as to agree not only on what is to be said but also on what is *not* to be said.

Identity as Emerging and Modified Through Dialogue

Personal identity can therefore be seen as a meaning system constituted with other people through dialogical processes. Maranhao

(1990) explains that the "traits of identity, however, do not precede dialogue; they are bestowed upon [the person] as he speaks and listens. The subject comes into being together with dialogue and is as much a meaning-content in the process as are the things talked about" (1990, p. 18). Identity does not fundamentally exist inside the isolated individual, waiting to be uncovered through an archeological exploration of the layers of an unconscious, but is a meaning system created through dialogue with others. Furthermore, personal identity does not form in an early developmental stage and then endure reasonably intact throughout life. It is constantly modified, created and recreated, in negotiations with interactive partners throughout a person's entire life.

Influences on Capacity to Create Meaning

Like identity, the capacity to create meaning may be more or less highly developed in general, and also like identity, it is not a static entity. Instead, it fluctuates in accordance with its operational context. We human beings are social animals, and the contextual element that most influences our capacity to create meaning is our relationship to other people. Children raised without contact with other humans do not develop language usage. Similarly, since the capacity to create meaning is interpersonally based, it can be expected to develop less well in children who have little access to empathic communicative interaction with other people.

Although the availability of another human being is a necessary condition if capacity to create meaning is to become highly developed, that availability in itself does not constitute a sufficient condition. Indeed, a number of other contextual factors affect this capacity and the likelihood of its being exercised. They include but are undoubtedly not limited to the following:

- Physical energy must be available. The person's creation of meaning will be facilitated if he or she is in good health, is in a rested state, and has an ability to devote attention to creating meaning rather than to another bodily activity. Clearly, problems in neurological functioning can affect meaning-making functioning.

- The individual's internal state must be experienced as sufficiently stable. There must not be so much conflict that it debilitates the person. However, some degree of conflict can motivate the person to create meaning in order to solve the problems involved.

- The environment must be experienced as both physically and emotionally safe. If the person must devote energy to remaining alert to potential danger or injury, that will clearly detract from his or her freedom to create meaning and from the energy available for that work.

- A history of reasonably attuned human relationships will make the person more likely to be able to engage productively in meaning-making, because the individual's capacity to create meaning develops over time and, once developed, can endure some adverse conditions.

- The specific content of the individual's picture of self and of the world—for example, whether these are seen as good, bad, helpful or evil—will either encourage or depress the capacity to create meaning.

- A cultural environment that is understood and that is expected to be understanding will facilitate the creation of meaning.

Interpsychic Space and Maintenance of Identity

As has been indicated, the most important of the influences on the meaning-creating capacity in any given context is the relationship to the other person(s) involved in that context. Winnicott's observation (1965) that it is not possible for an individual to retain a sense of self when either fused with or in isolation from other human beings is of major importance here. When interacting with others, the individual must constantly modulate *interpsychic space* in order to avoid either merger or isolation and to maintain optimal conditions for the creation and maintenance of identity (Saari, 1986). (While the idea of interpsychic space retains Winnicott's spatial metaphor, which has become familiar and useful to many clinicians, it is important from the standpoint of devising a functional theory to remember that what is being regulated here is *activity* rather than space.)

Functions of Affective-Cognitive Activity

In pointing out that affects influence the spatial distance between interacting humans, Winnicott specifically observed that anger creates distance and boundaries between people while love or affection pulls individuals closer. However, the affective-cognitive activity that is here understood to underlie meaning-making has at least four functions, discussed below, that serve to bridge the interpersonal/intrapsychic worlds of interacting human beings.

Regulation of Interpersonal Communication

The regulation of interpersonal communication is a function of affective-cognitive activity that can be seen in the example of the self-regulating other. Not only may one partner be aware of some dimensions of the interactive partner's inner experience but each partner's inner experience may also be altered out of a type of resonance with the affective state of the other. In addition, this communicative function includes the regulation of interpsychic distance through affect, with, as Winnicott noted, anger increasing the sense of distance and caring or love pulling a person closer.

Self-Organization

There is also a relationship between affective-cognitive activity and the relative degree of experienced organization of the self (Krystal,

1988). Experiencing a strong affect frequently becomes a focus around which an individual can maintain a sense of organization. For example, anger or a negative affect can help someone under stress continue to function, at least for a time. There is, however, also a relationship between the intensity with which an affect is experienced and the ability of the individual to experience affect without disorganizing. Strong affect can affirm self-boundaries but can also disrupt self-organization if the intensity exceeds the individual's tolerance level (Zetzel, 1970). In other words, strong affect can either hold the person together or lead to fragmentation, depending upon its intensity and duration.

Self-Esteem and Safety

Affective-cognitive activity also serves an evaluative function, assessing both the relative goodness or badness of the individual and the situation (Basch, 1976). Thus, affective-cognitive activity indicates not only self-esteem but also the degree of safety in the environment, as in Freud's concept (1920/1955) of signal anxiety. Through social referencing (Emde, 1989), affective-cognitive activities permit the communication of a caretaker or more experienced person regarding both the relative safety and social acceptability of particular behaviors.

Vitality

In addition, affective-cognitive activities can provide the individual with a sense of participation in or exclusion from a human community. In accord with Sullivan's idea (1953) of consensual validation and Seton's idea (1981) that people like to experience strong emotions because it makes them feel human, it is assumed here that a sense of aliveness or vitality, essential for continuing the process of creating meaning, is derived from affective-cognitive activities.

Complexity of Variables in Empathic Relating

The four functions of affective-cognitive activity, interacting together, can account for moment-to-moment fluctuations in the individual's experience of the self and relative ability to create meaning. Much of clinical empathy involves tracking the patient's current state in regard to the four functions as patient-therapist interactions proceed. The complexity of the functions' interaction, taken together with the factors influencing the capacity to create meaning, accounts for the difficulty clinical theoreticians have traditionally had in attempting to capture precisely what is involved in empathic relating.

Meaning-Making in the Holding Environment

Winnicott's concepts regarding what I have called interpsychic space include notions about a holding environment in therapy, in which the clinical work (and the client) is contained (Winnicott, Shepherd, & Davis, 1989). This environment is *transitional space*, the place where play and creativity occur (Winnicott, 1965). For young children, the transitional space contains three elements: the infant, the mother, and the soft toy or object. Treatment for adults involves a similar triad: the clinician, the client, and the client's experience, which is an object of contemplation (Werner & Kaplan, 1963). Winnicott's ideas about the treatment process, of course, include an understanding of treatment in which the relationship, rather than interpretation, is the critical curative element. In other words, the empathic clinician needs to be constantly aware of the state of the patient's affective-cognitive functioning and should interact with the patient so as to maximize the patient's capacity to create meaning during the treatment.

Growth in the Zone of Proximal Development

The idea of interpsychic space also refers to Vygotsky's "zone of proximal development" (1978, p. 86). Vygotsky noticed that a child could solve more complex problems when working in conjunction with an adult than when working alone. It was this difference between the child's ability when working alone and when working with an adult that he called the zone of proximal development, suggesting that educative efforts ought always to be targeted in that area, as it defines the current region for potential learning. This notion is similar to Loewald's idea (1980) that analysts should relate to patients as being slightly more developed than they are at present in order to stimulate growth. It is important for the therapist to be attuned to the client's zone of proximal development, therefore, for that attunement is a form of treatment that encourages growth, as opposed to treatment that focuses on eliminating pathology.

Relationship of Language to Identity

The effectiveness of the therapist's empathic use of interpsychic space in maximizing patient functioning can be further explained by addressing the question of how such patient-therapist interaction makes a difference in the creation of meaning. The creation of meaning, after all, encompasses more than the nonverbal experience of affect attunement. It involves language posited by Freud (1915/1957) to be that which makes the difference between what is conscious and what is not. Yet while Freud's ideas have been generally rejected owing to his associationist theory of language acquisition and his assumption of inherited symbolic meanings, there has been relatively little attention to the need for an alternative solution to the problem of how individual experience and language become linked. An understanding of language as a system of symbols or codes that may refer only to each other (Gergen, 1991; Saussure, 1916/1959) necessitates facing the fundamental question, How is it that the individual comes to be able to capture or express personal experience or meaning in this system of arbitrary signs?

Nelson's important work (1985) has approached this problem through understanding meaning as a tripartite phenomenon involving (1) the cognitive representation of meaning for the individual, (2) the communicative context through which the meaning of a word in a specific occasion of use is determined for the individual and that individual's interactive partners, and (3) the conventional meaning of a word for the lexical or cultural community at large. These aspects of meaning are both separable and interrelated over the course of the development of the individual human being. Drawing upon Nelson's and Stern's work, a series of general propositions about the relationship between language and experience can be suggested. These propositions will be introduced through the case illustrations that follow.

The Case of Paul: Stimulating the Growth of Inner Life

It is through experiencing another person's affect attunement that the individual comes to be able consciously to share personally or affectively meaningful experiences with others as well as with the self (self-reflexivity). This proposition has implications quite different from those found within orthodox psychoanalytic treatment. The most important is that the content of consciousness is constructed either following or concurrent with activity or experience; it does not preexist as biologically inherited meaning. Thus, some individuals may have very little constructed inner experience. Such people are likely to be prone to impulsive action.

> Paul was a thirty-five-year-old auto mechanic who sought treatment following a suicide attempt (through ingestion of headache medications) that had been serious enough to put him into a coma for two days. While indicating that he knew he needed treatment because his life was full of chaos, Paul was quite surprised that the hospital personnel and several therapists were taking his suicide attempt very seriously. While he knew that his medical condition as a result of the attempt had been serious, he pointed out that he had never meant to kill himself in the first place and so would never do it again.
> The suicide attempt had taken place the evening of the day after Paul broke up with the woman he had dated since his divorce. On the same day, he had had a

confrontation with his boss, who was critical of careless-ness in Paul's repair work and who threatened to fire Paul if his concentration did not improve. Paul went home from work with a headache and took some medication for it that did not work very well. Noticing that the pre-scription had passed its expiration date, Paul thought the pills might have lost some potency so he took another dose. Then, following a telephone call in which he ar-gued with his former wife regarding the amount of his child support, Paul simply decided to take the whole bot-tle. He could not describe his inner state at the time he decided to take the pills other than to say that things had simply gotten too much for him. A few minutes after taking the pills, he regretted his action and called a neighbor, who informed the police.

In treatment, Paul related that his childhood had been full of chaos, with an abusive alcoholic father and a mother who occupied herself with supporting the family and whom he remembered mostly as being absent. He had experienced many changes in caretakers, being looked after by grandparents, other relatives, and vari-ous friends whom his mother would recruit to help but who usually provided care only for short periods. In describing his life, Paul focused his language primarily on concrete facts and details of incidents. He offered lit-tle to no evaluation or narrative structure. Frequently, he wanted his therapist to tell him what the particular events of his life meant, clearly expecting such meaning to come from outside himself.

Although Paul seemed truly invested in the idea of bettering his life, his treatment seemed to have little effectiveness until he began attending Alcoholics Anon-ymous meetings with a friend. Paul became quite in-vested in these meetings, despite little evidence that his abuse of alcohol was significant. In his individual treatment, Paul would recount stories he had heard from other AA members and wonder if he had ever had similar experiences. His therapist's empathy for the people in these relayed stories seemed to be of critical importance to him. Over time, he began to recount stories from his own life with more affective and evaluative content. As this occurred, his life did seem to become less chaotic, and at the time he terminated treatment, he had begun working on a college degree through night classes, a goal in which he seemed, again, quite invested.

For individuals like Paul, who seem to have constructed little in the way of inner experience, group or family treatment in combination with individual treatment may be effective in stimulating growth in the inner life. This regime allows patient interaction with others in the group or family modality, in conjunction with time to reflect on the interactions with an affectively attuned therapist; thus, it affords more opportunity for the creation of consciously available and shareable experience than individual treatment alone. The initial sharing, however, may occur as much or more through action or nonverbal means of communication as through linguistic codes.

The Case of Bob: The Construction of Narrative Truth

Experience may be represented in the individual's cognitive system (which includes perception, memory, and the schematic representation of events as well as concepts and categories) without being either linguistically or consciously accessible. Such inaccessible experience will still have an effect on behavior even though it remains pre- or nonverbal. In Basch's (1981) view, this inaccessibility is what constitutes repression.

Bob sought treatment for marital problems that began after his wife had been diagnosed with multiple sclerosis. Although not severely hampered in her daily activities by the disease, his wife had been quite upset by its implications for her future. She had expected Bob, whom she normally experienced as supportive, to help her in dealing with this problem. Bob had, however, become increasingly distant from her both physically and emotionally, something neither of them saw as consistent with his previous behavior.

Bob was puzzled that his wife's concern over her illness seemed to infuriate him. In time, he discovered that for a period of about eight months, starting when he was twenty-eight months old, his mother had been preoccupied by the acute illness of a sister two years older than he. The sister had recovered with little resulting impairment, so the illness had not been an area of family discussion in later years. Bob's conversations with his mother now, however, revealed that she had retained a previously unarticulated but powerful sense of guilt over what she saw as her neglect of Bob during the time of his sister's illness. Following these conversations, Bob became convinced that his own experience of that time and the ensuing lack of discussion had affected his relationship with his wife after her illness was revealed.

Bob's conviction about the origin of his anger at his wife must be considered narrative rather than historical truth. Yet the fact that following his construction of this narrative truth Bob was able once again to be more empathic with his wife, along with the fact that similar instances are relatively common in therapists' experience, does suggest the likelihood that a type of repression exists that involves experiences for which there was no affect attunement at the time and that continue to have an effect on the individual.

The Case of Fran: Linking Inner Life with Linguistic Symbols

An individual may acquire and utilize conventional meanings of linguistic signs in ways that are socially appropriate, yet lack a personal cognitive meaning for those signs. An individual can memorize the lexical, or dictionary, meanings of words, and it may not be apparent to communicative partners that words referring to such ethereal things as feelings may have no reference in that individual's inner state. Thus, for example, an individual may be able to verbalize feelings of guilt or sadness when socially appropriate, without experiencing to any significant extent the inner state normally thought to be represented by these words. Basch (1981) has referred to this failure to connect words to the affective experiences as *disavowal*. Disavowal may, however, also frequently occur in individuals who do have an inner experience that is fairly well developed, but that inner experience and the linguistic symbols that refer to it may never have become linked with each other.

Fran was a thirty-eight-year-old woman who sought treatment after having left a fourteen-year marriage for a relationship with a woman she had originally known through a professional association. While generally pleased with her new relationship, she also found herself reluctant to make a permanent commitment to it, as her partner wished, because she no longer trusted her own ability to make judgments about others or about the quality of intimate relationships. She found herself comfortable with the idea of a lesbian identity and had immersed herself in activities in the local gay community but worried that she was adopting wholesale the culture and customs of this group. She wanted therapy to help her explore in more depth who she was as an individual.

Fran had been adopted into a middle-class family in a small town at the age of eighteen months. She knew little of her prior life but was under the impression that she had been in a foster family while awaiting her birth mother's decision whether to permit adoption. Fran described her childhood as generally quite reasonable, noting that she felt quite secure within the adoptive family. Although her parents were concerned that their children perform well in school and attain higher education, they had not been very verbal people themselves. They were supportive, but Fran was also taught to face life with a kind of "stiff upper lip" and to call upon her own resources to solve any problems she encountered.

To the pride of her parents, Fran had excelled in high school, winning a full scholarship to a well-known college. She recalled life in college, however, as extremely difficult. Feeling unable to learn how to deal with the wealthier and more sophisticated of her classmates, she nevertheless aspired to becoming a part of their group. Pursuit of this goal proved a matter of considerable frustration and sense of defeat. Particularly in her freshman year, Fran floundered academically; then she noted that she did far better in lecture classes than in seminars that demanded interactive participation. She then chose a major in a subject that had mostly lecture classes and managed to graduate with a respectable average, though she was left with a sense that she had failed intellectually.

Following college, Fran had married a young man whom she described as appealing because he seemed to have all the external qualities that should lead to social and financial success. While married, she completed a graduate professional program. Yet she described her married life as essentially empty, with her husband not wishing children but, instead, rather single-mindedly devoting himself to a career in a high-pressure field and encouraging her to do likewise. Though generally successful professionally, Fran felt herself unfulfilled and becoming irritable at work, even though she experienced fewer tensions in that setting than when alone with her husband.

The lesbian relationship, begun when Fran was pursued by a colleague at a conference, was both exhilarating and frightening. Fran experienced it as very natural for her and, in retrospect, believed there had been signs since her adolescence that she was more attracted to women than men. Yet it initiated her into a world of feelings and sensations with which she had previously been quite unfamiliar and with which she had not yet become comfortable. As Fran became more familiar with understanding and naming the sexual feelings related to her sexual orientation, she also found herself becoming able to connect words to her other experiences, both those reconstructed from childhood and those connected with her present life.

In contrast to Paul, who seemed to have little awareness of feelings in either himself or others, Fran appeared to have been very aware of her feelings, in at least a global sense, long prior to entering treatment. Since she could not connect these feelings well to words, however, she had difficulty using her inner experiences to construct stories that would explain her own or anyone else's behavior. Her affectively distant relationship with her husband had not demanded that their interactive behavior be regulated on the basis of such experiences, but her newfound intimate lesbian relationship did, thus creating the need for a better linkage between words and affect. Prior to the experiences that led Fran to treatment, she had been an intelligent and articulate professional woman who certainly knew and could employ words referring to affects appropriately. Her words had *not*, however, been effective in capturing her own inner experiences.

It is through the individual's experience with using the conventional meanings of words with others, in repeated but particular communicative contexts, that the conventional meanings are linked with experiences recorded in that individual's cognitive system. This is a type of associationist theory of the acquisition of meaning. However, it involves not an associative linking between a particular thing and a word but rather a contextual embeddedness of a particular meaning within a holistic experience. Vygotsky's idea (1978) that language has both a conventional dictionary *meaning* and an individualized and affective *sense* is relevant here. For each individual, the characteristic sense of any linguistic symbol will become both generalized and refined in relation to the affective-cognitive tone of the situations in which that symbol is either heard or evoked.

However, the linking of experience to the conventional meaning of words, which constitutes reference or representation, presupposes that the individual has the opportunity to participate in repeated communicative contexts with others. Those individuals who do not have, for whatever reason, a richness of repeated experiences in communicative contexts with others may have a highly developed ability to utilize words in conventional meanings yet not relate the same words well to personal experience.

> Following Fran's beginning lesbian experiences, she immersed herself nearly totally in the lesbian community and engaged in its activities with great intensity. She was particularly attracted to involvement in anything that allowed her both to be active in an event and to talk with others about their lives and experiences in relation to that event. In treatment, her initial descriptions of the same events seemed peculiarly couched in descriptive details about concrete externals, from which she seemed to infer human feelings and motivations, but as she became more experienced within the lesbian culture, this way of description shifted rather rapidly, and she became much more capable of describing her own experiences, which had both similarities with and differences from those of the people with whom she associated.

It can be speculated that Fran's adoption into a strange family at the age of eighteen months, when she would have just been learning to talk, and her having parents who were relatively non-verbal may have created a situation that made the linking of words and feelings difficult for her. This difficulty could have been compounded later by her lack of opportunity to explore fully sexual feelings prohibited in a homophobic society. Thus, in order to correct for these missed opportunities to acquire both meaning and sense for words in relation to intimate affective experiences, Fran propelled herself into extensive and repeated verbal experiences with others, both in the lesbian community and in treatment. These experiences of both active participation in events and an empathic relationship seem to have been quite effective in assisting her to connect her inner experiences with linguistic symbols.

Achieving Psychological Health Through Language

There are a number of ways to understand why the ability to capture inner experience through language enables the possibility of psychological health.

- Representation of the attributes of a complex identity through language enables those attributes to be manipulated mentally for the purposes of anticipating and planning behavioral choices.

- Language enables causal and temporal linkages in a narrative form, thus making possible an understanding of the relationship between the self and the environment.

- Representation of inner experience through language enables the conceptual transporting of self to other contexts in order to understand or anticipate the potential effects, both for oneself and for others, of those contexts upon functioning.

- Language enables the conceptual definition of a problem, including the setting of problem boundaries, in a manner that objectifies the problem and thereby creates the potential for a sense of mastery over it.

• Language enables the selective sharing of experiences with a broad community of human others, thereby creating the potential for a sense of participation in a human community.

Conclusion

This chapter has proposed that psychological health is evidenced through an identity that is complex in the sense of being highly differentiated, articulated, and integrated. Such identity complexity, it has been supposed, can be created only through a combination of active participation in social events and empathic interaction with others. The effectiveness of psychotherapy has then been explained as resting upon dialogical creation of meaning, involving a linkage of inner experience and language, between the client and the therapist.

References

American Psychiatric Association. (1994). *Diagnostic and statistical manual of mental disorders* (4th ed.). Washington, DC: Author.

Basch, M. F. (1976). The concept of affect: A re-examination. *Journal of the American Psychoanalytic Association, 24*, 759–777.

Basch, M. M. (1981). Psychoanalytic interpretation and cognitive transformation. *International Journal of Psychoanalysis, 62*, 151–175.

Becker, H. S. (1986). Culture: A sociological view. *Doing things together: Selected papers* (pp. 11–24). Evanston, IL: Northwestern University Press.

Bretherton, I. (1994). Infants' subjective world of relatedness: Moments, feeling shapes, protonarrative envelopes and internal working models. *Infant Mental Health Journal, 15*, 36–41.

Bruner, J. S. (1986). *Actual minds, possible worlds*. Cambridge, MA: Harvard University.

Bruner, J. S. (1987). Life as narrative. *Social Research, 54*, 11–32.

Bruner, J. S. (1990). *Acts of meaning*. Cambridge, MA: Harvard University.

Emde, R. N. (1989). The infant's relationship experience: Developmental and affective aspects. In A. J. Sameroff & R. N. Emde (Eds.), *Relationship disturbances in early childhood: A developmental approach* (pp. 33–52). New York: Basic Books.

Emde, R. N. (1994). Developing psychoanalytic representations of experience. *Infant Mental Health Journal, 15,* 42–49.

Epstein, S. (1973). The self-concept re-visited: Or a theory of a theory. *American Psychologist, 28,* 404–416.

Erikson, E. H. (1963). *Childhood and society* (2nd ed.). New York: W.W. Norton.

Fonagy, P. (1994). Mental representations from an intergenerational cognitive science perspective. *Infant Mental Health Journal, 15,* 57–68.

Freud, S. (1955). Beyond the pleasure principle. *The standard edition of the complete psychological works of Sigmund Freud* (Vol. 18, pp. 7–64). London: Hogarth Press. (Original work published 1920)

Freud, S. (1957). The unconscious. *The standard edition of the complete psychological works of Sigmund Freud* (Vol. 14, pp. 166–204). London: Hogarth Press. (Original work published 1915)

Gergen, K. J. (1991). *The saturated self: Dilemmas of identity in contemporary life.* New York: Basic Books.

Goffman, E. (1961). *Asylums: Essays on the social structures of mental patients and other inmates.* New York: Doubleday, Anchor Books.

Guidano, V. F. (1987). *The complexity of the self: A developmental guide to psychopathology and therapy.* New York: Guilford Press.

Hartmann, H. (1958). *Ego psychology and the problem of adaptation.* Madison, CT: International Universities Press.

Holquist, M. (Ed.). (1981). *The dialogic imagination: Four essays by M. M. Bakhtin* (C. Emerson & M. Holquist, Trans.), Austin: University of Texas.

Kleinman, A. (1988). *Rethinking psychiatry: From cultural category to personal experience.* New York: Free Press.

Krystal, H. (1988). *Integration and self-healing: Affect, trauma and alexithymia.* New York: Analytic Press.

Loewald, H. W. (1980). On the therapeutic action of psychoanalysis. *Papers on psychoanalysis* (pp. 221–256). New Haven, CT: Yale University Press.

Maranhao, T. (1990). Introduction. In T. Maranhao (Ed.), *The interpretation of dialogue* (pp. 1–24). Chicago: University of Chicago Press.

Nelson, K. (1985). *Making sense: The acquisition of shared meaning.* San Diego, CA: Academic Press.

Polkinghorne, D. E. (1988). *Narrative knowing and the human sciences.* Albany: State University of New York Press.

Saari, C. (1986). *Clinical social work treatment: How does it work?* New York: Gardner.

Saari, C. (1991). *The creation of meaning in clinical social work*. New York: Guilford Press.

Saari, C. (1993). Identity complexity as an indicator of health. *Clinical Social Work Journal, 21*, 11–24.

Saussure, F. de (1959). *Course in general linguistics* (W. Baskin, Trans.). New York: Philosophical Library. (Original work published 1916)

Searles, H. F. (1979). Dual- and multiple-identity processes in borderline ego functioning. In *Countertransference and related subjects: Selected papers* (pp. 460–478). Madison, CT: International Universities Press.

Seton, P. (1981). Affect and issues of separation-individuation. *Smith College Studies in Social Work, 52*, 1–11.

Stern, D. N. (1985). *The interpersonal world of the infant*. New York: Basic Books.

Stern, D. N. (1994). One way to build a clinically relevant baby. *Infant Mental Health Journal, 15*, 9–25.

Stolorow, R. D., & Atwood, G. E. (1992). *Contexts of being: The intersubjective foundations of psychological life*. Hillsdale, NJ: Analytic Press.

Sullivan, H. S. (1953). *The interpersonal theory of psychiatry. Collected works* (Vol. 1). New York: W.W. Norton.

Vygotsky, L. S. (1978). *Mind in society: The development of higher psychological processes*. Cambridge, MA: Harvard University Press.

Wachtel, P. L. (1993). *Therapeutic communication: Principles and effective practice*. New York: Guilford Press.

Werner, H. (1948). The concept of development from a comparative and organismic point of view. In S. Barten & M. Franklin (Eds.), *Developmental processes: Heinz Werner's selected writings* (Vol. 1, pp. 107–130). Madison, CT: International Universities Press.

Werner, H., & Kaplan, B. (1963). *Symbol formation*. New York: Wiley.

Wertsch, J. V. (1991). *Voices of the mind: A socio-cultural approach to mediated action*. Cambridge, MA: Harvard University Press.

Winnicott, C., Shepherd, R., & Davis, M. (Eds.). (1989). *D. W. Winnicott: Psychoanalytic explorations*. Cambridge, MA: Harvard.

Winnicott, D. W. (1965). *The maturational processes and the facilitating environment: Studies in the theory of emotional development*. Madison, CT: International Universities Press.

Zetzel, E. (1970). *The capacity for emotional growth*. Madison, CT: International Universities Press.

6

Women's Constructions of Truth, Self, Authority, and Power

Nancy Rule Goldberger

In the early 1980s, in a large interview study with a broad sample of rural and urban women of different ages, classes, ethnic backgrounds, and educational histories, three colleagues and I first explored with women the following questions: How do you know what you know? Where does your knowledge come from? To whom or to what do you turn when you want answers? Is there such a thing as truth or "right answers"? We wanted to understand and describe the variety of ways women go about making meaning for themselves in a world that devalues women's authority and voice. Ultimately, we arrived at a description of five knowledge perspectives or frameworks from which women view themselves and the world. These are described in our book *Women's Ways of Knowing* (Belenky, Clinchy, Goldberger, & Tarule, 1986).

Since our original work together, our professional paths have diverged, although each of us has continued doing research on individual epistemology with the aim of extending the thinking about diversity in ways of knowing that arise out of differences in personal history, culture, and social position.

In this chapter, I will summarize the original five meaning-making perspectives (ways of knowing) described by me and my colleagues and discuss how new interviews with women and men from a variety of ethnic backgrounds have extended my thinking about diversity in ways of knowing. I will also discuss my questions and new thoughts concerning how people know, and why and when people change their perspectives on knowing and truth. How this bears on the construction of meaning in the psychotherapeutic process will be a subtext in my discussion.

Assumptions, Context, and Positionality

My research was and continues to be guided by the belief that individuals have implicit theories about knowledge and truth that shape the way they see the world, the way they think about themselves, and the way they relate to authority. The ways-of-knowing interviews with women that formed the basis for my colleagues' and my early work (Belenky, Clinchy, Goldberger, & Tarule, 1986) were undertaken as a complement to William Perry's similar research on college men (Perry, 1970). Perry, a trained clinician and a keen observer of adolescents, was primarily interested in the changes in ethical and epistemological perspectives that occur during the college years. In his interviews with Harvard men, Perry captured the essence of how young men's thinking about the nature and origin of knowledge shifts in response to the challenges of study in an institution of higher learning. He showed how some students leave dualistic right-or-wrong thinking to arrive at an understanding of the relativism and contextualism of all knowledge and truth claims, and how a few individuals achieve a position of commitment within relativism in which truth (with a small "t") is embraced wholeheartedly yet tentatively. Although Perry clearly implied that shifts in ways of knowing affect conceptions of the self and assessments of self-efficacy and authority, he did not explore the ramifications of such self change in realms beyond the college environment.

Our work with women, which was designed both as an extension and a critique of Perry's scheme, built on the assumptions that learning is lifelong and that much of how human beings know and what they know is engendered, not just in schools, but throughout individuals' lifelong negotiation of social institutions and socializing forces. From the outset of our study of ways of knowing, we assumed that how a woman construes herself as a "knower" affects the way she orients herself to external valuations and social role expectations; it affects how she interprets and accommodates to or resists power differentials in her relationships with others. By including women from many different walks of life and educational backgrounds, we hoped to open up our study of women's epistemology to the voices of women who are often marginalized and unheard. By inviting women to speak about their lives and transformative experiences, we believed that we would hear indirectly about the situational, cultural, and historical factors that resulted in shifts in ways of knowing and concomitant shifts in conceptions of self and others. By choosing to focus only on women, we intended to bring to the forefront experiences perhaps common to women by virtue of their gender and to uncover developmental themes that have been ignored or are missing in major developmental theories but are prominent in the stories of women.

As theorists, my colleagues and I fall into what is now called the social constructionist movement in psychology (compare Gergen, 1985), a movement that has deep historical roots but that was just getting grounded in the discourse of psychology when we began our research. We believe, therefore, that personal theories of knowledge and experiences of gender and self, as they shift throughout the life cycle, are culturally embedded. One shapes and is shaped by one's cultural context; meaning-making is both an intrapsychic and extrapsychic phenomenon. All individuals grow up in families, communities, and cultures that affect the definitional boundaries for "male" and "female," but each individual also constructs narratives of self, gender, family, authority, and truth that evolve as she or he encounters new ideas and an ever-widening variety of people and outlooks on life. As we point out in our book, and as family therapists, too, often point out these days (Reiss, 1981; Hoffman, 1988; Feixas, 1990), even family histories are rewritten as people shift from one knowledge perspective to another. With the advent of the influence of social constructionism in family process theorizing, attention has turned to the culturally derived power relationships within the family and the processes whereby family members negotiate a common reality, which includes what is considered gender-appropriate behavior.

The process in which individuals engage of constantly revising and reinterpreting their own histories—as de Laurentis (1986) and Alcoff (1988) have pointed out—results in a shifting *positionality* for each woman's identity as *woman* or *knower*. That is, her definition of woman or knower changes as her position changes within an ever-shifting cultural context. At the moment we interviewed each woman, we captured a snapshot of her as both a natural epistemologist, with assumptions about the nature and acquisition of knowledge, and a developmentalist, with implicit theories about how and why people change. With few exceptions, the women were able to tell us their histories as makers of meaning and how they themselves had changed over time. In some cases, an individual's primary and current approach to knowing was clearly a manifestation of the approach to knowing valued by her immediate community or cultural reference group. In other cases, individuals were more conscious that ways of knowing are culture embedded and more interested in exploring alternative epistemologies beyond their cultural norms. Most women, in the process of describing their lives, reported transitional periods and changes in positional perspective that led to major shifts in the way they thought about knowledge and truth. Catalysts for such epistemological revolutions, we found, differed from person to person, although some common catalysts for change were education, childbearing, family trauma, difficult or challenging relationships, exposure to other cultures, and psychotherapy.

Psychologists and clinical theorists other than ourselves have pointed out the relevance of an individual's personal epistemology to everyday experience and decision making. Greeno (1989) has argued that children's beliefs about the origin and nature of knowledge have been understudied until very recently but are central to an understanding of the vast and disparate research on cognitive development and approaches to learning. Baxter Magolda (1989) has related epistemology to learning styles and cognitive complexity. The pioneering work of George Kelly (1955) has spawned a broad research agenda and clinical focus for those interested in personal meaning-making and the structure of personal knowledge. Other theorists and researchers (Chinen, 1984; Kitchener, 1983; Kitchener & King, 1981; Loevinger, 1976; Mahoney, 1991; Perry, 1970; Unger, Draper, & Pendergrass, 1986) have demonstrated how shifts in ways of knowing across the life cycle from adolescence throughout adulthood are directly related to self-concept, social perceptions and attributions, orientation to the future, and moral judgments.

The development of relativist thought has been shown to be related to a deepening capacity for empathic understanding (Benack, 1984) and reflective judgment (Kitchener & King, 1981), attainments that are presumably related to therapeutic communication and outcome. Watzlawick (1984) has drawn attention to how individual constructions of meaning and "inventions" of "reality" are manifest in the language and process of psychotherapy. Dell (1980), applying Bateson's ideas to family therapy, describes the "epistemological revolutions" that accompany family transformation. Family therapy theory has been greatly influenced not only by social constructionist theorizing but also by the writings of such radical theorists as Goolishian and Anderson (1987), who have emphasized the centrality of language and meaning-making in the therapeutic process. This new focus on therapeutic epistemology has led to the questioning of therapist privilege and the assumption of objective reality. In addition to Kelly (1973) and his followers, Basseches (1984), Guidano and Liotti (1983), Ivey (1991), Kegan (1982), and Mahoney (1991), among others, have developed clinically relevant theories of cognitive and epistemological development. Young-Eisendrath and Wiedemann (1987), who are feminist therapists, point out that "consensus about reality and other questions of meaning" (p. 5) is a common concern of people seeking psychotherapy. They pay particular attention in therapy to the social contexts in which women construct themselves and claim (or disclaim) their own authority.

The emphasis by social constructionists on the central role of social context in meaning-making has recently resulted in a similar focus for professional training in psychology. Clinical psychologists are now mandated to become culture sensitive and competent to work with culturally diverse patient populations. This implies that psychology should become more attuned to how psyche and culture construct each other, as well as to diversity in ways of knowing (Shweder, 1991; Goldberger & Veroff, 1995). Tyler, Sussewell, and Williams-McCoy (1985) recognize that many U.S. citizens, especially biracial or bicultural individuals, are shaped in part by divergent or even conflicting worldviews and ways of knowing that arise out of their minority status in the dominant culture. Tyler, Sussewell, and Williams-McCoy argue that in psychotherapeutic relationships, personal understanding and rapport are not enough: "the racial/ethnic social context [of therapist and client] must be incorporated as an integral component" (p. 318) of therapeutic theory and practice. Clinicians must also be alert to how culturally embedded constructions of "self" and "personhood" (Sampson, 1989) as well as "health" and "illness" (Kleinman, 1988; Landrine, 1992; Prilleltensky, 1990) affect the utilization of mental health services by nonmajority groups in this country as well the therapeutic interaction itself.

It seems clear that much recent developmental and clinical theory, including my colleagues' and mine, is part of *new paradigm psychology* (Guba, 1990) and reflects the shift from positivism to interpretive strategies and social constructionist epistemology. The growing emphasis within psychology on the value of narrative analysis, hermeneutics, and qualitative methodology in the study of human behavior (Bruner, 1986; Gergen, 1985; Gergen, 1988; Messer, Sass, & Woolfolk, 1988; Neilsen, 1990) is not unlike what my colleagues and I call "connected knowing"—the entering into the narrative text of the other.

Ways of Knowing

I will briefly summarize the five knowledge perspectives that Belenky, Clinchy, Tarule, and I have described (1986). As I have already argued, ways of knowing (including our five) should be considered frameworks for meaning-making that can evolve and change over time, rather than enduring traits or personality types. Although it is tempting to think about the five positions as a normative developmental sequence, we caution against this. Individual developmental timetables and routes to growth evolve as a function of life circumstances, opportunities, and cultural values. How, why, and when individuals develop or change is not easily captured by a single developmental prescriptive scheme. What is more, we developed and presented our scheme with the acknowledgment that our five positions are not fixed categories but rough schemata, which will undoubtedly be modified or elaborated as ways of knowing are studied across culture groups, genders, classes, and other sources of human difference. In spite of our warnings, there have already been misreadings of our theoretical position by those who assume we are describing either a fixed developmental sequence or some essential (enduring intrapsychic or biologically based) characteristics of women as a distinctive group (Bohan, 1993; Hare-Mustin & Maracek, 1990; Mednick, 1989).

Position I: Silence

Silence is a position in which women experience themselves as mindless and subject to powerful external authorities. In a sense, this is not a way of knowing but a way of *not* knowing. Women who have come out of this kind of silence tell us that their silence has been a way of surviving in what they experienced as a threatening and dangerous environment. Silence is the best policy. Although silence is also an issue for women in other epistemological positions (I will be discussing this later in this chapter), we decided to call this particular subgroup of our interviewees the *silent women*, because their absence of voice was as striking as their fragile and hidden sense of self.

For these women, *to know* or to use words to protest the actions of others—that is, to speak out—is to court danger and retaliation. It is the isolation, fearfulness, and acceptance of the status quo of silent women that makes them a challenge for clinicians. Silent women are women living out the most pernicious form of structural oppression and sexual abuse. They usually have grown up in families and communities and schools that have planted and then reinforced these women's belief that they are not smart and know nothing. Such women tend to drop out of school during or immediately after high school.

Silent women do not usually seek psychodynamic individual therapy since this move requires a modicum of sense of self-worth, sense of choice, and belief in the possibility of change. Self-reflection and group interaction are tremendous risks for silent women. They may be living with partners who actively discourage them, sometimes with threats, from seeking outside help. When they do show up in social and mental health agencies, clinicians must move cautiously in working with them. Silent women can experience further undermining of their self-esteem as they begin to speak because they have hidden from themselves as well as others for much of their lives. However, if the clinical encounter is made safe and trustworthy, if the early faltering voice of the silent woman is heard and affirmed, then clinical interventions can have powerful and empowering effects. We found in our study that silent women will seek help and initiate change in their lives on behalf of their children, if not for themselves. My colleague Mary Belenky has been pursuing the efficacy of reaching isolated rural silent women through their children in her new project, Listening Partners (Belenky, Bond, & Weinstock, 1992).

Position II: Received Knowing

Received knowing is a perspective in which a woman conceives of herself as capable of receiving, even reproducing, knowledge from external authorities but not capable of creating knowledge on her own. Knowledge, as far as she understands it, originates outside the self. The received knower tends to discount the importance of her own experience in the process of knowing.

The received knower listens carefully to the voices of authority outside herself; thus, at the outset of psychotherapy she is likely to yield power easily to the authority of the therapist. Not used to thinking about herself in psychological terms, the receiver knower is apt to seek treatment with physical complaints or problems in conforming to the expectations of others. There may be a high degree of self-blame. Highly suggestible and malleable, the received knower is usually eager to please the therapist (and thus may be at risk with unscrupulous therapists) and to be a good client. Her self-concept, in fact, is organized around social roles and expectations. She models herself after the cultural ideals of what "a good woman" should be, ideals transmitted by her church, her family, the teachers she grew up with. What she has learned from her "good authorities" (however "good" is constructed in her community), she can then transmit and teach to others. The received knower is a vehicle for the transmission of social stereotypes. When she speaks, her voice is a voice of imitation.

Alternative worldviews, even the perception of multiple choices in her life, may be experienced as a threat, making self-reflection and disclosure of discontent something to be avoided. Her fear of being different leads to self-editing and silence.

Clinicians who tend to view themselves as change agents are apt to assume that received knowers want to change or should want to change. This can be a serious misapprehension. We found that women at the perspective of received knowing are not necessarily unhappy with themselves in their world nor do they seek change or greater personal authority. There is both pleasure and security in trusting and listening to and learning from the voices of others. Discussion of change in beliefs or alternative ways to live can be threatening to someone who is secure in her community. This is especially so for individuals who grow up in relatively intact religious or indigenous communities in the United States. Clinicians should not assume that people from these communities who show up in mental health agencies seek personal growth and change and can benefit from individual or group self-disclosure therapies. Instead, clinicians must carefully assess how these clients construe "normality" and whether significant personal change might not jeopardize their positions in their home communities.

Position III: Subjective Knowing

The *subjective knower* turns inward for truth. She conceives of knowledge as personal, private, and subjectively known or intuited. People thinking out of a subjectivist perspective believe in multiple truths. The subjective knower believes, for example, that everyone has a right to his or her own opinion. She may say humbly, "It's just my opinion," or more assertively, "I have a right to my own opinion. It's what feels right to me!" Whatever her tone, she holds on ferociously to this right. Other people's opinions do not often change her mind, since she tends to be locked in her own subjectivity; however, she may seek out like-minded people, using them to affirm her opinions.

The protectionist stance of the subjective knower may not always be apparent to others. In our book, we identify a group we call "hidden subjectivists"—women who feel in their guts that they just know but keep it to themselves. Sometimes they speak what they know in intimate conversations with best friends; sometimes they hide their thoughts in private journals. On the surface, in public, they may look like conformists—toeing the line, doing what is expected, but underneath they are rebels and often quite resistant to the influence of others.

Subjective knowers do not see thought as central to the process of knowing, and they are generally unable to specify how they know. As one woman put it, "I try not to think. If you trust yourself, you just know the answer." They value gut knowledge or the inner voice over what they believe to be illegitimate theorizing by self-appointed authorities; thus, they display little respect for official, certified authority. In our study, many of the women who viewed the world from a subjectivist perspective had come to this way of knowing following a rejection of what they experienced as failed male authority. This makes the question of whether such women can work effectively in therapy with a male therapist an important one. In fact, it seems likely that female subjectivist knowers would gravitate to female therapists and feminist therapies. Whatever the therapeutic arrangements, the content of the therapy is likely to revolve around topics of power and disempowerment, gender relations, and anger and distrust. The theme of rebirth and reconstruction of the self is also likely to appear in therapy since, according to our interviews, many women who describe themselves as subjective knowers (almost half the women in our original sample fell into this category) also tell stories of revolutionizing their lives, discarding abusive relationships, and disengaging themselves from responsibilities to others.

Position IV: Procedural Knowing

The *procedural knower* is concerned with the acquisition of techniques that enhance critical understanding and evaluation of ideas in light of criteria held by and agreed upon by the members of a discipline, guild, or culture group. Blind or unexamined acceptance of external authority no longer works for these women and neither does sheer assertion of knowing without evidence to support opinion—the stance taken by subjective knowers who claim to "just know." In our original sample, procedural knowers—whether adolescents or adults—were primarily students that we interviewed in colleges and universities. Later interviews that I have done suggest that individuals other than students can be primarily procedural knowers if they are highly invested in the rules of inquiry and evaluation of some special group to which they belong and with which they identify.

Higher education, particularly the kind that students get in liberal arts colleges and universities and that introduces them to the ideals of critical analytical thinking, can push the received knower (less often the subjective knower) into the procedural knowing mode. This perspective, therefore, is common among women in schools and colleges who are being socialized into academic disciplines in which the emphasis is on learning and applying objective procedures for obtaining and communicating knowledge. For procedural knowers, authority is still external (as it is for received knowers), but it resides with the intellectual elite (not with *all* external authority, as received knowers assume). Once the student has mastered the appropriate right way to know, she is initiated into the community of scholars, the "charmed circle," as feminist philosopher Sarah Ruddick has put it (1984).

With the advent and use of reason and critical thinking comes a sense of mastery and personal competence. Many women are delighted to be initiated into the public world of the academy or the workplace, in which they assume they can attain the same degree of recognition, achievement, and power held by men. And many do succeed.

I have found, however, that there are serious psychological repercussions in the lives of other women who set out to learn the right way to know in a field. Our schools and colleges tend to care more about helping students analyze positions than about helping them develop opinions or establish values. In most classrooms, students are not taught how to discover and develop their own unique points of view and develop their own voices—a process that requires a turning inward for self-exploration. Instead, the student is urged to extricate the self from the process of knowing. The procedural knower, for example, is taught how to think analytically, how to "compare and contrast" alternative points of view and theories of other people, how to evaluate the trustworthiness of arguments. As we know from educational research studies, the female procedural knower, who has learned the right way to know can turn into the "good student" who has tremendous academic success. Teachers like this kind of female student; she is orderly, conscientious, thorough, and highly competent at what she does. However, we have found that a number of these highly competent women students suffer a feeling of alienation from their own successes and products. They express a feeling of nonownership of their work. They feel they are still learning by rote and thinking by someone else's recipe. They have lost touch with a sense of "I." Such students have "developed a public voice that aims to please the teacher" (Belenky, Clinchy, Goldberger, & Tarule, 1986, p. 109). A number of the stories we gathered from women suggest that this sense of alienation from the self can eventuate in a crisis of identity and meaning that bring such women into therapy. Others, who may not seek therapy, precipitously drop out of school or leave the disciplines in which they have been studying, claiming that the academy or the professions are not real life. They set out on a journey in search of the "unknown woman" (Koller, 1983), that is, themselves.

How are therapists to understand this kind of self-doubt? Why have these women not developed a voice that they can trust and claim as their own? Part of the problem, I believe, has to do with the powerful sex-role templates laid down for all individuals from childhood on, which lead women to deny or minimize their intellectual competencies. Another part has to do with the politics of mixed-sex group interaction and the sociology of knowledge—that is, who gets to speak in a group and whose questions and answers are considered valuable.

Listening to some "good students" talk about their educational experiences, one could conclude that they, too, are silent women. The questions asked within their discipline are not their questions; the answers are not their answers. The voice of reason that they have developed is powerful, but it is not experienced as their voice. Clance and Imes (1978), two clinical psychologists who have written about high-achieving women, have noted this phenomenon of distress and self-doubt in women who seem to have it made. They have labeled it "the imposter syndrome" because so many women, in spite of academic and professional accomplishments, "persist in believing that they are not really bright and have fooled anyone who thinks otherwise" (p. 241). This is, in fact, a common theme in women's psychotherapy; clinicians, however, too often explore early family roots of this "ego-disturbance" and neglect to examine the societal constructions of gender and achievement of women that are contributing to women's dis-ease.

Some women say it is the adversarial climate at certain levels of academia, business, and the professional world that bothers them. Many women, as I have indicated, say they find it uncomfortable to assume a stance of doubting, skepticism, and detachment when they engage others in conversation about ideas and opinions. They resist public debates, even on paper, that require them to treat others as adversaries and opponents. To raise their voices in disagreement, to shoot holes in other people's arguments, and to try to outmaneuver others feels too much like "attack and destroy"—like a field of war, in fact. However, skepticism, challenge, and detachment are central to the kind of academic discourse and analysis promoted by the positivist paradigm in the sciences and social sciences. The knower is supposed to stay separate and distant from the object of knowledge. Presumably, subjectivity clouds thought. The knower in these situations follows rules and procedures that allegedly ensure unbiased judgments.

This kind of detached, often adversarial, procedural knowing is what my colleagues and I call *separate knowing*. Separate knowing requires a harnessing, if not exclusion, of feeling and self from the process of knowing. Objectivity is attained by maintaining an impersonal distance and reasoning *against* the other; for the separate knower, being critical often means finding fault.

We contrast this with the procedural knowing that we call *connected knowing*, which is based on the premise that in order to understand another person's point of view or ideas, one must enter into the place of the other and adopt the person's own terms. Connected knowers are not dispassionate unbiased observers. They are biased in favor of that which they are trying to understand. They assume a stance of believing rather than doubting. The heart of connected knowing is active imagination, that is, figuratively climbing into the head of another. In connected knowing, objectivity is achieved by entering the perspective of the other and by reasoning along with the other.

My colleague Blythe Clinchy (1989) has found that male college students tend to be more comfortable with separate knowing and female college students with connected knowing. Unfortunately, in most educational environments, particularly the large competitive research universities and the so-called male professions such as law and business, separate knowing and adversarial interaction are the norm. Women who use connected knowing strategies in their learning or at work may be getting negative feedback; they may arrive in therapy blaming themselves, feeling disaffected, and feeling powerless to change themselves or the disturbing milieu. For example, such disaffection and frustration seems to be the case for female law students. Women are now being admitted to law schools in numbers equal to men and with the same academic credentials; however, the women report a high degree of alienation in law school (Weiss & Melling, 1988). A recent report about one law school detailed the female students' distress with, specifically, hostile competition and adversarial pedagogy that evidently were affecting their academic performance (Guinier, Fine, & Balin, 1994).

Position V: Constructed Knowing

The fifth perspective described in *Women's Ways of Knowing* is *constructed knowing*. From this perspective, all knowledge is viewed as contextual and relative. Truth, right answers, and even facts must always be evaluated within the contextual frame within which they arise. The constructed knower recognizes that to claim "I know" is to acknowledge the historical, cultural, and subjective position from which the "I" speaks. All knowledge is situated, a point Collins (1990) makes when she insists that to understand the epistemology of black women, for example, one must attend to the context and the communities in which black women live. To step outside one's subjectivity and to fathom other subjectivities and knowledge perspectives are goals for constructed knowers but ones they recognize as problematic, perhaps impossible. They understand that the knower is always a part of the known. The task for the constructed knower, as Collins sees it, is to value and draw on multiple ways of knowing—whether they be objective or subjective, separate or connected—to enlarge her reality and understanding of the world.

Our description of the epistemological position of constructed knowing reveals a belief on our part that this position may be a developmental endpoint (granted, we are speaking from our own situated perspective and value frame). We hold that once the epistemological revolution necessary to attain a constructed knowing perspective occurs, the world can never look the same. Once an individual understands that questions and answers grow out of contexts, there is no turning back to naïve objectivism or subjectivism, even though at times in her life the inner voice (so vivid for the subjectivist) or the convictions of external authorities (vital to the received knower) may override more tempered or complex thought or judgment.

Constructed knowing is a position from which women consciously confront the contradictions in how people know and are taught to know, consciously evaluate questions of "goodness" or "rightness" about many ways of knowing. They recognize that different routes to knowing have their place, their logic and usefulness. Constructed knowing is also the position from which women try to bring the self and passion back into knowing, or as Ruddick (1984) has put it, "to care about how I think and think about how I care" (p. 151).

Even though constructed knowers acknowledge the tentativeness of knowledge, they struggle toward a commitment within relativism (Perry, 1970). It is in this position that a person achieves a critical consciousness (Freire, 1971) and a capacity for reflective judgment that takes into account personal history, social and historical context, and structural inequality. It is from this position that a person makes informed choices and commitments and conceives of her life and acts as political.

Some critics have suggested that constructed knowing may be an artifact of good fortune and privilege. All the women in our original sample whom we placed in this fifth position were college educated; all were white. However, my new data on a more ethnically and educationally diverse sample (it includes more working-class people as well as Native Americans, immigrants from various Asian countries, and women of different Latina origins) suggest that the makeup of the earlier fifth-position group was an artifact of our original sampling procedures. Broader sampling has uncovered constructed knowers—wise women, if you will—among women of color and women of the working class, women who have become wise through their marginality and their life struggles, *not* through higher education. Wisdom, perspective taking, analytical thought, compassion and connection, and the ability to be self-critical are surely not the prerogatives of the advantaged or highly educated. As more stories of such wise women are included in studies of ways of knowing, they will undoubtedly change the conception of constructed knowing, although in ways I cannot now predict.

As one might suspect, even though diverse problems bring these constructed knowers into therapy (they are as susceptible to depression, disappointment, frustrated ambitions, and stunted anger as anyone else), they tend to use therapy well. They understand contradiction and can tolerate ambiguity; they use their constructivist perspective to try to enter into and understand other people's worlds. They are interested in exploring the history of their own constructions, deconstructions, and reconstructions. I have found that though they value analytical thinking, they also appreciate and respond to narrative and metaphor. Indeed, what strikes the observer most forcefully about these women is their passion and engagement with the world.

Normative and Personal Epistemology

My account of women's ways of knowing is concerned with how different women struggle to come to terms with the covert and overt social pressures to learn a normative epistemology, a right way to know. Some women yield to cultural norms; others do not. The families, schools, and communities in which women grow up affect the educational routes that they take and the perspectives on knowing that they develop. Although my work is, in part, about women's experiences of feeling silenced and intellectually devalued, it is also about women's efforts to gain a voice and claim the powers of their own minds.

Social acceptability, manifested as a preoccupation with a correct or right way to know, has been an issue in many of my interviews with women. Not all women feel their approach to knowing is socially acceptable or valid; many experience themselves as somehow out of the mainstream; many doubt themselves and their minds. Today, both men and women in the Western world are taught to value what is assumed to be the objective male mind and to devalue knowing that is identified as female and is assumed to be, among other things, overly emotional and personalized. Our androcentric culture sends out the message to women that in order to succeed they need to learn to think like a man.

In any society there are privileged epistemologies, socially valued ways of knowing for establishing and evaluating truth claims that assume normative standing. Such social norms affect and delimit individual ways of knowing. When a person or group subscribes to ways of knowing that fall outside the margins of the relevant culture's normative, or accepted, epistemology, any analysis of those divergent ways of knowing must necessarily also be an analysis of the power relationships within the community, workplace, or culture to which the person or group belongs (Miller, 1987; Howard, 1987; Collins, 1990). Certain world perspectives, ways of knowing, and value frameworks are more apparent in and more emphasized by women than men at this point in the history of Western culture. At other times and in other cultures, some of the ways of knowing often identified as female (particularly intuition, which is stressed by many subjective knowers) have been highly valued by the culture at large.

Although anthropologists have long been interested in the topic (Cole, Gay, Glick, & Sharp, 1971; Shweder, 1984; Whorf, 1956), lately the fields of psychology and women's studies have also been paying attention to how ways of knowing vary as a function of different racial, class, and cultural backgrounds. Collins (1990) has explored the politics and history of Afro-American knowledge and thought in her development of what she calls a "black feminist epistemology." She emphasizes the importance of concrete experience, dialogue and narrative, and the ethic of caring and connection in assessing knowledge claims. Wisdom, not knowledge, is given high credence among Afro-Americans since "mother wit" is needed to deal with "educated fools" (p. 208). These same values are echoed in the stories of the women we identified as connected knowers. Luttrell (1989) has analyzed how black and white working-class women define and claim knowledge. The women she interviewed relied on personal experience and common sense but also found intuition central to knowing (as did our subjectivists). Belenky, Bond, & Weinstock (1992) are studying ways of knowing and the development of voice in a group of disadvantaged rural mothers among whom silence and received knowledge are prominent. In my own recent work, I focus on the effects of acculturation on individuals from different ethnic communities, races, and immigrant groups as they are channeled into the U.S. educational system with its normative standards for the right way to know.

Members of marginalized cultural groups in the United States

whom my students and I have interviewed have told anguished stories about their loss of the familiar and standard ways of meaning-
making endorsed by their communities and cultures when they were
exposed to mainstream privileged American thought and interpretive frameworks. What is apparent to me, as I listen to stories about
the undermining of confidence in an individual's approach to knowing or the loss of an indigenous culture's approaches to knowing, is
the pain and compromise that accompany such social accommodation. As an Afro-American woman in one of my recent interviews
put it:

> What I've learned, I've learned through my culture,
> through my body, through my experience, but depending
> on which world I'm in, I express it differently. . . . If you
> want to be successful in this country, the United States
> of America, you have to be able to function in a white
> world. . . . You have to give up a lot of who you are, iden-
> titywise and culturewise, in order to make it through the
> system. And it's only after you've gotten to where you
> want to be that you can then re-take on who you are as
> a black person or an ethnic person. . . . It makes you crazy
> [to] try to do it in a manner that's not natural to you. You
> do it their way, which is not a bad way, it's just different
> . . . but at some point, if you're going to be healthy, you
> have to come back to yourself and reunite these two
> [ways of being] and make some peace with yourself.

This felt sense of coercion on the individual level is echoed in
feminist academic circles. Over the past decade or two, feminist
criticism has questioned the objectivity of a positivist science that
has for so long left out half the human experience—that of women.
As Westcott (1979) has argued, "to ignore women's consciousness
is to miss the most important area of women's creative expressions
of self in a society which denies that freedom in behavior" (p. 429).

She goes on to analyze the dialectical tension—that is, the discontinuities, oppositions, and dilemmas—that characterize women's concrete experiences in a patriarchal society. It is this tension between how women know, what women know, what they are supposed to know, and what they dare not know that originally propelled my colleagues and me into our investigation of women's ways of knowing.

Metaphors of Voice and Silence

Therapists who work with and listen to women know that the metaphors of *silence* and *voice* are very potent for women. Gaining a voice has come to be equated with personal empowerment. In my recent interviews, I have been paying close attention to how women speak about being silent and feeling silenced as they describe their lives and developmental histories. I have found that silence is not just an issue for a subset of women, as we implied in our book, but a common experience, albeit with a host of both positive and negative connotations, for almost all women, regardless of their prevailing epistemological position.

For most of this century, women have been taught that personal experience, subjectivity, values, and emotion have no place in scientific inquiry and dialogue. Instead, women have been taught to value the impartial cool intellect. Many women have told me and my colleagues that education seems to mean denial of voice, passion, and conviction, in the name of objectivity and science. As recent critiques of the positivist paradigm have shown, even though positivist standards of science have advanced the understanding of physical and social phenomena, this paradigm's ideals have not always served women well. In the name of objective science, scientists and scholars have ignored the experiences of marginalized peoples who do not fit into normative frameworks and theories. Standard paradigms, theories, and methods have silenced minority voices and women's voices.

From the woman's as well as the clinician's or educator's point of view, there is a big difference between self-imposed versus externally imposed silence. Feeling silenced and feeling unheard are clearly painful and frustrating experiences for women when imposed from without. But it is also clear from our interviews that sometimes there is self-silencing. A woman can be silent out of choice. Silence can be a place of retreat, of safety. It can be a place of self-renewal. Sometimes, in her wisdom about the situation and the moment, a woman may choose not to speak. Some women tell about learning how to temper their voices so that when they do speak they have a better chance of being heard. Patterns of silence and speech and women's assumptions about the rules of talk are obviously important data for a clinician working with women.

Most women would agree that, at times, women can lose their voices as they become engaged with others in the politics of talk— a loss of voice that occurs no matter how knowledgeable or eloquent they may feel they are. Why do women fall silent with certain kinds of people or in certain situations? Some may feel unheard even when they know they have something worthwhile to say. Many report the experience of being labeled backseat drivers and feeling that their voices and opinions have gone unsolicited, unheeded, and unappreciated. To speak and not be heard is another form of silencing.

In *Women's Ways of Knowing,* my colleagues and I described in some detail the distinctive family patterns and "politics of family talk" common to each epistemological perspective. There are rules of speaking and listening that children learn from early on. These rules (and the associated assumptions about where truth lies) are carried into adulthood and greatly affect the way an individual constructs "authority" and "expertise." One-way talk, inequality in parental communications, and disallowed questioning, on the one hand, all contribute to the silencing of children's sense of personal mind and voice. Mutuality in communication, listening and dialogue, and respect even for half-formed ideas, on the other hand, contribute to a growing sense of personal authority and voice. It is these lessons, learned first in families and then in schools, that greatly affect an individual's developing self-confidence and feelings of intellectual worth.

In psychotherapy, it seems imperative that the clinician honor the woman's point of view and experience, not by imposing expectations of developmental goals, but by listening to the woman's constructions of her problems within her own social context. Awareness of one's own ways of knowing and the assumptive base on which they rest seems obligatory in clinical work, since such awareness should sensitize a clinician to the possibility of matches and mismatches in her or his work with clients. All too often, therapists committed to (in some cases, entrapped by) a particular paradigm of clinical intervention operate as procedural knowers, rigidly applying a particular theory of psychopathology and particular therapeutic techniques without questioning their suitability for the particular client. Here, the danger lies in letting the procedures become the gospel and the clinician's ways of knowing supersede or overwhelm the client's ways.

Clinicians alert to context might ask these questions: What problems is this woman trying to solve? What is her experiential world? What are the social and psychological forces that limit or expand her vision? How does this woman know what she must do to survive and to flourish? This orientation to development as a process of interpretation and construction, in which the person's narrative or life story informs an understanding of individual developmental processes, is appropriately referred to by Freeman and Robinson (1990) in their thoughtful analysis of the problems in normative developmental theory as "the development within" (p. 53).

Conclusion

In conclusion, I argue that it is critical that clinicians focus on difference and listen carefully to the stories of marginalized people, so that they can better understand the logic of individual courses of action in different social contexts. Life stories can instruct clinicians that some people's lives simply do not conform to theoretical prescriptions and normative standards. By listening to different voices—voices from the margin—and exploring difference, therapists can challenge authority and old assumptions and paradigms. By understanding the epistemological biases behind different strategies of empowerment, they can evaluate strategies and choose the most effective one given the context. Such evaluations are as important to clinical intervention as they are to political action. In learning to live with diversity in a pluralistic world, all of us must learn how to make a connection with difference.

References

Alcoff, L. (1988). Cultural feminism versus post-structuralism: The identity crisis in feminist theory. *Signs: Journal of Women in Culture and Society, 13*, 405–436.

Basseches, M. (1984). *Dialectical thinking and adult development.* Norwood, NJ: Ablex.

Baxter Magolda, M. B. (1989). Gender differences in cognitive development: An analysis of cognitive complexity and learning styles. *Journal of College Student Development, 30*, 213–220.

Belenky, M., Bond, L., & Weinstock, J. (1992). *From silence to voice: Developing the ways of knowing.* Unpublished manuscript, University of Vermont.

Belenky, M. F., Clinchy, B. M., Goldberger, N. R., & Tarule, J. M. (1986). *Women's ways of knowing: The development of self, voice, and mind.* New York: Basic Books.

Benack, S. (1984). Postformal epistemologies and the growth of empathy. In M. L. Commons, F. A. Richards, & S. Armon (Eds.), *Beyond formal operations: Late adolescence and adult cognitive development* (pp. 340–356). New York: Praeger.

Bohan, J. S. (1993). Regarding gender: Essentialism, constructionism, and feminist psychology. *Psychology of Women Quarterly, 17*, 5–22.

Bruner, J. (1986). *Actual minds, possible worlds.* Cambridge, MA: Harvard University Press.

Chinen, A. B. (1984). Modal logic: A new paradigm of development and late-life potential. *Human Development, 27*, 42–56.

Clance, P. R., & Imes, S. A. (1978). The imposter phenomenon in high achieving women: Dynamics and therapeutic intervention. *Psychotherapy: Theory, research, and practice, 15,* 241–247.

Clinchy, B. (1989). The development of thoughtfulness in college women: Integrating reason and care. *American Behavioral Scientist, 32,* 647–657.

Cole, M., Gay, G., Glick, J. A., & Sharp, D. W. (1971). *The cultural context of learning and thinking.* New York: Basic Books.

Collins, P. H. (1990). *Black feminist thought: Knowledge, consciousness, and the politics of empowerment.* Boston: Unwin Hyman.

de Laurentis, T. (1986). Feminist studies/critical studies: Issues, terms and context. In T. de Laurentis (Ed.), *Feminist studies/critical studies* (pp. 1–19). Bloomington: Indiana University Press.

Dell, P. (1980). Researching the family theories of schizophrenia: An exercise in epistemological confusion. *Family Process, 19,* 321–335.

Feixas, G. (1990). Personal construct theory and the systemic therapies: Parallel or convergent trends? *Journal of Marital and Family Therapy, 16,* 1–20.

Freeman, M., & Robinson, R. E. (1990). The development within: An alternative approach to the study of lives. *New Ideas in Psychology, 8,* 1, 53–72.

Freire, P. (1971). *Pedagogy of the oppressed* (M. B. Ramos, Trans.). New York: Seabury Press.

Gergen, K. (1985). The social constructionist movement in modern psychology. *American Psychologist, 40,* 266–275.

Gergen, M. (Ed.). (1988). *Feminist thought and the structure of knowledge.* New York: New York University Press.

Goldberger, N., & Veroff, J. (Eds.). (1995). *The culture and psychology reader.* New York: New York University Press.

Goolishian, H. A., & Anderson, H. (1987). Language systems and theory: An evolving idea. *Psychotherapy, 24,* 529–538.

Greeno, J. G. (1989). A perspective on thinking [Special issue: Children and their development]. *American Psychologist, 44,* 134–141.

Guba, E. G. (Ed.). (1990). *The paradigm dialogue.* Newbury Park, CA: Sage.

Guidano, V. F., & Liotti, G. (1983). *Cognitive processes and emotional disorders: A structural approach to psychotherapy.* New York: Guilford Press.

Guinier, L., Fine, M., & Balin, J. (1994). Becoming gentlemen: Women's experiences at one Ivy-League law school. *University of Pennsylvania Law Review, 143,* 1–110.

Hare-Mustin, R. T., & Maracek, J. (Eds.). (1990). *Making a difference: Psychology and the construction of gender.* New Haven, CT: Yale University Press.

Hoffman, L. (1988). A constructivist position for family therapy. *Irish Journal of Psychology, 9*, 110–129.

Howard, J. A. (1987). Dilemmas in feminist theorizing: Politics and the academy. *Current Perspectives in Social Theory, 8*, 279–312.

Ivey, A. E. (1991). *Developmental strategies*. Pacific Grove, CA: Brooks/Cole.

Kegan, R. (1982). *The evolving self*. Cambridge, MA: Harvard University Press.

Kelly, G. A. (1955). *The psychology of personal constructs* (2 Vols.). New York: W.W. Norton.

Kelly, G. A. (1973). Fixed role therapy. In R. M. Jurjevich (Ed.), *Direct psychotherapy: 28 American originals* (pp. 394–422). Coral Gables, FL: University of Miami Press.

Kitchener, K. (1983). Cognition, metacognition, and epistemic cognition. *Human Development, 26*, 222–232.

Kitchener, K., & King, P. M. (1981). Reflective judgment: Concepts of justification and their relationship to age and education. *Journal of Applied Developmental Psychology, 2*, 89–116.

Kleinman, A. (1988). *Rethinking psychiatry: From cultural category to personal experience*. New York: Free Press.

Koller, A. (1983). *An unknown woman*. New York: Bantam Doubleday Dell.

Landrine, H. (1992). Clinical implications of cultural differences: The referential versus the indexical self. *Clinical Psychology Review, 12*, 401–415.

Loevinger, J. (1976). *Ego development: Conceptions and theories*. San Francisco: Jossey-Bass.

Luttrell, W. (1989). Working-class women's ways of knowing: Effects of gender, race, and class. *Sociology of Education, 62*, 33–46.

Mahoney, M. J. (1991). *Human change processes: The scientific foundations of psychotherapy*. New York: Basic Books.

Mednick, M. T. (1989). On the politics of psychological constructs: Stop the bandwagon, I want to get off. *American Psychologist, 44*, 1118–1123.

Messer, S. B., Sass, L. A., & Woolfolk, R. L. (Eds.). (1988). *Hermeneutics and psychological theories: Interpretive perspectives on personality, psychotherapy, and psychopathology*. New Brunswick, NJ: Rutgers University Press.

Miller, J. B. (1987). *Toward a new psychology of women*. Boston: Beacon Press.

Neilsen, J. M. (Ed.). (1990). *Feminist research methods*. Boulder, CO: Westview Press.

Perry, W. G. (1970). *Forms of intellectual and ethical development in the college years*. New York: Academic Press.

Prilleltensky, I. (1990). The politics of abnormal psychology: Past, present, and future. *Political Psychology, 11*, 767–785.

Reiss, D. (1981). *The family's construction of reality.* Cambridge, MA: Harvard University Press.

Ruddick, S. (1984). New combinations: Learning from Virginia Woolf. In C. Asher, L. DeSalvor, & S. Ruddick (Eds.), *Between women* (pp.137–159). Boston: Beacon Press.

Sampson, E. E. (1989). The challenge of social change for psychology: Globalization and psychology's theory of the person. *American Psychologist, 44,* 914–921.

Shweder, R. A. (1984). Anthropology's romantic rebellion against the enlightenment, or there is more to thinking than reason and evidence. In R. A. Shweder & R. A. LeVine (Eds.), *Culture theory: Essays on mind, self, and emotion* (pp. 27–66). New York: Cambridge University Press.

Shweder, R. A. (1991). *Thinking through cultures: Expeditions in cultural psychology.* Cambridge, MA: Harvard University Press.

Tyler, F. B., Sussewell, D. R., and Williams-McCoy, J. (1985). Ethnic validity in psychotherapy. *Psychotherapy, 22,* 311–320.

Unger, R., Draper, R. D., & Pendergrass, M. L. (1986). Personal epistemology and personal experience. *Journal of Social Issues, 42,* 67–79.

Watzlawick, P. (Ed.). (1984). *The invented reality: How do we know what we believe we know? Contributions to constructivism.* New York: W. W. Norton.

Weiss, C., & Melling, L. (1988). The legal education of twenty women. *Stanford Law Review, 40,* 1299–1369.

Westcott, M. (1979). Feminist criticism of the social sciences. *Harvard Educational Review, 49,* 422–430.

Whorf, B. L. (1956). *Language, thought, and reality.* Cambridge, MA: MIT Press.

Young-Eisendrath, P., & Wiedemann, F. (1987). *Female authority: Empowering women through psychotherapy.* New York: Guilford Press.

7

Narrative, Social Constructionism, and Buddhism

William D. Lax

The Western world, despite the many differences manifested by its population and local cultures, has continually tried to maintain the status quo, emphasizing culturally dominant or privileged views for our interactions and lives (Gergen, 1991). It is only recently, with the rise of postmodern thinking, that marginal or peripheral ideas and practices have been given greater attention by the larger society. In psychotherapeutic thinking and practices, this shift in attention is seen in the current rise of approaches framed within a postmodern and social constructionist orientation, such as the reflecting process (Andersen, 1987, 1991; Davidson, Lax, Lussardi, Miller, & Ratheau, 1988; Lax, 1989) and the conversational approach (Anderson, 1993; Anderson & Goolishian, 1988), the solution-oriented approach (Hudson O'Hanlon & Weiner-Davis, 1989; de Shazer, 1982), and the narrative approach of White and Epston (1990; Dickerson & Zimmerman, 1992; Zimmerman & Dickerson, 1993, 1994).

Rather than seeing the individual as the site of problems, these approaches see an understanding of social and historical relational networks and linguistic practices as central to both problem formation and resolution: they stress our relational nature to one another and how problems arise (and are dissolved) through language and through social interactions. In keeping with postmodern thinking, these approaches attend to the local and global contexts of our lives, both in and out of therapy, including issues related to politics and diversity (which includes gender, class and race, and local cultures). The role of the "other" is shifted from foreigner to extension of self, as self is viewed as arising out of the interaction between self and other. In addition, the role of the therapist is examined as it is raised to a more central position in therapy and falls under the same reflexive eye usually directed toward the client (see Madigan, 1991; Lax, 1995).

The same shift has also been evident in regard to Eastern spiritual practices such as Buddhism (see Epstein, 1995; Jones, 1994). The traditionally marginalized practices of meditation, with their questions about external "truths" or a permanent self, are receiving increasing public support that appears in keeping with the postmodern shift and its focus on self, relationship, narrative, multiplicity, diversity, and reflexivity.

In this chapter, I will comment on the relationship of both the Buddhist tradition, particularly the Theravada practice of *vipassana* meditation (Goldstein, 1994), and the narrative approach developed by Michael White and David Epston to social constructionism and postmodern thinking. After a brief overview of Buddhism and the narrative approach, I discuss how Buddhist thought and practice relate to narrative approaches, with a specific emphasis on the reflexive posture inherent in both practices. I also discuss how reflexivity facilitates the therapeutic process, emphasizing the importance of usually unsaid components within the therapeutic transaction.

The intention of this chapter is not to supplant existing models of therapy, but to enrich them through the integration of a 2,500-year-old tradition. It is my explicit hope that what follows will help to dissolve the distinctions between self and other, offering therapists a theoretical and practical approach to working with others in a manner that is less hierarchical than current approaches and that fosters growth for themselves as well as their clients.

Shifting Dualities: A Middle Path

Bateson (1972) was fond of talking about the dilemmas of living in an *either/or* world and urged us to shift to a *both/and* world in which both sides of a dilemma could be examined. The both/and perspective gives privileged status to neither side, recognizing the inherent reciprocity of each in interaction with the other. In the natural world, such reciprocity is seen in predator-prey relationships, where both predator and prey are necessary components of a larger ecological environment. In the social sciences, the shifting of theory away from the dualities of either/or can be seen in mind-body discourse and the examination of interconnections between body and mind, as in the field of psychoneuroimmunology. Such integrating views are not always employed in our "modern world," where hierarchy, specificity, and the privileging of one side over the other are often valued. In the social sciences, the current presence of both ways of thinking is evident in the ongoing debate between psychiatry and psychology regarding the nature of "mental illness," and it is even evident within psychology, in splits between such models of training as scientist-practitioner and scholar-practitioner.

Bateson's views were not new ones, as the same shift away from either/or was voiced by the Buddha, who called for a "Middle Way" between the extremes of asceticism and hedonism 2,500 years ago. His view led to a position of *neither/nor*: a position of seeing the delusion of the extremes. The Buddha explained his understanding of delusion and its end in the Four Noble Truths, describing how all of life is suffering. He described how we tend to cling to those experiences that we find pleasurable and push away those that we find unpleasurable. This process is based on our mistaken belief that there is a permanence to life, that we have a coherent, permanent self that we can hold on to from moment to moment. We live this illusion every day as we try to avoid difficulties and pain in most aspects of our lives. We seek out what is pleasurable through possessions and relationships. We marginalize death and old age, not wanting to see the suffering that will be there for each of us. However, the Buddha also said that there is a way to end this suffering; that way is the Eightfold Path.

Central to this path is the practice of meditation. It is through meditation that the individual can observe the ongoing movements of thoughts, recognizing their impermanence and not becoming immersed in them. As a meditation practice develops, observer and observed even merge, so that the meditator observes merely a continual flow of phenomena. The boundary between inside and outside blurs, with the distinction between self and other becoming less pronounced.

In Buddhism, it is a reflexivity between self and other that creates a sense of self (Mellor, 1991). There is no concept of a bounded masterful self, an ego, or even an unconscious. All concepts of self are considered attachments. In the Buddhist view, "Our sense of self is created by our thought processes and by the habit of grasping in the mind" (Goldstein & Kornfield, 1987, p. 145). And it is this sense of self, and a belief in it, that causes suffering. What we usually consider to be the self (*atta*), character, or personality is actually the "sum total of body parts, thoughts, sensations, desires, memories, and so on" (Goleman, 1988, p. 117). More specifically, our character or personality is *bhava*, that is, a continuity of consciousness over time. It is the moment-to-moment connections that we string together and make into a narrative, which we then hold on to. Moreover, each successive moment is conditioned by our *karma*: the causal factor that determines what is possible to happen next. One might even say that *karma* is the narrative that guides and begets actions in the future.

Buddhism emphasizes narrative construction as well as attention to the emerging components of the unfolding narratives, as it is from these narratives that all ensuing events emanate: "Guard the thought as it begets the action." Our minds move with little conscious control. Our individual thoughts occur almost as bubbles emerge in the ocean: they arise and pass away. They have nothing concrete about them, and they take a formal structure only when we hold on to them or try to push them away. They arise on their own accord from our background of personal experience and cultural contexts. They have no permanence.

Our sense of self is particularly made up of *skandas*, or aggregates, that include form, feeling, perception (including memory), mental formations (including volition), and consciousness. These aggregates, too, are continually changing as different states arise and pass away. Again, this process is what we come to believe is who we are. We often become most aware of these aggregates as a bundle; they are included in what we string together to forming a narrative structure with a beginning, middle, and end. The Buddhist text on psychology, the *Abhidharma*, describes these units of experience as mind moments. There are seventeen mind moments in every unit of experience and thousands of moments in any string of seconds. These massed mind moments arise as mental factors. Furthermore, mind moments are not random; each has a relationship to both its preceding and succeeding moments. This is the law of *karma*, of cause and effect.

Buddhism describes only two kinds of mental factors, healthy and unhealthy. They are opposing factors, with each supplanting the other, there being no middle ground. We can entertain only one kind at a time. When we are engaged in a healthy factor, there can be no unhealthy factor present. Among the healthy factors, mindfulness or awareness is one of the strongest, overriding any unhealthy factors. When the strong unhealthy factor of delusion is present, no healthy factor can arise. In Buddhism, the intention of meditation practice, and of life itself, is to cultivate healthy mental factors that will take precedence over any unhealthy factors.

Narrative and the Self

This section overviews the Western postmodern view of the self, while the subsequent section takes a second, closer look at the

Buddhist view of the self to illustrate the convergences between the two views. In the postmodern view, narrative has a particular role in our lives. Each individual develops a story about his or her life that becomes the basis of all identity. Thus, this view challenges any concept that an underlying unified self exists. As I have described elsewhere (Lax, 1992):

> The development of a narrative or story is something that we do in conjunction with others (see Gergen, 1989; Shotter, 1989). It is the process of defining who we are in interaction with other people's perceived understandings of us. This is a recursive process. We shape the world in which we live, thereby creating our own "reality" within a context of a community of others. The boundaries of our narratives are constructed through [historical], political, economic, social and cultural constraints and potentials, with our choice of narratives not limitless, but existing within prescribed contexts. This narrative or sense of self arises not only through discourse with others, but *is* our discourse with others. There is no hidden self to be interpreted. We "reveal" ourselves in every moment of interaction through the [continual] ongoing narrative that we maintain with others (p. 71).

A permanent self is merely an illusion that we cling to, a narrative developed in relation to others over time that we come to identify as who we are. As Kerby (1991) comments, the constructions of self are "acts of self-narration not only . . . descriptive of the self but, more importantly, . . . fundamental to the emergence and reality of that subject" (p. 5). He goes on to say that "the self is a fiction" (p. 34).

Buddhism and the Self

While postmodernism is a compilation of ideas borrowed from multiple sources, with roots in phenomenology, existentialism, French structuralism, critical theory, theories of literary criticism, and Marxism (Gergen, 1991), Buddhism has a single source, the Buddha. (For a comprehensive historical review of postmodern thinking, see Norris, 1991, and Jameson, 1992. For a review of the life of the Buddha, see Rahula, 1974.) Nevertheless, the Theravada Buddhist view of and approach to life is very consistent with the postmodern view and narrative approach. Both philosophies mirror their own processes, marked as they are by "uncertainty, frivolity, and reflexivity" (Parker, 1992, p. 71). For both, multiple voices, stories, and views are to be valued, with the individual's own experience given centrality, and contradictions are allowed (even encouraged). Although Buddhism ascribes to a specified cosmology of the world, both views challenge the reification of any global truths, hierarchies, or rationality of human interaction. In both, diversity of both thought and action are valued, a reversal of common dichotomies with a subsequent displacement of dominant discourses and what the culture may call common sense.

In Buddhism, for example, the Buddha encouraged his disciples not to listen to anyone expressing the truth; instead, each was to trust his or her own experience. Tibetan meditation teacher Trungpa Rinpoche has stated, "Buddhism doesn't tell you what is false and what is true, but encourages you to find out for yourself" (cited in Chödrön, 1991, p. 43). This approach, like that of postmodernism, can be seen as a direct challenge to the legitimation of any externally privileged position or truth.

Moreover, as mentioned previously, in Theravada Buddhism the self is conceived not as reified entity but as narrative. In addition, Buddhism, like postmodernism, attends to politics, with global human interactions understood on a personal, local level (see Gergen, 1991; Lyotard, 1988; Rosenau, 1992; Nhat Hanh, 1976).

In Theravada Buddhism, the path toward the end of suffering is laid out very clearly with many numerical steps, including the Eightfold Path, the seven factors of enlightenment, the five skandas, the three precepts, and so forth. The Eightfold Path describes Right

Understanding and Right Action as two of the steps in this path, offering them as guidelines to life. When the individual acts with them in mind, in any local context, he or she is guided to take both political and personal action. Taken together, the categories of steps offer a cosmology of the world that can be followed. The use of any metanarrative, such as a cosmology, is contrary to postmodern thinking (Lyotard, 1988), but the Buddhist cosmology differs from metanarrative in that it is seen as a story that can be interpreted in any number of personal ways. While many individuals will have similar experiences, what each individual experiences is considered to be based on her or his beliefs about what might be expected and her or his subsequent linguistic constructions of the experience. Thus, while there are laws in Buddhism, they are not normalized statements about how to be in the world or the way that the path *must* unfold.

In both the Buddhist and postmodern view, we all put our experiences into language based on our predominant narrative of the moment. This narrative guides our experience, and our experience shapes our narrative. The prior narrative constructions that we use have been described by others as *fore-understandings* (Gadamer, 1975), *quasinarratives* (Kerby, 1991), and *preunderstandings* (Andersen, 1992). Each of these arises through prior social exchanges and then shapes what follows. In the same manner, as stated by the laws of *karma*, our current narrative (which has been shaped by preexisting narratives) influences what will follow, and what follows then postfigures the previous narrative. While language can never truly represent experience, it shapes the experiences that we have. We are guided by our narratives to develop specific descriptions, and although they are not the "real" events, those descriptions often become our experience. Ram Dass (1974) captures this idea by relating a story told by his teacher, Neum Karoli Baba. A group of people gathered at a talk given by the Buddha. In attendance were a pickpocket and a saint. Neum Karoli Baba explained to Ram Dass, "You know, when a pickpocket meets a saint, all he sees are his pockets. He never sees the saint" (p. 162).

Thus, the things we "see" are only our concepts resulting from our narrative structures, not what are really "there." The Buddha's teaching is, "See things as they really are." This does not mean we are to return to the modern world, with its goal-seeking behaviors and search for external truths; instead, we are to view the world with the recognition that we construct it based on our desires and fears. We continually create our world based on our beliefs, grasping at what brings us pleasure and pushing away what causes us pain. It is because nothing can be held onto or repelled forever that the result of our endeavors is inevitably suffering, at least as long as we are caught up in this cyclical grasping and pushing away process.

A view of life as suffering may strike some as nihilistic. And the same charge of nihilism can be made about postmodernism. An alternative position is proposed by the postmodern critic Pauline Rosenau (1992), who distinguishes between the "affirmative" and the "skeptical" postmodernist. The affirmative postmodern thinker carries an optimistic view, seeing the individual as able to have an impact upon the world politically, socially, economically, and even ecologically. The affirmative postmoderist has a feeling of hope and belief in the progress of humankind in the future. She or he can be political, having strong beliefs in ideals and values yet knowing full well that these beliefs may change in the course of the next conversation. Conversely, the skeptical postmodern thinker carries a distrusting, gloomy view of the world, seeing it filled with "fragmentation, disintegration, malaise, meaninglessness, a vagueness or even absence of moral parameters" (p. 15). The feeling of doom carries over into political and the environmental fields as well as into the arts and sciences. The skeptic turns away from global metanarratives or universal theories and embraces multiple narratives, always deconstructing whatever is most dominant.

The affirmative and skeptic views can also be seen in Buddhism in that it carries a both/and perspective: life is composed of suffering through the continual seeking of comfort and avoidance of pain and at the same time it offers a Middle Path leading to the end of suffering. On the one hand, an individual can take the position that all is suffering, so we just must bear with it. On the other hand, the giving up of attachment and delusion leads the individual to immense joy and freedom, a sense of liberation. However, this freedom is not an end point, as a modernist might hope, but an awakening. Zen monks are fond of telling their students that before enlightenment one goes to the well and carries water, whereas after enlightenment, one goes to the well and carries water. The individual has the responsibility to live in the world with others, not only to sit and meditate.

The Buddha proposed the end of suffering through the process of "bare attention"; that is the process described earlier in which the individual simply observes the ongoing process of the arising and passing away of both desire and aversion. Paradoxically, it is a desire for liberation from suffering that keeps some on the path to achieving bare attention. Yet another paradox is that the Buddhist practitioner, like the affirmative postmodernist, needs to recognize the illusions of life yet to act knowing that her or his behavior counts. While the practice of bare attention is designed to be a part of everyday life, its formal development and cultivation comes about in the practice of meditation.

Insight Meditation

Meditation is one of the Buddhist practices that trains the mind to be more open and to generate healthy mental factors. While there are many different forms of meditation practice, in the Theravada tradition, the practice is called *vipassana*, or "insight" meditation. Insight meditation is the ongoing focus of attention on whatever arises in the senses and the mind, accompanied by a notation of the object of mindfulness. The meditator begins with attention to the breath, noting the in and out passage of air or the rising and falling of the abdomen. In this manner, the meditator can begin to experience the ever-changing nature of impermanence and see things as they really are. This seeing is a deconstructive venture.

Each mind moment is broken down into its components. The sound of a bird singing is labeled "hearing, hearing." The feeling of pain is "sensation, sensation." A "softness," or receptiveness, of mind is encouraged and is developed over time through an acceptance of the emerging phenomena. A harshness of observing generates only a self-rebuking quality; a gentleness of noticing generates kindness toward oneself and others. In postmodernist terms, this practice is a deconstruction. It focuses on process, not content: content is only grist for the mill. Insight meditation always takes into account opposing states, and the meditator is encouraged to view them without becoming captured by them, to shift away from the duality of holding onto or pushing away experiences. Different experiential phenomena are examined as the observer sees the independent arising into and passing away from awareness of each phenomenon.

Shifting Discourses and Reflexivity

The processes of meditation and of therapy share an emphasis on the shifting of discourses and on reflexivity. When we become able to take the reflective position of insight meditation in relation to our thoughts, feelings, and sensations, we are developing a state of equanimity. When we do not take this observing position, we become attached. We are immersed or captured by the *contents* of our interconnected mind moments. Our difficulties, then, result from our being stuck in a narrative that will often consist of unhealthy mental factors (for example, the perceptual/cognitive states of delusion, false views, shamelessness, recklessness, or egoism or the affective states of agitation, greed, envy, worry, aversion, contraction, or perplexity). One way out is to shift discourses, to move a narrative that can entertain a healthy mental factor (for example, insight, mindfulness, modesty, discretion, confidence, composure, nonattachment, impartiality, buoyancy, adaptability, or proficiency) (see Goldstein, 1994). It is this shift in discourse that is common to all therapies. It is the development, depending

on the therapy, of an observing ego, a cognitive reframing or restructuring, or a second-order shift. It is also often a move from
an either/or position to a both/and or neither/nor position. From
the Buddhist viewpoint, the individual who moves to a healthy
mental factor makes this shift, either by changing to a new narrative or by examining the former one from a distance. That is, the
individual takes a reflexive stance to her or his earlier discourse.
However, the view that a shift in discourse is possible does not
imply that there are absolute laws about what is healthy and
unhealthy, which would indicate a modernist view of ethics and
morality. Instead, the viewpoint is an offering, which individuals
may use as a guide in their decisions about their thoughts and
actions in the world.

In the Western world, clinicians' and theorists' attention to
reflexivity has been evident in family therapy, particularly those therapeutic models influenced by second-order cybernetics (Hoffman,
1992; Steier, 1991). Specifically, *reflexivity* is a process of making oneself an object of one's own observation, examining the narratives
that structure one's own experiences and visa versa. In the postmodernist view, as we continue to examine our self-narratives, we
are also engaged in the process of examining how we are seen, since
these narratives are generated through our interaction with the
other. Thus, by examining our own processes, we begin to see the
logic of the other. In this way, we break down subject-object barriers, opening a space for the other (Steier, 1991).

In addition, if we take seriously the idea of shifting discourses
and the impact of narratives on the unfolding reality that is co-
constructed between people, we need to watch our own thoughts
and their ensuing actions. The types of questions that we ask generate certain types of answers. If we are concerned about problems,
that is what we will get in our conversations with others. If we
believe that it is important to examine early childhood issues, then
those are the "realities" that we will be participants in creating. As
many have warned: "Be careful what you ask for. You may get it."

White's Narrative Approach

To extend and deepen the comparison of Buddhism and the postmodern narrative view, I turn to Michael White's narrative approach, which holds several ideas about problems and how people experience and solve them that are unique in postmodern theory yet in which I note affinities with Buddhist thinking. (White's work has been elegantly summarized by a number of writers: see Dickerson & Zimmerman, 1992; Zimmerman & Dickerson, 1993, 1994.) White believes that the narratives that we live by are not neutral, as they come from a dominant culture. Our narratives have specific effects on us and influence the way that we lead our lives. This is not necessarily to say that there are essential normalized good and bad narratives. For some people, however, dominant cultural stories have restrictive effects on their lives and interactions. These cultural stories "lead to constructions of a normative view, generally reflecting the dominant culture's specifications, from which people know themselves and against which people compare themselves" (Zimmerman and Dickerson, 1994, p. 235). People often have no perceived opportunity to decide if these narratives offer them the outcomes that they would desire or prefer in their lives. Through their interactions with the culture, their stories of who they are become rigid, with the cultural story often determining how they should be as well. As described above, these stories are formed in conjunction with others through social interaction, and the individual's subsequent sense of self arises through discourse with others. It is the other who helps the individual develop any alternative new story through continual renegotiation and who therefore becomes a member of the individual's "community of co-authors" (White, 1993b).

When a client identifies with a narrative about who she or he is and loses sight of alternative descriptions of self, she or he comes to take ownership of the narrative. This process of taking ownership is supported by our culture. We describe clients *as* their dilemmas, referring to them as "borderline" or "multiple," for example. To separate clients from problems, White (1989) has developed a procedure he calls "externalizing of the problem," for it is "not the person who is, or the relationship that is, the problem. Rather, it is the problem that is the problem" (p. 6). Through externalization, clients are enabled to name their problems and attain some distance from them in order to examine both how the problems influence them and how they influence the problems.

Externalizing the problem is similar to what happens in insight meditation. Once the client is no longer captured by the problem, as if the problem were who she or he actually is, the client becomes an observer of process, able to describe, examine, and comment on the unfolding narrative and not be affected by it as she or he is usually affected. The client can name a narrative, just as the meditator names her or his emerging thoughts, feelings, or sensations. Narratives can be named with generic categories such as anorexia, depression, anger, or temper or with very personal configurations such as "Wretched Randy" or "Wistful Thinking." As described above, the client can enter another discourse from the problematic narrative, to view the latter more clearly. The client can then begin to identify unique outcomes, times when the problem is not present and preferred thoughts, feelings, and behaviors, ones that she or he can also examine without attachment. Based on these exceptions to the problem, further alternative discourses can be developed and named.

Alternative discourses are akin to the healthy mental factors in Buddhism, they are ways out of unhealthy (undesired) narrative structures.

As White has described these narratives, clients can use them to resist the overwhelming pull of the problematic story, an action similar to meditation techniques to overcome unhealthy states of mind. For example, a meditator coming under the influence of restlessness can shift to a focused attention on counting breaths or naming the restlessness. The meditator develops a concentration *and* an alternative discourse that override the restlessness. When the meditator is counting or observing, she or he is not restless but count-ing or observing. Similarly, when a client is describing or engaged in a unique outcome, the old problematic story is absent, and the new story helps the client resist the pull to restore the old one. Soon the new one becomes the familiar narrative, supplanting the old one and giving the client a fuller range of experiences.

A narrative is not named with the intention of developing an-other reified narrative to which the person then becomes attached and takes as her or his identity. The narrative developed is an alter-native one, which the client can develop further, explore, and shed at some point, just as the earlier one was shed. The process forms a metaperspective that helps people guide both themselves and oth-ers to freedom from dominating restrictive narratives. White's nar-rative approach is grounded in the writings of Foucault (White, 1989), which have strong political implications for the relationship between power and knowledge. Influenced by these implications, White's therapy encourages political action in the form of assisting others to overthrow subjugating dominant discourses. For example, White and Epston (1990; Epston & White, 1992) give "Certificates" to clients who have become proficient at defeating a particular prob-lem, and then they enlist those clients to teach others to defeat mon-sters, tempers, or other nasty problems that affect children and their parents. Epston and Madigan's Anti-Anorexia Leagues (see Madi-gan, 1994) are another example of encouraging political action. Clients who have defeated anorexia have formed leagues to help others with anorexia free themselves from culturally supported mes-sages that encourage anorexia and bulimia. These leagues have developed into extensive networks of people striving toward libera-tion. The leagues are also an example of the postmodern challenge to the distinctions between self and other; in them, people come to see their shared narratives and are united on common ground. This outcome is very similar to the Buddhist view of the function of the spiritual community. One of the three "Jewels" in Buddhism is taking refuge in the *sangha*, the community of meditators. This spiritual community supports and encourages all its members to shed the shackles of suffering and attain liberation.

Because he believes that people are subjugated by the dominant political discourses and lose many aspects of their personal agency, White (1994b) sees the therapeutic process itself as a political act. Therapy as political act is clearly demonstrated in two examples: White's (1994c) work with Aboriginals, helping them reclaim both physical and emotional aspects of their lives, and Waldergrave's work (1990) with Maori tribespeople and other diverse groups in his practice of "just therapy." Buddhism's similar ideal of attending to politics is demonstrated by the continuing political activities of Nhat Hanh (1976), head of the Vietnamese Buddhist Peace Delegation during the Vietnam War, and others who address issues of ecology (Thornton, 1993), diversity and racism (Hooks, 1994), morality (Butterfield, 1994), and the politics of enlightenment (Thurman, 1992).

Liberation is another concept that links Buddhism and the narrative approach. Liberation as freedom from suffering is the endpoint of the Buddhist epistemology just as liberation as freedom from culturally dominant, repressive narratives is the focal point of White and Epston's work. People are seen to take on identities that restrict their interactions with the world and are inconsistent with who they truly believe they are. Each philosophy then offers a methodology to free people from the stories, developed through interaction with others, that demark the deficits that individuals have falsely assumed are who they are.

In the narrative approach, the therapist does not take an expert position. (This is also the case in several other models of therapy, for example the work of Anderson and Goolishian, 1988.) While the therapist does possess expertise, in a variety of areas based on life experiences and professional knowledge, that expertise is not used to put the therapist in a one-up position in relation to the client. The therapist enters the conversation attending to the client's words and stories about her or his experience. The therapist's position is very similar to that described by the Buddhist idea of having a "beginner's mind" (Suzuki, 1975) or "don't know mind." Pema Chödrön (Tworkov, 1993), a Buddhist-ordained nun for more than twenty years, refers to herself as a student/teacher. She says that by doing this she retains a "tension between confidence and humility" (cited in Suzuki, 1975, p. 18) that keeps her honest. The therapist, like the student of meditation, makes no prejudgments about what is to be said and maintains no commitment to a particular outcome. Each conversation or experience is seen as new; it exists in relation to what has happened before but is not dictated by prior conversations. In therapy, a joint improvisation of lives takes place, drawing on past performances and memories and creating something not scripted by either the therapist or the client (Bateson, 1994). Expertise itself becomes a "joint action" (Shotter, 1993, pp. 46–47), with new expertise developing for both client and therapist in the ensuing conversation. Thus, there is always the possibility that a unique outcome can occur in the present.

When therapy is conducted from this perspective—respecting the client, following the client's lead, searching for client strengths and successes, and honoring client choices for change—it is done with what the Buddhists describe as "loving-kindness." The goal is not "curing" someone, but helping that person (and the therapist) accept who the person is at that moment in time. As Chödrön (1991) has said, "Basically, making friends with yourself is making friends with all those [other] people too" (p. 5). As in the Buddhist view, we are to honor the other as having the same rights to happiness as ourselves, support that happiness, and seek the welfare and benefit of all with the simple wish, "May all beings be happy" (Goldstein, 1994, p. 143).

Reflexivity: Therapy for the Therapist

When therapy itself is viewed as a process of social construction, all participants involved are contributors. While each participant does not have an equal position in the social interaction, each does have a sense of collaboration, and the narrative that evolves from the therapeutic conversation is a collaborative product.

In most therapeutic encounters conducted from the modernist perspective, however, the process is very one-sided (Madigan, 1991), with the therapist in charge of the direction of the conversation and the client's narrative the focus of attention. The modernist sees the client's role primarily as one of seeking out "help" from a professional. By contrast, in social constructionist therapy, the therapist's narrative is just as available for examination as the client's. The narrative approach recognizes this aspect of therapy, with reflexivity built into the model.

In Buddhism, the reflexive self-examination that occurs in meditation is crucial and defines the meditator as a learner. In the narrative approach, we therapists, being coparticipants in the development of new alternative narratives, are also learners. This postmodern model encourages a joint learning process by emphasizing that not only should the therapist closely attend to the client's narrative but also both client and therapist should reflect on the therapist's narrative. White and Epston encourage us to be more transparent in our work, openly telling clients what is behind our comments and questions and asking clients to comment on our work. To accomplish this, we situate clients' comments within our own lives and experiences and encourage clients to ask questions of us in the therapy process (White, 1993a, 1994a).

When we disclose aspects of our lives, we become more aware of the different qualities of narrative that are carried into a conversation. No narrative is neutral; therefore, even as therapists, we have thoughts and feelings that are not always open and neutral. Sometimes these will color the therapy interaction, freezing us into a position that we come to believe is the right one.

Buddhism, of course, concerns itself very specifically with the way people become overwhelmed by thoughts, feelings, and sensations, particularly those that may be considered unhealthy, such as anger, delusion, agitation, greed, envy, or worry. Meditators are instructed to dissipate such thoughts and feelings by observing them. Therapists are susceptible to the same thoughts and feelings, sometimes developing such strong emotions and ideas as hopelessness, annoyance, or even anger in respect to clients. Some forms of therapy encourage a sharing of these thoughts and feelings with clients; others view them as the material of countertransference and have specific ideas regarding how to address them, either with clients or separately with a supervisor or another therapist. The central question concerns how useful these thoughts are to the therapeutic process. Do they promote further conversation, or do they direct the unfolding narrative in a specific direction? Should a therapist's narrative be privileged?

White (1993b) does not believe that it is useful for us to entertain feelings of hopelessness, anger, or any other negatively valenced thoughts or emotions when working with a client. For example, anger may arise when a client misses appointments or even hopelessness when a client couple continue to struggle with little sign of success despite their desires to improve their relationship.

Many therapists find it difficult to prevent these thoughts and emotions from entering their therapeutic lives. From a Buddhist perspective, both the therapist's immersion in her or his thoughts and feelings and White's point of view make perfectly good sense. First of all, it must be remembered that our lives are multi-storied, and when we become taken by a single version of a story, we are limiting our range of possibilities for engaging in the world. Our work becomes saturated by the chosen narrative, and we fall into the same position as our clients. They are coming to us because they are limited in their preferred actions, experiencing an incongruity between how they see themselves as individuals and how they conduct themselves in their lives. When we accept only one story of a situation (seeing a couple as "hopeless," for example) and are unable to see alternatives for action, we have shut off exploration of those possibilities. But do not clients come to us for exactly this service of examining other potentials?

Our job as therapists is consistent with both Buddhist practices and deconstruction (Derrida, 1976); it is to let go of any *singular* narrative to which we have become attached (even a narrative proposed in this chapter if it has become a dominant narrative). Buddhist nun Chödrön (1991) says, "Holding on to beliefs limits our experience of life" (p. 33). It is the exact opposite action that is desired in the narrative approach, where expanding our experiences enriches the narratives of these experiences. With clients, we can help them externalize their saturated problematic stories. With ourselves, we can do the same, making our ideas and feelings of anger, hopelessness, and frustration external to our thinking. We can all become observers of these processes from a meditative perspective, naming them and stepping away from them. We can see when they are signals that it is time to look for another story.

When prevailing narratives are examined and deconstructed, we are better able to see the social/cultural context out of which they arise. We can then understand how we have fallen into the cultural domain that privileges these narratives in our own lives. Often they can arise through a blind belief in the prevailing theories of our times—a belief in ideas about normal developmental stages, self-actualization, psychic lesions from childhood trauma, and most of the DSM-IV (American Psychiatric Association, 1994) categories that ascribe blame and pejorative connotations to people's lives. Through deconstruction, disembedding our narratives from their sociohistorical context, we acquire the possibility of freeing ourselves from their grasp, allowing alternative stories to be uncovered, emerge, and develop.

In the process of psychotherapy, narratives, along with their impacts and intentions, are subject to continual reexamination that notes both the subtle and profound effects they have on the lives of others. While the usual therapeutic process is to examine only the effects of clients' narratives on their own lives and the lives of those with whom they are in relationships, in the narrative approach, this examination is extended to the thoughts and actions of the therapist. The process takes a recursive form, examining both the effects that our preexisting narratives (that is, our "theories") have on the therapeutic interaction and the effects that clients have on our emerging narratives (and subsequent lives). This process is a radical shift from the one-way constructions of therapy that have been dominant in the profession (Madigan, 1991).

When we acknowledge that clients have an impact on our lives and we reverse the one-way model of therapy to a two-way process, a marked shift occurs in the subject-object relationship of client and therapist. Rather than being agents of change, we can be *changed agents,* affected by therapeutic interactions and gaining personal agency. We have the same opportunities to develop alternative narratives of our lives as our clients do, to make a small step in the lateralization of the client-therapist relationship. It is my belief that when a therapist engages in this type of reflexive practice, she or he is truly acting within the domain of Buddhist principles.

White (1994b) clearly identifies and articulates how therapeutic work changes our lives when we engage in it as a reflexive process, turning the gaze back on ourselves and further blurring the boundaries between self and other, accepting the idea of joint action in which each party has an impact on the other.

Specifically, White (1994b, p. 3) suggests that we acknowledge the following impacts that clients have on our lives and relationships:

The privilege that we experience as persons invite us into their lives in various ways, and the real effects of this privilege

The inspiration that we experience in our work as we witness persons changing their lives despite formidable odds and as we experience the real effects of this inspiration in our lives

The new and special associations that we experience and that enrich our lives

The joy that we experience as we are made privy to the extent to which persons are able to intervene in their own lives to bring about preferred changes and as we join with them in their celebration of these changes

The special metaphors persons introduce us to that provide us with thinking tools in other situations; the interactions they provide that enable us to extend the limits of our thinking and fill gaps in our own self-narratives; the contributions they make to the sustenance of our vision and our commitment to this work

White's acknowledgments are inspirational, containing a spiritual dimension. They privilege the relationship between self and other, a considerably different view than that found in most traditional psychology. Moreover, to think and act in this manner is consistent with Buddhist tradition. There is full recognition of the other as affecting self and even an exchange of self for the other (Chödrön, 1994).

Conclusion

One of the concepts I wanted to support and promote in this chapter is that when people are experiencing difficulties, they are stuck in a particular narrative from which they are unable to free themselves. It may be a narrative of depression, anger, pain, disappointment, or some similar feeling. Gaining relief from this narrative involves shifting to another narrative that is more desirable and does not generate the same uncomfortable feelings or actions. Both Buddhism and the narrative approach expound on this idea. In Buddhism, the uncomfortable narrative is generated by our clinging to what is pleasurable or pushing away what is unpleasant. These objects of attachment come from our social interactions. In the narrative approach, difficulties are generated when we are captured by dominant narratives supported by the local and larger culture.

Both the narrative approach and Buddhism privilege reflexivity. This process of using self-examination in our personal and professional everyday lives is a mode of liberating ourselves from falling blindly into subjugating narratives; it renews our sense of personal agency. While Buddhism cannot replace therapy, a therapy informed by Buddhism can offer an expanded view of the world and of the immediate real effects of our thoughts and actions on others, breaking down the barriers between self and other. Perhaps such an integration of East and West can help us distinguish, value, and accept both the similarities and differences of people in our diverse world.

References

American Psychiatric Association. (1994). *Diagnostic and statistical manual of mental disorders* (4th ed.). Washington, DC: Author.

Andersen, T. (1987). The reflecting team: Dialogue and meta- dialogue in clinical work. *Family Process, 26,* 415–428.

Andersen, T. (Ed.). (1991). *The reflecting team: Dialogues and dialogues about the dialogues.* New York: W.W. Norton.

Andersen, T. (1992). Reflections on reflecting with families. In S. McNamee & K. J. Gergen (Eds.), *Therapy as social construction* (pp. 54–68). Newbury Park, CA: Sage.

Anderson, H. (1993). On a roller coaster: A collaborative language systems approach to therapy. In S. Friedman (Ed.), *The new language of change: Constructive collaboration in psychotherapy* (pp. 323–344). New York: Guilford Press.

Anderson, H., & Goolishian, H. A. (1988). Human systems as linguistic systems: Preliminary and evolving ideas about the implications for clinical theory. *Family Process, 27,* 371–393.

Bateson, G. (1972). *Steps to an ecology of mind.* New York: Ballantine Books.

Bateson, M. C. (1994, October). *Conversations as ecology.* Paper presented at the conference New Voices in Human Systems, Northampton, MA.

Butterfield, S. (1994). Accusing the tiger: Sexual ethics and Buddhist teachers. *Tricycle, 1,* 46–51.

Chödrön, P. (1991). *The wisdom of no escape.* Boston: Shambhala.

Chödrön, P. (1994). *Start where you are.* Boston: Shambhala.

Dass, R. (1974). *The only dance there is.* New York: Anchor Books.

Davidson, J., Lax, W., Lussardi, D., Miller, D., & Ratheau, M. (1988). The reflecting team. *The Family Therapy Networker, 12,* 44–46.

de Shazer, S. (1982). *Patterns of brief family therapy: An ecosystems approach*. New York: Guilford Press.

Derrida, J. (1976). *Of grammatology* (G. C. Spivak, Trans.). Baltimore, MD: Johns Hopkins University Press. (Original work published 1967)

Dickerson, V., & Zimmerman, J. (1992). Families with adolescents: Escaping problem lifestyles. *Family Process, 31*, 341–353.

Epstein, M. (1995). *Thoughts without a thinker*. New York: Basic Books.

Epston, D., & White, M. (1992). *Experience, contradiction, narrative & imagination: Selected papers of David Epston & Michael White*. Adelaide: Dulwich Centre Press.

Gadamer, H. G. (1975). *Truth and method*. (G. Burden & J. Cumming, Trans.). New York: Seabury Press. New York: Continuum.

Gergen, K. J. (1989). Warranting voice and the elaboration of self. In J. Shotter & K. J. Gergen (Eds.), *Texts of identity* (pp. 70–81). Newbury Park, CA: Sage.

Gergen, K. J. (1991). *The saturated self: Dilemmas of identity in contemporary life*. New York: Basic Books.

Goldstein, J. (1994). *Insight meditation: The practice of freedom*. Boston: Shambhala.

Goldstein, J., & Kornfield, J. (1987). *Seeking the heart of wisdom: The path of insight meditation*. Boston: Shambhala.

Goleman, D. (1988). *The meditative mind*. Los Angeles: Tarcher.

Hoffman, L. (1992). A reflexive stance for family therapy. In S. McNamee & K. J. Gergen (Eds.), *Therapy as social construction* (pp. 7–24). Newbury Park, CA: Sage.

Hooks, B. (1994). Waking up to racism. *Tricycle, 4*, 42–45.

Hudson O'Hanlon, W., & Weiner-Davis, M. (1989). *In search of solutions: A new direction in psychotherapy*. New York: W.W. Norton.

Jameson, F. (1992). *Postmodernism, or, the cultural logic of late capitalism*. Durham, NC: Duke University Press.

Jones, S. (1994). A constructive relationship for religion with the science and profession of psychology: Perhaps the boldest model yet. *American Psychologist, 49*, 184–199.

Kerby, P. (1991). *Narrative and the self*. Bloomington: Indiana University Press.

Lax, W. D. (1989). Systemic family therapy with young children in the family: Use of the reflecting team. In J. J. Zilbach (Ed.), *Children in family therapy* (pp. 55–74). New York: Haworth.

Lax, W. D. (1992). Postmodern thinking in a clinical practice. In S. McNamee & K. J. Gergen (Eds.), *Therapy as social construction* (pp. 69–85). Newbury Park, CA: Sage.

Lax, W. D. (1995). Offering reflections: Some theoretical and practical considerations. In S. Friedman (Ed.), *The reflecting process in action*. New York:
Guilford Press.

Lyotard, J. F. (1988). *The postmodern condition: A report on knowledge* (G. Ben-
nington & B. Massumi, Trans.). Minneapolis: University of Minneapolis
Press.

Madigan, S. (1991). Discursive restraints in therapist practice: Situating therapist questions in the presence of the family. *Dulwich Centre Newsletter 3*,
13–20.

Madigan, S. (1994, November/December). Body politics. *The Family Therapy
Networker, 18*, 27.

Mellor, P. A. (1991). Self and suffering: Deconstruction and reflexive definition
in Buddhism and Christianity. *Religious Studies, 27*, pp. 49–63.

Nhat Hanh, T. (1976). *The miracle of mindfulness!* Boston: Beacon Press.

Norris, C. (1991). *Deconstruction: Theory and practice* (rev. ed.). New York: Routledge & Kegan Paul.

Parker, I. (1992). *Discourse dynamics: Critical analysis for social and individual psychology*. New York: Routledge & Kegan Paul.

Rahula, W. (1974). *What the Buddha taught*. New York: Grove Press.

Rosenau, P. (1992). *Post-modernism and the social sciences: Insights, inroads, and
intrusions*. Princeton, NJ: Princeton University Press.

Shotter, J. (1989). Social accountability and the social construction of 'you.' In
J. Shotter & K. J. Gergen (Eds.), *Texts of identity* (pp. 133–151). Newbury
Park, CA: Sage.

Shotter, J. (1993). *Conversational realities: Constructing life through language*. Newbury Park, CA: Sage.

Steier, F. (1991). Introduction: Research as self-reflexivity, self-reflexivity as
social process. In F. Steier (Ed.), *Research and reflexivity* (pp. 1–11). Newbury Park, CA: Sage.

Suzuki, S. (1975). *Zen mind, beginner's mind*. New York: John Weatherhill.

Thornton, J. (1993). Radical confidence: What is missing from eco-activism.
Tricycle, 3, 40–45.

Thurman, R.A.F. (1992). The politics of enlightenment. *Tricycle, 2*, 28–33.

Tworkov, H. (1993). No right, no wrong: An interview with Pema Chödrön. *Tricycle, 3*, 16–24.

Waldergrave, C. (1990). Just therapy. *Dulwich Centre Newsletter, 1*, 5–38.

White, M. (1989). *Selected papers*. Adelaide: Dulwich Centre Press.

White, M. (1993a). Deconstruction and therapy. In S. Gilligan & R. Price
(Eds.). *Therapeutic conversations* (pp. 22–61). New York: W.W. Norton.

White, M. (1993b, October). *The narrative approach*. Workshop presented at Ackerman Institute, New York.

White, M. (1994a, July). *The narrative approach*. Workshop presented at Family Institute of Cambridge, Cambridge, MA.

White, M. (1994b). *The politics of therapy: Putting to rest the illusion of neutrality*. Unpublished manuscript. Adelaide: Dulwich Centre.

White, M. (1994c, August). *Reclaiming our stories, reclaiming our lives*. Program presented at Camp Coorong, Australia.

White, M., & Epston, D. (1990). *Narrative means to therapeutic ends*. New York: W.W. Norton.

Zimmerman, J., & Dickerson, V. (1993). Separating couples from restraining patterns and the relationship discourse that supports them. *Journal of Marital and Family Therapy, 19*, 403–413.

Zimmerman, J., & Dickerson, V. (1994). Using a narrative metaphor: Implications for theory and clinical practice. *Family Process, 33*, 233–245.

Part IV

The Construction of Affect

8

Emotional Creativity
Theoretical and Applied Aspects

Elma P. Nunley and James R. Averill

*Man is a rational animal—so at least I have been
told. Throughout a long life, I have looked diligently
for evidence in favour of this statement, but so far I
have not had the good fortune to come across it,
though I have searched in many countries spread over
three continents.*

Bertrand Russell (1961, p. 73)

M any people view emotions in much the same light as teenagers and mothers-in-law—irrational, intolerable to live with,
and incapable of change. Psychologists use a more scientific jargon,
but they, too, have tended to treat the emotions as the wayward
adolescents or pesky in-laws of their discipline. Such an attitude on
the part of psychologists is paradoxical. Clinical syndromes are
almost synonymous with emotional disorders, and mental health
with emotional well-being. One might therefore expect mental
health professionals to be experts on the emotions. Such is not the
case. Much clinical knowledge about the emotions is intuitive and
applied rather than grounded in theory. That is not an indictment
of clinical psychology; rather, it is a comment on the field of psychology as a whole. Academic psychologists, even more than clinicians, have also neglected the emotions. Fortunately, the situation

is now changing, as evidenced, for example, by the recent *Handbook of Emotions* (Lewis & Haviland, 1993).

In this chapter, we present a social constructionist view of emotional development and change (Averill, 1980, 1984; Averill & Nunley, 1992). When the change is for the better, we speak of *emotional creativity;* when it is for the worse, of *neurosis.* The chapter is divided into two major parts: theoretical background and applications.

Theoretical Background

When analyzing emotions, two strategies are possible. The first is to analyze specific emotions, such as anger or fear; the second is to focus on processes, such as physiological arousal or cognitive appraisal, that are common to a variety of different emotions. With regard to the first strategy, a social constructionist approach has been applied to the analysis of anger (Averill, 1982, 1993), grief (Averill & Nunley, 1988), fear (Averill, 1986), hope (Averill, Catlin, & Chon, 1990), romantic love (Averill, 1985), and happiness (Averill & More, 1993). In this chapter, we adopt the second strategy; specifically, we focus on the role of concepts, beliefs, and rules in the construction of emotions in general (although, because of its centrality to the self and interpersonal relationships, we draw on the emotion of love for many of our examples).

Emotional Concepts and Vocabularies

In a philosophical one-liner, Wittgenstein (1953) observed, "If a lion could talk, we could not understand him" (p. 223). This is not because the lion would speak an unfamiliar language but because a lion's way of life is so completely different from that of a human being. What is true of language is also true of emotions: if a lion could emote, human beings could not understand the meaning of its emotions. Emotions—like languages—reflect a way of life apart from which they cannot be understood.

Lions do not talk, but people do. Hence, Wittgenstein's observation is even more applicable to cross-cultural than cross-species comparisons. Different societies encourage different ways of life, and these differences are reflected both in language and emotions. Language is, in fact, one of the primary vehicles by which people acquire the emotions of their culture. Whenever individuals learn a new emotional concept, they also learn how to be emotional in a way appropriate to the culture.

There are roughly 550 to 600 words (nouns, verbs, adjectives, adverbs) in the English language that have a clear-cut emotional connotation (Averill, 1975; Johnson-Laird & Oatley, 1989; Storm & Storm, 1987). By contrast, Lutz (1982) found no general term equivalent to "emotion" among the Ifaluk, a people of Micronesia, and only 58 words that she considered unambiguously emotional in connotation. Similarly, Howell (1981) found no general term for emotion among the Chewong of Malaysia, and only 7 words he considered indicative of specific emotions.

Do the number and kind of emotions *experienced* by the Ifaluk and Chewong differ from the emotions experienced by the typical American? We would assert yes. This is not to say that the Ifaluk or Chewong are less emotionally capable than are Americans or that they live less rich or meaningful emotional lives. Indeed, in cultures with fewer emotional terms, the terms that do exist may have a breadth and depth of meaning that is absent in more emotionally differentiated societies (Miller, 1994).

Individuals also differ in their emotional vocabularies. Some people have large and highly differentiated vocabularies; others have a more limited range of emotional concepts. Unless the range is too restricted (as happens in the case of alexithymia, discussed below), such differences do not necessarily pose a problem. In and of itself, a large or small emotional vocabulary is neither a blessing nor a curse. However, when persons with very different vocabularies need to interact, the potential for misunderstanding and conflict is great.

We do not mean to identify emotions per se with words or verbal concepts. Emotions can be conceptualized and given expression in many different ways, in art and music, for example, as well as in language. But however emotions are conceptualized and given form, the central point remains: the ways individuals think, feel, speak, and act are integrally tied to the concepts they use to categorize their emotions and make them meaningful.

Emotional Beliefs

Emotional concepts do not have meaning in isolation. Any concept is based on a network of beliefs, a kind of implicit theory or narrative structure. Beliefs about emotions can be divided into two categories: beliefs about what *is* and beliefs about what *should be*. We call beliefs of the first type *existential*, for they are about states of affairs that are presumed to exist. We call beliefs of the second type *rules*, for they comprise the shoulds and should nots of emotion.

Existential Beliefs

The category of existential beliefs can be further divided into beliefs that are factual (true in fact) and beliefs that are mythical (false but nevertheless held to be true). To illustrate this twofold distinction, consider cats. The ancient Egyptians presumably had many factual beliefs about cats (for example, that they climb trees, chase mice, and so forth), but the ancient Egyptians also believed that cats have godlike qualities. The later belief was part of their mythology.

It is often difficult to distinguish factual from mythical beliefs, especially when the myth is deeply embedded within a culture. And even when we recognize a myth as such, we may nevertheless act as though it were factual (compare the slight unease that many people experience if a black cat crosses their path—especially on Halloween or a Friday the thirteenth).

As with cats, so it is with emotions: Some beliefs about emotions are factual, based on empirical observation and scientific evidence, and some are mythical, false but held to be true based on folk tradition. The following are nine common myths of emotion that we have discussed in detail elsewhere (Averill & Nunley, 1992).

1. *The myth of the passions*. This myth finds popular expression in the notion that individuals are "gripped," "seized," and "overcome" by emotion, that the emotions are beyond personal control.

2. *The myth of emotional innocence*. This is the belief that individuals are not responsible for their emotions since, according to myth 1, emotions are out of people's personal jurisdiction.

3. *The myth of the emotional artichoke*. According to this myth, emotions—like artichokes—consist of superficial layers (leaves) and an underlying "heart." Only when the superficial layers (for example, overt behaviors) are peeled away is the heart (true essence) of the emotion revealed. The following three myths (4, 5, and 6) are common variations on this theme.

4. *The myth of primary emotions*. This myth postulates a few basic or primary emotions that presumably lie at the heart of more complex or compounded emotions. The primary emotions, according to the myth, are not further divisible, at least not in essence.

5. *The myth of true feelings*. This is the belief that the heart of the emotional artichoke consists of feelings that may or may not be recognized as such (compare the admonition, "Get in touch with your true feelings"). As in the case of primary emotions, true feelings are presumably simple and not subject to fundamental change.

6. *The myth of fervid viscera*. This is yet a third variant of the artichoke myth. It asserts that bodily changes (particularly of the viscera) are necessary, if not sufficient, conditions for emotions. Colloquially speaking, emotions are "gut reactions" and hence not subject to voluntary control.

7. *The myth of phylogenesis*. This myth reflects the belief that emotions are remnants of humans' evolutionary past (for example, of the animal in human nature). When this myth is combined with myth 4, the result is another very familiar proposition, namely, that primary emotions are innate, genetically determined patterns of response.

8. *The myth of paedogenesis.* According to this myth, individuals' emotions, if not inborn, are established during infancy and early childhood and remain basically fixed throughout life.

9. *The myth of emotional equality.* This is the belief that all people are created emotionally equal; individuals may differ in their physical or intellectual attributes, but according to this myth, everyone has the same emotional capabilities.

The myth of the passions (myth 1) has been particularly emphasized by Solomon (1976), and rightly so. It is the emotional equivalent of a creation myth. It finds expression in many common metaphors and folk sayings (Kövecses, 1990), for example, that emotions originate from "deep" within, occasionally "bubbling" to the surface like a hot fluid, only to "explode" if not released in a carefully controlled fashion. This myth also has had a profound influence on scientific theories of emotion, as discussed elsewhere (Averill, 1974, 1990).

We will resist the temptation to describe here what we believe the emotions to be "in fact," although shortly we will discuss the issue of emotional realism in general. For the moment, suffice it to say that we mean by emotion those states of affairs that in ordinary language are referred to as fear, anger, love, hope, and so forth. Fortunately, to dispel a myth, one does not need to know the complete truth, whatever that term might mean. For example, a person does not have to be versed in the latest discoveries in cosmology in order to know that the universe was not created in six tiring days. Similarly, a person need not be up on the latest research to realize that emotions are not primitive or gut reactions, beyond innovation and change. A little thought and reflection clearly indicates that human beings are the most emotional as well as the most intelligent of animals, and that human emotions vary considerably from one society to another and from one individual to another. Such would not be possible if these emotions were as primitive, invariable, and uncontrollable as the myths of emotion seem to imply.

Emotional Realism

At this point, a critic might object that by introducing a distinction between factual beliefs and myths we are reverting to a naïve realism with respect to the emotions. Our earlier reference to the beliefs of ancient Egyptians regarding cats, our critic might continue, is misleading in an important respect. Emotions are an aspect of human psychology and, unlike cats, have no existence apart from the way they are conceived and experienced. It would seem to follow that a myth of emotion, if sincerely held, would create its own reality and thus cease to be a myth in the ordinary sense.

A social constructionist position is not, however, incompatible with a kind of psychological realism. In some respects, standard emotional reactions (that is, those named in ordinary language) can be compared to hysterical conversion reactions but on a social rather than a psychological level of analysis. That is, the explanations current within a society to account for emotions need not correspond to the processes by which the emotions are constituted; and when they do not correspond, we may properly speak of the explanations as myths.

To illustrate the importance of distinguishing myth from reality, consider the case of childhood sexual abuse, currently a topic of considerable interest and controversy. Whether sexual activity with a child constitutes abuse depends, in part, on the social context. Mothers in Alorese society (Indonesia) may fondle the genitals of an infant while nursing it, and among the Hopi Indians of Arizona and the Siriono of Bolivia, it is (or at one time was) common for parents to masturbate their children. Before puberty, Ponapean girls (Caroline Islands) undergo procedures to enlarge the labia minora and clitoris. Ford and Beach (1951) describe the treatment as follows: "Old impotent men pull, beat, and suck the labia to lengthen them. Black ants are put in the vulva; their sting causes the labia and clitoris to swell" (p. 183).

In our own society, any of the above acts might be considered abusive, no matter how benign the intent. In this sense, sexual abuse is a social construction; its existence, however, is also a fact that few would want to deny. To complicate matters even further, evidence suggests that a child who has been sexually abused may forget (repress) the fact, presumably as a self-protective mechanism, only to recall the incident many years later, often under the guidance of a sympathetic therapist. The consequences for the presumed victim and alleged perpetrator can be very serious. We say "presumed" and "alleged," for memories of childhood abuse do not always correspond to reality. How often the memories are false is difficult to say. Loftus and Ketcham (1994) provide a comprehensive review of the relevant research. The title of their book, *The Myth of Repressed Memory,* suggests the need for caution when interpreting claims of childhood abuse when the *only* evidence is the recovery of long-forgotten memories and equivocal symptoms of psychological distress.

As the term "false memory syndrome" indicates, subjective (or even intersubjective) experience can be a poor guide to emotional reality. This is true not only of traumatic events ostensibly recalled but also of ongoing emotional experiences. Individuals are capable of interpreting and managing events, including their own emotional reactions, before and during as well as after an event. When the interpretation is informed by the myths of emotion described earlier, everyday emotional experiences may accrue features that are misleading at best and illusory at worst. (For a more detailed analysis, with particular emphasis on illusions of anger, see Averill, 1993.)

Rules of Emotion

Rules of emotion, the second broad category of beliefs about emotion, concern not what *is* (whether true or false) but what *should be*. Logically, *should statements* cannot be derived from *is* statements (because to do so is to employ the naturalistic fallacy), and vice versa. But that is in logic. Psychologically, there are close connections among existential beliefs, rules, and behavior: existential beliefs help determine the rules people hold, and the rules people hold help determine their behavior.

Three kinds of rules may be distinguished: constitutive, regulative, and procedural. To illustrate the distinctions, we find it helpful to begin with a nonemotional example, namely, rules in relation to language. (In actual practice, any given rule may have constitutive, regulative, and procedural aspects; for purposes of illustration, however, we have treated these aspects as though they derived from separate kinds of rules.) Thus, *constitutive rules* are the grammar of the language, without which the language would not exist. *Regulative rules* govern the way the language is spoken on particular occasions, stating, for example, that people should speak softly in a library. *Procedural rules* are the heuristics that allow people to speak effectively and fluently; they are taught, for example, in courses on rhetoric.

Similarly, we distinguish constitutive, regulative, and procedural rules of emotions. Constitutive rules help determine the kind of emotion that is experienced, for example, love rather than anger. If a constitutive rule of love is broken, the emotion of love that was being felt will be determined to have been not "true" love but some other emotion or condition (infatuation, say, or erotomania). Regulative rules determine how an emotion should be displayed. If a regulative rule of love is violated, the display will be recognized as a manifestation of love, but it will also be regarded as inappropriate under the circumstances. Finally, procedural rules determine how skillfully or effectively an emotion response is expressed. If a procedural rule of love is broken, the response may nevertheless be considered appropriate but the expression of it amateurish or boorish in execution.

Emotional Schemas

A phobic may fear a spider even though she sincerely believes it to be harmless, and a pedophile may sexually molest a child even though he honestly believes it to be wrong. How do we account for such anomalies in terms of concepts, beliefs, and rules? The answer is, we do not—at least, not entirely. From a constructionist point of view, emotions may be regarded as cognitive schemas for seeing and responding in ways characteristic of fear, anger, or any of the myriad of other emotions recognized in ordinary language. Emotional schemas (for example, that a spider is scary) differ from intellectual schemas (for example, that a particular spider is harmless) in a variety of ways (Averill, 1991; Calhoun, 1984; Epstein, 1994). Explicitly held concepts, beliefs, and rules are only part of the story.

To borrow a well-known metaphor from Freud, our consciously held concepts, beliefs, and rules are like the tip of an iceberg. What lies below the surface, however, is not a diffuse caldron of id impulses, as postulated by Freud, but rather a network of semi-articulated memories, expectancies, and response tendencies. This *cognitive unconscious* must be addressed if emotional change is to occur.

It is important to recognize that emotional schemas, considered in their entirety, differ in important respects from intellectual schemas. For example, in emotional schemas events are evaluated in terms of their relevance to the self (subjectivity) and not in terms independent of the self (objectivity). However, their differences must not be reified into separate systems of behavior, the one consisting of "lower" (biologically fixed) thought processes and the other of "higher" thought processes. To illustrate the fallacy of such reification, consider the following observation by Nietzsche in *Ecce Homo* (1908/1937) on his writing of *Thus Spoke Zarathustra:* "The notion of revelation describes the condition quite simply; by which I mean that something profoundly convulsive and disturbing suddenly becomes visible and audible with indescribable definiteness and exactness. One hears—one does not seek; one takes—one does not ask who gives; a thought flashes out like lightning, inevitably without hesitation—I have never had any choice about it" (pp. 99–100).

Creativity of the type exemplified by Nietzsche, whether in philosophy, science, or art, shares many of the features of emotional reactions. Such creativity, however, is among the highest of human achievements.

Creativity in any domain, from the most abstract to the most concrete, requires the organization and reorganization of the kind of mental activity that constitutes the cognitive unconscious. Rational discourse and problem solving form one route to change; so, too, do direct experience, observational learning, modeling, and active imagination (fantasy). In short, any technique that can facilitate intellectual creativity can also facilitate emotional creativity, and vice versa.

Emotional Creativity

The term *emotional creativity* may seem like an oxymoron. The emotional accompaniments of creative activity are well recognized, but people often find it difficult to conceive of emotions as creative products in their own right. Yet, if what we have said thus far is correct, emotions are as subject to creative change as are other forms of behavior. This point can be illustrated most easily with respect to rules of emotion, although similar considerations apply to other aspects of emotional schemas.

Due to innate predispositions and life experiences peculiar to him or her, each individual internalizes the rules of emotion differently; and when faced with a challenge to which the traditional rules of society do not seem to apply, the individual may formulate new personal rules. If the personal rules are sufficiently different from average, the resulting emotion will be idiosyncratic to the individual. On occasion, a new but idiosyncratic emotion may prove beneficial to the long-term interests of the individual or society. In the latter case, it is appropriate to speak of emotional creativity.

Stated more formally, an emotion can be considered creative if it meets, in varying degrees and combinations, three criteria: novelty, effectiveness, and authenticity (Averill & Nunley, 1992).

Novelty

An emotional response can be novel in an indefinite number of ways, depending on the standard against which it is compared. The minimal standard for an emotionally creative response is the individual's own past behavior. At a minimum, then, novelty implies flexibility, an openness to experience, a willingness to discard the old and try new ways of responding.

Effectiveness

No matter how open or flexible a response might be, it cannot be considered creative unless it is also effective in overcoming some obstacle or meeting some challenge. Stated most generally, an emotionally creative response is one that expands personal horizons and enhances interpersonal relationships.

Authenticity

An authentic response is one that stems from the self, that reflects the true interests and values of the individual. Too often a person tries to be different simply for sake of being different. Such behavior tends to be superficial; it lacks the discernment and insight required for further growth and creativity.

Neuroticism: Emotional Creativity Gone Awry

The term *neurotic* is no longer used in a technical sense to refer to a class of disorders distinct from the major psychoses. It is not even mentioned in the index of the fourth edition of the *Diagnostic and Statistical Manual of Mental Disorders* (American Psychiatric Association, 1994). Nevertheless, neurosis is a convenient generic term for those problems of living that are largely of psychological origin. That is the way we are using the term.

Neurotic disorders arise when emotional creativity goes awry. More specifically, neurosis involves behavior that is inflexible, ineffective, and inauthentic.

Inflexibility

This is the opposite side of the coin from novelty. From one point of view, neurotic behavior may be quite novel. For example, the person who torches buildings for the sheer excitement or pleasure of watching them burn (pyromania) is responding in an unusual way. The response, however, is novel only in the sense of being statistically rare within the population. When evaluated from the perspective of the person suffering from pyromania, the response has an inflexible, arthritic quality that makes it quite predictable as behavior. Unusual but inflexible responses are one of the primary characteristics of neurotic behavior in general.

Ineffectiveness

When evaluating the effectiveness of a response, it is important to keep in mind that behavior is not effective in-and-of itself but only with respect to some situation or goal. A response that is effective in one situation may be ineffective in another; and a response that is effective in the short run may be ineffective in the long run. This means that the criterion of effectiveness is often difficult to apply in practice. There is a sense in which all neurotic behavior is effective (for example, in warding off anxiety); otherwise, it would not be maintained. The situations in which neurotic behavior is effective are, however, so circumscribed that the person with this behavior is unable to live a full, productive life.

Inauthenticity

Even if a response is novel and effective, if it is also inauthentic, it is neurotic (as we are using the term). Con artists supply a good example. Such individuals may be quite flexible and effective in pursuit of their goals, and they may be relatively satisfied with life, but their behavior is a masquerade. A person does not have to feel miserable in order to be neurotic, any more than a person has to feel ill in order to be sick. There is comfort in the familiar, even if the familiar lacks authenticity.

Applications

Elsewhere (Averill & Nunley, 1992), we have explored many points of contact between emotional creativity and clinical practice, including transformations of the self, the paradoxes of pain (masochism) and pleasure (hedonism), near-death experiences and post–traumatic stress syndromes, the conflicting needs for solitude and intimacy, autonomy as the ability to mediate among conflicting needs, the role of imagination in facilitating change, and catharsis as an emotionally creative process.

In addition, laboratory studies have investigated the relation between emotional and intellectual creativity (Averill & Thomas-Knowles, 1991) as well as the creative expression of emotion in narrative and artistic form (Gutbezahl & Averill, 1994). A scale for the measurement of individual differences in emotional creativity has also been developed (Averill, 1994).

Our work on the applied level has included conducting workshops for individuals and couples on emotional creativity, and we have worked to develop new strategies for facilitating emotional change during individual psychotherapy. In the following discussion, we describe one such workshop and one individual case study.

In keeping with the theoretical issues presented earlier, we focus on three main strategies: first, clarification of the *concepts* a person uses with respect to the emotions; second, examination of the existential *beliefs* (both factual and mythical) that lend those concepts meaning; and third, exploration of the *rules* by which the existential beliefs are translated into action. (As emphasized in our discussion of emotional schemas, these are not the only strategies for change; they are, however, the only strategies that space allows us to illustrate in any detail.)

A Workshop for Couples

Seven couples participated in a weekend retreat workshop that was designed to allow them to learn more about their beliefs and rules of emotion and to improve their skills in communication and problem solving. Throughout the workshop, it was emphasized that one goal was for participants to become more emotionally creative.

Emotional Vocabularies

It is difficult for people to be emotionally creative if they do not have the appropriate words to express their feelings. So that they might gain insight into their emotional vocabularies, participants were asked near the beginning of the workshop to list the most important characteristics of a good relationship. The two concepts most frequently mentioned were love and happiness. Each participant was then asked to write (independently of his or her partner) ten synonyms and ten antonyms for love and for happiness. (We describe only the results for love.)

A total of twenty-six different synonyms for love were mentioned by two or more persons, and twenty antonyms. These synonyms and antonyms are presented in the following list. (Numbers in parentheses indicate the number of times the term was mentioned among the fourteen workshop participants. The participants mentioned a total of sixty-six synonyms and seventy-seven antonyms.)

Many of the terms listed here could be combined into broader conceptual categories. For example, among the synonyms, joy, happiness, laughter, and fun might be combined into a single category; and among the antonyms, arguments, yelling, anger, and fighting are conceptually related. The terms also differ in nuance, and depending on context, such differences can be important (for example, fun does not always lead to happiness, and not all arguments involve yelling and fighting). The main point we wish to emphasize is that no one term was mentioned by all fourteen participants. (Caring, the most frequently named synonym, was mentioned by ten participants; and hate, the most frequently named antonym, was mentioned by nine.) Even if single terms were combined in broader conceptual categories, the overlap would be less than might be expected. Although this particular sample is small, we have found such results to be typical.

When responses were compared for each couple separately, the number of shared synonyms ranged from one (one couple) to four

Couples Workshop Synonyms and Antonyms for Love.

Synonyms	Antonyms
Caring (10)	Hate (9)
Sharing (7)	Lies (6)
Trust (7)	Noncaring (5)
Joy (6)	Arguments (4)
Togetherness (6)	Hurting (4)
Understanding (6)	Untrustfulness (4)
Honesty (5)	Yelling (3)
Happiness (4)	Anger (3)
Forgiveness (4)	Fighting (3)
Intimacy (4)	Pious (2)
Touching (3)	Unforgiving (2)
Closeness (3)	Separation (2)
Dependable (3)	Cheating (2)
Laughter (3)	Not sharing (2)
Fun (3)	Leaving (2)
Commitment (3)	Apart (2)
Warmth (2)	Selfishness (2)
Loyalty (2)	Abuse (2)
Comfort (2)	Dishonesty (2)
Romance (2)	Resentful (2)
Caressing (2)	
Affection (2)	
Truthful (2)	
Friendship (2)	
Talking (2)	
Support (2)	

(three couples); and the number of shared antonyms ranged from zero (three couples) to three (three couples). Again, the lack of overlap is noteworthy.

When a couple do not share a common vocabulary with respect to a topic as central to their relationship as love, communication becomes difficult and misunderstandings are inevitable. One couple, whom we will call Al and Ginney, felt especially discouraged and frustrated. Al was temperamentally quiet, introverted, and uncommunicative; Ginney was expressive, extroverted, and fiery. These temperamental differences were exacerbated by disparity in their emotional vocabularies, especially when it came to expressions for love. Al believed that Ginney should just *know* he loved her without verbal expression, but Ginney desired to *hear* the words. Unfortunately, Al would often use an inappropriate or incorrect word according to Ginney's rules and she would then become frustrated, angry, and/or defensive. Discouraged in communication, Al would retreat further into silence, and Ginney would become even more confused and resentful. Thus, what started as sincere attempts at communication frequently ended in long periods of silence, with both partners feeling unheard and unloved. In the workshop, one of Al and Ginney's tasks was to gain a better understanding and acceptance of their temperamental differences, for such differences are unlikely to change to any great degree. Another task was to improve their pattern of communication through the development of a common emotional vocabulary.

Another couple had a somewhat different problem. Try as she might, Shannon could not list more than a few synonyms and antonyms for love. This was not because she lacked the relevant vocabulary. Rather, she had a difficult time putting her feelings into words. Shannon was later given the Toronto Alexithymia Scale (TAS-20); her score was well above the cut-off point for alexithymia (Bagby, Parker, & Taylor, 1994). Alexithymia literally means "absence of words for emotion." It is an inability to identify and name one's own emotional experiences, or perhaps it would be more accurate to say experiences in the making, for emotions that cannot be named are typically vaguely and poorly formed. People suffering from this clinical condition also tend to have an impoverished fantasy life, a reduced ability to experience positive emotions, and susceptibility to poorly differentiated negative affect (Taylor, 1994). With additional work in individual and group therapy, Shannon was able to increase significantly her capacity for fantasy and her ability to represent emotions symbolically.

Existential Beliefs

In addition to listing synonyms and antonyms, participants in the couples workshop were asked to describe (as written homework) their beliefs about, first, an ideal love relationship; second, the relationship they now had; and third, the kind of relationship they would settle for—their bottom line, so to speak. In a sense, their beliefs about ideal and bottom-line relationships bracketed or defined the space within which their current relationship might change.

The ideal that couples have of a relationship is often a kind of myth obtained from romance novels, television, or popular magazines. To the extent that such ideals present desirable goals toward which to work, they can have a valuable function. However, if the ideals are unrealistic (and they often are), they can have untoward consequences. Since few actual relationships match the ideal, a couple's current relationship may suffer by comparison. When the ideal is not made explicit, the source of dissatisfaction often remains obscure and only vaguely felt.

The bottom-line beliefs do not—or should not—represent the negative end of a continuum anchored at the positive end by the ideal relationship. Rather, the bottom line consists of the minimum requirements that must be present and whose absence suggests that a relationship should perhaps be terminated. The term *bankrupt* may be appropriate in this context. As in a business relationship, the bottom line in a love relationship should show a net gain after all costs are taken into account. Unfortunately, many people are willing to settle for less than they believe appropriate, simply because they are afraid to declare bankruptcy and move on.

When there are no overriding problems in a relationship (for example, fundamental incompatibilities in sexual matters), we have found that the bottom line typically has to do with respecting the other person's boundaries and wishes, even if the issues seem trivial to an outsider: for example, having an opposite-sex friend, inter-rupting when on the telephone, or paying (or not paying) for gro-ceries. Basically, the bottom line should be what any two long-term friends or roommates would require in order to continue to live together. Mutual respect and consideration for the other's auton-omy and tolerance for the other's idiosyncrasies are essential.

Rules of Emotion

Each individual brings into a relationship his or her own rules of emotion. As the relationship develops, those rules must be brought into congruence with each other so that emotions experienced in the relationship are compatible and mutually rewarding. Old rules must be refined to fit the new circumstances, and new rules idiosyn-cratic to the relationship must be developed. In this respect, rela-tionships are much like cultures in miniature. Each is characterized by its own set of rules and the emotions those rules help to consti-tute. Consequently, intimate relationships, if they are to last, require emotional creativity on the part of the individuals involved.

The idea that emotions can be constituted (not simply regu-lated) by rules is difficult for many people to grasp. The difficulty is due, in large part, to the myths of emotion described earlier. The best way we have found to introduce the topic of emotional rules to workshop participants is through historical and cross-cultural examples. The rules of courtly love as outlined by the twelfth-century cleric Capellanus (1180/1969) are particularly helpful as examples. For instance, one of the twelve "chief rules of love" enu-merated by Capellanus is, "Thou shall keep thyself chaste for the sake of her whom thou lovest." This sounds familiar to most listen-ers, until it is pointed out that courtly love was a relationship between a knight and his lady, each of whom might be married to someone else. Indeed, according to the courtly ideal, one could not love his or her marriage partner, for at its best, the love was to be "pure" (noncarnal).

Through a series of historical transformations, the rules of courtly love adumbrated by Capellanus still influence our current conception of love (see, for example, Hunt, 1959). Within such larger historical transformations, the norms and rules concerning love also show short-term variations. Cancian and Gordon (1988) provide numerous examples that illustrate this point. The following advice to brides from a 1932 article by Dorothy Dix in the *Ladies' Home Journal* is representative of how love and marriage were viewed earlier in the twentieth century: "Whether your marriage is a success or failure depends upon you, little bride. . . . For marriage is not only a woman's vocation, it is her avocation. It is her meal ticket as well as her romance. . . . So it is not only good ethics but good business for a young wife deliberately to set about keeping her husband in love with her (cited in Cancian & Gordon, 1988, p. 322).

Dix's advice can be contrasted with that offered in a 1974 issue of *Reader's Digest*: "If spouses are thoughtful toward each other on *all* occasions, they probably have a sick marriage" (Lederer & Jackson, cited by Cancian & Gordon, 1988, p. 309). By the 1970s, the norms for romantic relationships had shifted from an emphasis on self-sacrifice to an emphasis on self-assertion and personal fulfillment.

When we look across cultures, not just across time within a culture, we find even greater divergences in the norms and rules of love. For example, in some countries, a good Moslem may have three wives, and among the Nyinba, a group of Tibetan Buddhists, a woman simultaneously marries all the brothers in a family. Examples such as these serve to reinforce the point that romantic relationships can take many forms, all of them loving in their own way. There is no one belief system or set of rules that applies equally to all individuals or couples in love. Once the minimal requirements set by a couple are met, a wide range of possibilities exist. A couple need not be locked into one mythical ideal unless they choose to be.

Having been introduced through examples to the nature of emotional beliefs and rules, workshop participants are asked to prepare their own rules of love. Each person does this on his or her own and then shares those rules with his or her partner, working out differences and misunderstandings, if possible, but always building on the couple's bottom-line requirements for a sustainable relationship.

As we discussed earlier with respect to emotional schemas, simply stating or becoming aware of beliefs and rules does not necessarily lead to change. Once again, as an example, we draw an analogy between emotions and language. In school, people learn a foreign language (and improve their ability to write and speak their native language) with the help of books on grammar. Explicit knowledge of grammatical rules is neither necessary nor sufficient for learning a language, but it can be very helpful as part of a larger process. In a sense, the type of exercises described here provides participants with a little book of grammar (together with some vocabulary) for the emotions. However, as when people study a foreign language, the real work of learning must come through practice, and that is often a slow, arduous process extending over considerable periods of time.

Individual Psychotherapy

To illustrate further the application of a social constructionist approach to psychotherapy, we will examine in detail the case of a woman whom we will call Edie:

> Edie had an unstable and turbulent early childhood. Her mother often left her and a sibling alone for twenty to thirty hours at a time, frequently without adequate food or clothing. When Edie was five years old, she was adopted by a couple that abused her sexually, physically, and emotionally. At age eighteen, she married in order to get away from home. Two children later, she divorced her first husband because of neglect and abuse, after which he refused to be involved with the children or to assume any responsibility, financial or otherwise, for them. Edie remarried, but this second marriage also

ended in divorce. Edie was married to her third husband,
Nick, when she first came for counseling. The immediate precipitating incident was that Nick had threatened
to kill her. Shortly after starting therapy, Edie suffered a
major depression and was hospitalized for a short period.
After release from the hospital, she divorced Nick.

Due to the nature and severity of Edie's problems, her therapy was
multifaceted and lasted approximately three years. During the first
two years, she received therapy on a weekly basis. During the third
year, she came in on an as-needed basis (roughly once a month). For
part of this time, Edie was also on medication for depression.

The first year of therapy was devoted to traditional methods
(largely cognitive-behavioral). By the end of that year, Edie had
made considerable progress: she had gained fair insight into her
problems, and she had made some decisions about what she wanted
to do with her life. But try as she might, she could not be consistent
in her endeavors. During the second year, Edie systematically began
to examine her beliefs and rules about emotions, particularly love
and anger.

To make her beliefs explicit, statements that Edie made concerning relationships, love, men, and anger were rephrased in therapy sessions and pointed out to her. She was also instructed to
examine the relationships she had created (especially with men) and
to note the commonalities between them. This process required
numerous discussions over a period of six to eight months. Edie also
kept an ongoing journal in which she wrote down her thoughts, feelings, and images about relationships, love, anger, men, and women.
The following summary of Edie's beliefs about love is presented in
her own words (only slightly edited for consistency in style):

1. Love and friendship cannot coexist or mix. [Edie
   believed that she could be physically attracted only
   to men who treated her poorly, and she acted on

that belief. "Good guys" could be her friends, not her lovers.]

2. Hurt is a fundamental part of love; people who love you hurt you.

3. There is no such thing as a loving, caring relationship with a man, but if there were, it would be unbearably boring.

4. A man who cries or shows emotion is weak; therefore, a real man isn't sensitive or vulnerable.

5. Men cannot fend for themselves; they have to be pampered and taken care of by a woman. [Note the contradiction between this and the previous belief.]

6. Men are unreliable and untrustworthy.

7. A woman cannot be happy or complete unless she is in a romantic relationship.

Some of these beliefs draw on cultural stereotypes that in most contexts are relatively harmless. But when applied in an extreme and inflexible manner, even seemingly innocuous beliefs can wreak havoc in a person's life. Consider, for example, Edie's belief that "there is no such thing as a loving, caring relationship with a man; but if there were, it would be unbearably boring." Compare this with the question posed on the cover of a recent issue of the popular magazine *New Woman*: "Are nice guys boring in bed?" The answer given inside was, in effect, yes, all too often; but with proper instruction, they can be adept learners (Olson, 1994). Evidently, Edie was not alone in her belief that nice guys finish last.

After clarifying her beliefs, Edie explored her rules of love in a similar manner. As explained earlier, rules of emotion can be primarily constitutive, regulative, or procedural, and they typically combine aspects of all three types. Edie's chief rules of love were as follows:

1. One *should not* be romantically involved with a friend, because love and friendship cannot coexist.

2. A love relationship *should* be rocky, otherwise it is boring and cannot last.

3. One *should* accept the manner in which another person chooses to love even when it is hurtful; if love is refused, it may never be offered again.

4. When in love, one *should* see only the best in the other, and one *should never* be critical nor judgmental.

5. True love means total commitment of self and resources. One *should* always be available to the loved one, and one *should* share all of one's time and possessions.

6. One *should* love freely without expecting anything in return.

7. One *should* give unconditionally and constantly with no thought of herself or her own needs.

Like Edie's existential beliefs, her rules were not odd or unusual. Each can be found in one form or another in Cancian and Gordon's review (1988) of popular advice to women. Rules 4, 5, 6, and 7 were especially common during the early decades of this century. In the context of her beliefs, however, Edie's rules of love were highly dysfunctional. For example, when Edie's belief 2, "Hurt is a fundamental part of love; people who love you hurt you," was combined with her rule 3, "One *should* accept the manner in which another person chooses to love even when it is hurtful," the result was misery and self-recrimination.

Edie found it hard to acknowledge that her beliefs and rules had helped create the very type of relationships she feared. As we have noted, when considered in isolation, many of her beliefs and rules were relatively innocuous and even commonplace within the society. That is one factor that made them so difficult to recognize and modify.

After her beliefs and rules were made explicit, Edie realized that they were primarily based on her experiences as a child and reinforced by inappropriate cultural stereotypes. She was also in a position to understand why her relationships followed such a destructive pattern. However, even with this new insight, she still did not know how to change.

By necessity, Edie's therapy was multifaceted and many tricks of the trade were used. However, a central component of her therapy was for her to look for concrete evidence that would invalidate the damaging and limiting beliefs that she saw as true. Edie continued to record in her journal not only experiences with men that were destructive but also those that were satisfactory and contradictory to her beliefs and rules. An integral element of this exercise was to develop self-awareness for conscious versus automatic living, paying especial attention to her emotions, beliefs, behavior, and choices.

An important part of Edie's therapy was to imagine the kind of relationship she would like to have and the rules she would need in order to obtain what she wanted. Her new rules of love were these:

1. Love and friendship *should* go hand in hand.

2. To truly love, one *must* respect and value the other.

3. A love relationship *should* be mutually supportive.

4. Individuals *should* be willing to support spiritual growth and healing in the other, if they are truly in love.

5. To truly be strong, one *must* be gentle; and to be real, one *should* be able to cry.

6. One *should* be committed, willing, and able to resolve conflict in ways that enhance the relationship.

7. Relationships *must* be cultivated and nurtured.

8. One *should* set her own boundaries and respect the boundaries set by the other.

9. Love *should* be faithful, and it *should* honor its commitments to the other.

10. Laughter and fun *must* be an integral part of love.

These rules are hardly novel. They (or their near equivalents) can be found in many popular psychology books on love and relationships. But they were new and emotionally creative for Edie, and that is what matters. Edie was sickened, literally almost to death, of her old life patterns. Therefore, not only did she develop new concepts and rules, she made a firm commitment to assimilate them into her life. And she did just that. Within six months after developing these new rules, she met and fell in love with a *gentle*man who is kind *and* exciting. A year later, they were married, and Edie has never felt happier or been more productive in her work. Lapses have occurred, to be sure, but with the support of her husband and children, change is well established.

Conclusion

In this chapter, we have focused primarily on one aspect of a social constructionist approach to emotions, namely, that aspect that deals with concepts, beliefs, and rules. An examination of dysfunctional belief systems is a staple of most cognitive-behavioral therapies. Yet, most such therapies still treat the emotions (at least the "basic" emotions) as somehow primitive and unchanging. The distinguishing feature of a social constructionist approach is the notion of constitutive rules and their relation to emotional creativity on the one hand and to emotional disorders on the other.

Whether in group workshops or individual psychotherapy, five requirements need to be met for emotional creativity to occur (Averill & Nunley, 1992, ch. 25). The first is a sincere commitment to emotional innovation and change, in full recognition of the hardships that might be encountered at some point in the process. Emotions are inextricably related to a person's sense of self and values. Emotional innovation is likely to meet with strictures in the form of self-recrimination and/or social sanctions. The second requirement is knowledge and understanding of the emotions and creativity and of the way they may interact. Particularly important in this respect is an examination of one's beliefs, including myths and rules of emotion. The third requirement is increased awareness. When people learn to attend to their own thoughts, feelings, and reactions, they are often surprised, not only at the way they respond emotionally but also at the degree of control they actually have over their emotions. To meet the fourth requirement, people must set goals for themselves and their relationships. The more specific the goals, the greater the likelihood of change. The fifth and perhaps most important requirement is practice, practice, practice—through imagery, observation, and direct participation, people can learn to respond emotionally in different, more effective, and authentic ways.

References

American Psychiatric Association. (1994). *Diagnostic and statistical manual of mental disorders* (4th ed.). Washington, DC: Author.

Averill, J. R. (1974). An analysis of psychophysiological symbolism and its influence on theories of emotion. *Journal for the Theory of Social Behavior, 4,* 147–190.

Averill, J. R. (1975). A semantic atlas of emotional concepts (Ms. No. 1103). *JSAS Catalog of Selected Documents in Psychology, 5,* 330.

Averill, J. R. (1980). A constructivist view of emotion. In R. Plutchik & H. Kellerman (Eds.), *Theories of emotion* (pp. 305–340). San Diego, CA: Academic Press.

Averill, J. R. (1982). *Anger and aggression: An essay on emotion.* New York: Springer-Verlag.

Averill, J. R. (1984). The acquisition of emotions during adulthood. In C. Z. Malatesta & C. E. Izard (Eds.), *Emotion in adult development* (pp. 23–43). Newbury Park, CA: Sage.

Averill, J. R. (1985). The social construction of emotion: With special reference to love. In K. J. Gergen & K. Davis (Eds.), *The social construction of the person* (pp. 89–109). New York: Springer-Verlag.

Averill, J. R. (1986). The role of emotion and psychological defense in self-protective behavior. In N. Weinstein (Ed.), *Taking care: Why people take precautions* (pp. 54–78). New York: Cambridge University Press.

Averill, J. R. (1990). Inner feelings, works of the flesh, the beast within, diseases of the mind, driving force, and putting on a show: Six metaphors of emotion and their theoretical extensions. In D. E. Leary (Ed.), *Metaphors in the history of psychology* (pp. 104–132). New York: Cambridge University Press.

Averill, J. R. (1991). Emotions as episodic dispositions, cognitive schemas, and transitory social roles: Steps toward an integrated theory of emotion. In D. Ozer, J. M. Healy, & A. J. Stewart (Eds.), *Perspectives in personality* (Vol. 3a, pp. 139–167). London: Jessica Kingsley.

Averill, J. R. (1993). Illusions of anger. In J. T. Tedeschi & R. B. Felson (Eds.), *Social interactionist approaches to aggression and violence* (pp. 171–192). Washington, DC: American Psychological Association.

Averill, J. R. (1994). Emotional creativity inventory: Scale construction and validation. In N. H. Frijda (Ed.), *Proceedings of the VIIIth conference of the International Society for Research on Emotions* (pp. 227–231). Stovis, CT: International Society for Research on Emotions.

Averill, J. R., Catlin, G., & Chon, K. K. (1990). *Rules of hope*. New York: Springer-Verlag.

Averill, J. R., & More, T. A. (1993). Happiness. In M. Lewis & J. M. Haviland (Eds.), *Handbook of emotions* (pp. 617–629). New York: Guilford Press.

Averill, J. R., & Nunley, E. P. (1988). Grief as an emotion and as a disease. *Journal of Social Issues, 44*, 79–95.

Averill, J. R., & Nunley, E. P. (1992). *Voyages of the heart: Living an emotionally creative life*. New York: Free Press.

Averill, J. R., & Thomas-Knowles, C. (1991). Emotional creativity. In K. T. Strongman (Ed.), *International review of studies on emotion* (Vol. 1, pp. 269–299). New York: Wiley.

Bagby, R. M., Parker, J.A.D., & Taylor, G. J. (1994). The twenty-item Toronto alexithymia scale—I. Item selection and cross-validation of the factor structure. *Journal of Psychosomatic Research, 38*, 23–32.

Calhoun, C. (1984). Conceptual analysis and emotion. In C. Calhoun & R. C. Solomon (Eds.), *What is an emotion? Classic readings in philosophical psychology* (pp. 327–343). New York: Oxford University Press.

Cancian, F. M., & Gordon, S. L. (1988). Changing emotional norms in marriage: Love and anger in U.S. women's magazines since 1900. *Gender & Society, 2*, 308–342.

Capellanus, A. (1969). *The art of courtly love* (J. J. Parry, Trans.). New York: W.W. Norton. (Original work written approximately 1180)

Epstein, S. (1994). Integration of the cognitive and the psychodynamic unconscious. *American Psychologist, 49*, 709–724.

Ford, C. S., & Beach, F. A. (1951). *Patterns of sexual behavior*. New York: Harper-Collins.

Gutbezahl, J., & Averill, J. R. (1994). *Individual differences in emotional creativity as manifested in words and pictures*. Manuscript submitted for publication.

Howell, S. (1981). Rules not words. In P. Heelas & A. Lock (Eds.), *Indigenous psychologies: The anthropology of the self* (pp. 133–143). San Diego, CA: Academic Press.

Hunt, M. M. (1959). *The natural history of love*. New York: Knopf.

Johnson-Laird, P. N., & Oatley, K. (1989). The language of emotions: An analysis of a semantic field. *Cognition and Emotion, 3*, 81–123.

Kövecses, Z. (1990). *Emotion concepts*. New York: Springer-Verlag.

Lewis, M., & Haviland, J. M. (1993). *Handbook of emotions*. New York: Guilford Press.

Loftus, E. F., & Ketcham, K. (1994). *The myth of repressed memory: False memories and allegations of sexual abuse*. New York: St. Martin's Press.

Lutz, C. (1982). The domain of emotion words on Ifaluk. *American Ethnologist, 9*, 113–128.

Miller, W. (1994). The politics of emotion-display in heroic society. In N. H. Frijda (Ed.), *Proceedings of the VIIIth conference of the International Society for Research on Emotions* (pp. 43–46). Stovis, CT: International Society for Research on Emotions.

Nietzsche, F. (1937). *Ecce Homo* (C. P. Fadiman, Trans.). In *The philosophy of Nietzsche*. New York: Modern Library. (Original work published 1908)

Olson, K. (1994, December). Are nice guys boring in bed? *New Woman*, pp. 84–85, 134–135.

Russell, B. (1961). An outline of intellectual rubbish. In R. E. Egner & L. E. Dennonn (Eds.), *The basic writings of Bertrand Russell* (pp. 73–99). New York: Simon & Schuster.

Solomon, R. C. (1976). *The passions*. Garden City, NY: Doubleday, Anchor Books.

Storm, C., & Storm, T. (1987). A taxonomic study of the vocabulary of emotions. *Journal of Personality and Social Psychology, 53*, 805–816.

Taylor, G. J. (1994). The alexithymia construct: Conceptualization, validation, and relationship with basic dimensions of personality. *New Trends in Experimental and Clinical Psychiatry, 10*(2), 61–74.

Wittgenstein, L. (1953). *Philosophical investigations*. Oxford: Basil Blackwell & Mott.

9

Emotion and Cognition in Experiential Therapy

A Dialectical Constructivist Perspective

Jeanne C. Watson and Leslie S. Greenberg

Our primary objective in our approach to experiential therapy is the dialectical synthesis of reason and emotion. Experiential techniques help people to apprehend, symbolize, and integrate information from both their rational and experiential systems—two important parallel modes of processing information (Epstein, 1994; Greenberg, Rice, & Elliott, 1993). The relevance of a dialectical constructivist perspective for experiential therapy has been advocated by Greenberg, Rice, and Elliott (1993). As they state: "In a dialectical constructivist view, therapeutic exploration and change . . . are primarily generated by a dialectical process of synthesizing, or actively exploring contradictions between, concept and experience and by constructing new meaning through a process of differentiation and integration of experience. A dialectical constructivist view does justice both to the reality of immediate subjective emotionally based experience and to the active constructive cognitive processes by which people create meaning from immediate experience" (p. 56).

The essence of dialectics is the splitting of wholes into their constituent parts to reveal their interrelatedness, thereby making possible the creation of a new structure or framework for experience (Greenberg & Pascual-Leone, 1995). In this chapter, we focus on two dialectical processes, the first between inner experience and language and the second between symbolized experience and reflexive examination. These two processes occur in conscious awareness; however, conscious emotional experience results from a process that occurs out of awareness, an automatic dialectical synthesis of complex internal experience that produces a bodily felt response to situations. Although we will not focus here on this primary and unconscious dialectic, its product is a referent for conscious attention and is the starting point of our discussion of meaning creation in therapy.

In our view, clients confront two important tasks if they are to construct new meaning in experiential therapy. The first is to symbolize inner subjective experience and the second is to reflexively examine that experience. Both tasks involve the dialectical integration of different processes. Symbolization involves a dialectic between experience (the automatically synthesized levels of information that create a bodily felt sense) (Greenberg & Pascual-Leone, 1995) and the representation of that experience, that bodily felt sense, in language. Reflexive self-examination involves a dialectic between symbolized experience and its examination and evaluation in the light of current needs, goals, and values, in order to create new meaning and plans for future action. Both dialectical processes result in newly synthesized experience. For example, the result of experience symbolized in language might be: "I feel small and insignificant." This is a synthesis of symbol and experience. The result of reflexive examination might be: "I felt whipped by his comment and withdrew quivering. I hate myself for being such a wimp. I want to confront him and establish some limits." This is a synthesis of values, needs, and goals on the one hand and symbolized experience on the other.

In our view, emotions and action tendencies can be automatic, by which we mean they can be prereflective processes that developmentally precede representation and reflection and occur independently of them (Luria, 1976; Pascual-Leone, 1991; Taylor, 1990; Vygotsky, 1962). Much of the information about an individual's environment is apprehended, evaluated, and responded to at a preconscious level. Thus, an inherent difficulty for human beings in knowing and understanding their inner subjective experience and their social interaction is that these are continually in flux and less clearly perceptible to the actors than the experience of the physical environment. Consequently, subjective experience and social interaction with others are liable to distortion, misapprehension, and interpretation and may require negotiation with others who hold alternative views of events. This difficulty is in sharp contrast to individuals' experience of their physical environment. While representations of both the physical environment and the inner subjective experience constitute constructions of reality, representations of the physical environment are more grounded in the shared cultural and linguistic norms of an "objective reality," while representations of inner experience are more subjective. Moreover, the evanescence of inner subjective experience and social interaction makes them potentially less available to conscious awareness and thus to symbolization and reflexive scrutiny.

Symbolic representation and reflexive examination are the two fundamental activities in which clients engage during psychotherapy in order to carry out the two important tasks we have been discussing and gain knowledge and mastery of their emotions and actions. Symbolic representation and reflexive examination promote and facilitate each other as they both create and transform individuals' inner subjective experiences and their actions. Symbolic representation takes many forms, including works of visual art, musical compositions, rituals, and most ubiquitous of all, linguistic compositions. Experiential therapy emphasizes verbal modes of expression as the primary vehicle of symbolic representation. It is the symbolic representation of inner experience that makes it possible for clients to form usable representations of their expectations and characteristic ways of experiencing reality, and of the patterns of responding or personal styles of behavior that they have developed from emotionally significant past experiences (Epstein, 1994; Greenberg, Rice, & Elliott, 1993; Watson, 1992).

The second fundamental activity, reflexive examination, involves clients in consciously scrutinizing, questioning, and evaluating their experience and behavior, as well as their current needs, goals, and values, in the light of antecedents and consequences. The examination results in decisions and plans for future action. Together, clients' symbolic representation and reflexive examination of their experiences can produce moments of insight and new understanding; together, they allow clients to possess their feelings and actions rather than be possessed by them. To facilitate these ends, clients in experiential therapy are given a safe environment in which they can accomplish the two fundamental tasks of their therapy, with the aim of solving the specific affective-cognitive problems that are causing them distress.

We now turn to the role of emotions in experiential therapy and their relationship to action.

Emotions and Actions

Emotions are the result of a tacit synthesis of a variety of levels of information processing (Greenberg & Safran, 1987; Greenberg & Pascual-Leone, 1995, Leventhal, 1984). They are a fundamental human capacity, serving an adaptive problem-solving function. They inform individuals, at both conscious and preconscious levels, of the impact of their environment; they trigger reaction tendencies in response to environmental impacts; and they provide a means of communicating with others (Greenberg, Rice, & Elliott, 1993). However, an important assumption in experiential therapy is that an individual's feelings and perceptions are not truly accessible to that individual until he or she has symbolized them (Greenberg & Safran, 1987; Greenberg & Korman, 1993).

Promoting clients' access to their emotions through therapy serves a number of important functions (Greenberg & Korman, 1993). Emotions give individuals information about the significance and meaning of events; reveal individuals' needs, desires, and values; and organize individuals to prioritize goals and to act. Thus, a primary goal of experiential therapists is to evoke various emotional states in therapy so that clients can then symbolize these emotions, in awareness. Such symbolizing not only informs clients of the idiosyncratic significance particular events hold for them but also informs them of their implicit action tendencies. In addition, the evocation and arousal of emotion presents an opportunity for even traumatic experiences to be symbolized in language and for previously unexpressed or stifled emotional responses to be freely expressed and relieved, revealing and mobilizing unexpressed needs and goals. Clients' access to their emotions is an initial step toward changes in behavior and in the ways they view themselves and others (Greenberg, Rice, & Elliott, 1993; Watson & Rennie, 1994).

A process-experiential approach to therapy facilitates clients' access to their emotions and inner experiencing, using a variety of techniques (Greenberg, Rice, & Elliott, 1993). Clients can be asked to evoke past events vividly and concretely as a means of accessing the emotions they felt at the time. They can be asked to imagine a significant other in order to work on resolving lingering bad feelings toward that person. In this process, the dialectical synthesis of emotional arousal and its symbolic representation in language results in the construction of new meaning. Clients use their reevoked emotional experiences to differentiate the meanings implicit in their reactions and thus discern the impact on themselves of events and significant others. Once they have apprehended that impact, then clients can identify their characteristic responses to particular events. To put it another way, clients gain access to the tacit meaning structures that they have developed in response to specific environmental stimuli and that have been tacitly guiding their emotional responses (Greenberg, Rice, & Elliott, 1993).

Next we look more closely at symbolic representation and its instrumental role in meaning-making.

Symbolic Representation

The ability to symbolize an environment is one of the primary tools individuals use to master environments and to develop strategies for action (Dewey, 1933; Luria, 1976; Taylor, 1990; Vygotsky, 1962). In a similar vein, numerous writers have recognized that it is individuals' capacity to symbolize inner experience and thus understand it better that enhances their capacity for self-regulation and control (Harré, 1984; Orlinsky & Howard, 1986; Rennie, 1992). In psychotherapy, the human capacity to symbolically represent experience is harnessed to help clients acquire the self-knowledge and self-regulation that will allow them to formulate more satisfying strategies for acting and living. In the process of representing their internal and external experience in words, clients objectify it and make it perceptible. Thus, they consciously come to know and understand their experience in ways not possible as long as it remained out of awareness and unexpressed.

Meaning is created from the dialectical synthesis of language and *inner* experience. Thus, *conscious* experience is constituted by language, both created and transformed as it is represented in words (Dewey, 1933; Greenberg & Pascual-Leone, 1995; Taylor, 1990). Two points need to be stressed here. First, inner experience is inchoate and unclear. Only when it is translated into words or symbolically represented in some other way, a ritual or an art form, for example, does it become consciously known and understood. Second, the precise words chosen to represent the experience can transform and alter it. For example, an experience of being seen might be described as being "revealed" to the other or being "exposed" to the other. There is a great difference. "Revealed" does not connote the same sense of threat that "exposed" does. Thus, the kinds of emotions and action tendencies that the client finds implicit in his or her inner experience will depend to some extent on the terms used to describe the experience.

However, this is not to suggest that the meaning of an experience is arbitrary. The individual's dialectical construction of his or her experience in linguistic symbols is guided by an implicit, albeit inchoate, bodily felt sense and by the choosing of the words that constitute the best fit for representing the experience and giving it fuller form.

The mediation and expression of subjective experience through language results in a sense of self that can increase an individual's self-understanding. But before any of this can occur, emotional arousal must be induced.

Facilitating Emotional Arousal and Symbolic Representation

Experiential therapists can facilitate clients' emotional arousal and symbolic representation of their experience in the following ways. First, therapists can identify a focus of inquiry by attending to the problematic areas of experiencing manifested in clients' narratives. For example, a client's statements may reflect a negative self-evaluation, continued unhappiness with a significant other, or personal behavioral reactions that the client finds puzzling (Greenberg, Rice, & Elliott, 1993), the responses that Rice (1974) identified as "problematic reactions". The therapist can then have individuals appraise situations in relation to primary concerns (Frijda, 1986) or in relation to second-order needs and values.

Second, therapists can encourage clients to recreate, or reevoke, in awareness their subjective inner experience, their external environment, their interaction with others, or their internal dialogue. For example, clients might be encouraged to use either imagery or concrete and sensory language to reevoke specific situations and people. Using such kinds of language helps clients not only to recollect situations and people more clearly and accurately but also subsequently to access their own visceral, semantic, and emotional reactions to what is recollected.

Third, therapists will find that once clients have brought subjective reactions into awareness, they are in position to identify the subjective experience with words, representing its impact on them more precisely. For example, one client who entered therapy because she was very depressed and also confused as to the cause began to realize the negative impact on her of her husband's behavior. As she described the harsh, brutal way in which he spoke to her and his irresponsible activities outside the home that were detrimental to her and her family, she became aware of how humiliated and disempowered she felt in the relationship. She realized that she often suppressed her responses to his behavior for fear that he would retaliate.

Fourth, clients' symbolic representation of their experience can give them new awareness about the impact of their own feelings and actions. It offers them insight into their own characteristic behaviors and patterns of responding in different situations.

New awareness facilitates change in various ways. As experience is conceptualized, it is also circumscribed, so that some ways of viewing it may be brought into sharper focus while others recede. The symbolical representation forms a perceptual gestalt, capturing certain aspects of reality. However, as the gestalt is only a partial representation, it comes into dialectical opposition with other aspects of lived experience, against which it can be contrasted and checked. From this subsequent dialectical process, a newly organized gestalt can be formed, synthesizing novel information and providing alternative interpretations of events and inner experience.

Evaluation of a gestalt is not a rational or logical process; it is a shifting of focus, of the kind that occurs when a person shifts from seeing one image to seeing another as he or she views the well-known drawing that can be seen as the head either of a young woman or of an old hag. For example, a client who initially finds that a specific situation makes him feel overburdened and helpless may become aware almost immediately, as he symbolizes the experience, that this feeling is not a complete rendering of his experience in other aspects of his life. It may even be in sharp contrast with areas of his life in which he experiences himself as competent and in charge of his affairs. In this way, clients begin to see the links between their emotions, behaviors, other people, and events. As a result, they may be able to infer their general style of responding or a set of expectations that they have formulated from emotionally significant past experiences (Epstein, 1994; Greenberg, Rice, & Elliott, 1993; Watson, 1992). Subsequently, having attained a new level of awareness, they are able to evaluate their feelings and behavior in terms of their needs, values, and goals.

For example, one client was surprised to find herself anxious en route to a meeting with some friends whom she had not seen for some time. Exploring the problematic reaction, she realized that she was apprehensive that she might be rejected because she had initiated the contact. She recalled that she had been ostracized and humiliated as a child because her peers perceived her as too pushy. Thus, the proposition about reality that she might have inferred from her earlier experience was that if others perceive you as too intrusive or brash they are likely to reject you. And it might be this inference that was causing her present concern over initiating a meeting.

Note that it is the discovery of one's *subjective* construal that is therapeutic. Clients examine the personal validity and usefulness of their own propositions in current situations and decide whether they are appropriate or not. The objective is not to identify a personal rule in order to challenge it but merely to make it manifest so that the client can subject it to further scrutiny and evaluation to determine its personal validity and usefulness in current and future contexts.

Reflexive Self-Examination

Once clients have symbolized their experience and their personal styles of responding have become clear, both can be subjected to reflexive examination, through which events can acquire altered significance and alternative courses of action can be developed. Reflexivity, defined as radical self-examination (Taylor, 1990), has been regarded by some therapists as an intellectual exercise that deflects attention from the client's inner experience. Yet when a client engages fully in this self-reflection, his or her whole person is involved. It is *not* an intellectual exercise but a passionate commitment to the self in an attempt to come to know and realize that self in action more completely. Once clients have clearly articulated their feelings and are aware of their implicit action tendencies, they are in a position to reflect on and evaluate their actions and experiences and to create new meaning. Following this, they can choose those actions that will enable them to express themselves most fully in the present.

Reflexivity involves both individuals' instrumental and moral agencies and individuals' ability to think about feelings and actions as part of the moment-to-moment transactions in therapy (Rennie, 1988, 1992; Taylor, 1990). Instrumental agency is one's capacity to be goal oriented, independent, and autonomous in one's actions. Moral agency is one's ability to evaluate the significance of things for oneself in terms of high-order needs and values (Taylor, 1990). The significance that things have for an individual is revealed by the individual's emotions.

Clients' instrumental and moral agencies can be better understood if a distinction is made between first-order and second-order evaluations (Taylor, 1990). First-order evaluations are analogous to organismic experience: the automatic emotions that individuals experience and express. In contrast, second-order evaluations result after initial responses are subjected to reflective scrutiny and evaluation. The dialectical synthesis of information from both first-order evaluations and second-order evaluations is an important process in experiential psychotherapy, designed to facilitate enhanced well-being and greater understanding of self and others. If clients act on the basis of first-order evaluations only, their behavior remains automatic and outside of conscious control. If they act on the basis of second-order evaluations only, then their actions may become dim reflections of their own innermost needs, desires, and goals. (This result has been at the root of Rogers' observation (1959) that accessing values in therapy was unproductive.) However, if clients adequately represent both their inner experience and their second-order values, then they are in a position to negotiate a satisfying compromise between the two.

Additional Reflexive Self-Examination

In addition to evaluating their inner experience in terms of its personal meaning, clients can also use cognitive processes that are necessary to problem solving and to performing creative acts in other domains as means of additional reflexive self-examination. Three of these important activities have been identified as essential components of clients' reflexive self-examination in therapy (Watson & Rennie, 1994). First, clients need to formulate questions about, or *inquire* into, their inner experience (comprising their emotions and perceptions) and their outer experience (comprising their physical and social environments). Second, clients need to examine and *explain* their behavior and feelings as they represent them. Third, clients need to *evaluate* their behavior and experience, once they have gained an understanding of the relevant antecedents and consequences. They can also continually evaluate their representation of their experience in terms of both its goodness of fit and its strategic implications. It is in order to properly evaluate their experience once it has been adequately represented that clients need to articulate their desires, needs, goals, and values, as we have been describing.

If clients are to feel and act differently, they need to acquire a sense of control over themselves and the events in their life. An important by-product of inquiry is that it provides the inquirer with a sense of control even as it allows the relationships among various aspects of experience to be revealed (Dewey, 1933). The thinking through of alternatives and the examination of their possible implications and consequences affords people the freedom of informed choice. Inquiry is often prompted by discord, conflict, perplexity, and doubt. For example, both Dewey and Peirce see perplexity and doubt as motivating forces that propel people to seek solutions to resolve dilemmas and ambiguities and to devise methods with which to cope with them. Moreover, the nature of the problem determines its solution, which in turn determines the process of thinking (Bernstein, 1971).

Negative emotions, in particular, alert people to problematic aspects of experience that require attention, and it is often these problems that clients bring to therapy. Thus, we see the person in therapy as engaged in a search motivated by unpleasant affective arousal and by a desire to know and understand the significance of his or her experience in order to create new meaning. In experiential therapy, the questions clients pose about inner experience are termed *markers*. Therapists use these markers to identify the aspects of experience that clients may be ready to work on and to determine the information that needs to be accessed to facilitate clients' emotional arousal, symbolic representation, and reflexive examination. For example, for behavioral or emotional reactions that clients see as puzzling or too extreme in some way, therapists promote the recollection and symbolic representation of the problematic situation. In contrast, for unfinished business such as the presence of lingering bad feelings toward a significant other, therapists promote the recollection and symbolic representation of the other (Greenberg, Rice, & Elliott, 1993).

The role of reflexivity in promoting change is further illustrated by the following example. A depressed client, who felt humiliated and defeated in her marriage, began to reevaluate the extent of her husband's power in the relationship and to question whether he would really harm her if she became more assertive in her behavior with him. After some reflection, she became aware that she had seen him as more powerful than he was and recognized that he was more dependent on her than she had previously acknowledged. She resolved that she wanted to express her feelings in the relationship and to inform him when his behavior was hurtful to her. Instead of allowing her husband to dictate the rules of the house, she began to stand up to him more and assert her own priorities.

In the next section, we examine a specific change event to exemplify the dialectical processes involved in the construction of new meaning.

Exploring Problematic Reactions

Problematic reactions, as described above, are reactions that clients feel are too extreme in some way or that they find puzzling and do not understand fully. Thus, a client may be concerned about feeling and expressing intense anger toward a parent for interrupting a telephone conversation or may be puzzled at feeling constrained, as if in a straightjacket, after a minor disagreement with a family member. Often clients do not clearly understand what triggered their reactions. Their tacit self-in-the-world schemes do not match their conscious view of themselves.

During the exploration of their problematic reactions, clients reflect on and inquire into their experiences to reveal the underlying tacit meaning structures. Their own perplexity prompts them to question and examine their experience in order to understand it better. This understanding then enables them to determine alternative ways of acting in the future that will enhance and optimize their functioning. The exploration of problematic reactions facilitates clients' synthesis of their self-concept and their experience, as the therapist helps them to work with emotional arousal, symbolic representation, and reflexive examination in the way we have been discussing.

Steps Toward Resolving Problematic Reactions

Rice and Saperia (1984) are among those investigators who have advanced what is known as process-oriented research, as opposed to outcome-oriented research, in the field of psychotherapy. The approach to therapy that they have researched is grounded in

Rogers's client-centered therapy, but it has to some extent been "reconceptualized in cognitive, information-processing terms" (p. 31). On the basis of their research, Rice and Saperia developed a six-step model of the operations that clients need to perform to resolve problematic reactions successfully in therapy. The approach we have been discussing clearly draws upon this model, which has also been elaborated on by Greenberg, Rice, and Elliott (1993). It is worth noting, therefore, that the formulation in this chapter is rooted in empirically based, process-oriented research, resulting in a highly differentiated, sequenced, and operationalized set of therapeutic steps.

The first step is a statement of the problematic reaction. The second is a vivid description of the scene in which the problematic reaction was experienced. In the third step, clients differentiate their affective reactions and the salient aspects of the situation. Then, in the fourth step, they understand the impact of the stimulus situation; in the fifth, they broaden and deepen the exploration to identify a personal mode of functioning across situations; and in the sixth, they resolve the problematic reaction.

According to this model, after reevoking their situations, clients are prompted to identify important aspects of the situations to determine the stimulus that triggered their reactions, for example, an expression on a friend's face, or a tone of voice. Subsequently clients are encouraged to explore their construal of the stimuli in order to understand the subjective impact. The point in the session when clients understand their reaction and create new meaning is termed *the meaning bridge* (Rice, 1986).

The Meaning Bridge

The meaning bridge results from the dialectical synthesis of experience and symbol and illuminates the personal meaning that clients' experiences have for them, enabling them to understand their behavior differently. Subsequently, their new understanding can be subjected to reflexive examination, as they broaden and deepen their exploration of themselves to gain an understanding of a more pervasive mode of functioning that is preventing them from meeting their current needs and goals. Clients resolve their problematic reactions when they acquire a new view of their mode of functioning in the world. The dialectical synthesis of symbolized experience and reflexive examination that results in the construction of new meaning is accompanied by an awareness of how they would like to function, the self-changes necessary to do so, and a sense of being empowered to make those changes.

The empirically validated change process of the resolution of problematic reactions (Rice & Saperia, 1984; Wiseman & Rice, 1989; Watson, 1992) is illuminated by the following example. A client observed that he became very angry when his father called to him to come downstairs while he was talking to a friend on the phone. After vividly reevoking his experience and representing the situation more concretely and with greater differentiation in the therapy session, the client realized that he felt insignificant and that his father was oblivious to his needs and activities. As he represented the meaning of his father's behavior to him in the specific situation, he became aware that he often felt that his parents treated him like a child. They constantly questioned his judgment and monitored his activities as if anticipating that he was going to make a mistake. He realized that their attitude toward him had eroded his self-confidence, frequently leaving him anxious and uncertain.

The discovery of the personal significance he ascribed to his parents' attitude and behavior toward him prompted him to examine his actions, values, and goals in order to determine whether his parents' concerns were warranted on the basis of his past behavior. After careful scrutiny, he determined that while his values and goals were sometimes at odds with those of his parents, he nonetheless acted responsibly and in his own best interests. As he examined the differences between his expectations and those of his parents, he gained a better sense of his current needs and future goals. Further, he became more confident in his ability to make and implement

important life decisions successfully. He not only came to trust himself and his judgment more, but he was also able to enlist his parents' support and cooperation in implementing some significant life
changes that they had previously opposed.

During the exploration of problematic reactions, therapists attempt to promote recall expressed in vivid and evocative language
of the situation in which the reaction occurred. This vivid recall
heightens clients' access to their subjective affective experience as
it was when the external situation happened and facilitates the current representation of the experience in words (Greenberg, Rice, &
Elliott, 1993). The act of reevoking vivid internal representations
of prior external environments enhances recollection and arousal,
so that clients are in a better position to distill the essence of their
experience. After differentiating their feelings and developing more
and more adequate articulations of their inner experience, clients
become clear about the meaning of the events. As clients create
new meaning and recognize the significance to them of specific
events, schemes for action become evident and can be evaluated in
terms of clients' current desires, needs, goals, and values (Greenberg & Pascual-Leone, 1995; Piaget & Inhelder, 1941/1974).

In addition to evaluating their behavior and experience, clients
continually evaluate the accuracy of their representations by means
of an inner bodily felt sense (Gendlin, 1982). Feelings of relief and
excitement follow when the right label is found and clients have
made sense of their inner experience (Watson & Rennie, 1994).
These feelings may be accompanied by a sense of excitement and
discovery if the symbolization of subjective sense results in the creation of new meaning that enables clients to see themselves or the
world differently. Clients also examine the implications and consequences of their actions and behavior. Subsequently, they are able
to evaluate the consequences and implications of their actions, feelings, goals and values, using the empirical observations generated
by representing both their external and internal experience. They
gain insight in the form of retrospective knowledge or understand-

ing, and they see links between behaviors and feelings and identify the antecedents and consequences of these behaviors and feelings.

It is as a result of accurately labelling their subjective felt sense that clients reach a meaning bridge and are able to see why they reacted as they did (Rice, 1986). For example, a young female client was puzzled at her desperate attempts to reach out to an ex-boyfriend. After exploring the situation, she realized that she had felt bereft and isolated upon recently terminating a destructive relationship with another man. At around the same time, a number of her close friends had moved away from her city. The sense of abandonment she experienced made her panic, leading her to desperately and impulsively reach out to her ex-boyfriend to confirm that she was not totally alone. After gaining this understanding of her reaction and a better appreciation of the meaning of the events to her, she was able to reevaluate her sense of isolation. She realized that she was not as helpless and alone as she had felt and that she had more than sufficient reserves to carry on independently while circumspectly seeking and building new supports.

Emerging Patterns and Rules of Behavioral Responses

In the performance model, the meaning bridge is currently conceptualized in terms of clients' understanding of their reactions (Greenberg, Rice, & Elliott, 1993). Subsequently, clients are thought to broaden and deepen their exploration of self to identify a mode of functioning in the world. A qualitative analysis of clients' reports of their subjective experiences during the exploration of problematic reactions (Watson, 1992; Watson & Rennie, 1994) suggests that it might be more accurate to view the meaning bridge as the point at which clients formulate an inference about a general pattern of responding in various situations or about a personal style of behavior: for example, impulsively reaching out when feeling abandoned or alone or withdrawing in fear when someone is angry.

The understanding that clients acquire about why they reacted as they did in specific situations can be abstracted to indicate to clients a more pervasive mode of functioning across a variety of situations. Therapists can help clients' identify a general proposition or personal style of functioning that they may have extrapolated from previous significant emotional experiences and that they are tacitly using to guide their behavior in the current context (Epstein, 1994; Watson, 1992). Thus, if a client realizes that when she perceived a friend as angry and threatening in a specific encounter she became silent and withdrawn, the therapist can inquire whether there is something about seeing other people as threatening and angry that somehow makes the client more guarded and restrained. This type of inquiry suggests that there may be a general pattern of responding that clients engage in to organize their behavior even in different contexts.

Abstracting a personal style or a general rule that guides behavior across different situations is an important step for clients in the resolution of problematic reactions. If the meaning bridge is conceptualized as a client hypothesis about his or her general mode of functioning, the task of creating that bridge becomes clearer. First, clients' explorations of their experience may broaden as they attempt to verify whether they respond in a similar way in other contexts. Second, their exploration may deepen as they try to identify the origins of the personal style. This investigation enables them to evaluate whether the hypothesis is effective in the current situation. Third, clients can examine the implications and consequences of their responses so that reaction patterns and experience can then be looked at in the light of client values, needs, and goals, in an active attempt to devise strategies for acting that may be more personally satisfying and congruent with current life situations and goals.

The questions clients pose about their experiences can be used to orient them, directing their attention toward the salient aspects of current and past experience. They can also heighten the emotional arousal experienced by clients in the session. The questions act like compasses to guide clients and help them determine whether they have reached their destination or not. Following the exploration of problematic reactions, clients construct new meaning as they gain increased understanding of their way of being-in-the-world and their transactions with their environment. In other experiential tasks, clients construct new meaning about other aspects of their experience. For example, in resolving unfinished business, the client comes to see a significant other in new ways (Greenberg, Rice, & Elliott, 1993).

Clients often acquire a sense of control during their exploration of problematic reactions, as they come to realize that they have already formulated propositions about reality from their prior experience and have developed patterns of responding in the face of specific environmental cues and stimuli. As the architects of these propositions and patterns, clients realize that they can continue to endorse them or can revise them in the light of present experience, needs, goals, and values. In this approach, client rules are not viewed as either irrational or dysfunctional; rather, they are regarded as explaining puzzling behavior and aspects of experience. Clients of their own accord and initiative evaluate the current appropriateness of a given rule. The process of acquiring control is augmented further in experiential therapy to the extent that clients are seen as the experts on their own experience and as capable of determining the significance of things for themselves. Solutions to problems are found through the act of inquiry; they are not made for clients through the process of interpretation by the therapist.

Conclusion

The application of a dialectical constructivist perspective to experiential therapy emphasizes the dialectical synthesis of reason and emotion. The construction of new meaning may be further broken down into a dialectical synthesis between emotional experience and its symbolic representation in language and the dialectical interaction of symbolized inner experience and reflexive examination. In therapy, experiential therapists work to augment the three client

processes of emotional arousal, symbolic representation, and reflexive examination, in order to facilitate resolution of the specific
affective-cognitive problems that are causing client distress. As they
symbolize their experience, clients are in a position to gain fuller
access to their inner experience, heightened by increased emotional
arousal. Increased arousal enables them to distill the essence of their
experience and symbolize it accurately to create new meaning. In
the process, they may become aware that their descriptions of
events color the way they see the world and learn that language is
constitutive of experience. Thus, they may learn that through the
act of symbolizing experience they can alter its impact and feel differently about it.

The symbolization of experience enables clients to apprehend
the significance of events for themselves and to identify the personal styles they have developed in response to their constructions
of experience. Subsequently, they are in a better position to reflect
on their discoveries in a dialectical synthesis that enables them to
formulate alternative ways of acting and responding in specific situations. These alternatives can then be similarly examined, and
their implications and consequences assessed. In so doing, clients
achieve greater freedom to choose those courses of action that are
most likely to help them realize themselves as fully as possible in
the future.

References

Bernstein, R. J. (1971). *Praxis and action: Contemporary philosophies of human
    activity*. Philadelphia: University of Pennsylvania Press.

Dewey, J. (1933). *How we think*. Chicago: Henry Regnery.

Epstein, S. (1994). The integration of the cognitive and psychodynamic uncon-
    scious. *American Psychologist, 49*, 709–724.

Frijda, N. H. (1986). *The emotions*. New York: Cambridge University Press.

Gendlin, E. (1982). *Focusing*. New York: Bantam Books.

Greenberg, L. S., & Korman, L. (1993). Assimilating emotion into psychother-
    apy integration. *Journal of Psychotherapy Integration, 3*, 249–267.

Greenberg, L. S., & Pascual-Leone, J. (1995). A dialectical constructivist approach to experiential change. In R. A. Neimeyer & M. J. Mahoney (Eds.), *Constructivism in psychotherapy* (pp. 169–194). Washington, DC: American Psychological Association.

Greenberg, L. S., Rice, L. N., & Elliott, R. (1993). *Facilitating emotional change: The moment-by-moment process.* New York: Guilford Press.

Greenberg, L. S., & Safran, J. (1987). *Emotion in psychotherapy.* New York: Guilford Press.

Harré, R. (1984). *Personal being.* Cambridge, MA: Harvard University Press.

Leventhal, H. (1984). A perceptual motor theory of emotion. In L. Berkowitz (Ed.), *Advances in experimental social psychology* (pp. 117–182). San Diego, CA: Academic Press.

Luria, A. R. (1976). *Cognitive development: Its cultural and social foundations.* Cambridge, MA: Harvard University Press.

Orlinsky, D., & Howard, K. (1986). The psychological interior of psychotherapy: Explorations with the therapy session reports. In L. S. Greenberg & W. Pinsoff (Eds.), *The psychotherapeutic process: A research handbook* (pp. 477–502). New York: Guilford Press.

Pascual-Leone, J. (1991). Emotions, development and psychotherapy: A dialectical-constructivist perspective. In L. S. Greenberg & J. Safran (Eds.), *Emotion, psychotherapy and change* (pp. 302–335). New York: Guilford Press.

Piaget, J., & Inhelder, B. (1974). *The child's construction of quantities.* London: Routledge & Kegan Paul. (Original work published 1941)

Rennie, D. L. (1988). *Clients' agency in psychotherapy: I. The quest for personal meaning.* Paper presented at the First International Conference on Developmental Counseling, Porto, Portugal.

Rennie, D. L. (1992). Qualitative analysis of the client's experience of psychotherapy: The unfolding of reflexivity. In S. G. Toukmanian & D. L. Rennie (Eds.), *Psychotherapy process research: Paradigmatic and narrative approaches* (pp. 211–233). Newbury Park, CA: Sage.

Rice, L. N. (1974). The evocative function of the therapist. In D. A. Wexler & L. N. Rice (Eds.), *Innovations in client-centered therapy* (pp. 289–312). New York: Wiley.

Rice, L. N. (1986). *Therapist manual for unfolding problematic reactions.* Unpublished manuscript, York University, North York.

Rice, L. N., & Saperia, E. P. (1984). Task analysis and the resolution of problematic reactions. In L. N. Rice & L. S. Greenberg (Eds.), *Patterns of change* (pp. 29–66). New York: Guilford Press.

Rogers, C. R. (1959). A theory of therapy, personality, and interpersonal relationships, as developed in the client-centered framework. In S. Koch (Ed.), *Psychology: A study of a science: Vol. 3. Formulations of the person and the social context* (pp. 184–256). New York: McGraw-Hill.

Taylor, C. (1990). *Human agency and language*. New York: Cambridge University Press.

Vygotsky, L. S. (1962). *Thought and language*. Cambridge, MA: MIT Press.

Watson, J. C. (1992). *The process of change when exploring problematic reactions: An inquiry into self*. Unpublished doctoral dissertation, York University, North York.

Watson, J. C., & Rennie, D. (1994). A qualitative analysis of clients' reports of their subjective experience while exploring problematic reactions in therapy. *Journal of Counseling Psychology, 41*, 500–509.

Wiseman, H., & Rice, L. N. (1989). Sequential analyses of therapist-client interaction during change events: A task-focused approach. *Journal of Consulting and Clinical Psychology, 57*, 281–286.

Part V

Constructivist Metatheory in
Psychotherapy Integration

10

Psychoanalysis and Constructivism

Convergence in Meaning-Making Perspectives

Stephen Soldz

When I first became interested in psychology, I, like many others, was attracted to Freud and psychoanalysis. Psychoanalysis, it seemed, offered a perspective through which I could glimpse and give structure to the "deeper," more primitive aspects of human existence. Why were decent people often full of rage? Why were so many people obsessed with sex while simultaneously feeling humiliated about this obsession? Why do most curse words focus on a few body parts and on forbidden sexual relations with mothers? Psychoanalysis addressed these and myriad other issues that were ignored by other schools of psychological and social thought.

Simultaneously with my interest in psychoanalysis, I was focused on the possibilities of social change. Serious social change, it seemed, resulted from people's engaging in activity out of the ordinary and consequently construing the world in profoundly different ways. Psychoanalysis, however, provided little understanding of these processes. Psychoanalysis could help us understand why people failed to change, as Reich (1933/1970, 1934/1972) emphasized, but it contributed little to an understanding of the processes by which change did occur. A similar difficulty faced psychoanalytic contributions to the therapeutic process as well: psychoanalysis could explain patients' consistencies and resistances to change but had little to say about the processes through which change could occur. Classical psychoanalysis postulated some mysterious effect of "insight," but the great import given to the concept could hardly be understood in the terms of classical analytic theory. Furthermore, psychoanalysis seemed to have difficulty with the assumption that action and changed behavior frequently precede rather than follow changed thoughts and the insight that was so valued.

While confronting these dilemmas, I became aware, through a friend who had been George Kelly's student, of the existence of constructivist approaches to psychology. These approaches emphasized the importance of activity in human thinking and were more consistent with the awareness I had derived from my social concerns. Nearly simultaneously, I began psychoanalytic training in an institute where the dominant theory, called *modern psychoanalysis*, downplayed insight as a cause of change and, instead, emphasized the complexities of the relationship between the patient and analyst.

In the years since then, I have struggled with the relationships between the psychoanalytic and constructivist ways of understanding human functioning and the therapeutic endeavor. Kelly (1955), in his fragmentation corollary, postulated that people can maintain mutually inconsistent construct subsystems. I feel as if I am a living example of this Kellyan phenomenon, drawing as I do from psychoanalytic and constructivist theories as well as from personality trait theory (Soldz, Budman, Davis, & Demby, 1993; Soldz, Budman, Demby, & Merry, 1993a, 1993b, in press a, in press b), work in cognitive science and artificial intelligence (Soldz, 1993a), and a broad spectrum of empirical work in psychotherapy research (Soldz, 1990; Soldz, Budman, & Demby, 1992; Soldz, Budman, Demby, & Feldstein, 1990). A stream running throughout most of this theoretical and empirical work is the relation between reality and the multiplicity of perspectives we can have on it. Thus, even my most unconstructivist research has implicitly dealt with constructivist themes.

In this chapter, I explore a little of the territory I have just outlined, examining the interface of psychoanalysis and constructivist thinking, with a special emphasis on the personal construct psychology (PCP) of Kelly (1955). I first briefly examine the history of the interactions both psychoanalytic theory and constructivism have had with alternative psychological approaches. I then discuss several theoretical issues, such as the nature of reality, that workers in both traditions necessarily confront. In order to elucidate the potential for cross-fertilization between psychoanalysis and constructivism, I also present a brief account of my use of PCP in developing theoretical explanations of therapeutic phenomena inadequately construed by traditional theories. I give special emphasis to my attempts to reconstrue modern psychoanalytic clinical technique in PCP terms that make greater sense to me than do the traditional drive theory concepts in which this technique is usually couched.

Relation of Psychoanalysis to Other Schools of Thought

Psychoanalysis was developed in an applied setting, far from the university. The theory was largely developed as an explanation of the analytic practice. Shortly thereafter, analysis became institutionalized in freestanding institutes that were primarily devoted to the training of future analysts. While Freud and a number of the early analysts were extremely interested in and conversant with other intellectual traditions, this was less likely to be true of later analysts. What interest there has been in other intellectual traditions has been far more likely to be focused on the humanities and social sciences than other psychological approaches. Indeed, until recently, most psychoanalysts (at least in the United States) were M.D.s who had little psychological training other than their psychiatric residency and analytic training, neither of which were likely to involve in-depth exploration of other psychological theories. In addition, psychoanalysis had a radical self-conceptualization of its relation to previous thought that did not encourage analysts to explore other contemporary psychological theories. The sense of having developed a radically new approach, the insularity of the institutes, and the training that focused on application all contributed to the development of generations of analysts who had at best a nodding acquaintance with other psychological theories. As a result, psychoanalysis developed its own language, constructs, and traditions of theorizing, which were alien to most other psychotherapies.

During the period in which behavioral theory dominated most academic psychology, such insularity may have made sense. However, even when the cognitive revolution returned theories of the mind to psychology, relatively few thinkers tried to bridge the gaps between the psychoanalytic tradition and academically studied psychological approaches. The few efforts that were made (for example, Wolff, 1960) were largely ignored by the mainstream. In recent years, however, there has been a convergence in thematic focus among analysts and contemporary psychologists (Barron, Eagle, & Wolitzky, 1992), although, so far, this convergence has had relatively little influence on mainstream analytic thinking. For example, thinkers such as Atwood and Stolorow (1984), whose work clearly reflects constructivist themes, have preferred to orient their recent work toward phenomenology and existentialism, despite the awareness of Kelly's constructivist approach shown in their earlier work (Stolorow & Atwood, 1979; compare Soldz, 1988b).

The one major exception to the analytic authors' neglect of nonpsychoanalytic work is their interest in recent research on infants' object relations processes (Demos, 1992; Lichtenberg, 1984; Stern, 1985). However, even in this instance, it is not uncommon for those analytic authors primarily interested in clinical matters to pick and choose among the research for findings that are congruent with the authors' preexisting beliefs, rather than engage with the details of the research and its potential challenges to those beliefs. The details of the research studies have therefore yet to penetrate far into the analytic world.

Even as analytic authors have moved toward the concept that

meaning structures are at the core of psychological functioning, they have often remained ignorant of much parallel work conducted by constructivists. The main exceptions to this generalization are theoretical works based on the schema concept (Dorpat & Miller, 1992; Slap & Saykin, 1983); however, the few works that exist in this area have so far had little impact on mainstream psychoanalytic thinking or clinical practice.

Within the broader spectrum of psychodynamic theory, a number of recent works have attempted to integrate the best of psychodynamics with cognitive psychology. Much of this work is based on solid empirical research into patients' repetitive patterns of construing and behaving (Horowitz, 1987; Luborsky & Crits-Christoph, 1990; Westen, 1991). It remains to be seen, however, if this body of work will exert any significant impact on clinical practice or on psychoanalytic theorizing. Unfortunately, so far, psychoanalysts have remained largely refractory to the influence of research-based findings (Talley, Strupp, & Butler, 1994).

Nevertheless, despite the insularity of analytic thinking, psychoanalysis has been going through its own quiet revolution. Constructivist themes and conceptualizations have invaded the bastion, often with their authors unaware of, or at least not acknowledging, the broader trends in psychology with which they are in synchrony.

Since its inception, psychoanalysis has been confronted with a duality in its conceptualization of psychological functioning. One aspect of psychoanalytic thinking has employed a biological frame of reference, based upon an emphasis on unconscious derivatives of instinctual drives. A second aspect of psychoanalytic thinking has primarily investigated the individual patient's structures of meaning-making.

Both aspects of thought have roots in Freud's work. It is well known that psychoanalysis was created on the basis of Freud's work as a neurologist and under the influence of the evolutionary thought prevalent at the time (Sulloway, 1979). Thus, Freud's work as it relates to neurology and evolutionary thought can be seen as a precursor of much of both modern sexology and the biologically based approach to cognitive modeling known as connectionism, which models brain functioning in terms of neural networks of simple neuronlike structures, the strength of whose links is modified through experience (Glymour, Ford, & Hayes, in press).

The second aspect of psychoanalytic thought (that is, structures of meaning-making) has led to concentration on conceptualizing about the knowledge structures of individuals. Freud's controversial shift from conceiving of the Oedipal conflict as reality to conceiving of it as peoples' fantasy can be seen as a crucial step in the direction of a focus on knowledge structures. While this tendency was largely implicit in early analytic thought, it has become stronger in recent years. Numerous psychoanalytic authors have developed "schema" models (Dorpat & Miller, 1992), conceptualized the mind in terms of "structures of subjectivity" (Atwood & Stolorow, 1984), or emphasized the role of the reconstruction of patient narratives in therapeutic and analytic treatment (Spence, 1982). This recent work appears to increase the potential that psychoanalysis will engage with other schools of thought. A prime area for such cross-fertilization is constructivist psychology, since it, too, is concerned with the understanding of structures of subjectivity.

Relation of Constructivism to Other Schools of Thought

Recent constructivism, like psychoanalysis, has had a complex relation with other schools of thought. As much of the psychological terrain has already been mapped out by others, constructivists have often found themselves reframing classical conceptualizations in new terms, in the hope of developing a more comprehensive theory, one with human activity at its core. Thus, constructivist thinking, especially in the clinical domain, has consistently borrowed from other clinical approaches. Cognitive therapy, psychoanalysis, client-centered approaches, and gestalt therapy have all been drawn upon, while behavioral principles exert subtle influence on virtually all psychologists.

Constructivism has grown in popularity at the same time that cognitive science has developed as a new synthesis of cognitive psychology, philosophy, and artificial intelligence. While there are common themes in the two movements (Ford & Bradshaw, 1993; Soldz, 1993b), the relations between the two approaches are still unsettled. Many cognitive scientists see constructivism as a natural framework within which to conceptualize their work. However, a number of constructivists, especially the clinicians, see cognitive science as a threat to the humanistic values that they endorse. My personal opinion is that an alliance between cognitive science and constructivism is among the most exciting developments in psychology. We need to use the most advanced theoretical developments in psychology and cognitive science and combine them with psychotherapy process research to help us understand how people change and how therapy can facilitate this process. Constructivism, with its theoretical basis in human activity, seems a natural basis for this undertaking.

Convergence of Therapeutic Schools

The effort to draw upon differing approaches is part of a larger tendency in the therapy world. That tendency is the increasing recognition that no therapeutic school has a monopoly on wisdom. Efforts toward the development of eclectic and integrative approaches to therapy have flourished. They have been aided by research suggesting that while psychotherapy is effective in general, there is little evidence that one type of therapy is more effective than any other (Lambert & Bergin, 1994; Smith, Glass, & Miller, 1980). This finding has been referred to as the *dodo bird hypothesis* (Luborsky, Singer, & Luborsky, 1975), because it is the dodo bird in Lewis Carroll's *Alice in Wonderland* who declares, after a race, "*Everybody* has won, and *all* must have prizes."

Psychotherapy researchers have had two primary responses to the dodo bird hypothesis. The first has been a search for nonspecific elements that underlie therapies and to which much of their success can be attributed. For example, much research has investigated the hypothesis of Rogers (1975) that warmth, genuineness, and empathy underlie the curative power of all therapies (Soldz, 1990). This line of research has, however, gradually fizzled out, at least partly due to methodological difficulties. More recently, much research has focused on the quality of the working, or therapeutic, alliance between patient and therapist (Horvath & Greenberg, 1994). Both these lines of research explore the curative powers of the therapeutic relationship and implicitly or explicitly claim that these powers are relatively independent of particular schools of therapy.

A second response to the dodo bird hypothesis has been a greater search for an understanding of particular change processes (Rice & Greenberg, 1984). In this approach, psychotherapy researchers attempt to model precisely, in ways akin to task modeling in cognitive psychology, particular change processes that occur in psychotherapy sessions. One of the main contributions of constructivism to the understanding of psychotherapy may be a language that can describe these change processes without tying them to any one therapeutic school. Constructivist theory and personal construct psychology (PCP) in particular, because of their emphasis on structural change through human activity, are uniquely placed to play the role of common therapeutic language for describing therapeutic change processes. In fact, it is this role of metalanguage and metatheory for therapy that is, in my opinion, the primary role for constructivism. While the systematic pursuit of constructivist themes may lead to new therapeutic approaches, they should not be the primary goal. The world has more than enough schools of therapy; the last thing we need is another school. What is needed, rather, is a better understanding of the factors in our current therapies that lead to successful patient outcomes. Only then are we as clinicians likely to make real therapeutic advances.

Issues Faced by Both Psychoanalysis and Constructivism

Most comprehensive psychological theories necessarily confront a core set of theoretical issues. An examination of the way that psychoanalysis and constructivism deal with these issues elucidates areas of overlap and of continued tension between the two approaches. Thus, I briefly discuss several of these issues.

Personal Perspective and the Nature of Reality

A conceptualization of the relationship between the individual and reality is a cornerstone for any psychological theory. All theories must situate themselves somewhere between the external reality orientation of empiricism and the internal reality orientation of idealism.

Psychoanalysis and constructivism share an emphasis on reality structured by the personal perspective of the individual. In both approaches, the individual filters new experiences through already existing psychological structures. Thus, psychoanalysis has always emphasized that the present is seen through lenses developed earlier in life. Freud's famous turn toward seeing internal conflict and unconscious fantasy as playing primary roles in neurosis was a turn in this direction. No longer is the individual seen as solely the victim of fate, of the traumas that befell him or her. Rather, the individual's internal wishes, defenses, and fantasies play a primary role in how he or she will perceive the present.

However, psychoanalytic schools have differed in exactly how they see the role of reality versus fantasy and internal life. Classical ego psychology, which was the dominant tendency in American psychoanalysis in the 1950s and 1960s, was firmly wedded to a Darwinian adaptationist view in which psychological development was seen as a progressive adaptation to external reality (Hartmann, 1958; Hartmann, Kris, & Lowenstein, 1964). In this theory, psychological structures develop in order to help the individual better adapt to his or her environment. A special psychic organ, the ego, is formed largely to mediate conflicts among the internal drives manifest in the id, the superego's ideals and pangs of conscience, and the threats from the external world. The ego, fortunately, is endowed with various capacities, such as perception and cognition, that aid it in this task. Unlike earlier forms of analytic theory, ego psychology did not see the ego capacities as derived fundamentally from conflict, though they may become embroiled in psychic conflicts.

Other analytic schools took almost the opposite view. The Kleinians (Klein, Heimann, & Money-Kryle, 1955), for example, emphasized the importance of internal unconscious fantasy ("phantasy" in their literature) almost to the exclusion of external reality. For Klein (1975), various complex forms of psychic conflict are inevitable very early in life, largely irrespective of the actual experiences of the individual. Thus, unconscious fantasies of destroying the mother are omnipresent in the first few months of life, based on internal drives. Such a view tends toward pure idealism, in which psychological life unfolds driven by internal imperatives.

Others have risen to defend the honor of reality in its unmediated forms, insisting that pathology is the result of childhood trauma. While this position has had the laudable effect of reminding us that terrible things can happen to children, it has also tended to distract our attention from the individual's construal of that trauma. In the extreme view of some, any attempt by the therapist to explore an individual's personal meaning of a traumatic experience is a deplorable blaming of the victim.

For constructivism, the role of the individual's way of construing has always been primary. Existing constructs, schemas, or other psychic structures guide what individuals pay attention to in their current interactions with the world. To understand the individual is, at least partly, to understand his or her personal way of making meaning out of experience.

However, within this larger frame, constructivists, like psychoanalysts, have differing opinions of the role of reality in psychological development. The radical constructivists (Maturana & Varela,

1987; von Glaserfeld, 1984) have tended toward a solipsistic idealism in which there is no reality except for that constructed by the
individual. Kelly (1955), in contrast, adopted a pragmatic view in
which individuals develop their psychological structures, systems of
personal constructs, in order to anticipate the world. Unsuccessful
anticipations lead individuals to modify their constructs. While reality is not directly knowable in this view, people are constantly bump-
ing up against it. As a result, they develop "fallible but functional
knowledge" (Agnew & Brown, 1989), which allows them to make
sense of much of the world much of the time. It is this pragmatic
constructivism that I have in mind when I refer to constructivism.

Despite sharing a label with more moderate constructivists, radical constructivism seems to me to be radically different in intent,
as well as incoherent. After all, if the radical constructivists are right
that we each live in a solipsistic world, that it makes no difference
which interpretation of events we choose, and that "reality" plays
no role in the choice, then what is the point of their trying to convince us that they are right? Under their premises, the argument
cannot possibly have an effect on its recipient, and it would make
no difference if it did.

Neither the psychoanalytic nor the constructivist worlds have
come to a consensus regarding the nature of reality. What is needed,
in my opinion, is a form of pragmatic constructivism that acknowledges the existence and importance of the external world while
simultaneously accepting the variability of individuals' constructions of that world. Furthermore, as the label of pragmatic is meant
to indicate, such an approach would recognize that some construals work better than others, while accepting that absolute truth may
always elude us.

Psychic Structure

Both psychoanalysis and the personal construct variant of constructivism have placed great emphasis on the development of psychic structures. However, psychoanalysis emphasizes the content of

these structures, while PCP emphasizes the form. Classical psychoanalysis postulated those three psychic structures, the id, ego, and superego, which represented the individual's drives, adaptive capacities, and conscience and ideals, respectively. Opinions have differed whether these structures should be thought of as metaphorical divisions of a unitary psyche or as literal structures.

Later developments, in object relations and interpersonal theories, postulated the existence of structured representations of self and others as primary psychic structures (Greenberg & Mitchell, 1983). Recently, so-called psychoanalytic *self psychology* has put great emphasis on the development of articulated self-structures (Kohut, 1971, 1977). From the perspective of all these theories, successful development consists, at least in part, of the development of better organized and articulated psychic structures.

In constructivist theory and, most notably, in PCP, psychic structure has been a prime concern from the beginning. Much of constructivism has been guided by the Wernerian principle that the individual's development consists of differentiation accompanied by hierarchic integration (Werner, 1948). Kelly's "organization corollary" postulated that "each person characteristically evolves, for his convenience in anticipating events, a construction system embracing ordinal relationships between constructs" (1955, p. 56). A major portion of the PCP research literature has explored the implications of cognitive complexity or differentiation, supplemented in more recent years by the implications of cognitive integration (Bieri, 1955; Crockett, 1982; Landfield & Cannell, 1988; Soldz & Soldz, 1989).

Similarly, neo-Piagetian approaches concentrate on the individual's developing ability to separate the perspective of the self from that of others and to distinguish his or her own point of view from that of others (Rosen, 1985). Kegan (1982), for example, presents a developmental theory in which what was originally equated with the self is re-cognized as only part of the self and hence becomes an object available to inspection by the self. It is in this way that the acted-upon impulses of the impulsive individual become desires that can be reflected upon at a higher stage of development.

This brief survey suggests that one of the prime differences between constructivist and psychoanalytic approaches to development is whether or not one assumes that the mental lives of all individuals are concerned with the same contents. Constructivists tend to emphasize the formal development of construct systems, while psychoanalysts are more concerned with the contents of these systems. The differences are not as great as the present necessarily limited discussion suggests, however. Most constructivists in fact assume that people are embedded in an interpersonal matrix and that the individual's self and the others he or she interacts with are among the prime objects of the individual's psychic structures. Psychoanalysts, in turn, have paid increasing attention to the formal properties of psychic structures. Atwood and Stolorow (1984), for example, have written extensively about structures of subjectivity, while others (Modell, 1990; Ogden 1990; Searles, 1965) have speculated upon the structures of infantile cognition that they maintain are preserved in regressive phenomena in adulthood.

The common interest in the nature of psychic structures suggests that here is an area where cross-fertilization between constructivism and psychoanalysis could be beneficial to both. The Kellyan emphasis on cognitive differentiation and integration, along with the PCP concepts regarding the microstructure of individual construal, could usefully be combined with recent psychoanalytic emphases on the development of (largely unconscious) structures of subjectivity.

Role of the Past and of Development in Adulthood

Psychoanalysis is the paradigmatic instance of a psychology predicated on the importance of the past. Virtually all psychoanalytic schools emphasize that the "child is father to the adult," that adulthood can only be viewed as the result of forces and pressures that occurred long ago, early in life. In extreme forms, this position assumes that *most* important psychological development occurs early in life, a position with dubious research support (Vaillant, 1977).

Constructivists, in contrast, tend toward the position that life can (or should) consist of continuous growth and change. Constructivists are not likely to see the past as simply preserved in the present, as many psychoanalysts do. In the process of development, the individual's past ways of construing are applied to present experience. These ways are, however, transformed in the process. Thus, childlike symptoms in an adult cannot be understood simply as a replication of past experience; instead, the meaning of those symptoms must be understood, at least in part, in the context of the adult's present construal processes.

Most constructivists are sympathetic to the adult developmental perspective (for example, Kegan, 1982, 1994; compare Soldz, 1988a). In extreme forms of constructivism, this position tends toward a romantic view that all possibilities are open, if only we can think of them. However, this view has difficulty explaining recent research findings. McCrae and Costa (1990), for example, have presented strong evidence that personality traits are remarkably stable in adulthood (defined by them as after age thirty), contradicting most adult developmental approaches. Furthermore, McCrae and Costa explain contrary findings by showing that we remember ourselves as having changed much more than our longitudinal data warrant. Interestingly, the latter finding is consistent with constructivist thinking, dating back to Bartlett (1932), on the reconstructive nature of memory (Loftus, 1980).

It appears that the role of the past in the present and the nature of adult development are far from settled. A comprehensive theory will have to explain the place in development of both stability and change. Such an approach is fundamental if we are to understand the nature of longer-term psychotherapy with adults. Does such therapy induce fundamental personality change, or does it merely help clients accept their existing personality? Under what circumstances does change in construing processes lead to change in personality traits?

The Body and Sexuality

Perhaps the most radical impact of classical Freudian theory was to lead to (or facilitate an ongoing) reconceptualization of the role of bodily experience in the formation of the psyche. Freud's theory of psychosexual stages was more than a set of stages for development. It transformed the mind-body debate. No longer could the mind be conceptualized as independent of the baser bodily processes such as hunger, urination, and sexuality. In the Freudian view, early childhood bodily experience was constitutive of psychological structures. While often carried to the point of ridiculous extremes, this Freudian view is still the only psychology that puts many of the everyday concerns of people at the core of its theory. For example, people spend an outrageous amount of time and energy on sexual fantasy, a fact that virtually all nonpsychoanalytic theories totally ignore.

Unfortunately, psychology's ignoring of the body and of bodily experience largely carries over to constructivism. Kelly (1955), for example, suggests that core constructs can involve bodily processes but does not elaborate on the idea. His 1,200-page *The Psychology of Personal Constructs* contains only one index reference to sex (as distinct from sex role). Sexuality and bodily experience in general hardly figure in Kegan's *The Evolving Self* (1982), despite its frequent focus on adolescent development. Evidently, constructivist adolescents and adults are not like the rest of us in being obsessed with sexuality whenever we get a chance to be distracted. (It should be noted, however, that Kegan's more recent book, 1994, does discuss adolescent sexuality more fully and explicitly.)

Recent trends in psychoanalysis have resulted in a reduction of the attention given to sexuality and other bodily experiences. Reacting against early sexual reductionism, recent object relations and self psychological theories emphasize the importance of relationships in psychological development, while simultaneously downplaying the role of bodily experiences and concerns in these relationships. Many students of psychoanalytic psychotherapy today hardly hear a word about sex and the body, and many contemporary patients regard sexuality as too private to be discussed.

The role of bodily experience and sexuality in psychological functioning is an area where none of our theories are even remotely adequate. The early psychoanalytic reductionism posed certain crucial issues but failed to resolve them. The flight from the body in much contemporary cognitive psychology does not help us in this domain either. The constructivist emphasis on meaning and meaning structures can be of help if it is remembered that much of our lives are devoted to construing less lofty phenomena than the meaning of life.

After saying all of this about theory, I, too, have little to say about sexuality and the body themselves, as I, too, am at a loss to conceptualize this form of the mind-body problem. I only know that such a conceptualization is necessary if we are to develop a psychology relevant to much of daily life. I have always assumed that what we would need is a psychology of activity, in which activity is defined broadly enough to encompass what are traditionally conceptualized as thought, fantasy, and action. Some recent works by Johnson (1987) and Lakoff (1987) on bodily origins of metaphor provide intriguing first steps. One always hopes that work in neurophysiology and neuropsychology will provide illumination (Damasio, 1994). Feminism has certainly returned attention to the bodily bases of social and personal experience. But beyond these rudimentary steps, I am at a loss to proceed further.

Narrative Thinking

One of the most interesting areas of convergence between psychoanalysis and constructivism lies in the recent wave of interest in storytelling (see Chapters One, Seven, and Eleven). Many psychologists (and computer scientists) have realized that people spend much of their time constructing and telling stories (Bruner, 1990; Mishler, 1986; Riessman, 1993; compare Soldz, 1992b). It is as if a narrative wave swept over the field and many thinkers who thought they were being wildly original were, in fact, only riding a wave they had not yet consciously seen.

The narrative approach is a natural one for psychotherapists. After all, patients spend much of their time telling stories to their therapists. Why not focus some of the therapists' and theorists' attention on the act of storytelling rather than devote it solely to story content? Therapy, from this perspective, can be viewed as the process of the construction of alternative stories (Efran, 1994; Neimeyer, 1994; Vogel, 1994). This conceptualization can be traced back to Kelly (1969), at least. In his account of the development of PCP, Kelly describes his coming to realize that the therapeutic effect of Freudian interpretations was not due to their "accuracy," but rather to their placing the client's disturbing and inexplicable psychological phenomena in a context in which they make sense. Similarly, I have always assumed that the effectiveness of some of the more bizarre interpretations of Jungians or the students of Melanie Klein is due to their allowing patients to make some sense of, and grant an importance to, extremely disturbing "primitive" psychological experiences. It is the placing of these experiences in a larger context that makes them less frightening to patients.

Spence (1982) brought the narrative approach to psychoanalysis in his classic work, *Narrative Truth and Historical Truth*. In that work, he argued that historical reconstruction in psychoanalysis consists of patient and analyst creating a new story of the patient's life with better narrative qualities than the story the patient used previously and that the narrative truth of this story should not be confused with its historical accuracy. While rarely referring to explicitly constructivist work, Spence thus recreates, in a psychoanalytic context, much of the constructivist perspective on the nature of therapy. His work also poses questions about the characteristics of patient narratives that are more or less successful. Such questions implicitly introduce external reality via the back door.

Unfortunately, the narrative trend provides an opening for radical relativist views (Gross & Levitt, 1994), in which all construals of reality are of equal value. Yet it also provides exciting new directions for psychology that will be explored for years to come. This area is one particularly ripe for cross-fertilization between psychoanalytic and constructivist thinking (Luborsky & Crits-Christoph, 1990; compare Soldz, 1993c).

Shifting Frameworks of Psychotherapy

As psychoanalytic theory has moved in more constructivist directions, the conceptualization of the nature of therapy has also moved in that direction. If the individual's development of psychic structures is conceptualized as driven by a search for meaning, then therapy must involve the creation or modification of these meaning structures. One core issue in this therapeutic process is the form the new structures will take: will they derive from the client or the therapist? The psychoanalytic world is full of therapists and theorists who know exactly what issue the client is, or should be, concerned with. For some therapists, it is the return of repressed sexual drives; for others, it is splitting of the internal unconscious representations of self and others. Still other analysts, the self psychologists, are sure that clients are concerned with a fragmentation of their self-experience. These therapists emphasize that therapy should concentrate on the experience of the client; it should be *experience-near*, they say. However, that experience seems always to be conceptualized through the *therapists'* conceptual system. The client's experience turns out to be focused on exactly those issues that theory says are important.

Of course, constructivists face the same problem of imposing their constructs on clients. If human nature is centrally concerned with meaning-making, then clients must be facing difficulties in making meaning, even if they think they are concerned with how bad they feel or their difficulty in stopping using drugs. What this discussion points up, is that there is always a disjuncture between the client's point of view and that of the therapist. The therapist is always applying his or her professional constructs (Soldz, 1989, 1992a) to clients and their experience. While this occurs universally in the practice of psychotherapy, there is a criterion that provides a justification for making a commitment to some forms of psychotherapy rather than others. The claim for the superiority of some theoretical systems over others is that they facilitate the understanding of larger portions of clients' experiences and that they suggest more useful ways to facilitate client change. That is, theories are pragmatic constructions and are to be judged by their ability to generate the "fallible but functional knowledge" mentioned earlier.

Cross-Fertilization Between Psychoanalysis and Constructivism

From the perspective I have been presenting, what might cross-fertilization between psychoanalysis and constructivist psychology focus on that would be of benefit to therapists? I would argue that the reasons why psychoanalysis and constructivist psychology should be giving ideas and practices to each other are threefold.

1. Psychoanalysis is the most well developed nonbehavioral clinical approach. In particular, until very recently, psychoanalysis was relatively unchallenged as an approach for elucidating the more primitive aspects of psychological functioning that are common among our more severely disturbed clients.

2. Constructivist ideas provide a unique lens through which to view clinical material, resulting in technical innovations. For example, Kelly's emphasis on the bipolarity of personal constructs suggests to me that I should ask clients for the opposite of their problematic constructions.

3. Constructivism provides a principled theoretical approach to clinical phenomena; that is, it provides the most well developed approaches to conceptualizing the nature of structures of subjectivity and, even more importantly, the processes of change in these structures. Thus, constructivist theory can elucidate clinical phenomena that remain mysterious in other theoretical approaches.

Psychoanalytic Clinical Wisdom

Psychoanalytic ideas and practice have been under continuous development for approximately a century, far longer than any rival clinical approach except behaviorism. To the extent that clinical practice and reflection upon it are capable of generating knowledge, a proposition that is under attack these days (compare Dawes, 1994), one would expect the practice of psychoanalysis to have generated much knowledge about clients and their problems. While psychoanalysis has been challenged for decades as an approach to the psychological problems of the walking wounded, it has until very recently been virtually the only clinical approach to the severe personality disorders. And until recently, other therapists were largely unable or unwilling to treat the latter people. It should not be surprising, therefore, that psychoanalytic theory has framed much of the thinking about these difficult patients. For example, Leitner (1980) has discussed the treatment of a borderline woman within the framework of PCP; nevertheless much of his thinking clearly derives from psychoanalytic object relations approaches to severe personality disorders. Similarly, Phenninger (1994) presented a thorough discussion of the conceptualization and treatment of severely disturbed patients, which, while based in PCP, draws extensively on psychoanalytic thinkers. Much of my clinical writing, too, has reframed in constructivist terms phenomena first commented upon by psychoanalytic writers. It appears that the wisdom gained by psychoanalytically oriented therapists does provide guideposts in this difficult territory, even if we choose to encapsulate this guidance in different theoretical frameworks.

Reconceptualizing Hostility

As an example of this reconceptualizing process, I can describe the way I have puzzled over and conceptualized the hostility that is prevalent among severely disturbed patients (Soldz, 1983). Rage attacks are common among patients who receive the borderline diagnosis, and other forms of hostility are frequent among most patients who receive personality disorder diagnoses. That hostility is one reason clinicians often dread or avoid treating these patients.

In psychoanalytic thinking about personality disorders, however, hostility has played a regular part. Thus, in patients with what he calls a borderline personality organization, Kernberg (1975) postulates a splitting of self and object representations due to the prevalence of hostility. But where does this hostility come from? For Kernberg, it arises largely from an overabundance of a genetically endowed aggressive drive. Such an explanation is extremely speculative and is far removed from either the patient's or clinician's experience as manifested in therapy.

In pondering this phenomenon, I drew upon Kelly's definition of hostility (1955): "Hostility is the continued effort to extort validational evidence in favor of a type of social prediction which has already proved itself a failure" (p. 510). When first encountered, this definition seems rather abstract. Yet, for me, it makes more sense than do competing conceptualizations. Kelly implies that hostility arises when a person tries to understand others who are important to him or her and the explanation proves inadequate. When this inadequacy becomes apparent, the individual is faced with two choices: modify the understanding, or attempt to get the other to fit the inadequate explanation. If an individual's construct system is not very well developed or that particular explanation of the other is especially central for the individual, reconstrual may prove difficult or impossible. The hostile solution may prove preferable: try to get the other to confirm the already disconfirmed construal. Thus, for example, a patient may insist that a therapist take care of his or her every need despite the recognition that no one can always do this.

The Kellyan conceptualization of hostility has several advantages over other approaches. It can help therapists understand why patients with severe personality disorders are particularly prone to use hostility. They are the same patients whose interpersonal construct systems are not very well articulated, resulting in difficulties with understanding others. As they are not able accurately to predict others' behavior, they are regularly faced with invalidation of important interpersonal predictions, resulting in the danger that their interpersonal world will appear extremely chaotic to them. In an attempt to avoid this chaos, they therefore try to get important others to conform to the invalidated predictions. If therapists are not strong enough to withstand these patients' demands (or nurturant enough to meet them), the patients will provide further opportunities for their therapists to demonstrate strength (or nurturance), through out-of-session crises.

This conceptualization of hostility can also unify our understanding of other phenomena in severely disturbed patients. Thus, those patients labelled borderline will often construe the therapist as perfect at one moment and as an awful monster at the next. Theories of an aggressive drive have difficulty perceiving a unity between this phenomenon and the phenomenon of hostility. The PCP conceptualization, however, provides just such a unifying framework. Both the therapist's perfection and monstrousness are manifestations of hostile construing. The patient insists on forcing the therapist into a mold already known not to fit. Insisting on the therapist's perfection is as hostile as is insisting upon the opposite. The PCP view is thus able to unite a broad spectrum of clinical phenomena under one umbrella.

Object-Oriented Questions

The conceptualization of severely disordered patients in terms of insufficiently articulated construct systems can also help therapists understand the effectiveness of certain modern psychoanalytic interventions (Spotnitz, 1976) that are not well grounded in traditional theory (Soldz, 1986, 1987, 1993a). The essence of these techniques is not to challenge the constructions of the patient directly but to support them in ways that make the patient feel understood, leading to more active elaboration. Object-oriented questions, for example, accept the patient's projections onto the external world, primarily the therapist, and actively elaborate these projections (Soldz, 1986, 1993a). Thus, if a patient complains that the therapist is uninterested in her, an object-oriented approach might be to inquire what was making the therapist uninterested, thus accepting the patient's construal but asking the patient to elaborate it. Further questions could explore the patient's view of the therapist's motivations. These object-oriented questions encourage the elaboration of the patient's interpersonal construal system, leading, ideally, to greater differentiation and integration of the system. As the patient gradually develops a more articulated construct system, she is likely to feel greater safety, leading her to experiment with some of her construals. As this aspect of her system becomes more articulated, she can more afford the danger of invalidation, which no longer will lead to chaos and the loss of the ability to make sense of others.

Joining and Mirroring

Another set of modern psychoanalytic interventions is called *joining* and *mirroring*. In joining, the therapist accepts and goes along with the patient's (conscious or unconscious) belief or attitude, while in mirroring, the therapist adopts the patient's belief or attitude. An example of joining (albeit in a nonclinical context) comes from a work group that I had been leading and that was very upset about the prospect of new members coming into the group after it had been working hard for several years. Group members felt it was not right that others could come in and get the benefit of all the hard work that we had done over the years. After at first being astounded by the vehemence of the reaction, I started thinking like a clinician and grasped the underlying emotional issue: people felt that the newcomers would displace them in my eyes (much as the older child fears being displaced by the new arrival). I intervened by joining their reaction and telling them that they would always be the special ones in my eyes and that we both knew that the newcomers would never be as special. A wave of smiles swept through the group, as they both recognized their unexpressed desire and realized that it could not be met in reality. Everyone then readily agreed that it would be fine to bring newcomers into the group. In this incident, we can see the essence of joining: my acceptance of the group members' point of view allowed them freedom to reconstrue that view. If I had interpreted their unexpressed wish to be special, I think I would have induced guilt, which would also have led to an acceptance of the new members but with resentment. By accepting and joining their wish to be special, I created a safe environment in which their perceptions were not challenged, allowing them to move to a new position. In PCP terms, we can see that my joining allowed them to stop engaging in hostility, that is, repetitively attempting to elicit confirmation of a social prediction (insisting on being special forever) that has already proven invalid (they knew at some level that this was not really possible). Of course, as these group members were not seriously disturbed patients, the reconstrual took place relatively easily, once I recognized the underlying issue and responded by joining the members, in the technical sense of that word.

A Common Language for Change Processes

The previous examples have illustrated how personal construct concepts can be used to comprehend change processes that owe their origins to a variety of clinical traditions. Since the personal construct concepts are theoretically coherent formalizations of the processes through which people make sense of the world, and since these concepts are focused on processes of change, they (and concepts from related traditions in constructivism and cognitive science) can provide a common language through which hypotheses about human change processes can be formulated and tested in a theoretically coherent manner.

Conclusion

Psychoanalysis has a long and noble history, and despite recent assaults, it is not about to disappear any time soon. The clinical knowledge and intuitions developed out of the psychoanalytic tradition exert great influence on most contemporary schools of therapy. Furthermore, the issues posed by psychoanalysis regarding the role of sexuality and the body in the psychological life of both children and adults have nowhere been adequately conceptualized by rival theories. Successful understanding of these issues will be essential if a comprehensive psychology capable of understanding the frequently unexpressed concerns of people is to be developed. However, in the long run, psychoanalysis, like all theoretical approaches, will be either abandoned or superseded. It is to be hoped that the best of the psychoanalytic tradition will be retained (and transformed) in the process.

Constructivism is at an earlier stage of its development and is still striving to develop a comprehensive framework for psychological theorizing. To this task, it brings great promise. The level of meaning-making structures with which constructivism is concerned is among the most promising for uniting the disparate phenomena of everyday life and clinical practice. Constructivism, however, means many things to its adherents. It remains to be seen if the current large-scale interest will continue and if the theoretical tensions will be resolved or will lead to fragmentation and the development of rival schools. Personally, I am skeptical that there is enough convergence between radical and pragmatic constructivists for the two to share a common label. In any case, the evolving constructivist traditions will need to confront the issues raised by the psychoanalytic tradition if they are to develop into a comprehensive framework for understanding and guiding the process of psychotherapy, much less into a comprehensive psychological theory.

References

Agnew, N. M., & Brown, J. L. (1989). Foundations for a theory of knowing: II. Fallible but functional knowledge. *Canadian Psychology, 30*, 168–183.

Atwood, G. E., & Stolorow, R. D. (1984). *Structures of subjectivity*. Hillsdale, NJ: Analytic Press.

Barron, J. W., Eagle, M. N., & Wolitzky, D. L. (Eds.). (1992). *Interface of psychoanalysis and psychology*. Washington, DC: American Psychological Association.

Bartlett, F. C. (1932). *Remembering: A study in experimental social psychology*. New York: Cambridge University Press.

Bieri, J. (1955). Cognitive complexity-simplicity and prediction behavior. *Journal of Abnormal and Social Psychology, 51,* 263–268.

Bruner, J. (1990). *Acts of meaning*. Cambridge, MA: Harvard University Press.

Crockett, W. H. (1982). The organization of construct systems. In J. C. Mancuso & J. R. Adams-Webber (Eds.), *The construing person* (pp. 62–95). New York: Praeger.

Damasio, A. R. (1994). *Descartes' error: Emotion, reason and the human brain*. New York: Putnam.

Dawes, R. M. (1994). *House of cards*. New York: Free Press.

Demos, E. V. (1992). The early organization of the psyche. In J. W. Barron, M. N. Eagle, & D. L. Wolitzky (Eds.), *Interface of psychoanalysis and psychology* (pp. 200–232). Washington, DC: American Psychological Association.

Dorpat, T. L., & Miller, M. L. (1992). *Clinical interaction and the analysis of meaning: A new psychoanalytic theory*. Hillsdale, NJ: Analytic Press.

Efran, J. S. (1994). Mystery, abstraction, and narrative psychotherapy. *Journal of Constructivist Psychology, 7,* 219–228.

Ford, K. M., & Bradshaw, J. M. (1993). *Knowledge acquisition as modeling*. New York: Wiley.

Glymour, C. N., Ford, K. M., & Hayes, P. J. (in press). The prehistory of android epistemology. In K. M. Ford, C. N. Glymour, & C. N. Hayes (Eds.), *Android epistemology*. Cambridge, MA: AAAI/MIT Press.

Greenberg, J. R., & Mitchell, S. A. (1983). *Object relations in psychoanalytic theory*. Cambridge, MA: Harvard University Press.

Gross, P. R., & Levitt, N. (1994). *Higher superstition*. Baltimore, MD: Johns Hopkins University Press.

Hartmann, H. (1958). *Ego psychology and the problem of adaptation*. Madison, CT: International Universities Press.

Hartmann, H., Kris, E., & Lowenstein, R. M. (1964). *Papers on psychoanalytic psychology*. Madison, CT: International Universities Press.

Horowitz, M. J. (1987). *States of mind: Analysis of change in psychotherapy* (2nd ed.). New York: Plenum.

Horvath, A. O., & Greenberg, L. S. (Eds.). (1994). *The working alliance: Theory, research, and practice*. New York: Wiley/Interscience.

Johnson, M. (1987). *The body in the mind*. Chicago: University of Chicago Press.

Kegan, R. (1982). *The evolving self*. Cambridge, MA: Harvard University Press.

Kegan, R. (1994). *In over our heads: The mental demands of modern life*. Cambridge, MA: Harvard University Press.

Kelly, G. A. (1955). *The psychology of personal constructs* (2 Vols.). New York: W.W. Norton.

Kelly, G. A. (1969). The autobiography of a theory. In B. Maher (Ed.), *Clinical psychology and personality: The selected papers of George Kelly* (pp. 46–65). New York: Wiley.

Kernberg, O. (1975). *Borderline conditions and pathological narcissism*. Northvale, NJ: Aronson.

Klein, M. (1975). *Love, guilt, and reparation, and other works, 1921–1945*. London: Hogarth Press.

Klein, M., Heimann, P., & Money-Kryle, R. (Eds.). (1955). *New directions in psychoanalysis*. New York: Basic Books.

Kohut, H. (1971). *Analysis of the self*. Madison, CT: International Universities Press.

Kohut, H. (1977). *Restoration of the self*. Madison, CT: International Universities Press.

Lakoff, G. (1987). *Women, fire, and other dangerous things: What categories reveal about the mind*. Chicago: University of Chicago Press.

Lambert, M. J., & Bergin, A. E. (1994). The effectiveness of psychotherapy. In A. E. Bergin & S. L. Garfield (Eds.), *Handbook of psychotherapy and behavior change* (4th ed., pp. 143–189). New York: Wiley.

Landfield, A. W., & Cannell, J. E. (1988). Ways of assessing functionally independent construction, meaningfulness, and construction in hierarchy. In J. C. Mancuso & M.L.G. Shaw (Eds.), *Cognition and personal structure* (pp. 67–89). New York: Praeger.

Leitner, L. M. (1980). Personal construct treatment of a severely disturbed woman: The case of Sue. In A. W. Landfield & L. M. Leitner (Eds.), *Personal construct psychology: Psychotherapy and personality* (pp. 102–121). New York: Wiley.

Lichtenberg, J. (1984). *Psychoanalysis and infant research*. Hillsdale, NJ: Analytic Press.

Loftus, E. (1980). *Memory*. Reading, MA: Addison-Wesley.

Luborsky, L., & Crits-Christoph, P. (1990). *Understanding transference: The CCRT method*. New York: Basic Books.

Luborsky, L., Singer, B., & Luborsky, L. (1975). Comparative studies of psychotherapy. *Archives of General Psychiatry, 32*, 995–1008.

McCrae, R. R., & Costa, P. T. (1990). *Personality in adulthood*. New York: Guilford Press.

Maturana, H. R., & Varela, F. J. (1987). *The tree of knowledge: The biological roots of human understanding*. Boston: New Science Library.

Mishler, E. G. (1986). *Research interviewing: Context and narrative*. Cambridge, MA: Harvard University Press.

Modell, A. H. (1990). The roots of creativity and the use of the object. In P. L. Giovacchini (Ed.), *Tactics and techniques in psychoanalytic therapy: Vol. III. The implications of Winnicott's contributions* (pp. 113–127). Northvale, NJ: Aronson.

Neimeyer, R. A. (1994). The role of client-generated narratives in psychotherapy. *Journal of Constructivist Psychology, 7*, 229–242.

Ogden, T. H. (1990). On potential space. In P. L. Giovacchini (Ed.), *Tactics and techniques in psychoanalytic therapy: Vol. III. The implications of Winnicott's contributions* (pp. 90–112). Northvale, NJ: Aronson.

Phenninger, D. T. (1994, July). *Personal construct approaches to severe psychopathology*. Paper presented at the Sixth North American Personal Construct Network Conference, Indianapolis, IN.

Reich, W. (1970). *The mass psychology of fascism*. New York: Farrar, Straus & Giroux. (Original work published 1933)

Reich, W. (1972). *What is class consciousness?* In L. Baxandall (Ed.), *Sex-Pol* (pp. 277–358). New York: Vintage Books. (Original work published 1934)

Rice, L. N., & Greenberg, L. (Eds.). (1984). *Patterns of change*. New York: Guilford Press.

Riessman, C. K. (1993). *Narrative analysis*. Newbury Park, CA: Sage.

Rogers, C. R. (1975). Empathic: An unappreciated way of being. *Counseling Psychologist, 5*, 2–10.

Rosen, H. (1985). *Piagetian dimensions of clinical relevance*. New York: Columbia University Press.

Searles, H. (1965). *Collected papers on schizophrenia and related subjects*. Madison, CT: International Universities Press.

Slap, J. W., & Saykin, A. J. (1983). The schema: Basic concepts in a non-metapsychological model of the mind. *Psychoanalysis and Contemporary Thought, 6*, 305–325.

Smith, M. L., Glass, G. V., & Miller, T. I. (1980). *The benefits of psychotherapy*. Baltimore, MD: Johns Hopkins University Press.

Soldz, S. (1983, June). *Hostility and the severely disturbed personality*. Paper presented at the Fifth International Congress on Personal Construct Psychology, Boston.

Soldz, S. (1986). Construing of others in psychotherapy: Personal construct perspectives. *Journal of Contemporary Psychotherapy, 16*, 52–61.

Soldz S. (1987). The flight from relationship: Personal construct reflections on a psychoanalytic therapy. In G. J. Neimeyer & R. A. Neimeyer (Eds.), *Personal construct therapy casebook* (pp. 76–89). New York: Springer.

Soldz, S. (1988a). The construction of meaning: Piaget, Kegan and psychoanalysis. *Journal of Contemporary Psychotherapy, 18,* 46–59.

Soldz, S. (1988b). Constructivist tendencies in recent psychoanalysis. *International Journal of Personal Construct Psychology, 1,* 329–347.

Soldz, S. (1989). Do psychotherapists use distinct construct subsystems for construing clients and acquaintances? A repertory grid study. *Journal of Social and Clinical Psychology, 8,* 98–112.

Soldz, S. (1990). The therapeutic interaction: Research perspectives. In R. A. Wells & V. J. Giannetti (Eds.), *Handbook of the brief psychotherapies* (pp. 27–53). New York: Plenum.

Soldz, S. (1992a). Negativity in psychotherapist evaluation of clients and personal acquaintances. *International Journal of Personal Construct Psychology, 5,* 393–411.

Soldz, S. (1992b). [Review of J. Bruner, *Acts of meaning.*] *Modern Psychoanalysis, 17,* 108–110.

Soldz, S. (1993a). Beyond interpretation: Elaboration of transference in personal construct therapy. In L. M. Leitner & N.G.M. Dunnet (Eds.), *Critical issues in personal construct therapy* (pp. 173–192). Malabar, FL: Krieger.

Soldz, S. (1993b). [Review of K. M. Ford & J. M. Bradshaw (Eds.), *Knowledge acquisition as modeling.*] *SIGGART Bulletin, 4*(4), 11–13.

Soldz, S. (1993c). [Review of L. Luborsky & P. Crits-Cristoph, *Understanding transference: The core conflictual relationship theme method* (followed by a response from the authors).] *Psychotherapy Research, 3,* 69–73.

Soldz, S., Budman, S. H., Davis, M., & Demby, A. (1993). Beyond the interpersonal circumplex in group psychotherapy: The structure and relationship to outcome of The Individual Group Member Interpersonal Process Scale. *Journal of Clinical Psychology, 49,* 551–563.

Soldz, S., Budman, S. H., & Demby, A. (1992). The relationship between main actor behaviors and treatment outcome in group psychotherapy. *Psychotherapy research, 2,* 52–62.

Soldz, S., Budman, S. H., Demby, A., & Feldstein, M. (1990). Patient activity and outcome in group psychotherapy: New findings. *International Journal of Group Psychotherapy, 40,* 53–62.

Soldz, S., Budman, S. H., Demby, A., & Merry, J. (1993a). Diagnostic agreement between the Personality Disorder Examination and the MCMI-II. *Journal of Personality Assessment, 60,* 486–499.

Soldz, S., Budman, S. H., Demby, A., & Merry, J. (1993b). Representation of personality disorders in circumplex and five-factor space: Explorations with a clinical sample. *Psychological Assessment, 5,* 41–52.

Soldz, S., Budman, S. H., Demby, A., & Merry, J. (in press a). Personality traits as seen by the self, therapists and other group members: The big five in personality disorder groups. *Psychotherapy.*

Soldz, S., Budman, S. H., Demby, A., & Merry, J. (in press b). The relation of defensive style to personality pathology and the big five personality factors. *Journal of Personality Disorders.*

Soldz S., & Soldz, E. (1989). A difficulty with the Functionally Independent Construction measure of cognitive differentiation. *International Journal of Personal Construct Psychology, 2,* 315–322.

Spence, D. P. (1982). *Narrative truth and historical truth: Meaning and interpretation in psychoanalysis.* New York: W.W. Norton.

Spotnitz, H. (1976). *Psychotherapy of preoedipal conditions.* Northvale, NJ: Aronson.

Stern, D. N. (1985). *The interpersonal world of the infant: A view from psychoanalysis and developmental psychology.* New York: Basic Books.

Stolorow, R. D., & Atwood, G. E. (1979). *Faces in a cloud.* Northvale, NJ: Aronson.

Sulloway, F. (1979). *Freud: Biologist of the mind.* New York: Basic Books.

Talley, P. F., Strupp, H. H., & Butler, S. F. (1994). *Psychotherapy research and practice: Bridging the gap.* New York: Basic Books.

Vaillant, G. E. (1977). *Adaptation to life.* Boston: Little, Brown.

Vogel, D. (1994). Narrative perspectives in theory and therapy. *Journal of Constructivist Psychology, 7,* 243–262.

von Glaserfeld, E. (1984). An introduction to radical constructivism. In P. Watzlawick (Ed.), *The invented reality: How do we know what we believe we know? Contributions to constructivism* (pp. 17–40). New York: W.W. Norton.

Werner, H. (1948). *Comparative psychology of mental development* (rev. ed.). Madison, CT: International Universities Press.

Westen, D. (1991). Social cognition and object relations. *Psychological Bulletin, 109,* 429–455.

Wolff, P. H. (1960). The developmental psychologies of Jean Piaget and psychoanalysis [Monograph 5]. *Psychological Issues, 2* (Madison, CT: International Universities Press).

11

Narrative and the Process
of Psychotherapy

Theoretical Foundations and Empirical Support

Robert L. Russell and Mary L. Wandrei

Narrative permeates life. The meanings we construct and the ways in which we tell them to each other are often given form through narrative. In fact, narrative is a primary means by which we build representations of the past, exchange objective and subjective information in the present, and forecast the future. Stories are the symbolic threads that hold together the meanings we orient to and exchange in our everyday lives.

An extensive theoretical and empirical literature focuses on narrative as a, if not *the*, fundamental means humans use to structure their everyday experience (for example, Bruner, 1986; Labov, 1972; Russell, 1991; Russell & van den Broek, 1988; Sarbin, 1986; White, 1980). In narrative, we structure the continuous stream, the chaotic and protean manifold of human experience, and gain thereby a certain degree of understanding and control over it. For this reason, as Fisher (1984, 1985) points out, narrative has become an anthropological descriptor of human existence: humans are construed as Homo narrans and not simply as Homo symbolicus or Homo sapiens. Our narrativity distinguishes us as a species.

During the last decade, substantial subareas of clinical, cognitive, and developmental psychology have been reoriented to the use of narrative concepts and narrative research (for example, Bettelheim, 1977; Bruner, 1987; Gardner, 1971; McMullin, 1986; Polkinghorne, 1988; Russell, 1987; Russell & van den Broek, 1988;

1992; Schafer, 1980; Spence, 1982; Stein, 1982; Trabasso & van den Broek, 1985). This reorientation has led scholars in these fields to face the enduring capacity of individual human beings to actively construct representations of their and others' experience. But why this reorientation now?

In section one, we tentatively trace this turn to narrative to the growing interest in expressivist and speech act theories of language. Further, we trace it to developments in the philosophy of science, in which the ban on idols of reason, such as narrative itself, has been dismissed as futile. (We use the term *idols of reason* to describe imaginative and religious forms of meaning-making activities, ones that go beyond modes of reasoning associated exclusively with logic and science and thus create an expanded version of reason.) In this way, we show that narratives share key features and functions with explanatory formalisms in science and with what have come to be called *performatives*, types of sentences that do, rather than simply describe, things. Performatives' function is not simply to describe states of affairs already in existence but instead to bring states of affairs into existence in a person's public and private life (as occurs when the bride and groom say, "I do," at a wedding).

Following this brief attempt to contextualize psychology's concern with narrativity and construction within larger intellectual developments, we catalogue in section two some of the taken-for-granted uses of narrative and narration in the common practices of clinical assessment and treatment. This catalogue will serve to highlight the many ways in which clinical psychology has previously recognized and clinically exploited the central role of narrative processes in the construction of meaning and in the processes giving rise to adaptive and maladaptive functioning. We note, however, that this use of narrative was more implicit than explicit and had not until relatively recently been run through the gauntlet of empirical exploration and validation.

In section three, we review some of our own empirical work on the role of narrative in the study of psychopathology and treatment processes. We first review the simplified three-dimensional model of narrative structure that has oriented our studies, highlighting how constructive processes take place on and through each dimension. Next, we selectively review several studies on psychopathology and treatment processes in adult and in child psychotherapy. We highlight how narrative dimensions can become targets of clinical intervention strategies.

In section four, the concluding section, we recommend how research on narrative and its use in clinical psychology can proceed in a more integrated way than at present. Because narrative is fundamental to meaning-making in both everyday life and the interaction of psychotherapy, we suggest that a focus on narrative will make the research-practice divide easier for therapists and theorists to bridge.

Narrative in Context

What is narrative? It is, first and foremost, a linguistic structure. Therefore, to talk about the therapeutic use of narrative is to implicate a large body of theoretical and empirical literature regarding the role of language in everyday life and in formal knowledge seeking in the natural and social sciences. Here, we contextualize (and, in a certain sense, motivate) clinical psychology's concern with narrative by outlining two larger but overlapping areas of intellectual concentration. We hope to lead others to appreciate how narratives are not simply instrumental pathways, by which individuals reach physical or mental realities from which they are personally detached and disembodied, but are rather the fundamental means through which lives acquire form and quality and through which science constructs its traditions and its revolutions.

Expressivism Versus Positivism

Expressivism, as a formulation of the function of language, is best understood in contrast with nominalism or positivism, in which words are understood to stand for or signify things: "If we use [words] to marshal ideas, they must be transparent. We must be able to see clearly what the word designates" (Taylor, 1985, p. 226). In the empirical tradition, words were to be clear signs or labels that pointed to objects or their attributes that were thought to exist independently from the word or label. By the late nineteenth and early twentieth century, positivism had taken a firm hold on the sciences, to the point where an empiricist terminology was suggested to be the only language "pure" enough to adequately describe the world. This observation language comprised words that could be ostensively defined by observable characteristics of things or by the relations of the empirically assessable objects described (Hempel, 1959).

The Rational Paradigm

The paradigm of language as a denotative set of descriptors has clear implications for philosophical conceptions of what it means to be human and to engage in activities designed to acquire knowledge. For example, Fisher (1984, 1985) characterizes the *rational paradigm*, in which a denotative view of the relation of words to things is presupposed. This paradigm derives from a long tradition originating with Plato and Aristotle, but it especially gained prominence and formalization in the Enlightenment. It restricted logic and rationality to cases in which valid inference and demonstrative reasoning were present, to the exclusion of dialectical and rhetorical reasoning and of all the idols of reason, whether conceived as myths, opinions, traditions, authority, values, desires, stories, or nonsense. In this view, there is little room for narrative to perform a constructive role in the search to understand reality. When reality is thought always to be already "there," language functions only to refer to that prior-existing reality.

Four presuppositions of the rational paradigm capture the positivist view of human cognition and knowledge seeking. These presuppositions implicitly underlie many theories of therapy, especially cognitive therapy, as well as scientific methodology: (1) "humans are essentially rational beings"; (2) "the paradigmatic mode of decision making and communication is argument—clear-cut inferential (implicative) structures"; (3) "rationality is determined by subject matter knowledge, argumentative ability, and skill in employing the rules of advocacy in given fields"; and (4) "the world is a set of logical puzzles which can be resolved through appropriate analysis and application of reason conceived as an argumentative construct" (Fisher, 1984, p. 4).

With the ascendence of this paradigm, narrative was relegated to literary studies. It was thought neither to provide access to valid knowledge nor to function in important ways as a cognitive form of representation.

The Narrative Paradigm

The expressivist view also has a rich philosophical history. Explicit in the work of Herder and Humboldt and other Romantics, expressivism was taken up by Nietzsche and Heidegger in the nineteenth century and later was most comprehensively formulated by Cassirer (1946) and Taylor (1985) in philosophy and by Werner (1940) in psychology. Expressivism protests against the purely designative function of language, instead emphasizing the creative reflective awareness and world-making beyond mere description that the use of language affords, insisting that ideas as such do not exist prior to their expression in language (Taylor, 1985). From this perspective, people do not first come up with ideas about the world and then invent words to describe their internal concept, with everyday language being "both too rich and too poor to represent experience adequately" (Spence, 1982, p. 36). Instead, language is the means by which they congeal particular bits of an inchoate world (Taylor, 1985) that are salient and personally or socially relevant. The expression and articulation of sense data are what make an object real to a person or community; language is therefore necessary to all higher forms of thought or memory. Thus, narratives are not fashioned out of veridical experience; rather, experience is fashioned out of narratives.

The contribution of expressivism to a narrative constructivism is its insistence that people do not have access to a reality that lies behind language as the immaculate target of reference. Instead, language creates reality: "The special symbolic forms [including language] are not imitations, but *organs* of reality, since it is solely by their agency that anything real becomes an object for intellectual apprehension" (Cassirer, 1946, p. 8). Fisher (1984) outlines the *narrative paradigm* alternative to the rational paradigm as follows: (1) "humans are essentially storytellers"; (2) "the paradigmatic mode of human decision making and communication is 'good reasons' which vary in form among situations, genres, and media"; (3) "rationality is determined by the nature of persons as narrative beings—their inherent awareness of narrative probability, what constitutes a coherent story, and their constant habit of testing narrative fidelity, whether the stories they experience ring true with the stories they know to be true in their lives . . ."; and (4) "the world is a set of stories which must be chosen among to live the good life in a process of continual recreation" (p. 78).

This alternative paradigm has been growing as the influence of the Enlightenment project has waned.

The shift in paradigms, even their opposition, may seem rather abstract. However, the way in which language helps to create reality and express who individuals are in relation to others can be shown by looking at how individual sentences function in context. There it is seen that the functions of sentences cannot be delimited to picking out bits of reality that are already there or to saying things that can be assessed for their truth values. Instead, language creates the world in which we function.

Speech Act Theories

Austin (1962), Searle (1969), and other speech act theorists also consider many, if not all, forms of language to be related to the world of "given" facts in a far more complex way than just through describing these facts. Especially in the realm of performative language, words do not describe or report things or events so much as create them. Such verbalizations (termed *illocutionary* by Austin) are neither true nor false; instead, the utterance of certain words is a constituent part of the performance of an action (Austin, 1962). Prototypic examples of performatives are, "I name this baby Elizabeth," or, "I bet you fifty dollars that the incumbents will not get reelected." Here the statement does not merely describe an inner representation of an occurrence of an event or predict that an action will take place; instead, the expression, the saying of the words, is the action itself: naming or betting.

Do only special occasions and special expressions carry out actions and thereby construct the reality individuals live in? Austin's conclusion is that the distinction between performatives and other utterances that are *constatives* (for example, "[I assert that] the world is round") is not at all clear or decisive. The constative utterance looks different from the performative utterance only because its performative stem (shown in brackets in the example) has been suppressed and deleted. Not surprisingly, Austin provides enough examples and argument to end up rhetorically asking, "When we issue any utterance whatsoever, are we not 'doing something'?" (p. 92).

Performative Language

We place narrative construction squarely in the realm of performative language, but in a triple sense. First, the very telling of a personal narrative performs a meaningful act of self-creation, one that can be analogically related to the formal act of christening, as in, "I name this ship *Adventurer*." Similarly, to tell a personal narrative, an individual must christen himself or herself as the narrator, saying perhaps, in effect, "My first person narration creates me as the adventuresome narrator/protagonist." In this way, a formal causal link becomes apparent between narrative and human agency and character. If we think of narratives as metaphors standing for who we are, the therapeutic use of a new metaphoric narrative may create a "kind of reverberation down through the network of entailments that awakens and connects our memories of our past . . . experiences, and serves as a possible guide for future ones" (Lakoff & Johnson, 1979, p. 140). Particularly in therapy, clients learn who they are through the stories that they are asked to tell and retell.

Second, the act of narration not only constructs a person as a certain type of narrator, it also constructs the listener as a certain type of *narratee* (Prince, 1988). There is a certain structural complicity, with its own politics, in the formation of the identities of the tellers and the told. What people listen to makes them who they are no less than what they say. Character is bound up in the buzz of narrative discourse at both creative poles. This circularity partially explains why narratives of oppression (concerning race, age, religion, and so forth) harm the characters of the tellers, those to whom they are told, and those about whom they are told.

The relation of narrative to character becomes evident when it is understood that the telling of stories is meant to do something interpersonally: "I the narrator assert, declare, boast, or warn the addressee that I am an [the] adventurer." The narrative constructivist model does not suppose that inside a person there is an isolated subjective world that can be transported to another person, as one would flash signals across a wasteland. Instead, construction of meaning, interpersonal acts, happen within dialogue, in the communicative public space between two or more people. According to theorists such as Vygotsky, Mead, Habermas, and Bakhtin, the development of selves, and their internality, takes place through intersubjective experience; this development is an essentially social act, as is the telling of stories.

The potential impact of narrative also lies at the heart of transformation at more global levels of human organization. For example, many liberatory political projects, including the black civil rights, women's rights, and gay rights movements have emphasized the necessity for subordinated groups to reclaim the language that constructs their experience and their power to name themselves. Women in patriarchal societies, for instance, are encouraged to tell their own stories in order to legitimize their voices and experiences (for example, Gilligan's "different moral voice," 1982) within the mainstream and/or to create transformative narratives that revalue their subordinated experience (for example, growing in connection and relation with other individuals, as stressed by Belenky, Clinchy, Goldberger, and Tarule, 1986, and Jordan, Kaplan, Miller, Stiver, and Surrey, 1991). In these senses, then, narrative does not just describe experiences; its expression helps to make me, the narrator, who I am, to make the narratee who she or he is, and to place the construction of the events in the narrative on the performative, social plane.

Narration and Knowledge

That there is a performative and expressive element to narrative does not mean that it is useless to attempt to secure knowledge about the physical, mental, or interpersonal worlds. In fact, many philosophers of science see narrative as having a fundamental role in the succession of paradigms in the hard sciences, and in the codification not only of the history of science but also of some of its specific content domains.

This new look at the role of narrative in science can be partially explained by the failure of attempts to understand the relation between scientific theories and the world in realist rather than constructivist terms. The arduous road to accepting the use of narrative runs through the successive attempts to ground scientific theory in the ostensive relations, first, between words and world; then, between sentences or propositions and the world; and finally, through whole theoretical networks of propositions and the world. Even the latter attempt fails, because the meaning of the theoretical networks of propositions is always underdetermined by the facts that the networks are meant to explain (Thagard, 1992, pp. 191–224).

Furthermore, narrative tasks are implicated in the attempt of one paradigm to succeed another. For a revolutionary paradigm to replace an accepted paradigm, it must first show narratively how the old paradigm made sense, given its structure and content, but also how it is unacceptable, given the new paradigm's structure and content (MacIntyre, 1980). In a sense, the new paradigm must supply a better, a richer understanding of the accepted paradigm, even as it purports to render the accepted paradigm obsolete. In other words, even if the paradigms are incommensurate, the progress of science requires that the new paradigm secure the narrative continuity of the scientific tradition (see Russell & van den Broek, 1988, for application of this theory to therapy).

This narrative moment in scientific progress is not the sole function of narrative in science. As Danto (1985) has pointed out, the structure of scientific explanations and the structure of everyday narratives are similar in their explanatory sequence. Both try to explain a change from A to C by positing some occurrence of law-like regularity, B, in between. Similarly, as has become rote via Kuhn (1970), Feyerabend (1975), and Rorty (1989), it is now generally known that the process of science is replete with rhetorical gambits, ripostes, and ploys. The cloth of scientific knowledge is woven in rhetorical casuistries (see Burke, 1986). Even the most arcane scientific theories have their competitors, and the rules of engagement for this competition are now understood not to be solely about accounting for data but to be also about persuasion and influence. Words advocate realities, after all. This makes sense: the process of knowledge acquisition and dispersion is a process wrought with human personalities and desires. Like the other processes that make humans human, it too taps a fundamental symbolic resource: the ability to tell stories.

If the hard sciences are coming to terms with their constructivism and reliance on narrative, some in the social and personality sciences see narrative as providing *the* formalism appropriate to understanding human lives conceived as integral wholes. Syllogisms and theoretical and/or statistical generalizations are all seen as inadequate to grapple with the structural and temporal complexities involved in living. When lives are the objects to be explained, the formalism most adept at comprehensive explanation seems to be that of narrative (Bruner, 1987; MacIntyre, 1980).

The present turn toward narrative is, therefore, motivated both by the realization that our language serves deeper purposes than simply accurate reference and by the slow acknowledgment by the hard and soft sciences that narrative processes are not only permanently with us but are constitutive of the process of gathering and transforming knowledge. We see this move from the implicit to the explicit in clinical psychology as well, as people move from simply using narrative to systematically studying it in clinical assessment and treatment.

Narrative as a Foundation of Assessment and Therapy

Given the fact that humans use language, and specifically narrative, in the most basic to the most complex meaning-making activities, it comes as no surprise that clinical psychologists use narrative in almost all aspects of assessment and intervention. Typically, however, it has been used in making subjective clinical inferences as opposed to objective assessments or interventions. After we document the implicit clinical role of narratives in assessment and treatment, we will review some ways in which research has begun to tap the richness of narrative as a resource for understanding adjustment and therapeutic change.

Assessment

Attention to clients' verbal output in general and to narrative abilities more particularly, has obviously played a major role in the development of clinical assessment techniques and test instruments. Both cognitive and personality functioning have been assessed using strategies that tap clients' narrative competencies and their use in specific tasks. Such assessment measures rely on clients' narrative production and comprehension and, typically, on professionals' narrative competencies in employing clinical judgment and, to a lesser degree, narrative coding schemes.

Personality Structures

Narratives have been used to assess personality structures of both needs and motivations. Perhaps the most popular use of narrative productions for assessment is embodied in the Thematic Apperception Test (TAT) (Henry, 1973) and the Children's Thematic Apperception Test (CAT) (Bellak, 1986). Clearly, these tests require the ability to create a story with beginning, middle, and end. Of significance to the interpretation of test results are not just *which* intra- and interpersonal thematic contents are demonstrated in the story but *how* the subject presents these themes within the narrative: how simple or complex are the expressions of themes? Similarly pointed questions routinely orient clinicians' appraisals of their clients' narrative expressions. At what emotional and interactional levels are various needs and desires and their frustration narratively articulated? How do the stories relate to issues of autonomy and relation: are they interwoven and connected or disjointed and random? What do the stories tell us about the client's achievement motivation or self-doubt? Is the language used in a story natural or belabored? Does a story incorporate self-reflective or impulsive construction of events? Should the therapist worry about criminality, moral degradation, or self-harm? These types of questions, which are confronted in interpreting test results, suggest the richness of narratives as a resource for personality assessment.

Means-Ends Problem Solving

The Means-Ends Problem-Solving Task (Platt & Spivack, 1975) taps a more narrow band of narrative skills, namely, the pragmatic ability to narrate sets of strategies that can connect the protagonist's need states at the story's beginning with the protagonist's need fulfillment at the story's ending. Here, it can be seen how central narrative is to everyday problem-solving activity. In other words, in addition to seeing narrative productions as providers of personality trait and state information, evaluators tap narrative competencies to assess levels of cognitive problem solving. The ability to tell differentiated and complex story middles indexes a person's ability to deal with the hassles and crises of everyday life.

Intelligence Tests

Tests of intelligence also incorporate basic word usage and comprehension tasks into their data gathering, as illustrated by the subtests of vocabulary and verbal comprehension on general tests such as the Wechsler Adult Intelligence Scale—Revised (WAIS-R) (Wechsler, 1981), Wechsler Intelligence Scale for Children—Third Edition (Wechsler, 1991), and Stanford-Binet Intelligence Scale: Fourth Edition (SB:FE) (Thorndike, Hagen, & Sattler, 1986), and specialized tests such as the Peabody Picture Vocabulary Test—Revised (PPVT-R) (Dunn & Dunn, 1981) and the Illinois Test of Psycholinguistic Abilities (ITPA) (Kirk, McCarthy, & Kirk, 1968). In addition, more complex linguistic and narrative skills can be tapped, as they are on the WAIS-R and WISC-III Similarities and Picture Arrangement subtests. The ability to participate in verbal exchange, through both comprehension and production of narratives, is clearly implicated on such measures.

Cognitive and Neuropsychological Assessment

Both cognitive and neuropsychological assessment strategies make use of narrative techniques even more specifically than intelligence tests do. Generally speaking, mental status examinations have always incorporated an assessment of language capabilities, including evaluation of such abilities as verbal fluency, expressive language errors and omissions, comprehension of spoken language, and naming and word finding. Ascertaining the level of a patient's disturbance on these and other verbal abilities involves both structured questions and, usually, careful observation of the patient's spontaneous, unprompted speech. For example, according to one widely used text on mental status examinations, "Listening to the patient's spontaneous speech for even a brief period of time may provide invaluable information that cannot be obtained during more formal aspects of the language examination" (Strub & Black, 1985, p. 51). It is likely that interpretation of such less-structured verbal output requires using implicit narrative principles. In addition, tests of memory such as the Wechsler Memory Scale (WMS) (Wechsler, 1945) and the Babcock memory subtest (Babcock & Levy, 1940) employ both story memory and story production tasks. Implicitly, the constructors of these tests have acknowledged narrative as a major form in which information is stored.

Conclusions

Narrative techniques are, thus, routinely used to assess aspects of personality, intelligence, and cognitive subsystems like memory. *However, the data derived from these techniques traditionally have been either interpreted clinically or assessed objectively in terms that do not directly deal with the narrative form of the client's productions.* Consequently, research on the specifically narrative properties of clients' verbal behavior has been lacking. This same trend can be seen, on an even larger scale, when we consider the role of narrative in clinical treatment.

Narrative in Therapy

The representation of subjectivity and of relations between persons and events is pivotal in clinical treatment. Clinicians work hard to attend to, and to prompt the client to attend to, the client's specific manner of symbolizing events. Every clinician knows by now Freud's view (1893/1981) that there is "an intimate connection between the story of the patient's suffering and the symptoms of his illness" (p. 161). Insert "narrative schemas" or "scripts" for Freud's "story," and you will find yourself nearly at the forefront of cognitive therapies. Both Freud and those engaged in cognitive therapies seem to be embracing a simple fact of life: individuals' talk discloses who they are. This truism, expanded and particularized, is at the center of much of therapeutic training. "Listen not only to what the client is saying but to how the client is saying it" is an injunction trainees hear over and over. Less often heard perhaps, but no less important, is the injunction to orient oneself to what a client is doing interpersonally in saying whatever he or she says. Often, neurotic types of adult psychopathology are flagged when there are discrepancies between the what, the how, and the interpersonal verbal action. For example, a male client may say to a female therapist that his deportment with women is always proper, while simultaneously speaking in a seductive tone and smiling in a sexually suggestive manner. Similarly clinical progress is often noted when these different facets of communication are brought more systematically into line in the course of treatment. Thus, not only in assessment but in therapeutic treatment as well, adult therapists focus on verbal cues embedded in the client's narratives.

Neo-Freudian Theory

More recently, there has been a return to language and narrative in neo-Freudian theory. In fact, Schafer (1980) maintains that therapy proceeds as the patient reconstructs his or her life story in the analytic terms of sexual and aggressive action and defenses against taking such action within the transferential relationship. Purportedly, this more coherent narrative enables the client to experience and understand his or her life history differently and facilitates the adoption of novel strategies with which to confront the future.

Child Psychotherapy

Child therapists also are instructed to pay close attention to the metaphorical meaning of a client's play and storytelling. Such instruction is based on fairly sophisticated theories regarding cognitive or personality development and the facilitating functions of symbolic play and fantasy (see, for example, Schaefer, 1993; Schaefer & Cangelosi, 1993). In fact, the importance of the use of stories in treatment of children is explicitly recognized by practicing clinicians. Koocher and Pedulla (1977) reported that 32 percent of the practicing clinicians they surveyed said that storytelling was at least occasionally useful and 12 percent said that it was often useful. Moreover, narrative intervention techniques have been formalized and clinical explications have appeared in several publications (Gardner, 1971, 1993). Recognition of the usefulness of narrative in child treatment has, in recent years, given rise to detailed prescriptions and suggestions as to how and when narrative procedures should be employed in the treatment of a variety of childhood disorders (for example, Franzke, 1989).

Form (over Content)

As dependent as clinical assessment and treatment are on narrative and the language it embodies, the lion's share of both the clinical and the research focus has been on the content or thematic structure of clients' stories. Clinicians and researchers have, for the most part, failed to incorporate the time-honored focus on narrative form that permeates the fields of literary criticism and narrative study. However, if the insights of narrative constructivism are to be fully tapped by clinicians, it is to the formal properties of narrative that the focus must turn. It is these properties that make narrative narrative.

Narrative in Psychotherapy Research

What are some of the important structural features of narratives that can be observed? Russell and van den Broek (1988, 1992) have presented an empirically testable, three-dimensional model of narrative structure, emphasizing (1) the structural connectedness of narratives; (2) the representation of subjectivity in narratives (that is, the motivational and psychological relation that subjects assume toward the events being talked about); and (3) the elaboration/complexity of narratives. These three dimensions concern formal properties of narrative structure that have received extensive empirical and/or theoretical investigation in other fields of psychology and in literary criticism, and these same dimensions can produce important clinical information about clients' phenomenal experience. For example, the way in which individuals employ and interconnect events via such devices as the definition of event categories and of causal and temporal relationships, provides information about the salience of and interrelationships between disparate autobiographical events, and suggests how the events figure psychologically in clients' attempts to fashion a coherent understanding of their lives. Two main classes of structural variables (the first dimension of the model) have received intense investigation: first, abstract event categories (for example, setting, initiating event, internal responses, attempt, consequence, and reaction) that employ the content of the narrative (see, for example, Mandler & Johnson, 1977; Stein & Glenn, 1979) and, second, abstract sets of relations, such as temporal and causal ones, that connect the events in the different categories (see, for example, Kintsch & van Dijk, 1978; Trabasso & van den Broek, 1985).

The second dimension of the model, subjectivity, has been called by Bruner (1987, p. 20) "the landscape of consciousness." This dimension concerns the way in which individuals construct and qualify their psychological relation to the events being talked about. Linguistic markers of subjectivity in a narrative provide information about the speaker's motivation and intention, and they situate the protagonist's actions within the realm of what is possible or necessary, illusory or real. This information is crucial to clinicians, who are always assessing how clients portray their psychological relation to the concrete events and episodes in their life; to what degree clients can overcome their egocentrism and consider action from another point of view; and the level of reflective awareness that clients can attain in understanding their own activity and conduct.

The third dimension concerns the type and level of language that clients use in constructing their narratives. Is the language monosyllabic or polysyllabic? Does clients' talk employ long highly qualified sentences or short direct sentences. Are the narratives multi-episodic or restricted to single episodes? Attention to the third dimension can provide information about the complexity or poverty of clients' experience, their attunement to characteristics of possible audiences (such as children), and their level of knowledge about their narrative topics.

With these dimensions in mind, we present the findings of a few of our studies that focus on the relationship of narrative properties to the assessment and treatment of psychopathology, both in adult and child therapy. We have arranged our findings as answers to the following set of simple questions: Can types of therapists and types of clients be differentiated on the basis of their narrative language? Can severity of psychopathology be predicted by narrative performances? Can the quality of individual psychotherapy sessions be characterized by their narrative characteristics? Can explorations of narrative construction give therapists clues about the form and function of clinical interventions? Affirmative answers to these questions will suggest that research and clinical attention to narrative processes in assessment and treatment will spawn new understanding of psychopathology and the processes leading to therapeutic change.

Can Types of Therapists and Types of Clients Be Differentiated on the Basis of Their Narrative Language?

Several studies have supported hypotheses that narrative factors are useful in distinguishing clinically relevant patterns of meaning-making: patterns in the language of therapists of different therapeutic orientations and patterns in the language of patients with different diagnostic characteristics. For therapists, different theories of psychotherapy prescribe and proscribe different sets of speech acts (for example, speech acts of interpretation and confrontation are prescribed by dynamic theories, whereas speech acts of reflection and clarification are prescribed by Rogerian therapies). More subtle than these prescriptions, however, are the implied differences between therapists of differing orientation in their degree and type of use of representations of subjectivity (the second dimension in Russell and van den Broek's model).

Therapist Subjectivity and Self-Disclosure

Essig and Russell (1990) devised a linguistically sophisticated coding scheme to identify sixteen different types of elaboration of subjectivity, and they used this system to investigate whether the therapists Rogers, Perls, and Ellis could be distinguished on this narrative dimension. This study seemed important, not only because it would assess the discriminative validity of the coding scheme but also because most theories of psychotherapy proscribe the disclosure of subjectivity on the therapist's part. In fact, several studies on self-disclosure (defined as a therapist technique aimed at intentional disclosure of private information) had found that therapists' disclosing utterances occurred relatively infrequently and that there were no significant differences between therapists in terms of the frequency of disclosures in their discourse (Elliott et al., 1988; Hill, Thames, & Rardin, 1979).

When self-disclosure was defined in terms of the narrative representation of subjectivity, however, Essig and Russell (1990) found that such self-disclosure is in fact quite prevalent in therapist discourse and is also differentially employed, in ways consistent with therapists' avowed theoretical orientation. When the well-known Rogers, Perls, and Ellis tapes (in which each of three therapists separately conducted a session with a voluntary patient known as Gloria), which had served in the Hill, Thames, and Rardin (1979) study, were reanalyzed, Rogers and Ellis were shown to use speech more densely marked with indicators of subjectivity than the speech of Perls, and Rogers used more densely subjectivity marked speech than Ellis. Even in Perls's speech, a full 30 percent of utterances were marked with subjectivity in simple sentences, and a full 22 percent of utterances were marked with subjectivity in complex sentences.

When the specific types of subjective elaboration were investigated, it could be shown that Rogers used markers of subjectivity for conveying affirmation, in and through the highly marked tentativeness of his reflective formulations of Gloria's experience. Ellis, on the other hand, used markers of subjectivity that placed Gloria's experience in a landscape that questioned its necessity or possibility, its appearance or reality from a point of view that was "objective" and "given." Perls, quite differently from the other two therapists, was more interested in suppressing the elaboration of a subjective perspective on behavior and concentrated his interventions on accenting Gloria's need to act. These different uses of the elaboration of subjectivity in practice seemed motivated by differences in client-centered, rational-emotive, and gestalt theories.

Patients' Narratives and Psychopathology

Narrative representation of subjectivity has also been shown to distinguish patients with differing underlying psychopathologies. For example, Rothschild and Russell (1995) report findings, obtained as part of Rothschild's dissertation research (1989), that compare high-functioning opiate versus cocaine addicts, patient types whose psychological treatment seems not only often unrelated to their differential diagnosis but also notoriously problematic in realizing long-term positive results. On traditional tests of sensation seeking and levels of psychological defensiveness, these unusually high-functioning substance abusers could not be distinguished as hypothesized. The opiate addicts, traditionally thought to have less-developed defenses, scored significantly higher on the Defensive Style Questionnaire than did the cocaine addicts, and there was no significant difference between the two groups in terms of the patients' self-reported sensation seeking, a dimension on which cocaine addicts had been theorized to show more extremity than opiate addicts.

However, when their narratives of their first experience with their drug of choice were examined for type and level of representation of subjectivity, theory-consistent findings were obtained. A psychodynamic view of opiate addiction postulates that opiate addicts choose their drug in order to achieve a cessation of experience, which is felt as too painful to withstand. Cocaine addicts are thought to choose stimulants as their drug of choice in order to heighten and intensify experience and thus relieve an underlying depression. Translated into linguistic terms, this would mean that the use of modality (that is, the development of a subjective perspective about the persons, events, and things that figure in the discourse) should differ between the two groups, especially when the self figures as the object of experience to be elaborated. Rothschild (1989) indeed found that the opiate and cocaine addicts' elaboration of subjectivity significantly differed in cases where the addict's self was the event to be elaborated, and differed in the direction expected. The cocaine addicts elaborated the basic event of the self through subjectivity markers proportionately more than the opiate addicts. The latter seemed to dampen the basic event of the self. In other words, the opiate addicts constrict whereas the cocaine addicts expand the self as a center of subjectivity.

Can Severity of Psychopathology Be Predicted by Narrative Performances?

Another crucial empirical question regarding the clinical relevance of narrative in meaning-making has been its relation to levels of psychopathology. Hambleton, Russell, & Wandrei (1995) coded stories told by clients on four commonly used assessment instruments (TAT, Means-Ends Problem-Solving Test, Babcock Memory Subtest, and a prompt to tell a story about a significant life event). When the stories were scored on measures derived to capture information on the three dimensions of Russell and van den Broek's model of narratives (structural connectedness, subjectivity, and elaboration/complexity), it was found that these dimensions of narrative performance displayed stable individual differences and that mean levels varied systematically across the different assessment instruments.

In a series of regression analyses, the narrative measures were assessed for their ability to predict subjects' levels of symptoms of three types: depressive, anxious, and cognitive-mediational. These symptoms had been previously assessed with standard instruments (for example, the Beck Depression Inventory, the State-Trait Anxiety Test, and the Self-Control Index). Results indicated that substantial amounts of the variance on each of the three indices of psychopathology (about 33 percent in depressive symptomatology, 31 percent in anxiety symptoms, and 17 percent in cognitive-mediational difficulties) could be predicted. In these analyses, the structural connectedness of the narratives was most related to levels of psychopathology: the poorer the narrative form of the stories, the more severe the pathology.

Can the Quality of Individual Psychotherapy Sessions Be Characterized by Their Narrative Characteristics?

Empirical studies have also demonstrated links between clients' elaboration of subjectivity and the depth of the experiencing in psychotherapy. For example, Lord, Castelino, and Russell (1990) found a significant relationship between objective measures of client depth of experiencing in sessions and the degree of client subjective elaboration in speech. This finding was considered especially important because the measures of subjectivity concern specific linguistic markers that are used not simply to express feeling or emotion but also to express expectations, perspective taking, and other aspects of clients' worldviews.

Similarly, Essig and Russell (1989) reported that therapy sessions judged highest in good therapy process components could be differentiated from sessions judged lowest in good therapy process components (as rated by clinical observers using the Vanderbilt Psychotherapy Process Scales) on the basis of the degree of representation of subjectivity in therapist, patient, or their combined discourse. For example, significant differences between low-rated and high-rated sessions were found on several different subtypes of the representation of subjectivity. These markers encoded clients' or therapists' attempts to embed events they were talking about into subjective and dynamic time frames, that is, frames that define the time of action over and above the definition supplied by verb tense. In addition, in the high-rated good process sessions, events were more often placed in multiple subjective perspectives oriented toward the process of knowledge acquisition, events' appearance or reality, and events' power of provoking attitudinal reactions in the speaker. It is perhaps the presence of this dynamic use of perspective in conjunction with modality-marked reference to temporality that signals good process in therapy.

Can Explorations of Narrative Construction Give Therapists Clues About the Form and Function of Clinical Interventions?

Russell, van den Broek, Adams, Rosenberger, and Essig (1993) showed that a master therapist's retellings of children's stories had more structural connections in the form of causal and temporal relationships and many more markers of subjectivity than the stories on which they were based, but they also contained more conceptual redundancy. In addition, elaborations of subjectivity figured more often in causal sentences in the therapist's narratives than in the children's. Such findings were interpreted to indicate that the therapist was attempting to impart both more knowledge about the representation of events and more coherent and elaborate theories of mind, to assist clients in reaching higher developmental levels of narrative explanation.

A second study (Russell, Castelino, Wandrei, & Jones, 1995) compared original child client stories and the reformulation of those stories by therapists to lay participants' versions of those stories told under three different contextual prompts. In this research, a story told by a child client is subsequently recorded on tape by a child actor. The tape is listened to by lay participants. They are first asked to tell the story exactly as they heard it. Then they are asked to retell the story, assuming the role of a helpful parent. Finally, they are requested to reformulate the story the way they think a therapist might communicate it back to a child client. Comparisons of the narratives indicated that, first, the expert therapist provided a richer depiction of internality and, especially, intersubjectivity than both the children and the lay participants across all three experimental conditions; second, the lay participants emphasized internality and intersubjectivity somewhat more than the children under the first prompt but to an equal degree under the parent and therapist prompts; and third, the therapist limited the complexity of his language far more than the lay participants. These findings illustrate some of the specialized ways therapists use narrative interventions to promote clients' acquisition and use of the landscape of consciousness that is constituent both to individuals' storytelling and to their mental well-being. The strategy seems to follow a surprisingly simple dictum: provide the richest model of interiority and intersubjectivity through the simplest narrative language required by the client's cognitive-linguistic development level.

Conclusion

The development of narrative structures can be understood to have at least two functions that ultimately may be correlative to each other. Narrative plays a role for the individual both in terms of the organization of event knowledge and self-knowledge and in terms of the moment-to-moment negotiation of identities and relationships. We have emphasized these two functions in this chapter. However, an additional major emphasis on narrative has emerged in poststructuralism/postmodernism and in social constructionism: in this view, not only do individuals or small groups of individuals use language to structure personal experience, but by community disavowal of culturally dominant master stories and community advocacy of locally constructed contextually sensitive stories, communities can derive new ways of conceiving what things and people are and how they come to be and do. The degree of rigidity of the culturally dominant stories no longer constrains the degree of creation and legitimation of the locally constructed stories.

This is a new move in the use of narrative constructions, and it could be incorporated into theories of therapy. It is no longer the individual's purely personal constructions but the societal constructions that need alteration in order to facilitate contextually diverse narratives that may affirm and thus partially alleviate an individual's or community's struggle. The necessity of attending to sociohistorical master stories may be especially felt when therapists attempt to assist individuals in subordinated groups. When dominant groups control social institutions and the narratives that sustain them, the target for intervention may actually lie less "in" the individual than in the symbolic media that mask or distort the true interests embedded in the current structure of society (Unger & Crawford, 1992).

Research on the role of narrative constructivism, consequently, needs to proceed both at the micro- and the macroanalytic levels. Both have an impact on all aspects of the mental health profession. Moreover, since familiarity with narrative is widespread already in the clinical community, research findings about narrative structure and function have a reasonable chance of seeming relevant to practice. Narrative studies can thus provide a two-way bridge between research and practice, a bridge of the kind not crossed often enough. However, we are encouraged by the progress of narrative-focused research into psychopathology and the processes by which it can be treated and by the relevance to practice of the growing body of findings. This progress gives us confidence that macrolevel research will also be productive. From our perspective, the future truly contains an exciting research story yet to be told.

References

Austin, J. L. (1962). *How to do things with words*. Cambridge, MA: Harvard University Press.

Babcock, H., & Levy, L. (1940). *Revision of the Babcock examination for measuring efficiency of mental functioning.* Chicago: Stoelting.

Belenky, M. F., Clinchy, B. M., Goldberger, N. R., & Tarule, J. M. (1986). *Women's ways of knowing: The development of self, voice, and mind.* New York: Basic Books.

Bellak, L. (1986). *The TAT, CAT, and SAT in clinical use* (4th ed., rev.). Philadelphia: Grune & Stratton.

Bettelheim, B. (1977). *The uses of enchantment: The meaning and importance of fairy tales.* New York: Vintage Books.

Bruner, J. (1986). *Actual minds, possible worlds.* Cambridge, MA: Harvard University Press.

Bruner, J. (1987). Life as narrative. *Social Research, 54,* 11–32.

Burke, K. (1986). *Language as symbolic action.* Berkeley: University of California Press.

Cassirer, E. (1946). *Language and myth.* New York: Dover.

Danto, A. C. (1985). *Narration and knowledge.* New York: Columbia University Press.

Dunn, L. M., & Dunn, L. M. (1981). *Peabody Picture Vocabulary Test—Revised.* Circle Pines, MN: American Guidance Service.

Elliott, R., Hill, C. E., Stiles, W. B., Friedlander, M. L., Mahrer, A. R., & Margison, F. R. (1988). Primary therapist response modes: Comparison of six rating systems. *Journal of Consulting and Clinical Psychology, 55,* 218–223.

Essig, T. S., & Russell, R. L. (1989, June). *The Vanderbilt Psychotherapy Process Scales and self-disclosing features: Good process and subjectivity during inpatient psychotherapy sessions.* Paper presented at the meeting of the Society for Psychotherapy Research, Toronto.

Essig, T. S., & Russell, R. L. (1990). Analyzing subjectivity in therapeutic discourse: Rogers, Perls, Ellis, & Gloria revisited. *Psychotherapy: Theory, Research, Practice, and Training, 27,* 271–281.

Feyerabend, P. (1975). *Against method.* London: Verso.

Fisher, W. R. (1984). Narrative as a human communication paradigm: The case of public moral argument. *Communication Monographs, 51,* 1–22.

Fisher, W. R. (1985). The narrative paradigm: An elaboration. *Communication Monographs, 52,* 347–367.

Franzke, E. (1989). *Fairy tales in psychotherapy: The creative use of old and new tales.* Lewistown, NY: Hogrefe & Huber.

Freud, S. (1981). Case five: Fraulein Elisabeth von R. In J. Breuer & S. Freud, *Studies on hysteria* (pp. 135–181). New York: Basic Books. (Original work published 1893)

Gardner, R. A. (1971). *Therapeutic communication with children: The mutual story-telling technique*. Northvale, NJ: Aronson.

Gardner, R. A. (1993). *Storytelling in psychotherapy with children*. Northvale, NJ: Aronson.

Gilligan, C. (1982). *In a different voice*. Cambridge, MA: Harvard University Press.

Hambleton, G., Russell, R. L., & Wandrei, M. L. (1995). *Narrative performance as a predictor of psychopathology*. Manuscript submitted for publication.

Hempel, C. G. (1959). The empiricist criterion of meaning. In A. Yoder (Ed.), *Logical positivism* (pp. 108–129). New York: Free Press.

Henry, W. E. (1973). *The analysis of fantasy*. Malabar, FL: Krieger.

Hill, C. E., Thames, T. B., & Rardin, D. K. (1979). Comparisons of Rogers, Perls, and Ellis on the Hill Counselor Verbal Response Category System. *Journal of Counseling Psychology, 26*, 198–203.

Jordan, J. V., Kaplan, A. G., Miller, J. B., Stiver, I. P., & Surrey, J. L. (1991). *Women's growth in connection: Writings from the Stone Center*. New York: Guilford Press.

Kintsch, W., & van Dijk, T. A. (1978). Toward a model of text comprehension and production. *Psychological Review, 85*, 363–394.

Kirk, S. A., McCarthy, J. J., & Kirk, W. D. (1968). *The Illinois Test of Psycholinguistic Abilities*. Urbana: University of Illinois Press.

Koocher, G. P., & Pedulla, B. M. (1977). Current practices in child psychotherapy. *Professional Psychology, 8*, 275–287.

Kuhn, T. S. (1970). *The structure of scientific revolutions* (2nd ed.). Chicago: University of Chicago Press.

Labov, W. (1972). *Language in the inner city: Studies in the black English vernacular*. Philadelphia: University of Pennsylvania Press.

Lakoff, G., & Johnson, M. (1979). *Metaphors we live by*. Chicago: University of Chicago Press.

Lord, J. J., Castelino, C. T., & Russell, R. L. (1990, June). *Linguistic aspects of client discourse: Affect, subjectivity, and client experiencing levels*. Paper presented at the meeting of the Society for Psychotherapy Research, Wintergreen, VA.

MacIntyre, A. (1980). Epistemological crises, dramatic narrative, and the philosophy of science. In G. Gutting (Ed.), *Paradigms and revolutions* (pp. 54–73). Notre Dame, IN: University of Notre Dame Press.

McMullin, R. E. (1986). *Handbook of cognitive therapy techniques*. New York: W.W. Norton.

Mandler, J. M., & Johnson, N. S. (1977). Remembrance of things parsed: Story structure and recall. *Cognitive Psychology, 9*, 111–151.

Platt, J. J., & Spivack, G. (1975). *Manual for the Means-Ends Problem-Solving Procedures (MEPS): A measure of interpersonal cognitive problem-solving skills*. Camden, NJ: University of Medicine and Dentistry of New Jersey.

Polkinghorne, D. E. (1988). *Narrative knowing and the human sciences*. Albany: State University of New York Press.

Prince, G. (1988). Introduction to the study of the narratee. In M. Hoffman & P. Murphy (Eds.), *Essentials of the theory of fiction* (pp. 314–345). Durham, NC: Duke University Press. (Original work published 1973)

Rorty, R. (1989). *Contingency, irony, and solidarity*. New York: Cambridge University Press.

Rothschild, D. (1989). *Differentiating cocaine and opiate addicts: Affect management, defensive functioning, and narrative style*. Unpublished doctoral dissertation, New School for Social Research.

Rothschild, D., & Russell, R. L. (1995). *The talk of cocaine versus opiate addicts*. Unpublished manuscript.

Russell, R. L. (1987). Psychotherapeutic discourse: Future directions and the critical pluralist attitude. In R. L. Russell (Ed.), *Language in psychotherapy: Strategies of discovery* (pp. 341–351). New York: Plenum.

Russell, R. L. (Ed.). (1991). Narrative [Special issue]. *Journal of Cognitive Psychotherapy, 5*.

Russell, R. L., Castelino, C., Wandrei, M. L., & Jones, M. A. (1995). *Building theories of mind through narrative exchange: Therapeutic and lay strategies*. Manuscript submitted for publication.

Russell, R. L., & van den Broek, P. (1988). A cognitive developmental account of storytelling in child psychotherapy. In S. R. Shirk (Ed.), *Cognitive development and child psychotherapy* (pp. 19–52). New York: Plenum.

Russell, R. L., & van den Broek, P. (1992). Changing narrative schemas in psychotherapy. *Psychotherapy: Theory, Research, Practice, and Training, 29*, 344–354.

Russell, R. L., van den Broek, P., Adams, S., Rosenberger, K., & Essig, T. S. (1993). Analyzing narratives in psychotherapy. *Journal of Narrative and Life History, 3*, 337–360.

Sarbin, T. R. (1986). *Narrative psychology: The storied nature of human conduct*. New York: Praeger.

Schaefer, C. E. (Ed.). (1993). *The therapeutic powers of play*. Northvale, NJ: Aronson.

Schaefer, C. E., & Cangelosi, D. M. (Eds.). (1993). *Play therapy techniques*. Northvale, NJ: Aronson.

Schafer, R. (1980). Narration in the psychoanalytic dialogue. In W.J.T. Mitchell (Ed.), *On narrative* (pp. 25–50). Chicago: University of Chicago Press.

Searle, J. R. (1969). *Speech acts: An essay in the philosophy of language.* New York: Cambridge University Press.

Spence, D. (1982). *Narrative truth and historical truth: Meaning and interpretation in psychoanalysis.* New York: W.W. Norton.

Stein, N. L. (1982). What's in a story: Interpreting the interpretations of story grammars. *Discourse Processes, 5,* 319–335.

Stein, N. L., & Glenn, C. G. (1979). An analysis of story comprehension in elementary school children. In R. O. Freedle (Ed.), *Advances in discourse processes: Vol. 2. New directions in discourse processing* (pp. 53–120). Norwood, NJ: Ablex.

Strub, R. L., & Black, F. W. (1985). *The mental status examination in neurology* (3rd ed.). Philadelphia: Davis.

Taylor, C. (1985). *Human agency and language.* New York: Cambridge University Press.

Thagard, P. (1992). *Conceptual revolutions.* Princeton, NJ: Princeton University Press.

Thorndike, R. L., Hagen, E. P., & Sattler, J. M. (1986). *Technical manual, Stanford-Binet Intelligence Scale: Fourth Edition.* Chicago: Riverside.

Trabasso, T., & van den Broek, P. (1985). Causal thinking and the representation of narrative events. *Journal of Memory and Language, 24,* 612–630.

Unger, R., & Crawford, M. (1992). *Women and gender: A feminist psychology.* New York: McGraw-Hill.

Wechsler, D. (1945). A standardized memory scale for clinical use. *Journal of Psychology, 19,* 87–95.

Wechsler, D. (1981). *WAIS-R manual: Wechsler Adult Intelligence Scale—Revised.* San Antonio, TX: Psychological Corporation.

Wechsler, D. (1991). *Manual for the Wechsler Intelligence Scale for Children—Third Edition.* San Antonio, TX: Psychological Corporation.

Werner, H. (1940). *Comparative psychology of mental development.* Madison, CT: International Universities Press.

White, H. (1980). The value of narrativity in the representation of reality. *Critical Inquiry, 7,* 5–27.

· ·

12

Metaphor, Meaning-Making, and Metamorphosis

Mary Baird Carlsen

The alternative to numbers is words. Whereas numbers are signs, words are symbols, and therefore by their very nature equivocal; their ambiguity can be reduced but never eliminated. This bars them from the needle's eye of absolute precision, but the loose ends that prevent them from piercing that eye endow them with a texture that numbers cannot match. . . .
<u>*From the adversity of verbal ambiguity, opportunity opens.*</u>
Huston Smith (1976/1992, p. 13, emphasis added)

"From the adversity of verbal ambiguity, opportunity opens." Those words are key in this examination of metaphor as both a window into client change and a means to client change. Hold onto them and reconsider them during this exploration of metaphor, meaning-making, and metamorphosis.

Evolving Metaphors in Psychotherapy

This search into the meanings and therapeutic applications of metaphor was born of an intuitive sense that spontaneous metaphoric expressions, shared in the course of psychotherapy, have a great deal to reveal about a client's evolution in meaning-making.

Working to clarify and name this intuition, I collected sample metaphors from differing stages of therapy, to compare and contrast those metaphors that came early in therapy with those that appeared later in the process. In doing this, I came to the conclusion that metaphors are not only innovative, imaginative forms of comparison and contrast, they are also conceptual windows into evolution and change.

To illustrate, the following metaphors, spontaneously expressed by clients during the early hours of therapy, reveal emotional pain, identity confusion, and a sense of utter meaninglessness:

> *I feel a void within me.*
>
> *It is dark, overwhelming—I'm falling apart from the inside out.*
>
> *I feel like I'm in a whirlpool—grasping to stay alive.*

In contrast, these expressions from the middle hours of a therapeutic sequence reveal one woman's effort to sort destructive behaviors even as she named new hope for herself.

> *I put my foot out and trip myself [this woman is gaining enough perspective on her destructive tendencies that she can begin to put them into words for the first time].*
>
> *I am a young plant . . . able to push through a boulder of granite and emerge [there is hope here; she does recognize strengths that she can use].*

And, finally, these metaphors from three different clients demonstrate their transformational shift from living inside their problems to "having" those problems and being able to work with them (Kegan, 1982, pp. 118–120, calls this a "subject/object transition"):

My relationship is not so cut and dried; the hard edges are softening and that is happening in lots of areas.

I feel more myself, more integrated, a lot more self-accepting. I don't think I can go back. It's interesting to look back; it's not so judgmental. I am making decisions by finding but not by seeking; I'm not so simple; some of my rules have broken.

I am becoming real . . . I'm taking off this big coat that I have been lugging around for so long . . . I carried a belief—from the media, from the culture. Now I am shedding it, getting in touch with the genuine.

These evolutions of metaphoric expression display the ways these individuals are learning to "speak into being" a knowledge of themselves (compare Neimeyer, 1994).

Lest we generalize too quickly from these examples, however, we do well to remind ourselves that every therapeutic sequence is its own unique unfolding of experience. And certainly, many clients do not complete a fully developed sequence of developmental meaning-making: meaning-makings can abort, distort, or simply lose their way. Also, the kinds of meaning-making described here usually result from long-term investments, but clients may not have the motivation, the means, or the capability to follow through with an extended therapeutic sequence.

Additionally, many clients do not spontaneously create fresh metaphoric expressions. Why is this so? Several possibilities come to mind: some clients may never break free of their repetitions of old memories, of their habits of vocabulary and expression, of their simmering resentments, of their conceptual loadings of old assumptions. Others may never have developed the creative capacity to expand their ideas through the playing off of words and ideas. Often limited in intuition and imagination, they stay close to their "facts," preferring concrete, definitive language that brings them more rapidly to the security of cognitive certainty, closure, and personal control (compare Stewart & Thomas, 1986).

Then there are those others who may simply have no practice in using metaphors, coming from communities of discourse where verbal expression did not include metaphoric usage (although I do ponder the four-letter expletives of the streets and the metaphors of violence and rape or the metaphors of battle that permeate contemporary competitions of sports, business, and yes, the win-lose battles of relationship). Or they may not use metaphors because they simply lack a knowledge base that can fuel the transport of ideas from one domain to another. Not only does metaphoric usage take a capacity to play with ideas, it also takes a certain level of vocabulary and enough understanding of a domain of knowledge to put words together in the fashion of metaphor (compare Gardner, 1983, pp. 290–293). Our musician clients may well use terms from music, engineers from the precisions of their technologies, and computer specialists from the intricacies of their machines' branching systems. Indeed, one client who spent the hours of his day working with systems analysis confessed to being caught in a "do-loop" that prevented him from expressing himself in spontaneous, expressive ways. His expertise provided a metaphor that shaped our therapy in many productive ways.

Without judging those clients who do not use metaphor, without negating any form of expression—whether visual, verbal, emotional, or behavioral—and without being insensitive to the developmental levels of our clients, we can learn a great deal by studying our most metaphor-using clients in their most metaphorical moments. We might even come to believe with Miall (1982) that such moments can be insights into the "crucible in which meaning is born," even as they show us "something about the nature of concept formation . . . of the mystery of how new meaning is created" (pp. xviii–xix).

Interpretations and Perspectives

In the manner of constructivist meaning-making, this discussion tracks themes that weave in and around its key words: *metaphor*, *meaning-making*, and *metamorphosis*. The object of this inquiry and articulation is not to build a case, data piece upon data piece, or to prove or disprove the influence of one thing or another, but rather to open up our thinking about the topics at hand so that we can translate new insights and new findings into more effective ways to understand and help our clients. For these reasons, this investigation is heuristic in its inquiry, as its theme unfolds, as Douglass and Moustakas (1985) have described: "Like the spokes of a wheel, a theme or question radiates and presents myriad avenues for exploration, pointing to related meanings, places, people, and situations in which the phenomenon under investigation is precipitated and intensified in its precise meaning" (p. 52).

Definition and Family of Metaphors

In tracking definition and interpretation, it is helpful to look first at the word *metaphor* itself, its root (*meta-*), its base meaning, and its extended meanings. (The following three definitions are from the *Oxford English Dictionary*, 2nd ed.)

> **Meta-** *prefix [representing the Greek meta-]. . . . Joined chiefly to verbs and verbal derivatives, the principal notions which it expresses are: sharing, action in common; pursuit or quest; and, especially, change (of place, order, condition, or nature), corresponding to [the] Latin [prefix] trans-.*
>
> **Meta** *[substantive]. One of the conical columns set in the ground at each end of the Circus, to mark the turning-place in a race. Hence, [transferred sense]. A boundary.*
>
> **Metaphor** *[formed on Greek metapherein to transfer, which is formed on Greek meta- + pherein to bear, carry].*

The figure of speech in which a name or descriptive term is transferred to some object different from, but analogous to, that to which it is properly applicable.

Metaphoric usage frequently encompasses not only the narrowly construed rhetorical device of metaphor but the techniques of *simile, model*, and *analogy* as well. For example, Gruber (1980) concluded that "metaphors, analogies, and models are part of a group of comparison processes by which we use some parts of our knowledge to illuminate others. There are many names for such comparison processes, but there is no adequate taxonomy of them" (p. 122). With our present state of knowledge, he believed that it is "idle to fuss over definitions"; that what is needed is a large and generous term to cover the whole family of comparison processes and that term is metaphor. In this manner, "*Metaphor, image, figure of thought*, and the abbreviated *figure* [are used] interchangeably for such comparison processes" (Leary, 1990c, p. 28).

The family of metaphors that shapes and reflects the developmental, organic model of constructivist meaning-making includes among its root metaphors many of the meanings named above and found in the term metaphor itself. These root metaphors—turning place, pursuit, quest, boundary, transition, and transformation—are all descriptive terms that can be used to characterize either the processes of meaning-making or shifts in personal knowing. Metaphoric clusterings like these demonstrate the thesis of Gruber and Davis (1988) that "metaphors do not function in isolation from each other, but in articulated ensembles, each metaphor having its special role in the complex whole" (p. 260) (compare Lakoff & Johnson, 1980).

Development and Structural Transformation

In his "root metaphor" theory, Pepper (1942, p. 91) named clusterings of metaphor, thought, and interpretation that create four principal world hypotheses, or fundamental ways of viewing the world:

formism, *mechanism*, *contextualism*, and *organicism*. The organismic hypothesis is particularly significant for developmental constructivists because it is "based on the root metaphor of the complex, integrated organic process that is presumed to underlie the structural development and transformation of a phenomenon. Within this worldview, phenomena are perceived as dynamic and developing 'organic wholes'" (Lyddon, 1989, p. 443; compare Royce & Mos, 1981).

A process that is organic allows for the deconstruction and reconstruction of the systems that create the whole. These shifts in logical or conceptual structure, in the patternings of method, metaphor, and hypothesis, are very much what Kuhn (1970) has described as the paradigm shifts that occur when the historical perspective or worldview of a particular scientific community is altered. Although Kuhn did not assign preeminence to considerations of metaphor in his earlier analyses, in 1987, writing about his characterization of scientific revolutions, he stated that what "has been the most difficult . . . for me to see, but now seems the most obvious and probably the most consequential [is the common occurrence of a] central change of model, metaphor, or analogy—a change in one's sense of what is similar to what, and of what is different" (cited in Leary, 1990c, p. 20). Kuhn's assertions about paradigm shifts and scientific revolutions could just as well be applied to the work of psychotherapy. Indeed, if we adopt Kelly's characterization (1963) of the client as a scientist working on his or her own behalf (p. 15), then we can believe that when a client's paradigm becomes inadequate, a kind of mini–scientific revolution can be set in motion when the old paradigm is abandoned in favor of a new and more encompassing conceptual structure (compare Rosen, 1985, p. 126). In that manner, constructivist transformation takes place.

Contemporary Scholarship

In this section, I widen the perspectives of this discussion by sampling the thinking and assumptions of contemporary scholars involved in the study of metaphor. To preserve their styles of thought and language and to open windows into metaphoric epistemologies, I more frequently quote than paraphrase them. Metaphor all too easily loses its conceptual power in translation and analysis (compare Polanyi & Prosch, 1975, p. 79).

The Great Psychological Questions

In varying fields of scholarship, from linguistics to cognitive psychology, from the development of scientific models to the study of client narrative, inquiry into the uses of metaphor is multiplying at the present time. This willingness to entertain the less tangible in considering the mysteries of the mind is granting new status to questions often avoided within the positivistic traditions of psychology. Bruner (1990) affirms this shift: "In spite of the prevailing ethos of 'neat little studies,' and of what Gordon Allport once called methodolatry, the great psychological questions are being raised once again—questions about the nature of mind and its processes, questions about how we construct our meanings and our realities, questions about the shaping of mind by history and culture" (p. xi).

Contemporary interest in the use and influence of metaphor (see Leary, 1990a) is a part of this willingness to study great psychological questions. Further impetus comes from three contemporary trends: a broadening interest in the history of psychology; a growing attention to the nature of cognitive processes, particularly those underlying creative activity; and an expanding exploration of the nature of language, especially the incidence and functions of metaphor (Leary, 1990b, p. xi).

Out of their refocusing of theoretical attention, a number of scholars are coming to similar conclusions: "Metaphor permeates all discourse, ordinary and special" (Goodman, 1976, p. 80). "Our ordinary conceptual system, in terms of which we both think and act, is fundamentally metaphorical in nature" (Lakoff & Johnson, 1980, p. 3). "A large part of self-understanding is the search for appropriate personal metaphors that make sense of our lives" (Lakoff & Johnson, 1980, p. 233). "All knowledge is ultimately rooted in metaphorical (or analogical) modes of perception and thought" (Leary, 1990c, p. 2). And, "Metaphor characterizes human thought and language in a truly fundamental way" (Leary, 1990c, p. 3). Bruner and Feldman (1990) point out that in the history of consciousness and cognition, "even on the shallowest inspection, it is apparent that there have been *nothing but* metaphors." They go on to say that "these metaphors have been so varied and so riotously luxuriant, at least where consciousness is concerned, that we can only stand back and wonder: Of what or of whom does one speak in such cascading metaphors? Consciousness as a spotlight, a footlight before which scenes are enacted, a flowing river, a stream of thoughts, a seamless web, a set of sets, a graph, a powerless rider, a recursive loop, an internalized running back and forth, a readout, a pandemonium, a stage or display—there is no end to the parade" (p. 230).

Creative Function

Bruner and Feldman (1990) separate the metaphors of cognitive theory into two broad categories: one that tends to cluster interpretive metaphors into "reproductive" models and one that shapes "productive" models. On the one hand, the reproductive metaphors depict cognitions as "a cycle of reflecting and then reproducing the world—a kind of selective, but order-preserving copying machine"; on the other hand, the productive metaphors depict cognition as "a creator, imposing its categories on whatever it encounters, ending by making a world of its own" (pp. 230–231). It is in that second, creative arena that metaphor offers its special contribution.

But what is this contribution? One answer comes from Goodman (1976), who wrote that metaphor "springs not merely from love of literary color but also from urgent need of economy. If we could not readily transfer schemata to make new sortings and orderings, we should have to burden ourselves with unmanageably many different schemata, either by adoption of a vast vocabulary of elementary terms or by prodigious elaboration of composite ones"

(p. 80). Furthermore, metaphor is not simply ornamental, for it "participates fully in the progress of knowledge: in replacing some stale 'natural' kinds with novel and illuminating categories, in contriving facts, in revising theory, and in bringing us new worlds" (Goodman, 1984, p. 71). Indeed, as Gruber and Davis (1988) have pointed out, it is in the creative, generative functions of metaphor that a great deal of cognitive work takes place—activity that can range from serving as a "modality of thought," to "highlighting the mismatch between the literal and metaphoric forms of an idea," to serving an "affective role, as when the evocative power of a metaphor charges an idea with new excitement" (pp. 254–255).

For those concerned about the legitimacy—or illegitimacy—of metaphoric usage in scientific investigation and evaluation, neuropsychologist Karl Pribram (1990) has had something to say that can help us understand we are not dealing with simple either/or's. It is not a question of rejecting or accepting metaphoric usage in scientific study. Rather, it is a matter of understanding the individual functions of metaphor, reason, and empirical investigation in contributing to the creative evolution of scientific thought and conclusion (compare Lyddon, 1989; Rosen, 1985). It is also a matter of increasing our understandings of the human cognitive capacity to move back and forth from the imaginative explorations of metaphoric thought to the precisions of analytical and logical scientific thinking (compare Bruner, 1986).

Pribram (1990), who used the metaphor of the hologram in developing his brain research, follows a relatively simple sequence in refining his scientific investigation. To keep his meanings clear, he gives specific definitions of his key words and their functioning: *metaphor* is classified as "a broad and somewhat undefined sense of the similarities between two things," *analogy* as "a way of reasoning about metaphor," and *model* as "a precise coupling of an organization of data to another mode of organization such as a mathematical formulation" (p. 97).

In Pribram's exploratory design, the sequence starts with a general metaphor that shows similarities between two things; then the sequence "trims" the "metaphor into more and more precise shape, primarily through reasoning by analogy back and forth between the two things being compared." The process continues this "reasoning by analogy" until the original metaphor is "transformed into a precise scientific model." Pribram describes this sequence from metaphoric conception to scientific application as "a straightforward and accurate way of tracing the manner in which human brains have gone about understanding themselves" (pp. 97–98). In tune with Pribram's analysis, Hoffman, Cochran, and Nead (1990) propose that "the metaphor [that is, the picture theory of imagery] is doing exactly what a scientific metaphor should do" (p. 214) as it generates theoretical classification systems and ideas for experiments. They point out that through its conceptual contribution, metaphor helps to define the specific ways in which the phenomenon of interest requires further investigation and theorizing.

Self-Reflexive Understanding

A few additional observations from Pribram (1990) seem particularly significant for constructivist psychology. He states that although the "skeptics are indeed correct in doubting our ability to achieve an existential understanding of our own brains," and although "existential understanding is essentially private, whereas scientific understanding is essentially and eminently shareable," when it comes to the innovation of understanding and the broadening of knowledge, "the proper use of analogical reasoning sets in motion a self-reflective process by which, metaphorically speaking, brains come to understand themselves" (pp. 79–80).

But how might this analogical reasoning and self-reflective process show itself in psychotherapy? This is what resulted when a client I will call Ellen transported her statement of "burnout" into a set of analogical reasonings:

> *Burnout is what happens when the flame has been turned too high for too long. I have gotten charred.*

> *Burnout is what occurs in a closed room where the fire exhausts its oxygen and builds up toxic gases.*
>
> *Burnout occurs when there is not enough fuel for the fire; when it dies from a lack of fuel.*

Playing these analogies off against each other and against her real-life situation, Ellen was more adequately able to define her current dilemmas of overwork, psychological pressure from her employers, and lack of time for rest and creative work. With new insight into what was happening in her life she formed plans to reduce her fatigue and tension, even as she started an in-depth evaluation of her meanings of career.

Cognitive Synergy

Continuing this sampling of contemporary scholarship, I find Apter's (1982) conception of metaphor as "cognitive synergy" provides a way to name the surprise element in metaphor—the element that makes us come to attention when an apt metaphor shakes our thinking. In defining his terms, Apter used the root metaphors of synergy: "The term synergy (from the ancient Greek *ergon* meaning work, and *syn* meaning together) is intended to imply that two processes are working together to produce an effect which neither could produce alone. In the case of *cognitive synergy*, this new effect produced by the conjunction of mutually exclusive meanings is experiential, and can be described as increased vividness associated with enhanced arousal" (p. 56).

I interpret this to mean that use of a metaphor creates new meaning, yet in some interesting, paradoxical manner, the integrity of the original terms in that metaphor remain intact. It appears that the contradictions inherent in metaphor are held in place by their paradoxical similarities; what develops is "something like an electrical potential [that] is set up between the contradictions" (Apter, 1982, p. 61). As contradictions are held in tensive juxtaposition by the metaphoric nexus, excitement, attention, surprise, and innovative thought are generated.

Olds (1992) came to similar conclusions when she characterized metaphor as drawing on "imagery or affective associations as part of its power for sharpening thought. Metaphor 'carries us,' allowing the rich subsidiary meanings we bring to both points of contrast to be organized around the creation of new meanings. Metaphor creates 'semantic resonance.'" From Olds's perspective, "the power of metaphor resides in its capacity to hold in interactive tension both similarities and differences between two compared objects or events, the two poles of the metaphor." In this manner, the "power of analogy opens up fruitful contrasts and comparisons; an inappropriate metaphor can even be useful in suggesting more precisely how two fields in fact do differ. *Negations play as crucial a role as affirmations in 'analogical imagination'*" (p. 24, emphasis added).

Emotion and Verbal Expression

But what about metaphor and emotion? And what about emotion and meaning-making? My own metaphoric characterization of emotions as "barometers of meaning" is an acknowledgment of the mysterious dynamics that provide a running report of how well we think and feel we are doing (compare Frijda, 1988). Lazarus and Folkman (1984) describe the running evaluation this way: "humans are meaning-oriented, meaning-building creatures who are constantly evaluating everything that happens. . . . These evaluations are guided by cognitive structures that orient the person with respect to what is relevant and important for well-being" (pp. 276–277). Miall (1989) also acknowledged the interactive dynamics of meaning and emotion when he wrote, "The development and fate of the self are monitored continually, with emotions forming the anticipatory reference points that help to determine behavior and thought" (p. 196). Miall holds the conviction that "emotion is not the result of shifts in the core constructs that define the self; it is the cause and agent of the shifts" (p. 194). For these reasons, meaning-making is not just a detached analytical intellectual enterprise. It involves our excitements, our griefs, and our passions as well.

If emotions are barometers of meaning and if metaphor can be an expression of meaning or meaninglessness as well as a prod to meaning-making, then metaphors would seem to serve a very important role in translating the intangibles of emotion into some sort of verbal expression. Indeed, clients do struggle to put their sense of meaninglessness and emotional turmoil into words that the therapist can understand. As a result, many metaphors early in therapy contain the phrase, "I feel," as clients stretch their languages to convey their sense of loss, emptiness, fear, or confusion.

In contrast, preliminary examination of case histories suggests that during the closing hours of therapy, "I feel" statements are frequently replaced by "I have," "I understand," or "I am changing" statements. Clients appear to move from being in the middle of emotional and cognitive dissonance into broader, more fulfilling perspectives on self. They become more able to live in the present, more accepting of the unexpected in their life process and more capable of taking charge not only of new explorations and activity but of reflective adaptive monitoring and redirection of thought and emotion. They no longer feel so much at the mercy of mood and emotion, as brief closing statements from another client, Natalie, illustrate:

> I am able to step back outside of this and then look in again. And I can take everything that I was emotionally involved in previously and look at them in separate packages. I am more able to see how they have affected my behavior up to this point and I also see how they are still affecting me. Being able to look at it this way now, makes it as though I can take it and rearrange things a little bit, which is intriguing to me. . . . I feel like I am enjoying the freedom of being outside of the emotional web [cited in Carlsen, 1988, pp. 106–107].

On that reflective note, this preliminary exploration moves into more precise description and illustration of the therapy called meaning-making.

Meaning and Meaning-Making

In earlier writing (Carlsen, 1988), I discussed how the term *meaning* can be conceptually enlarged to link the elements of the noun and the verb: on the one hand, meaning; on the other, mean-ing. Meaning as a noun contains the elements of constructs, word systems, cognitive schemata, matrices of belief, orienting mechanisms, and reference points for ordering personal reality (compare Kreitler & Kreitler, 1976)—in other words, the descriptors of that which orders and makes sense of the inputs of life experience. But when meaning is mean-ing, it becomes the predicate that incorporates the activities of process, movement, growth, personal anticipation, and intending—the "from-to" growths and developments that take us both from what we do not know to what we know and from what we know to what we do not know (compare Polanyi & Prosch, 1975). In these transitions, we often move from being inside our problems (from "being the problem," in other words) to cognitively and emotionally stepping outside our problems to understand them and to have them.

As its hyphen suggests, *meaning-making* interconnects nouns that are reference points for meaning—love, vocation, learning, for example—and the verbs of processing, doing, creating, and developing. Indeed, meaning-making is active; meaning-making is process; meaning-making is the doing that we are. This usage is in the tradition of Fingarette (1963), who concluded that the individual's presumed meaning-making may refer to a "scientific . . . process of developing a logical, reliably interpretable and systematically predictive theory" or to an "existential . . . process of generating a new vision which shall serve as the context of a new commitment" (pp. 64–65). This usage of meaning-making is also in the tradition of Kegan (1982), who asserted, "it is not that a person makes meaning, as much as that the activity of being a person is the activity of meaning-making" (p. 11).

Meaning-making, then, is about the journey of development and the creation of self—the activity of each person who is both shaping a self and shaping a coherent, meaningful life. This journey constitutes our life project—"often misunderstood as a lonely and radically free decision—that is actually the cumulative structure of meaning that unfolds slowly in the course of life and links together a person's past, present, and future into a coherent whole" (Charme, 1984, p. 2). Here are enacted our evolutionary tendencies toward greater order, interrelatedness, and complexity. Development is a transformational shift that occurs as a person moves from one system of structuring the world to another. It is not a simple cumulative process but a transformational one. With increasing complexity of thought and self-knowledge comes increasing capacity to achieve personal creative solutions and new forms of knowledge (Carlsen, 1988, pp. 12–13). In this process are the movements of personal knowing that can take a person into "more epistemologically powerful (inclusive, viable, integrated) ways of making sense of the world" (Lyddon & Alford, 1993, p. 32).

It seems that if there is any truth, it is a truth of process—of form moving to and through form in an epigenetic, organic manner that grows from the unfolding of the seed that is at the heart of human development. Indeed, the original metaphoric meanings of develop include "to unwrap, to disentangle, to rid free; to open out of its enfolding cover; to unveil or lay bare to oneself; to discover, detect, find out; to cause to grow (what exists in the germ): to grow into a fuller, higher, or more mature condition" (Oxford English Dictionary, 2nd ed.). How this evolutionary tendency toward greater order, interrelatedness, and complexity is fostered and encouraged both in ourselves and in our clients is the exploratory question that carries this discussion into the activities of a developmental-constructivist psychotherapy.

Meaning-Making as Psychotherapy

Although our designs and strategisms for psychotherapy might suggest otherwise, therapeutic change cannot be legislated in any predictable fashion: therapy does not follow a schedule, it is neither predictable nor linear, and it is definitely not neat and tidy in its sequences. Too much happens both inside and outside the therapy room—think of the vast numbers of inputs between sessions—for us to arrive at any simple conclusions about what makes therapy work. Often, it is the intangibles of belief, respect, or dialogue that make the difference, not some special technique. Nevertheless, we do not give up our expertise, nor do we abandon our theories and methods to the whims of chance. What we need to give some order to the mysterious and the unexpected in psychotherapy is a guiding theory and a flexible design. With these to shape our process, we can better determine our techniques, our forms of communication, our dynamics of relationship, and the kinds of roles we want to incorporate.

The design adopted in my own formulation of sequential meaning-making unfolds in four cycling/recycling stages of *establishment, data gathering, patterning,* and *closure and reconciliation.* In the first phase of psychotherapy, the therapist *establishes* a relationship with each client, working to make him or her feel listened to, understood, and respected in his or her presenting concerns. In the safety of the therapy room, what is offered is the possibility of a "holding environment" (Kegan, 1982, pp. 256–257) that will provide not only confirmation and a sense of continuity during the course of the therapy but also an opportunity for learning, growing, and evolving through the point-counterpoint experience of the therapeutic dialogue. From a constructivist perspective, this means a time for probing the differing ways the client interprets, relates to, and acts upon the world.

Even as the initial relationship is being established, the work of *data gathering* is begun—what Loder (1981, p. 54) has called the "scanning of the environment"—as client and therapist work together to name presenting concerns, history, beliefs, disillusionments, emotional reactions, and whatever seems of primary importance in the early hours of therapy. Varieties of therapeutic technique and assessment—genograms, for example, or autobiographical writing—are available to be used according to client need, all with the purpose of building mutual trust and of opening the presenting problems to expanding exploration. And even as assumptions, beliefs, attitudes, meanings are explored, so are the dynamics of personal emotion. "What are you feeling right now?" is a common question that joins with the other central question, "What do you mean by that?"

As therapy progresses, the continual questionings, searchings, wonderings, sharings of experience, ideas, and feelings interact to form tentative hypotheses, tentative theories, of what is going on and what needs to go on. Emerging self-knowledge and self-understanding may bring experimentation with a new scenario for self. This can be the time of *patterning*, of assembling the pieces of the personal puzzle in entirely new ways, of creating new patterns of self-description, of building theories, of experimenting with new life experience. In other words, this third stage (although, of course, there are no neat and tidy stages—they intermingle, cycle, and recycle throughout a single session and throughout the course of therapy) is the ongoing search for patterns and process as the deconstruction/construction evolution continues. Here the concept of play is frequently introduced, to lighten the comparisons and contrasts that feed insights and new awareness. I use the word play a great deal, as I remember Einstein's idea of "free play with concepts" (cited in Holton, 1979, p. 158). Metaphor and its accompanying analogical reasoning can be very much a part of this play.

Finally, through establishing a relationship, varying, intertwining, data gathering, and patterning, therapy moves into a time of *closure and reconciliation* (compare Loder, 1981). In reconciliation, new understandings bring former understandings, former ways of framing the world, into a fresh accommodation when that which is familiar is worked into the fabric of the strange and unfamiliar. This time of accommodative reconciliation signals movements into closure, as the therapist continues to reinforce and affirm each client's broadened conceptions of self. What is also named and emphasized is the ongoing challenge of *process*—that there is no final cure for the problems of life, that they will reappear in new form (compare Rogers, 1956). What makes this negative-sounding assertion more positive is that transformed knowings give promise that future problems will be more quickly and easily resolved. The validity of this statement is demonstrated repeatedly when former clients come back for "tune-ups" that build on what was learned and worked through before. They are almost always in a much different conceptual and emotional place, much more able to work through their new problems in a speedy, insightful manner (compare Carlsen, 1988, pp. 167–182; Rogers, 1956).

Meaning-Making as Heuristic Process

To keep our meaning-makings alive and active, we do well to feed our thinking and our therapies with fresh knowledge and insight. For these reasons, part of my meaning-making has been the continuing search for patterns of process that affirm the evolution of developmental design within the relatively brief sequences of psychotherapy (compare Bateson, 1958; Keeney, 1983; Rogers, 1956). To serve that purpose in this freshening of my study of therapeutic meaning-making, I have tapped conceptions and models of heuristic inquiry. Why? Because the patterning of heuristic process is so much like the meaning-making model and because it allows and cultivates the mystery of discovery and creation. Constructive insight emerges from within rather than being imposed from without.

Because constructive insight emerges from within, the objective of heuristic search is not to prove or disprove the influence of one thing or another but rather "to discover the nature of the phenomenon itself and explicate it as it exists in human experience" (Douglass

& Moustakas, 1985, p. 42). In this heuristic manner, therapy tracks particular themes and questions, particular dilemmas of meaning and meaning-making, always working to stimulate new thought, emotion, and action in a kind of "passionate and discerning personal involvement in problem solving, an effort to know the essence of some aspect of life through the internal pathways of the self" (Douglass & Moustakas, 1985, p. 40). Adopting this heuristic approach, therapy is more open to the speculations created by imagination, intuition, and self-reflection and to the creative insights and cognitive expansions stimulated by the use of metaphor.

Moustakas (1990, pp. 27–32) frames a six-stage heuristic process that clarifies what I have suggested above: (1) an initial engagement with the presenting questions; (2) an "immersion" in the related questions around the central topic, a central questioning; (3) a time of gestation and incubation when the subconscious can tackle the problem in ways illustrative of creative process; (4) the times of new understanding and insight—the "ah, ha, and aha," of creative insight; (5) a time of naming and explication; and finally, (6) a coming together of the new ideas into a meaningful synthesis. In the manner of meaning-making, heuristic inquiry steps back from personal knowings to challenge them in order to more fully understand them.

In adopting the heuristic approach in my research, writing, and psychotherapy, I have allowed for gullibility in my speculations, as defined by Arieti (1976). Building on his study of creative process, he concluded that "gullibility means a willingness to explore everything: to be open, innocent, and naive before rejecting anything. It means accepting (at least temporarily or until proved wrong) that there are certain underlying orderly arrangements beyond and within us. More than the inventing of new things, creativity often implies the discovery of these underlying orderly arrangements" (p. 377).

To help clients discover and appreciate these underlying orderly arrangements, I frequently teach Arieti's (1976) "conditions of creativity" (pp. 372–383) to my clients so that they understand more of what it takes to arrive at creative solutions: cultivation of constructive quiet and aloneness (in contrast to destructive loneliness), free thinking, gullibility, remembrance and inner replaying of past traumatic conflict, and movement from divergent thinking into the alertness and discipline that brings the problem solving to pragmatic resolution and application. I present these conditions as steps, an ordering that provides another "truth of process," another sequential patterning, to help clients learn new ways to handle their problems in the future, when the therapist is no longer around. That learning includes the self-reflective ability to observe, for example, the differences between being gullible and being skeptical, between being too trusting and not trusting enough, between being creatively alone or destructively depressed and lonely. Understandings like these inform and affirm the personal power of the client.

Meaning-Making and Metaphor

In the spirit of meaning-making and of heuristic inquiry, metaphor is purposefully tracked and stimulated in this approach to therapy. Although not much research has been carried out on metaphor in psychotherapy (compare Angus & Rennie, 1989; Rothenberg, 1988), constructivist thinking is reaching out to embrace approaches that pay attention to language and to narrative process (Neimeyer, 1994). These approaches would seem to lead directly and naturally into the use of metaphor.

Therapist-Generated Metaphors

In conceptualizing the use of metaphor as a tool for psychotherapy, the therapist can view the use of metaphors in two contrasting ways. First, metaphors can be structured, set up in advance as interventions or reframings—strategies for psychotherapy. In this approach, the therapist initiates the metaphoric expression—whether through an image, symbolic activity, or an exploration of language—deciding in advance that a particular metaphor will be appropriate, helpful, and facilitative of therapeutic change. This strategic approach is now evident in marriage and family therapy, where metaphor has assumed a very important role both in the training of therapists and in work with family systems (see Duhl, 1983, for an excellent overview). There is much to learn from the research and application in these therapeutic fields; nevertheless, I take a different tack from those who strategize their metaphorical interventions.

Client-Generated Metaphors

In the second use of metaphor, the one that more fully reflects my own, the therapist joins in with the spontaneous expressions of the client, within the particular contexts of each therapy session. This does not mean that a metaphor that appeared in one session cannot be reintroduced by the therapist as an ongoing leitmotif that provides special understandings between therapist and client. Nor does it mean that the therapist squelches his or her own expressions, which can feed the freewheeling play of the therapeutic dialogue. What is most sought, however, is the novelty and spontaneity of client expression that contributes to the shaping of a common language, a set of themes, a group of windows, even as this fresh expression stimulates the comparisons and contrasts that can open the mind and suggest new solutions.

My client Mike provided a metaphorical theme in our first therapy session when he used the phrase, "I am 'out of synch' with my peers." Although fairly sophisticated in his understandings of psychology, he was going through a kind of early-thirties identity crisis and needed a way to sort through his confusions. His words, "I am 'out of synch' with my peers," became an immediate point of departure for our dialogue, a kind of shorthand that formed a third language, one that we shared. The repeated use of his phrase not only made him feel heard but also expanded our explorations in some very fruitful ways.

Kegan on Metaphor in Psychotherapy

Kegan (1994) also discusses the use of metaphor in psychotherapy. He cautions that "any successful approach will have to be both 'cognitive' and 'psychodynamic.' That is, it must be aware of the actual contours of a client's way of knowing and match it closely." And if a therapist introduces "images, 'frames,' malleable maps, or metaphors" to further the facilitative process of therapy, they must be "introduced tentatively, with an ear to the client's own use of images and a readiness to abandon the offered metaphor if the client does not incorporate it into her own discourse." In addition to these suggestions, Kegan offers a "why" for the impact of metaphor when he writes, "Metaphorical language offers the benefit of engaging the left and the right side of the brain simultaneously, combining the linear and the figurative, the descriptive and the participative, the concrete and the abstract" (p. 260).

Root Metaphors of the Therapist's Orientation

Even with a sensitivity to the client's metaphor and a wish to use that metaphor rather than his or her own, the therapist brings personal language to the session, often personal language so much in the background of awareness that the therapist does not realize how much it influences the therapeutic dialogue and experience. Each of us uses such language so automatically that we are often unaware of the dead metaphors that hover in the wings of our consciousness. By identifying these and naming them, we can bring them into the foreground of awareness (where an active metaphor works) to examine them and to decide whether they accurately reflect what we believe. This seems particularly important when we use traditional languages of psychology and of prescribed forms of therapy. Are we attuned to "treatment," "cure," or "adjustment"? Or do we prefer the language of "growth," "development," and "process"? Do we find ourselves adopting the belief that the "mind is a brittle object," a belief that shows up when we characterize clients as quite likely to "fall apart at the seams," "crack up," or be "easily crushed"? (Lakoff & Johnson, 1980, p. 28). How easy it is to internalize therapeutic languages rife with metaphors that we never carefully examine! Indeed, metaphors all too easily take on the colorings of literal truth. This is why we need to call them to our attention—to bring them into awareness in order to analyze them and make choices about them (Leary, 1990b).

New understandings of the dynamic relationship between language and thought can help us accept Kegan's recent suggestion that therapists need to be "experts in discourse" (I appreciate Kegan's ideas conveyed in a December 1994 conversation). To be an expert in discourse means to recognize, name, and sort not only our clients' languages but our own. It also means to be a teacher of discourse, as we help clients to notice and analogically work with their spontaneous expressions. It means to stimulate and encourage the dialogues that bring therapy to life (Friedman, 1985), to activate listening that leads to more than paraphrasing (Stewart & Thomas, 1986), and to join in creative theorizing and the playing off of ideas and language—all to shake loose old ideas and behavior and to stimulate the new.

To be an expert in discourse also means to reach across disciplinary lines in order to incorporate a diverse range of scholarship into the process of discourse and to draw upon the field of communication theory for application to that same process. I have had my client dialogues enriched, for example, when I adopted the metaphor of dialogical listening as the "sculpting of mutual meanings" advanced by communication theorists Stewart and Thomas (1986). This sculpting, they write, "runs with metaphors" (p. 190), by which I understand them to mean that a reciprocal construction of meaning occurs as the partner in dialogue listens creatively for both subtle and obvious metaphors in order to weave them into his or her response. "When the other person hears his metaphor coming back at him, he can get a very quick and clear sense of how he's being heard." Also, there is a "co-building" of talk that produces fresh responses to the issues being faced together (pp. 190–191).

Continuing in the manner of meaning-making, this discussion now moves into its closure/reconciliation stage, as themes and interpretations of metamorphosis are woven into and around examples of client change.

Metamorphosis

Metamorphosis means "the action or process of changing in form, shape or substance;" "a complete change in the appearance, circumstance, condition, character of a person" (*Oxford English Dictionary,* 2nd. ed.). In constructivist and Piagetian terms, metamorphosis includes reconstructions that will be maintained over time and will generalize to other contexts. These reconstructions, or constructivist gains, "are predicated upon a *reorganization of knowledge structures.*" Further, they derive from a *"structural transformation* [that] provides a new foundation upon which to build the next evolutionary step" (Rosen, 1985, p. 190, emphasis added). This is the reason that clients who have achieved a metamorphosis seem to continue growing after their therapeutic sequence is completed. "The larva that has emerged from the cocoon as a beautiful butterfly has not simply become a better larva, but has been transformed in its essential being and will never again be a larva" (Rosen, 1985, p. 190).

At the simplest levels of change, once a person is aware of something, he or she is already different. And on more complex levels, once individuals are able to step outside of fixed opinions, fixed stories of self, fixed repetitions of emotion and behavior, they are more able to move into new experiences of themselves and their worlds. What has been transformed includes their processings of personal reality as well as their reconstituted form of that reality—a developmental shift that takes the person from one way of knowing into another. Developmental theorists describe these shifts in a variety of ways. Basseches (1984), for example, has asserted, "The most equilibrium one will find in adulthood will come from a way of thinking which recognizes all theories—all answers to life—as provisional, awaiting new data, new experiences, new relationships with other people, to be reconstructed in ways that incorporate more." He states further that "the constant epistemic task of life is building better and better understandings" (p. 337).

And what about that "better and better understanding"? Is that not a statement of values, one that might give constructivists pause? Perhaps. But I listen to Basseches when he asserts that "frameworks which help distinguish changes for the better from changes for the worse are essential to an inquiry into human development" (1984, p. 15). Indeed, my study of creative aging clearly demonstrates Basseches's thesis and my own that there is a *better* way (if not a *best* way or a *right* way) to live out life and that this better way includes the cultivation of wisdom, generativity and care; a willingness to entertain new ideas; an acceptance of being in process; and an ongoing sense of curiosity and wonder that can carry a person through the difficult times of life (Carlsen, 1991, pp. 44–46). These developmental goals have been articulated in the work of Erikson (1961) and are being further explored in contemporary studies of wisdom (Sternberg, 1990). The study of these ideals and an observance of the dissonant states that result from the failure of many people to develop their human potential, is leading this meaning-making therapist to foster those client changes that offer promise for more fulfilling programs for life.

Coming to Closure

In this time of closure, I return to client metaphor as I track the constructivist shifts in the ways that clients Becky, Tina, and Arthur made sense of themselves. Even as I do this, I remind the reader that transitions in metaphorical thinking are more likely to be revealed and accomplished in long-term sequences of therapy that allow time for in-depth exploration. It does takes time to practice the dialogical, to reason with the analogical, and to come to the point where the mysteries of process and the sometimes painful surprises in the unexpected are accepted as a part of the engagement of life.

Becky

The story of Becky illustrates some of these transformational achievements. Becky came into therapy when she was dissolving a destructive marriage. Still caught by her husband's abuse and his continual discounting of her capability, it took some intensive therapeutic work for her to fully describe the negative power of his influence. Little by little, she began to break free, to name and affirm her need to assert herself even as she practiced that assertion. What was revealing was that as she broke free from her past and from her relationship, she became increasingly metaphorical even to the point of experimenting with poetry. Her realization that she had stifled her emotional response to abuse was painful at times, and she used metaphor to describe both her recognitions and her new awareness: "It is like looking down a dark, narrow tunnel, with a terrible sadness at the bottom that just makes me weak." Out of the pain, she moved into the naming of self in more definitive ways as she declared, "There is no stuff chipping into what an experience can be," and, "It is so nice to wear myself comfortably," and had the insight that "I don't think about life in the same way at all." Becky left therapy soon after she made these statements, and occasional contact between us has convinced me that there is no way she will allow herself to be caught again in the negative passivity of her former relationship.

Tina

Tina's metaphors were spotted through a fairly extended therapy that also dealt with identity concerns. Again, many of her metaphors started coming as she made a major developmental change that enabled her to believe in her own identity even as she found pleasure in a mix of family and career. Out of her struggle to find herself, she could allow this mix, describing herself "growing toward wholeness" even as she remembered that she started out feeling "like a china doll, like a child." She also recognized in the course of therapy that she had not seen herself as a "whole person," only as someone with "scattered pieces." None of these metaphors was fed by me. There was clear evidence of her metamorphosis in her spontaneous expressions. Later visits, single session tune-ups, confirmed the durability of her reconstructions.

Arthur

With Arthur, the owner of a highly successful engineering firm, the course of therapy was sometimes vague and ill-defined. However, what became increasingly evident was the depth of the developmental transition and existential crisis that he was experiencing. What became equally clear was how much he needed an empathic therapist to serve as listener and facilitator, teacher, and companion-explorer. Even more, because he was unusually intuitive, as well as sensitive to nuances of idea and language, it meant a great deal to him to have a therapist/writer to serve as a sounding board for his written thought pieces. These spontaneous expressions (often done in the middle of the night) served a very important role in his coming to new insight about himself.

At first, sentences like these appeared: "Doors that were open are closing"; "I'm fascinated by my preoccupation"; "I live by default, by not setting boundaries"; "Darkness equals creativity equals search equals something I am seduced by." Each of these statements provided springboards for discussion, opening topics that he and I might have missed if these metaphors had not been expressed. Arthur's words reflected his loneliness as a man whose intuition and creative drive were not common in his profession. Although he was successful, well liked, and respected, he yearned for ways to incorporate his intuitive, introverted nature into the enactments of his job. In his therapeutic talking and writing into meaning, he gained increased understanding of himself and his unique dilemmas, even as he plotted a future that would allow him to be more genuine in his relationships with his family, his colleagues, and his clients.

Even more, Arthur found increasing enjoyment in his creative efforts, both at work and in the privacy of his writing and thinking. He also found himself less impatient, more willing to allow for the natural unfolding of answers and new experience: "I am savoring the joy of the unexpected"; "I will float on the wind rather than buck the wind"; "The journey is more important than the destination." He also came to understand his need for adventure—an inner desire to be "superman, a hero in the Tolkien model"—and to make business more of an adventure. He realized that he did not "do well in a box." And there was a sadness sometimes as he named the dilemmas of a man who had grown up living out adventure, yet wanted the structures of home and work in a contemporary world. There is a "sadness among men my age with nobody to guide us."

Arthur's breakthroughs accelerated as he quit using alcohol, joined a male support group where his style was accepted and affirmed, and as he articulated awareness of the "little larcenies" of his life that eroded his basic integrities and distorted his values. The "little larcenies" phrase served as a springboard for explorations and reasoning that were still going on as our therapy came to a close. I felt that this man had arrived at a new level of development, with a balanced interdependence, a constructivist ability to compare and contrast present awarenesses and choices with those of the past, and an awakening investment in the plotting of his future even as he accepted the hard work that lay ahead.

Conclusion

In my case explorations and discussion in this chapter, I have explored the languages of metaphor, meaning-making, and metamorphosis even as I have allowed them to run free at times. The purpose of this heuristic exploration has been to immerse myself and the reader in the themes of key words in therapy, to gather samplings of contemporary thought and interpretation in order to gain more understanding of their meanings, and to use those enriched understandings to further discover and illustrate the meaning-making potential of metaphor for the work of constructivist psychotherapy. The case studies have affirmed the value of metaphor to interrupt thought, to surprise, to express feelings and ideas, to shake preconceptions, to call to attention, and to shake people's thinking and knowing in the creation of the new. By paying more attention to the constructive, creative power in metaphorical usage, constructivist psychotherapy has an opportunity to enrich and expand its practices and conceptions.

References

Angus, L. E., & Rennie, D. L. (1989). Envisioning the representational world: The client's experience of metaphoric expression in psychotherapy. *Psychotherapy*, 26, 372–379.

Apter, M. (1982). Metaphor as synergy. In D. S. Miall (Ed.), *Metaphor: Problems and perspectives* (pp. 55–70). New Jersey: Humanities Press.

Arieti, S. (1976). *Creativity: The magic synthesis*. New York: Basic Books.

Basseches, M. (1984). *Dialectical thinking and adult development*. Norwood, NJ: Ablex.

Bateson, G. (1958). *Naven* (2nd ed.). Stanford, CA: Stanford University Press.

Bruner, J. (1986). *Actual minds, possible worlds*. Cambridge, MA: Harvard University Press.

Bruner, J. (1990). *Acts of meaning*. Cambridge, MA: Harvard University Press.

Bruner, J., & Feldman, C. F. (1990). Metaphors of consciousness and cognition in the history of psychology. In D. E. Leary (Ed.), *Metaphors in the history of psychology* (pp. 230–238). New York: Cambridge University Press.

Carlsen, M. B. (1988). *Meaning-making: Therapeutic processes in adult development*. New York: W.W. Norton.

Carlsen, M. B. (1991). *Creative aging: A meaning-making perspective*. New York: W.W. Norton.

Charme, S. L. (1984). *Meaning and myth in the study of lives: A Sartrean perspective*. Philadelphia: University of Pennsylvania Press.

Douglass, B. G., & Moustakas, C. E. (1985, Summer). Heuristic inquiry: The internal search to know. *Journal of Humanistic Psychology*, 25, 39–55.

Duhl, B. S. (1983). *From the inside out and other metaphors: Creative and integrative approaches to training in systems thinking*. New York: Brunner/Mazel.

Erikson, E. H. (1961). The roots of virtue. In J. Huxley (Ed.), *The humanist frame* (pp. 147–165). New York: HarperCollins.

Fingarette, H. (1963). *The self in transformation*. New York: HarperCollins.

Friedman, M. (1985). *The healing dialogue in psychotherapy*. Northvale, NJ: Aronson.

Frijda, N. H. (1988). The laws of emotion. *American Psychologist*, 43, 349–358.

Gardner, H. (1983). *Frames of mind: The theory of multiple intelligences*. New York: Basic Books.

Goodman, N. (1976). *Languages of art: An approach to a theory of symbols*. Indianapolis, IN: Hackett.

Goodman, N. (1984). *Of mind and other matters*. Cambridge, MA: Harvard University Press.

Gruber, H. E. (1980). The evolving systems approach to creative scientific work: Charles Darwin's early thought. In T. Nickles (Ed.), *Scientific discovery: Case studies* (pp. 113–130). Boston: Reidel.

Gruber, H. E., & Davis, S. N. (1988). Inching our way up Mount Olympus: The evolving-systems approach to creative thinking. In R. J. Sternberg (Ed.), *The nature of creativity* (pp. 243–270). New York: Cambridge University Press.

Hoffman, R. R., Cochran, E. L., & Nead, J. M. (1990). Cognitive metaphors in experimental psychology. In D. E. Leary (Ed.), *Metaphors in the history of psychology* (pp. 173–229). New York: Cambridge University Press.

Holton, G. (1979). What, precisely, is 'thinking'? Einstein's answer. In A. P. French (Ed.), *Einstein: A centenary volume* (pp. 153–165). Cambridge, MA: Harvard University Press.

Keeney, B. P. (1983). *The aesthetics of change*. New York: Guilford Press.

Kegan, R. (1982). *The evolving self*. Cambridge, MA: Harvard University Press.

Kegan, R. (1994). *In over our heads: The mental demands of modern life*. Cambridge, MA: Harvard University Press.

Kelly, G. A. (1963). *A theory of personality: The psychology of personal constructs*. New York: W.W. Norton.

Kreitler, H., & Kreitler, S. (1976). *Cognitive orientation and behavior*. New York: Springer.

Kuhn, T. S. (1970). *The structure of scientific revolutions* (2nd ed.). Chicago: University of Chicago Press.

Lakoff, G., & Johnson, M. (1980). *Metaphors we live by*. Chicago: University of Chicago Press.

Lazarus, R. S., & Folkman, S. (1984). *Stress, appraisal, and coping*. New York: Springer.

Leary, D. E. (Ed.). (1990a). *Metaphors in the history of psychology*. New York: Cambridge University Press.

Leary, D. E. (1990b). Preface. In D. E. Leary (Ed.), *Metaphors in the history of psychology* (pp. xi–xiii). New York: Cambridge University Press.

Leary, D. E. (1990c). Psyche's muse: The role of metaphor in the history of psychology. In D. E. Leary (Ed.), *Metaphors in the history of psychology* (pp. 1–78). New York: Cambridge University Press.

Loder, J. (1981). *The transforming moment*. San Francisco: Jossey-Bass.

Lyddon, W. J. (1989). Root metaphor theory: A philosophical framework for

counseling and psychotherapy. *Journal of Counseling and Development, 67,*
442–448.

Lyddon, W. J., & Alford, D. J. (1993). Constructivist assessment: A
developmental-epistemic perspective. In G. J. Neimeyer (Ed.), *Constructivist assessment: A casebook* (pp. 31–57). Newbury Park, CA: Sage.

Miall, D. S. (Ed.). (1982). *Metaphor: Problems and perspectives.* Atlantic High-
lands, NJ: Humanities Press.

Miall, D. S. (1989). Anticipating the self: Toward a personal construct model of
emotion. *International Journal of Personal Construct Psychology, 2,*
185–198.

Moustakas, C. E. (1990). *Heuristic research design, methodology and applications.*
Newbury Park, CA: Sage.

Neimeyer, R. A. (1994). The role of client-generated narratives in psychotherapy. *Journal of Constructivist Psychology, 7,* 229–242.

Olds, L. E. (1992). *Metaphors of interrelatedness: Toward a systems theory of psychology.* Albany: State University of New York Press.

Pepper, S. C. (1942). *World hypotheses: A study in evidence.* Berkeley: University
of California Press.

Polanyi, M., & Prosch, H. (1975). *Meaning.* Chicago: University of Chicago
Press.

Pribram, K. M. (1990). From metaphors to models: The use of analogy in neuropsychology. In D. E. Leary (Ed.), *Metaphors in the history of psychology*
(pp. 79–103). New York: Cambridge University Press.

Rogers, C. R. (1956). What it means to become a person. In C. E. Moustakas
(Ed.), *The self* (pp. 195–211). New York: HarperCollins.

Rosen, H. (1985). *Piagetian dimensions of clinical relevance.* New York: Columbia
University Press.

Rothenberg, A. (1988). *The creative process of psychotherapy.* New York: W.W.
Norton.

Royce, J. R., & Mos, L. P. (Eds.). (1981). *Humanistic psychology: Concepts and
criticisms.* New York: Plenum.

Smith, H. (1976/1992). *Forgotten truth: The common vision of the world's religions.*
San Francisco: HarperSanFrancisco. (Original work published 1976)

Sternberg, R. E. (1990). *Wisdom: Its nature, origins, and development.* New York:
Cambridge University Press.

Stewart, J., & Thomas, M. (1986). Dialogic listening: Sculpting mutual meanings. In J. Stewart (Ed.), *Bridges not walls: A book about interpersonal communication* (4th ed., pp. 180–197). New York: Random House.

Part VI

Constructivist and Social
Constructionist Psychotherapy:
Examples of Personal Implications

13

Process Interventions for the Constructivist Psychotherapist

Robert A. Neimeyer

In their initial letter of invitation to each of the contributors to this book, Kevin Kuehlwein and Hugh Rosen announced their desire "to give voice to the underlying theme underpinning all versions of constructivism as well as to its many variations and amplifications." Similarly, they expressed their hope that the various chapters would "demonstrate to the reader how one might translate the implications of constructivism into the theory and practice of effective therapy," prompting each contributor to speak to the ways in which his or her adherence to a constructivist epistemology "makes a difference in [his or her] practice, attitudes, strategies and techniques." They suggested that these goals might be best achieved by clarifying how we would distinguish ourselves from nonconstructivist clinicians in these respects but, beyond that, granted us free rein to develop our ideas in whatever way seemed congenial to us. Intrigued by the prospect of collaborating with a broad range of other constructivists in articulating our positions and impressed by the generous degree of latitude granted us by the editors to pursue these goals, I eagerly accepted the invitation.

As time passed, however, I began to experience a vague sense of unease whenever I contemplated putting finger to keypad to begin writing this chapter. It was not that my commitment to this project specifically or to constructivism more generally had waned; if anything, my advocacy of a constructivist base for psychotherapy had become increasingly evident in the domains of presentation, publication, and practice. Why then the curious reluctance to set down and illustrate the implications of my constructivist convictions in black and white?

As I began to struggle with this question, it suddenly struck me that the answers were all around me in my recent "conversations" with other constructivists, whether in public discourse, printed debates, or private discussions. Indeed, it came to me that nearly every aspect of that apparently straightforward invitation had somehow become problematic for me. While I myself had attempted in various contexts to identify "underlying themes" that would give coherence to constructivist perspectives (Neimeyer, 1988; Neimeyer, 1993b; Neimeyer, 1993c; Neimeyer & Feixas, 1990), I had also become increasingly aware of the important points of divergence among constructivist theorists (Neimeyer, 1993a; Neimeyer, 1995a; Neimeyer, Neimeyer, Lyddon, & Hoshmand, 1994) on issues as fundamental as basic epistemology, ontology, and therapeutic strategy. With so much dissensus within the constructivist camp, could my own work meaningfully be seen as a "variation or amplification" of a unifying theme? Moreover, I had become more critical of the abstractness of much constructivist discourse (Neimeyer, in press), raising serious questions whether my own theoretical principles could be sufficiently distilled to permit their clear "translation" into practice. Finally, I had begun to experience a kind of conceptual vertigo, which accompanied the blurring of familiar boundaries as proponents of apparently contrasting philosophical and psychological traditions began to identify themselves as constructive or narrative theorists. If advocates of critical realism (Noaparast, 1995), cognitive-behavioral modification (Meichenbaum, 1993), and rational-emotive (Ellis, 1993) approaches are to be considered constructivist, could I hope to distinguish between constructivist and nonconstructivist positions?

The net result of these background misgivings is a chapter that is highly personal in its content. I have attempted to enunciate those themes that seem to unify my own (current) work; explicate and, where possible, illustrate their application to practice; and distinguish my present provisional principles for doing therapy from those alternatives I know best, namely, my own past convictions. I begin by taking a brief backward glance over the evolution of my practice as a psychotherapist and then "unpack" for the reader my working (constructivist) definition of psychotherapy, to erect a framework for the consideration of therapeutic techniques that follows. I then move on to several forms of process intervention that are compatible with this overall framework, referring to the work of other constructivist authors when it extends, supports, or refines my own preliminary attempts at specifying what I do. Finally, I conclude with some thoughts on where these clinical and conceptual currents seem to be carrying me, with the recognition that most of our attempts to forecast the course of our own development rely upon a rather dusty crystal ball.

One Therapist's Journey

Looking back at my early development as a psychologist, it is hard to see how I could have become anything other than a constructivist psychotherapist. As an undergraduate, I had been steeped in the European philosophic tradition and was particularly influenced by Kant's argument (1781/1952) that human perception was inherently constrained by our "categories of intuition," forever barring us as a species from having direct access to a "noumenal" reality of things-in-themselves. Merleau-Ponty's phenomenological perspective (1962) deepened this essential insight by asserting the primacy of the lived world of human experience over artificial attempts to distinguish between the knower and the known. Polanyi (1958) effectively dismantled the related myth of scientific objectivity, arguing that passionate and often tacit personal knowledge undergirded even the most vaunted scientific achievements. Finally, Foucault (1970) added a critical historical perspective in his analysis of

the "ordering codes" by which different cultures and epochs organized their experience in language, sometimes with socially oppressive results. Thus primed, I was ill-prepared to accept the then-
dominant behavioristic forms of psychological discourse, which I
found to be arid and insulting at the conceptual level and simplis-
tic and prescriptive at the clinical practice level.

Traveling the Path of Kelly's Personal Construct Psychology

What I was prepared to accept was personal construct theory,
George Kelly's ambitious attempt (1955) to lay a different kind of
assumptive base for psychology and, in particular, psychotherapy.
As the founding father of clinical constructivism, Kelly rejected the
foundationalist doctrines of both idealism and materialism, which
attempted to find a secure anchor for human knowledge in transcendent principles on the one hand or sense data on the other. He
conceded that it may be "disturbing to visualize ourselves trying to
make progress in a world where there are no firm points of departure immediately accessible to us, no 'givens,' nothing that we start
out by saying we know for sure" (Kelly, 1977, p. 5). Yet he maintained that

> The "known realities" keep slipping out from under us.
> Our senses play all kinds of tricks and prove themselves
> to be the most unreliable informants. And our theolo-
> gies, far-seeing as they appear to be, do, in time, lead to
> such indecent practices that sensitive men refuse to take
> them literally. Thus we find ourselves repeatedly cut off
> from what we thought we knew for sure, and we must
> reluctantly abandon the very faiths from which we orig-
> inally launched our most fruitful enterprises.
>
> The upshot of all this is that we can no longer rest
> assured that human progress may proceed step by step in
> an orderly fashion from the known to the unknown.
> Neither our senses nor our doctrines provide us with the

immediate knowledge required for such a philosophy of science. What we think we know is anchored only in our assumptions, not in the bed rock of truth itself, and that world we seek to understand remains always on the horizons of our thoughts [pp. 5–6].

Rather than lapsing into nihilism in the face of this foundationlessness, however, Kelly sought to respond affirmatively by sketching the outlines of a new kind of psychological theory whose focus was the processes by which human beings posit, test, and revise their constructions of a world to which they are forever denied direct access. In elaborating upon this basic postulate, Kelly (1955) systematically teased out the further implications of his position through a set of corollaries bearing on the construing process, the structure of knowing, and the social embeddedness of personal knowledge (Neimeyer, 1987). Thus, he viewed human beings as "set" to attend to recurring patterns in the flow of events, punctuating and thematizing them in an effort to find sufficient regularity to anticipate the future in meaningful ways. He viewed all action as anchored in implicit anticipation, representing a behavioral commitment to our often passionately held personal and communal interpretations. Kelly's was not a solipsistic position, however. To the extent that our own concrete perceptions of events might fail to validate our more abstract assumptions, we would need significant restructuring of our construct systems, to permit their extension and refinement. Yet despite his emphasis on the reconstruction and elaboration of our systems of meaning, Kelly recognized that deep-going change in our most basic constructions of self and world was rarely easy. Indeed, all of us experience the perturbation that attends such change when the central constructs on which our personal theories depend are challenged, much as scientists resist modification of the "metaphysical hard core" of their most cherished formal theories (Guidano & Liotti, 1983, p. 63).

One of the unique features of Kelly's theory was his attempt to specify the *structure* of knowing, both in terms of the essential properties of our basic units of meaning and of the broader organization of these units into viable systems for anticipating events and guiding our action. At the most basic level, Kelly held that meaning is a matter of contrast, that we frame discriminations in terms of *bipolar constructs* that identify what things are by distinguishing them from what they are not. From this perspective, every assertion implies an unstated negation: for example, the compliment delivered by a husband in marital therapy that the therapist is "refreshingly intelligent" can be understood only in terms of its implicit contrast (perhaps to the client's spouse or previous therapist). On a more general level, these constructs are viewed as hierarchically arranged, with some functioning as relatively durable core identity constructs for the person who uses them, and others being more peripheral and hence more open to modification without necessitating major reorganization of the individual's system. Ultimately, however, even the most elaborate personal construct system has its limits, which are revealed all too clearly when the individual anxiously confronts urgent experiences that cannot be accounted for in the light of his or her prevailing understandings.

Finally, Kelly made at least a preliminary attempt to place the self in social context, by acknowledging that our personal elaboration of meaning is grounded in the common field of constructions afforded by our language and cultural systems. At a more molecular level, he also provided a starting point for a constructivist analysis of interpersonal relationships, through his emphasis on "construing the construction processes of the other" as the basis for developing social roles (Neimeyer & Neimeyer, 1985). In the therapeutic setting, this view suggests the necessity of our developing an awareness of the client's core role structure, his or her "deepest understanding of being maintained as a social being" (Kelly, 1955). However, whether in the context of counseling or other intimate relationships, access to this core construction of self is rarely permitted by the individual in a casual or direct way, since such permission would open the person to the potential "terror" of invalidation by the individual who has been "allowed in" (Leitner & Faidley, in press).

Much of Kelly's portrayal of persons resonated with me, particularly as I began my training as a psychotherapist. I was drawn to his respectful depiction of struggling human beings as wrestling not with the demons of a traumatic past or the unfavorable reinforcement contingencies available in their immediate environment but with the distressing implications for the future and limitations of their best attempts to construct a reality within which they could live. Moreover, unlike the classificatory diagnostic systems in which I was being trained, personal construct theory leveled the playing field, inviting me to construe myself in the same terms—or at least along the same dimensions of evaluation—as my client. This emphasis on reflexivity put *me* clearly in the therapy and consistently reminded me that my construction of my client's position was just that—my construction. At the same time, Kelly prodded me to surmount, as best I could, the constraints of my own system and to bend every effort toward seeing the client's world through his or her eyes, to see the options available from his or her perspective. While some of these themes informed other humanistic psychologies as well, construct theory offered a richness of vocabulary that revealed human change processes at a level of specificity that I had never before (or since) encountered. Thus, while it offered occasional novel suggestions for therapeutic strategies and assessment techniques (Leitner & Dunnett, 1993; Neimeyer, 1993; Neimeyer & Neimeyer, 1987), its great value for me as a developing therapist lay in its functioning as a permeable metatheory that allowed me to organize and assimilate a broad field of clinical concepts and strategies that cohered with its essentially constructivist perspective.

A View from the Frontier

After some years of working within personal construct psychology and the growing international theory group that was applying, testing, and elaborating this perspective (Neimeyer, 1985), I felt thoroughly at home with the theory. Not only did its basic respect for the deep individuality of each person fit my experience as a psychotherapist but even its more esoteric terminology began to feel like second nature, providing a comfortable frame of reference in which I could interpret and organize my interactions with clients. Like a well-designed and spacious old house, its various rooms and views of the surrounding terrain continued to intrigue me even after many years of habitation, and it offered a convivial meeting place for conversations with fellow travelers, whose journeys often originated within quite different traditions. (Dalton and Dunnett, 1992, provide a reader-friendly introduction to the terminology of the basic theory, while contributors to Mancuso and Adams-Webber's 1982 book offer chapter-length excursions into the research deriving from each of Kelly's corollaries.)

And yet, without my fully realizing it, my way of living within the theory had begun inevitably to change as I evolved as a therapist and person. Ironically, in a passage on human (and scientific) development, Kelly (1977) himself had captured in metaphor some of the subtlety of this evolution: "with each new step that brings into focus some new facet of the universe, something, which before we thought was all settled, begins to look questionable. It is not that each new fact displaces an old one, but that gradually, almost imperceptibly as our ventures progress, a darkening shadow of doubt begins to spread over the coastline behind us" (p. 7).

For me, the "shadow of doubt" that began to darken the once-safe harbor of personal construct theory took the form of a vague dissatisfaction with the basic emphasis of Kelly's theory itself. It was not so much that it began to feel *wrong* to me, as that it began to feel *confining*, in need of enlargement, remodeling, or joining together with some adjacent theoretical structures. Indeed, the contemporary construct theorists whose work I found most exciting were precisely those who stepped outside the formal structure of Kellian theory, boldly envisioning extensions into such domains as family construct psychology (Feixas, 1990; 1992; Procter, 1987), language-based therapy (Efran & Clarfield, 1992; Efran, Lukens, & Lukens, 1990), or conversational psychology more generally (Mair, 1989).

In retrospect, I realize that what distinguished these perspectives was their attention to the processes that *connect* people, that link the individual subjectivities envisioned by Kelly. In fairness, Kelly had in fact attempted such intersubjective bridging through his attention to social role construction and to the individual's struggle to "join" with the core identity constructs of another; Kelly's effort has been considerably advanced by subsequent construct theorists (Leitner, 1988; Leitner & Faidley, in press). But for the most part, scholars working within this tradition have continued to grant primacy to the personal, as distinct from the interpersonal, aspects of human existence. In contrast, systemic constructivists like Anderson and Goolishian (1992), Hoffman (1992), and White and Epston (1990) gave focal attention to the *conversational construction of meaning* (Loos & Epstein, 1989) and its implications for therapeutic practice. As illustrated by the chapters by Friedman, McNamee, and others in this book, the language-based social constructionist perspective afforded new vistas on human change, describing processes facilitated by a form of therapeutic dialogue that weaves narratives imparting a sense of coherence, relevance, and elaborative possibility to clients contending with a problem (Loos, 1993). At the same time, personal construct theory still seemed to hold the edge in offering a fine-tuned depiction of the evolution of meaning systems at the individual level.

But even with the complementary perspectives afforded by systemic and personal versions of constructivism, something still seemed missing. At one level, systemic and narrative theorists had undertaken a telling analysis of the ways in which particular styles of "languaging" about problems constrain the persons subordinated to those styles, and had even sketched the outlines of alternative therapies that empowered clients to approach difficulties in fresh ways (Epston & White, 1995). Too often, however, the discussion of language by systemic authors seemed too abstract, too remote from where the rubber meets the road, namely, the actual give-and-take of therapeutic conversation between client and therapist. Likewise, most of the personal construct tradition sidestepped the task of spelling out in a concrete way the "structural coupling" between client and therapist systems (Maturana & Varela, 1987, p. 75). Thus, as a therapist, I found myself still groping for ways to convey (especially in training contexts) my distinctive *patterns of engagement* with clients, the particular ways in which I entered into therapeutic conversations with individuals and families whose personal and communal constructions of reality had somehow become foreclosed, conflictual, or chaotic. What follows, then, is a preliminary attempt to articulate some of my prereflective awareness of those conversational practices in which I tacitly engage as I attempt to assist clients in the process of therapeutic reconstruction. Because constructivism has come to mean different things to different authors (Lyddon, 1995; Neimeyer, 1995a), I begin with a brief overview of the conceptual terrain in which this approach is grounded and then progress to a consideration of several specific process interventions for the constructivist psychotherapist.

A Definitional Beginning

Elsewhere, I have discussed what I take to be the defining epistemological features of constructivist therapies, including their adherence to nonrepresentational theories of knowledge; their pluralistic conception of personal and scientific "truth"; their depiction of the proactive, systemic, and discriminative form of construing; and their emphasis on the constitutive role of language, broadly defined, in bringing forth the very realities with which we contend (Neimeyer, 1995a). Several of these themes have also been competently addressed by Rosen and Kuehlwein in the opening and closing chapters of this book. For this reason, I will intentionally steer away from what Schön (1983) aptly referred to as "the high, hard ground" of formal theory, and instead wade directly into "the swampy lowlands" of professional practice.

What features of this shifting and largely unmapped domain of practice emerge as salient when viewed through a constructivist lens? My response begins with a definition of psychotherapy as

> The variegated and subtle interchange and negotiation of (inter)personal meanings . . . in the service of articulating, elaborating, and revising those constructions that the client uses to organize his or her experience and action. Such a definition emphasizes several features of the psychotherapy process, including the delicacy with which the therapist must grasp the contours of the experiential world of the client, the dialogical and discursive basis of their interaction, and the contributions of both to their mutual inquiry. . . . Although psychotherapy conceived along these lines can have many different concrete objectives, at an abstract level all of these involve joining with clients to develop a refined map of the often inarticulate constructions in which they are emotionally invested and that define what they regard as viable courses of action and, then, extending or supplementing these constructions to enlarge the number of possible worlds they might inhabit [Neimeyer, 1995b].

From this conceptual vantage point, what we as therapists have to offer our clients is not an expert set of prescriptions for "correct" ways of thinking, acting, or feeling, but a hard-won and carefully honed expertise in the *therapeutic use of language*. Metaphorically, I think of the work of therapy as *sculpting conversational realities*, giving form to a joint construction that embodies something of the intentionalities of both client and therapist. As is true of the sculptor working with clay or marble, the shape taken by the sculpture as the work unfolds must respect the limitations imposed and the affordances offered by the medium being shaped—in this case, the malleability or recalcitrance of those personal, family, or cultural constructions that define the "problem" in the client's eyes. The shape taken by this linguistic sculpting is similarly constrained by the fineness or coarseness of the conversational tools available to the therapist as well as his or her proficiency in using them. Like all metaphors, of course, this one highlights some features of therapeutic discourse (for example, the delicate, form-giving nature of the therapist's interventions) while obscuring others (for example, the extent to which such sculpting occurs in a more temporal than spatial dimension). But for me, the analogy is instructive, reminding me that an indefinite (but not infinite) range of conversational forms might emerge from the therapeutic interaction, in spite of the stubborn substantiality of the preexisting constructions that clients present to us (Efran & Fauber, 1995).

Of course, other, quite different metaphors could also aptly convey some of what I have in mind as I unpack the conversational artistry that typifies psychotherapy. One alternative that has particular appeal to me is therapy as an exercise in *rhetoric*, understood as an artful use of discourse to accomplish pragmatic ends. Unfortunately (and unfairly), rhetoric acquired a bad name among many psychotherapists trained in "scientifically" oriented graduate programs and pervaded by an ethos of positivism that distrusted any attempt to embellish the unvarnished "facts" upon which attempts at persuasion, communication, or evaluation of arguments were supposed to hinge. But a reconsideration of the utility of rhetoric as a symbolic discursive form of reality construction may now be possible, as constructivist epistemology has begun to make room for alternatives to the dominant objectivism of our discipline. Viewing the psychotherapy office as a stage that grants rhetorical status to both (or all) participants in the conversation also has an affinity to the narrative metaphor adopted by many constructivists, insofar as the "text" of the therapeutic dialogue can be opened to various forms of reading and analysis (Gonçalves, 1995; Russell, 1991; White & Epston, 1990). Many of the process interventions I will describe next could be seen as rhetorical *tropes* (conversational turns or figures of speech) directed toward therapeutic ends. (For a wide-ranging discussion of the resurgence of rhetoric in the social sciences, see Simons, 1989.)

What follows describes and briefly illustrates those conversational tools that I use in my own practice. Because the interventions focus on the process of meaning-making rather than upon content per se, I refer to them as *process interventions for the constructivist psychotherapist*. I make no claim that they are in any sense an exhaustive listing of what we as therapists do; this preliminary taxonomy is a far less than comprehensive description of my practice. But by explicating, exemplifying, and elaborating upon these fairly specific strategies for sculpting the conversations of therapy, I hope to help bridge the gap between the occasionally disembodied conception of language among systemic therapists and the sometimes highly embodied and individualistic conception of construing among personal construct theorists. In emphasizing what transpires *between* therapist and client as partners in therapeutic inquiry, this chapter can be seen as part of a broader effort to envision a "psychology in an intermediary mode" (Mair, 1989, p. 39), one that sees new forms of personal knowledge emerging from the coupling of therapist and client systems of meaning (Glover, 1995).

Process Interventions for the Constructivist Psychotherapist

To explicate some of the conversational practices that inform my own hybrid version of constructivist psychotherapy, I have tried to tease out particular patterns of discourse from the larger fabric of my interaction with clients. In many cases, I found this a challenging task, not only because particular interventions derived their meaning from a broad and difficult to specify conversational context but also because any one intervention often embodied multiple intents, blended multiple categories. Moreover, some intentions seemed to pervade nearly the entirety of my therapy, such as my attempts to encourage greater self-awareness on the part of clients about the implications of their present constructions and their affective significance for clients' lives. In this respect, my efforts as a therapist cohere with the experience of clients studied by Rennie (1992); for these clients, "reflexivity" (encompassing both a sense of awareness and agency) represented a core category implicit in much of their functioning in therapy.

Finally, it is important (and consistent with a constructivist prejudice) to acknowledge that my attempt to formulate a taxonomy of conversational practices is constrained by the structure of my current professional construct system for understanding and organizing the therapeutic encounter. Thus, while there are some common features of my intervention style that I have consciously ignored because they are shared by most forms of therapy (for example, the use of verbal and nonverbal "encouragers" such as saying, "umm hmm," or leaning forward in my chair and the use of open-ended questions), there are undoubtedly many more that may be invisible to me although they would be obvious to other observers. My aim, therefore, is to offer a suggestive and admittedly perspectival taxonomy of interventions for sculpting the process of therapy, which readers (including myself at a future point!) will likely find necessary to refine, revise, or replace to yield a more adequate depiction of therapeutic practice.

The categories of interventions that emerged for me are listed below, along with succinct definitions that I flesh out in the remainder of the chapter.

A few general observations can be made about this taxonomy as a whole. First, all of the interventions take the form of *verbal* nouns, in keeping with the process focus of this approach to therapy. They are the names of the interventions, but they also are *actions*. (Also, I have stretched conventional linguistic usage in labeling some cat-

Selected Process Interventions in Constructivist Psychotherapy.

Intervention	Description
Empathizing	Indwelling the client's meanings and communicating an understanding of them
Analogizing	Developing an image or metaphor to explore or capture an experience
Accentuating	Focusing the client's attention on an important feature of experience that might be overlooked
Nuancing	Highlighting in passing an aspect of the client's communication for further elaboration
Dilating	Widening the field of discussion to include broader issues or implications
Constricting	Narrowing discussion to a single focal issue
Contrasting	Exploring a sensed conflict or discrepancy in the client's experience
Structuring	Articulating or organizing diffuse material in a way that clarifies its implications for action
Ambiguating	Fostering a looser or more approximate meaning
Weaving	Overlaying or connecting strands of related material

egories—for example, "ambiguating"—a semantic infelicity for which I beg the reader's indulgence.) Second, I caution that most of these interventions can be expressed in technically eclectic forms, not all of which are language based, in the narrow sense of that term. To take but a single example, a therapist can engage in contrasting by framing an implied conflict in the client's construing, using a two-chair exercise from gestalt therapy to explore the split, or encouraging a written dialogue between two aspects of the self in a journal format. Thus, although my focus here is on the sorts of conversational gambits that can be found in a therapy transcript, I believe that this taxonomy is compatible with a view of language as "any form of symbolic display, action, or communication within human communities—verbal or nonverbal—intended to establish, question, or otherwise negotiate social and personal meanings and coordinate behavior" (Neimeyer & Mahoney, 1995, p. 406). Finally, several interventions are discussed as complementary counterparts (for example, dilating and constricting), highlighting the point that none of these interventions is a good thing all by itself and that the timing of intervention in the client's change process and its appropriateness to particular *tasks* of therapy (Greenberg, 1992) is a critical consideration in the facilitation of therapeutic reconstruction.

Empathizing

The importance of the therapist's empathic attunement to the client has been considered commonplace in most forms of therapy, at least since the work of Rogers (1951). But *empathizing* has a special significance for the constructivist therapist; in a sense, it provides the necessary grounding for all other interventions. In constructivist terms, empathizing entails the therapist's attempt to build a bridge into the lived experience of the client in order to indwell there, to "try on" the often idiosyncratic meanings the client attributes to events and to communicate an understanding of the predicament embodied in the client's understanding of the presenting problem. While the dimensions of the problem construction may be reshaped in the course of subsequent therapeutic discourse, forming an empathic connection with the client is often a precondition for prompting a therapeutic restructuring of that problem.

An example of this form of empathizing was provided by my recent work with Clara, a dignified and intelligent woman of seventy-six, whose husband, Ed, had entered a nursing home following a series of debilitating strokes that left him confined to a wheelchair and only semilucid. Clara had sought therapy at the insistence of her thirty-eight-year-old son, Richard, who was concerned about her "depression," which peaked dramatically following each of Clara's frequent visits to Ed in the nursing facility. Indeed, her anguish over Ed's "dying by degrees" had been so pronounced that it had resulted in her attempting suicide a few months before, at which point she had been hospitalized and administered ECT and various forms of pharmacotherapy. But despite Richard's increasingly exasperated efforts to "protect" her from further distress by insisting she not visit Ed, Clara had been unable to comply. Instead, she had begun "sneaking" out to see him, even at the risk of driving a wedge of secrecy between her and Richard, whom she regarded as the most "loving and devoted" figure in her life.

It quickly emerged in the first session that the relationship between Clara and her husband had been a strained one at best for decades, characterized by Ed's marital infidelity and verbal and physical abuse of her, the latter stopping only when Richard had grown large and strong enough to intervene. But it also became clear that the "compassion and love" that Clara had learned in her family of origin had been a major resource for her throughout her marital travail; she and Richard recounted numerous incidents of her "unselfish caretaking" toward various family members in distress, from her young adulthood through her older age. Thus, as we struggled with her obvious resistance to Richard's pleas that she spare herself (and by implication, him) the pain of frequent visits to Ed, I observed: "I'm really struck by the impossible choice that you face. On the one hand, you can visit Ed, but in doing so you open yourself to painful reminders of all the things that will never be resolved between you, which deepens not only your own distress, but also that of someone you love [*gesturing to Richard*]. On the other hand, you can protect yourself and Richard by not visiting Ed, but at the cost of being inconsistent with a core part of who you are as a devoted and compassionate caretaker."

As Richard looked on quietly for the first time in the session, Clara responded, "Exactly," the moisture in her eyes belying her otherwise stoic self-presentation. Once I had empathized with the apparently irresolvable dilemma arising from the intersection of her self and circumstances, I was then in a better position to explore constructive alternatives with both her and Richard (such as employing symbolic forms of resolving the status of her marital relationship, and examining the implications of Richard's "caretaking" of her). Having begun to indwell the problematic particulars of Clara's construction of life, I was more readily able to envision elaborating her understanding in ways that did not invalidate her core constructs of self and relationships.

Analogizing

By *analogizing*, I mean elaborating an image or metaphor—sometimes suggested by the therapist, sometimes by the client—to explore, capture, or crystallize an experience. Because highly personal and novel meanings are not easily conveyed in the standardized lexicon of public discourse, therapists must frequently stretch the capacity of literal language to help a client articulate an elusive but important awareness or to bring features of the client's constructions into vivid relation through the use of an apt metaphor. For the constructivist therapist, whose overarching goal is to facilitate the extension and clarification of the client's system of meanings, analogizing is a staple intervention that can serve many specific functions (see Chapter Twelve and Gonçalves & Craine, 1990).

One such use of analogy is illustrated by my exploration of a spontaneous image offered by Jack, a sixty-eight-year-old man who saw me during the disintegration of his marriage. Jack reported that his wife's request for a separation had "blindsided" him, coming on the heels of her recent bout with cancer, which reportedly had left her circumspect about spending her remaining years with a man she saw as increasingly depressive and self-isolating since his retirement. A successful officer in the Air Force, Jack had subsequently had a distinguished career at the highest levels of government service and education, and he considered his loss of his wife, Lee, the most vivid "failure" of his life. As the relationship began to fracture, Jack described to me the awkward, stilted interactions with her that had come to replace the "real intimacy" they had once enjoyed. He then alluded to the "curtain of rejection" that he felt when he was in her presence. Sensing that a great deal of significance was being compressed into this three-word phrase, I invited him to unpack it with me more systematically.

BOB: I'm intrigued by that image of the curtain. Can you say more about what it looks like?

JACK: The curtain itself is transparent, like in an old movie. It's not visible, but your hand does not go through. Even though it looks like you're in the same room, there's a clear rebuff.

BOB: Who has put the curtain there?

JACK: It's because of my behavior, my past reclusiveness. I can't really blame Lee for it.

BOB: What feeling does that leave you with?

JACK: Just the irresolution of the whole thing. When we're together, things will be moving down the former path, then she suddenly becomes aware of succumbing to me again, and there's an abrupt change. She scrambles behind the barricades. She says it would be terrible not to see me again—as a friend. . . . But that just doesn't give me the companionship and warmth that I need and want, so I'm always pushing at the curtain when I'm there, although I later restrain myself.

Even this brief exploration of Jack's casually offered metaphor was revealing, bringing into sharper focus (for both of us) the subtle distancing he ascribed to Lee during their interactions, his explanation for this behavior in terms of his own past reclusiveness, and the protective function of the curtain or barricade behind which she scrambled in the face of his all-too-familiar advances. This led us into a useful discussion of Lee's fear that permitting too much closeness would result in her falling under his spell once more, as she had at the beginning of their then-clandestine relationship, a decade before his proposal of marriage.

A rather different use of a "boundary" metaphor occurred in my therapy with Jessie, a thirty-four-year-old social worker trying to sort out the complexities of her relationship to her lesbian partner, Sarah, and her male lover, Michael. Although she had been able to maintain both relationships with her monogamous partners for nearly two years, the "open negotiation" of time commitments and mutual expectations had become increasingly complicated as Michael neared the completion of his graduate program and considered the feasibility of a move to another city. At the same time, Sarah began to make unclear, unsettling requests, such as wanting to lease Jessie's house (which she had helped build) after Jessie vacated it. Jessie experienced these subtly competing emotional demands as in some respects intrusive on the part of both of her partners and was confused by the way in which her implicit agreements with each of them seemed to change from day to day. As she struggled to convey this elusive feeling, I suggested that the "boundaries that define your life seem like walls of sand in a desert world, solid, but sculpted by the wind and constantly rebuilt." The analogy evidently fit for Jessie, and she went on to describe Michael's and Sarah's places in the image ("parts of the wall, but too close"), and her own quest across the course of several relationships for some "flexible boundaries" that would give her a sense of "control." As was also true for other co-constructed metaphors that emerged from our therapy, Jessie spontaneously elaborated on the "walls of sand" image in future sessions, to track the emerging redefinition of her relationships and sense of self. Her recollection and restructuring of the analogy accords with the findings of constructivist researchers who report that therapeutic dialogues rich in the use of appropriate imagery and figurative language seem to promote internalization of the therapeutic conversation and revision of the client's personal theories, events that may represent the core process of therapeutic change (Martin, 1994).

Accentuating

While the fostering of greater client reflexivity is, as I have stated, an overarching goal of my therapy, certain interventions seem specifically relevant to augmenting clients' awareness of the process and content of their construing. One such conversational intervention is *accentuating,* the attempt to focus clients' attention powerfully on some important feature of their experience (or my experience of them) that might otherwise be marginalized or overlooked. An example of this intervention occurred during my contact with Chris, a forty-three-year-old woman who had suffered two major losses in the last year—first of her father, who died suddenly of heart failure, and then of her close friend David Alan, who experienced a protracted death from AIDS.[1] As we spoke at some length about the different ways in which she responded to each of these deaths, I was struck by a perceptible difference in her manner of telling each tale, despite the manifest similarity in the grief she felt for the loss of these two beloved people in her life, and I accentuated this change.

BOB: I don't know if you have the same awareness about this, but it seemed to me as if, when you speak about your relationship with David Alan, I see some of the pain here. I see some of the moisture in your eyes, some of the trembling in your jaw, and so on, that seem to reflect the deep sadness that you felt with him as you anticipated his death. . . . But when you speak about your father, there's a kind of subtle cooling, a kind of backing off, almost as if your style of interacting with me here reflects the kind of communication you had in those two contexts. [*Pause.*] Do you notice that difference?

CHRIS [*voice trembling at first*]: I didn't notice it till you said that, but I think that's true. Even when I talk about how I relate to my family about my grief, I minimize it. No, I don't minimize it, I control it. The tremor goes out of my voice a little bit. And I didn't notice that, but I think that's true. I think every time I'm interacting with them, I flip into a different mode.

BOB: Does that suggest something about the different role you play in your family of origin, as compared to your role with David Alan?

CHRIS: Yes, I am the communications satellite in my family. . . . But I'm not following the old pattern. I'm not willing to be the telegraph anymore. I can't do it. I have needs that need to be met.

A primary aim of accentuating is to lift particular patterns or processes to a higher level of cognitive awareness (Kelly, 1955), so that they can be clearly construed, discussed, and perhaps revised. In Chris's case, this entailed recognizing and eventually modifying the habitual ways in which she modulated her own affective experience in the family context in order to permit a familiar communication pattern, even though that pattern maintained a systemic equilibrium that was dysfunctional for her on a personal level.

Nuancing

A related intervention is *nuancing,* which I define as highlighting certain aspects of a client's presentation for further elaboration. Like accentuating, it draws attention to one aspect of what the client has offered, but typically does so succinctly and in passing, in a way that subtly deflects, rather than dramatically alters, the flow of the conversation. An example of nuancing arose in my work with Jack, the career diplomat and educator who was reeling under the impending breakdown of his marriage to Lee. As we explored the way in which he had negotiated previous losses and transitions in his life, he exemplified the steely-eyed analytical style that had so typified his climb to power in government service.

JACK: In fact, every time I have made a career move, I have not maintained any of the relationships or friendships that were most important to me at any stage of my life. I don't maintain relationships past their effective life. That was true when I was president of [three colleges and universities], when I was a consultant for [a large corporation], and when I worked with [a past presidential administration]. Once a person is no longer relevant to my future, I close the book on him.

Bob: And yet this contrasts with your incredible attempt to maintain your connectedness to one person, Lee.

Jack: Maybe the life of this relationship's not over yet.

Bob: The "*effective life*" of this relationship is not over.

Jack: Yes. It still operates for me in a faltering way. . . . I suppose that sounds rather cold-blooded.

In this instance, the nuancing of one facet of Jack's communication—the effective life of his relationships—led to a more extended consideration of his habitual pattern of coping with loss and whether this was a pattern that was shifting as a function of his investment in one specific person.

Dilating and Constricting

Originally applied by Kelly (1955) to the widening or narrowing of the client's perceptual field, that is, the range of elements of experience that need to be construed, I find *dilating* and *constricting* to be equally useful terms for describing conversational interventions designed to achieve this same effect. In dilating, I attempt to widen the field of the discussion between me and the client to include broader issues or implications; whereas in constricting, I try to restrict our attention to a single focal issue. A somewhat unusual example of the former process occurred in my counseling with Veronica, a capable attorney in her mid forties, who vacillated between a characteristic "over concern" with her family's finances and a "depressive shutdown" when she perceived other family members (particularly her husband) to be undercutting her micromanagement of the family budget. Recounting one such incident, when her husband, Ted, impulsively bought a motorcycle for one of their sons, Veronica defiantly concluded, "If he won't be thrifty, then I won't be either. That's just the way it is with men, and I'm tired of it." Almost immediately, however, she retracted the angry force in this proclamation by adding, "Or is all of this just my perception? I do believe I'm *spoiled*, and if I don't get my own way, I like to pout." At this point, I accentuated her shift of position by asking if she noticed how quickly she silenced herself by switching from anger to self-criticism. After she responded affirmatively, I asked her how she had come to construe herself as spoiled, a term frequently reserved for children. She responded that as a child, she had often been labeled spoiled by her siblings, who resented her favored treatment in the family. This caused her to feel guilty, something she continued to feel vividly whenever she spiraled into a cycle of self-criticism. Intrigued by the apparent significance of this form of self-accusation in maintaining her cycle of assertive engagement and guilty withdrawal in her marriage, I decided to dilate our discussion to tease out the broader implications of her feeling "spoiled" within her present construct system. As one means of doing this, I engaged in a pattern of recursive questioning called the *downward arrow technique*, described by Burns (1980) from a cognitive therapy standpoint and further elaborated for use in constructivist therapy (Neimeyer, 1993d).

BOB: Suppose that it were true, that you really were *spoiled*. If that were so, what would that mean to you?

VERONICA: It would mean that Ted is right to be in control in the relationship.

BOB: I see. And if that were true, that Ted should be in control in the relationship, what would that mean?

VERONICA: I don't know, it's just a sad, dangerous feeling, like an image of Darth Vader, dark and vicious.

BOB: Hmm. . . . And if he really were a kind of dark, Darth Vader figure, what would that mean to you?

VERONICA: That he'll hurt me.

BOB: And if it were true that he'd hurt you?

VERONICA: I'd die, like a candle melting. . . . I'd become nonexistent.

I was impressed at how the metaphor of a candle melting was an apt description of Veronica's passivity and acquiescence during her self-critical phases, but also at how discrepant the Darth Vader image was with her previous description of Ted. I therefore asked if she had any idea where her Darth Vader image came from. She replied, "I don't know exactly. I do have a fear of him, but he's fairly passive. He's not violent, but kind, even when he's angry. There's no reason for that image in his family background." Alerted to the unstated contrast, I then asked if there were any reason for the image in *her* family background. What came to light was her own father's alcoholic bouts of temper, during which he would unmercifully paddle her younger brother, once threatening to shoot him for stealing money to buy marijuana. A teenager at the time, Veronica was aware of her father's angry violence but helpless to stop it. Indeed, her feelings of powerlessness and distress were so acute that she forgot the most extreme instances of her father's rage for some fifteen years, although she continued to meekly withdraw in the face of men's displeasure in subsequent relationships. Thus, in dilating the implications of the term spoiled, through the use of the downward arrow questioning, we tapped into a vein of emotional imagery that connected her paralysis in relation to Ted to an older and still relevant paralysis in relation to a far more controlling man in her life, her father.

The opposite movement, *constricting,* is often useful when a client presents a litany of concerns, obfuscating any relevant therapeutic direction. In such instances, I will sometimes ask, "If you were to select the *one* thing in this session that you really want me to hear, what would it be?" By putting other considerations (temporarily) out of bounds, we are then in a better position to make progress on a focal issue.

Contrasting

As a conversational practice, *contrasting* involves exploring a sensed conflict or discrepancy in a client's experience. While contrasting, like many of the interventions described here, may be employed by therapists working within quite different traditions, it has a special role in constructivist therapies predicated upon a coherence theory of truth (Neimeyer, 1995a). If one assumes that the viability of a perspective is determined more by its internal consistency than by its alignment with an objective reality as defined by an observer, then it follows that the most profound challenges to the adequacy of a construction system will arise from its internal tensions and inconsistencies, rather than its failure to square with the facts as perceived by the therapist. The idiosyncratic polarities, dialectics, pulls, contradictions, and competing programs of action that are thematic in clients' experiences have attracted the attention of numerous constructivists, who have considered how they might be conceptualized, assessed, and used as stimuli to growth in psychotherapy (Greenberg & Pascual-Leone, 1995; Guidano, 1995; Kelly, 1955; Mahoney, 1991; Neimeyer, 1993).

An example of contrasting as a conversational intervention occurred during my work with Jack, whose accommodation to his seemingly inevitable divorce from Lee was complicated by an unexpected event. The catalyst for her separation from him had been her brush with cancer, which although apparently successfully treated, remained an ever-present threat. In the midst of Jack's therapy, just before the holidays, the specter of the cancer rematerialized. Lee discovered a knot on her spine and scheduled a bone scan to evaluate it. Jack's response, understandably "not resisted" by Lee, was to "take charge" of the medical regimen, showing quite tender and unselfish attention to her needs. When I inquired how this whole development left him feeling, Jack responded that it "intensified his sadness and loneliness," in so far as the divorce documents arrived in his mailbox the same day he returned from the hospital.

He then began to shift discussion to some particularly insulting language in the divorce papers; at which point, I returned the focus to the discrepant emotional pulls of the situation he faced.

BOB: Let's slow down for a moment here. I was really struck by the strong contrast between your very intimate and thoughtful caretaking of her, on the one hand, and the arrival of these quite legalistic divorce documents, on the other. What is that like for you?

JACK: It's not a whipsaw for me. With Lee, I expect at some point to just pick up my shirts and leave, just like I did with my first wife. Her illness shifts attention away from our discussion of our relationship, but I'm still feeling more and more like I want to be a minimal presence during the holidays.

BOB: So there's a tug in two directions—to be there for her, versus to be a "minimal presence."

JACK: Yes. . . . But if she were seriously ill, I'd move right back in, even if she objected. It's like when I headed the Emergency Response Team [during his years as a diplomat], if an emergency arose, my cardinal plan was to get onsite to where the problem was. You can't manage a crisis efficiently at a distance.

BOB: That sounds like a fundamental principle for you, superseding any personal feelings you might have.

JACK: Yes. It's very clear. It's not even a decision.

BOB: Is there any particular feeling attached to that?

JACK: Responsibility. My presence is needed. I get a little adrenaline rush just thinking about it! Like when our man was abducted in [a third-world capital]. I just went. And in this case, Lee accepts this and is grateful for my being there. It's like in sports. You do what you do on the field, and then the adrenaline rush subsides, and you go back to the locker room having won or lost.

In this case, our exploration of the sensed contrast pointed out the apparent incompatibility between two response subsystems—efficient crisis management and a bereaved withdrawal—which made competing and inconsistent demands on Jack's action. Not surprisingly, given Jack's historical organization of his identity around the former role, emergency management provided a compelling construction for channeling his actions during Lee's (momentary) health crisis, temporarily eclipsing his need to realign his relationship with her over the long haul. But the tension between a well-rehearsed professionalism and an emerging personalism remained and continued to serve as an impetus for the reconstruction of his sense of self and life priorities over the course of therapy.

Structuring and Ambiguating

A major function of therapeutic conversation is to clarify linguistic quandaries (Efran & Fauber, 1995), resolving some of the ambiguity of presenting problems in a way that allows for more effective decision making. One means of accomplishing this is through *structuring*, defined as organizing diffuse material in a way that clarifies its implications for action. Such structuring is related to Kelly's concept (1955; Neimeyer, 1988) of "tightening" a construction, articulating it in precise and concrete terms that allow the client to experiment with novel behavior. However, structuring need not terminate in an explicit action plan to be useful. In working with Jessie, for example, our conversations rarely yielded explicit plans for what to do differently, although Jessie herself made profound changes in her two central relationships across the span of our brief contact. Instead, the contribution of structuring the problem domain may come at a more conceptual but nonetheless satisfying level—as Jessie noted after our first three sessions, "from our contacts, slippery, vague things are much more firmed up and not nearly as threatening."

An instance of gradual structuring that did lead to an explicit action plan occurred in therapy with Chris, the woman who had suffered the loss of both her friend and father within the past year. After encouraging her to flesh out in some detail her contrasting reactions to the two deaths, her ways of communicating with relevant others about them, and so on, I gently prompted her to tighten her construing of this contrast further and explicate what it implied for her future grief work.

BOB: Chris, do you have any sense of what it would take at this point to have the same feeling of your grief moving forward in connection with your father's death that you felt with David Alan's?

CHRIS: I know that there are some tangible things I need to do that I've been avoiding. I've been avoiding it because it would really concentrate my emotions and bring them to the surface. As long as I was overwhelmed with grief about David Alan, I was unwilling to do that. [*She describes a seaworthy boat, handcrafted by her father shortly before he died, which had been dry-docked since the time of his death. Moisture wells in her eyes.*] And I need to say good-bye to him through that boat, but I don't know when. . . . My mother knows I need to do that, and she has made arrangements for me to have access to a key to go whenever I want to. It's just up to me to do it.

BOB: When you want to, literally and metaphorically, take that key and open that door, and see the last construction of your father's life.

CHRIS [*tears visible now*]: It symbolizes so much of his life, his dreams, his hopes, things I admire about him most. It's much more him at this point than visiting the grave or my family home—which he also built. I've avoided it, and I know I need to do that. And I think I'm almost ready to do that.

BOB [*clarifies briefly what form this visit might take—with her mother or by herself*]: As you speak of this, I almost get a sense that there are a series of tasks, each of which is a further step on the path of perspective taking or perspective making toward the death of your father. One would be visiting the family home, another would be visiting his grave, and a third would be visiting the boat. It starts to seem like a hierarchy of experiences, each of which comes a little closer to the core.

CHRIS: Yes. With David Alan, the work of letting go was done when he was alive, so it was not the same kind of task. . . . [*She notes that her family had had a simple memorial service following her father's cremation, but because the whole period had been such a "blur" for the survivors, it seemed perfunctory and unfulfilling. She then spontaneously begins to associate to what she wanted to do differently.*] What I'd like to do with my mother is organize some kind of family ritual, something at the gravesite, which I think will be helpful.

BOB: And not only in terms of your private grief, but also in terms of reconstituting the family in a way that was not possible last year, letting you acknowledge the importance that your father had in all your lives.

CHRIS: And I hope in a way that lets us express what he meant to all of us. The pain is somewhat less. It's easier to speak, easier to reminisce, to get out the pictures, mementos. That, as an experience, is something I would like to bring to my family, and it would be good for all of us.

BOB: And you could do this without simply assuming the role of the family facilitator; you could not only create, but also fully participate in the experience.

CHRIS: Exactly. I could be supported by that, and support them as well. It's important for me, before I can learn to relate to them differently.

BOB: Well, I look forward to hearing how these plans turn out.

In this case, as is often true in my form of constructivist therapy, concrete and fairly rapid directions for change (at the levels of both self and system) emerged from the therapeutic dialogue, but without such direction being imposed from the alien perspective of the helping professional. This form of emergent co-structuring of an action plan seems clearly different to me from the "homework assignments" made by most cognitive-behavioral therapists and from the therapeutic prescriptions given by most systemic therapists. In the latter two instances, the therapist typically takes the lead in shaping the task assignment (and in many cases, is solely responsible for its formulation), leaving the client with only the responsibility to comply with the prescribed action. I agree with Hoffman (1992) that the unequal power relationship implied by such an arrangement is incoherent with a constructivist stance and is inimical to the conversational reconstruction of meaning that characterizes a language-based therapy.

In fact, there are many points in the flow of therapy when sculpting the conversation in the direction of greater structure, however gently this is done, is inappropriate. Indeed, I often find myself moving in quite the opposite direction, engaging in *ambiguating* interventions, defined as fostering a looser or more approximate meaning in place of the habitual or literal constructions that a client has used to organize a problem experience. For example, Veronica, the woman who was by her own assessment overly concerned with her family's finances, could at first envision only problem solutions that entailed more careful budgeting, rationing of the shampoo, and other such actions. What was called for in this case was not a tighter but a looser formulation of the problem domain, one that might suggest quite different constructions of the solution. I therefore attempted to ambiguate the problem, saying: "And yet, however much effort you exert along those lines, the problem only gets worse. . . . I wonder, if we were to back off a few steps, what kind of an *image* you get when you view yourself contending with these financial difficulties?" The aim here was to prompt a vaguer, but potentially richer, construction of the difficulty. Veronica eventually arrived at a metaphoric image in which she was constantly "pushing" against the collective inertia of the children while her husband stood outside the scene looking on with apparent noninvolvement.

Alternative strategies for ambiguating the problem might have included asking Veronica how each of the other family members might describe the problem, how I might formulate the issues if I were in her shoes, her "theory" of how the problem came to exist, or whether she had any "vague ideas" about how she might think about the problem in a different light if she could remove the pressure to "solve" it. As Kelly (1955) notes, this kind of loosening is useful insofar as it "releases facts, long taken as self-evident, from their rigid conceptual moorings" (p. 1,031), thereby allowing for the emergence of alternative solutions. It is worth emphasizing, however, that conversational structuring (tightening) and ambiguating (loosening) can be accomplished not only through the content of the therapist's intervention but also through systematic modulation of the therapeutic ambiance, judicious selection of techniques, and artful regulation of the therapist's nonverbal, coverbal, and verbal style, as described elsewhere (Neimeyer, 1988). By tacking back and forth between the structuring and ambiguating styles of intervention, therapist and client are better able to engage in the circular process of entertaining novel speculative constructions of the problem domain and then testing these constructions' specific relevance to the client's need to act differently.

Weaving

While I have intentionally emphasized here the moment-to-moment conversational practices that are latent in my work, it is worth underscoring that these interventions are informed by both my ongoing reading of the flow of my interaction with the client and the more durable recurrent themes that I have winnowed from our therapy. While this thematic undercurrent often serves as a tacit guide to my practice, it is sometimes helpful to bring it into the session in a more public way by formulating it as a conversational intervention. One form of this public thematizing is *weaving*, which

I define as overlaying or connecting strands of related material. From the client's standpoint, the immediate effect of this juxtaposition of issues can range from exhilarating to disconcerting, but weaving ultimately tends to promote a greater coherence in the client's experience and a sense of reckoning with larger issues.

An instance of such weaving occurred in mid-therapy with Jessie, the social worker trying to sort out a fluctuating field of relationships centering on her male and female partners. In the course of some emotionally demanding sessions during which I met with all three partners together and in every possible combination, Jessie had begun to reach the liberating but painful decision to deescalate her long-distance relationship with Sarah in order to commit herself more consistently to emerging possibilities with Michael. As she began to consolidate this choice, however, she started to receive what she regarded as "mixed signals" from several of the important figures in her life. Not surprisingly, Sarah reflected her ambivalent support for Jessie's movement by referring to their relationship in the present tense in her letters, but Jessie's mother and brother also directly and indirectly expressed their expectations that she would remain in the community rather than explore joint career opportunities with Michael in another city. Reporting each of these quandaries as separate developments, Jessie was confused and angered by them, and she was unable to make them fit with each person's professed support of her decision and genuine affection for Michael. As a result, she felt herself subtly withdrawing from all three: Sarah, her mother, and her brother. Weaving these plots together at a thematic level, I wondered aloud, "whether there might not be an invisible thread of connection in your relationships with Sarah, your brother, and mother, each one wanting you in a way that is beginning to feel outmoded and leading you to reassert your boundaries and distance." Jessie paused for a moment and then reported "a starburst" of insight that left her feeling excited and affirmed and better able to talk to each of these important figures about the changing patterns of her life.

A second brief example, this time from my contact with Jack, illustrates how weaving can occur between, as well as within, sessions. After months of separation had begun to dim Jack's hope for a reunion with Lee (particularly following the "false alarm" of her second cancer scare), we began to focus more consistently on his need to construct an alternative life in which she would not be his linchpin. With characteristic creativity and more than a little seriousness, Jack began to envision leaving the United States to pursue life once more in the foreign service, conceding his attraction to the "somewhat heroic and romantic image of sending her a postcard from Sierra Leone." I shared his chuckle but then asked if "that might not be an elegant but ultimately desolate attempt to repeat the pattern of 'closing the book' on all of his current relationships," as we had discussed several sessions before in connection with his earlier career moves. He then acknowledged that this form of "running off to join the Foreign Legion" at best delayed the critical decision of what kind of future was worth living for him as he moved into the "endgame" of his life.

Conclusion

In this chapter, I have tried to write honestly, from the growing edge of my awareness as a therapist, rather than comfortably, within the secure base of a familiar theory that I still work *from* but no longer quite work *within*. This has meant that I have tried to translate into communicable terms processes of therapeutic co-construction that are not yet fully consolidated for me and not neatly packaged for convenient conveyance to the reader. The process interventions provisionally articulated here have for me more the feel of a rough sketch or work in progress than a final rendering of the landscape of conversational practice.

At the outset of this chapter, I signaled my misgivings whether my approach to conceptualizing the work of therapy would be shared by other constructivists or even distinguished reliably from the approaches of nonconstructivist therapists. With respect to the first part of the question, I am encouraged by the occasional convergence of my path with that of other constructivists, who, while respectful of the contribution of *languaging* to the construction of clinical realities, nonetheless accord an important role to the *local knowledge* of the families and individuals with whom we typically work. Attempting to explicate more clearly those concrete conversational practices that we use to help clients articulate, refine, and renegotiate such personal meanings strikes me as a legitimate effort for those of us attempting to bridge these two worlds.

The second half of the question, whether the practices I outline correspond to those of nonconstructivist therapists, is perhaps better answered by the nonconstructivist therapists reading this chapter! While it is my hope that this taxonomy of process interventions has sufficient generality for its contents to be recognized by therapists of many persuasions, it is also my impression that practitioners of various approaches use these tools with different frequencies, in different combinations, and toward different ends. To take but a single example, practitioners of conventional cognitive-behavioral therapies tend to be much more structuring than ambiguating in their intervention styles, more literal than metaphoric, and more constricting than dilating, thereby shaping a distinctive therapeutic process. To acknowledge that sculptors, carpenters, and bricklayers all use hammers and chisels is by no means to claim that they are indistinguishable in the way they conceive of their work, approach their materials, wield their tools, or craft their products.

Where might the pursuit of a process intervention approach to therapy lead, if my preliminary forays in this chapter were extended creatively by other theorists, researchers, and practitioners of constructivist psychotherapy? Inevitably, any attempt at forecasting represents an indistinguishable blend of preferences with predictions. With this caveat in mind, I nonetheless believe that a process intervention approach could contribute to the ongoing refinement of a constructivist model of therapeutic practice in at least five ways.

First, and most fundamentally, it could place greater inflection on a therapy of engagement, one that highlights the delicate interplay of therapist and client construing, in the service of restructuring, the personal realities of one (or both) participant(s). In so doing, it could give greater ontological and epistemological status to the discursive basis of actual practice, complementing the somewhat compartmentalized attention to supra-individual processes of "languaging" and intra-individual processes of "construing" featured in other constructivist models.

Second, the further elaboration of the process intervention approach could contribute to the development of a more concrete constructivism, one that balances an enthusiasm for epistemology with a penchant for pragmatics. To date, constructivists have been more outspoken in enunciating their principles than procedures; an emphasis on conversational practice could help rectify this imbalance.

Third, the specification of a comprehensive set of naturally occurring conversational practices for meaning-making would help counter an unfortunate trend toward the trivialization of constructivist practice. Currently, there is a danger that constructivism will come to be identified with a few glib narrative procedures or standardized patterns of questioning. While novel, these procedures and questions require serious expansion to yield a more convincing portrayal of a strategically flexible practice.

Fourth, a move to contextualize various process interventions, by considering their specific relevance to particular patterns of client construing, could further bridge the divide that separates public conversation from private construction. Identifying contextual markers that indicate when engagement in a particular process intervention is likely to be useful would also explicitly guide therapists attempting these procedures.

And fifth, with sufficient specification, some process interventions might be incorporated into psychotherapy process research as a taxonomy for analyzing conversational heuristics, as "verbal response modes" were studied in past research (Hill, 1995). However, in keeping with the subtlety of the processes to be studied, I suspect that useful analyses will have to make use of intensive interpretive designs, ones that take therapist intentionality into account and do not rely on "objective," observer-rated features of discourse alone (Rennie, 1995).

In closing, it is worth emphasizing that constructivism is not a separate school of therapy, distinguishable from other schools, but a particular mind-set for approaching the work of therapy, whatever the therapist's theoretical orientation (Neimeyer & Mahoney, 1995). Indeed, there are vigorous expressions of constructivism in clinical traditions ranging from the psychodynamic (Spence, 1982) and the humanistic (Mahrer, 1989) to the family systemic (McNamee & Gergen, 1992) and cognitive-behavioral (Mahoney, 1995). Thus, I believe that constructivism has something of value to offer to all therapists, irrespective of the traditions from which they draw conceptual sustenance and practical inspiration. I hope that my own attempt to bring to the foreground several process interventions for the constructivist therapist makes a modest contribution to this goal.

Note

1. My interaction with Chris is included in a videotape training program entitled *Death in the Family: Individual and Systemic Responses to Loss,* distributed by PsychoEducational Resources, P.O. Box 2196, Keystone Heights, FL 32656. It is part of a series of studio-produced videotapes presenting the work of various constructivist therapists and targeted toward both professional continuing education and classroom use.

References

Anderson, H., & Goolishian, H. A. (1992). The client is the expert: A not-knowing approach to therapy. In S. McNamee & K. J. Gergen (Eds.), *Therapy as social construction* (pp. 25–39). Newbury Park, CA: Sage.

Burns, D. (1980). *Feeling good.* New York: Signet.

Dalton, P., & Dunnett, G. (1992). *A psychology for living.* New York: Wiley.

Efran, J. S., & Clarfield, L. E. (1992). Constructionist therapy: Sense and non-sense. In S. McNamee & K. J. Gergen (Eds.), *Therapy as social construction* (pp. 200–217). Newbury Park, CA: Sage.

Efran, J. S., & Fauber, R. L. (1995). Radical constructivism: Questions and answers. In R. A. Neimeyer & M. J. Mahoney (Eds.), *Constructivism in psychotherapy* (pp. 275–304). Washington, DC: American Psychological Association.

Efran, J. S., Lukens, M. D., & Lukens, R. J. (1990). *Language, structure, and change: Frameworks of meaning in psychotherapy.* New York: W.W. Norton.

Ellis, A. (1993). Reflections on rational-emotive therapy. *Journal of Consulting and Clinical Psychology, 61*, 199–201.

Epston, D., & White, M. (1995). Termination as a rite of passage: Questioning strategies for a therapy of inclusion. In R. A. Neimeyer & M. J. Mahoney (Eds.), *Constructivism in psychotherapy* (pp. 339–356). Washington, DC: American Psychological Association.

Feixas, G. (1990). Personal construct theory and the systemic therapies: Parallel or convergent trends? *Journal of Marital and Family Therapy, 16*, 1–20.

Feixas, G. (1992). Personal construct approaches to family therapy. In R. A. Neimeyer & G. J. Neimeyer (Eds.), Advances in personal construct psychology (Vol. 2, pp. 215–255). Greenwich, CT: JAI Press.

Foucault, M. (1970). *The order of things: An archaeology of the human sciences* (A. Sheridan, Trans.). New York: Pantheon.

Glover, R. (1995). Personal theories in psychotherapy: Toward an epistemology of practice. In R. A. Neimeyer & G. J. Neimeyer (Eds.), *Advances in personal construct psychology* (pp. 191–226). Greenwich, CT: JAI Press.

Gonçalves, O. F. (1995). Hermeneutics, constructivism, and the cognitive behavioral therapies: From the object to the project. In R. A. Neimeyer & M. J. Mahoney (Eds.), *Constructivism in psychotherapy* (pp. 195–230). Washington, DC: American Psychological Association.

Gonçalves, O. F., & Craine, M. H. (1990). The use of metaphors in cognitive therapy. *Journal of Cognitive Psychotherapy, 4*, 135–149.

Greenberg, L. S. (1992). Task analysis. In S. G. Toukmanian & D. L. Rennie (Eds.), *Psychotherapy process research* (pp. 22–50). Newbury Park, CA: Sage.

Greenberg, L. S., & Pascual-Leone, J. (1995). A dialectical constructivist approach to experiential change. In R. A. Neimeyer & M. J. Mahoney (Eds.), *Constructivism in psychotherapy* (pp. 169–191). Washington, DC: American Psychological Association.

Guidano, V. F. (1995). Constructivist psychotherapy: A theoretical framework. In R. A. Neimeyer & M. J. Mahoney (Eds.), *Constructivism in psychotherapy* (pp. 93–108). Washington, DC: American Psychological Association.

Guidano, V. F., & Liotti, G. (1983). *Cognitive processes and emotional disorders: A structural approach to psychotherapy*. New York: Guilford Press.

Hill, C. E. (1995). Musings about how to study therapist techniques. In L. T. Hoshmand & J. Martin (Eds.), *Research as praxis* (pp. 81–103). New York: Teachers College Press.

Hoffman, L. (1992). A reflexive stance for family therapy. In S. McNamee & K. J. Gergen (Eds.), *Therapy as social construction* (pp. 7–24). Newbury Park, CA: Sage.

Kant, I. (1952). *Critique of pure reason*. Chicago: Encyclopedia Britannica. (Original work published 1781)

Kelly, G. A. (1955). *The psychology of personal constructs* (2 Vols.). New York: W.W. Norton.

Kelly, G. A. (1977). The psychology of the unknown. In D. Bannister (Ed.), *New perspectives in personal construct theory* (pp. 1–19). San Diego, CA: Academic Press.

Leitner, L. M. (1988). Terror, risk, and reverence: Experiential personal construct therapy. *International Journal of Personal Construct Psychology, 1,* 251–261.

Leitner, L. M., & Dunnett, N. G. (1993). *Critical issues in personal construct psychotherapy*. Malabar, FL: Krieger.

Leitner, L. M., & Faidley, A. J. (in press). The awful, aweful nature of ROLE relationships. In R. A. Neimeyer & G. J. Neimeyer (Eds.), *Advances in Personal Construct Psychology* (pp. 289–312). Greenwich, CT: JAI Press.

Loos, V. E. (1993). Now that I know the techniques, what do I do with the family? In L. M. Leitner & N. G. Dunnett (Eds.), *Critical issues in personal construct psychotherapy* (pp. 239–263). Malabar, FL: Krieger.

Loos, V. E., & Epstein, E. S. (1989). Conversational construction of meaning in family therapy: Some evolving thoughts on Kelly's sociality corollary. *International Journal of Personal Construct Psychology, 2,* 149–167.

Lyddon, W. J. (1995). Forms and facets of constructivist psychology. In R. A. Neimeyer & M. J. Mahoney (Eds.), *Constructivism in psychotherapy* (pp. 69–92). Washington, DC: American Psychological Association.

McNamee, S., & Gergen, K. J. (1992). (Eds.). *Therapy as social construction*. Newbury Park, CA: Sage.

Mahoney, M. J. (1991). *Human change processes: The scientific foundations of psychotherapy*. New York: Basic Books.

Mahoney, M. J. (Ed.). (1995). *Cognitive and constructive psychotherapies*. New York: Springer.

Mahrer, A. R. (1989). *The integration of psychotherapies*. New York: Human Sciences Press.

Mair, M. (1989). *Between psychology and psychotherapy*. London: Routledge & Kegan Paul.

Mancuso, J. C., & Adams-Webber, J. R. (1982). *The construing person*. New York: Praeger.

Martin, J. (1994). *The construction and understanding of psychotherapeutic change*. New York: Teachers College Press.

Maturana, H. R., & Varela, F. G. (1987). *The tree of knowledge: The biological roots of human understanding*. Boston: New Science Library.

Meichenbaum, D. (1993). Changing conceptions of cognitive behavior modification: Retrospect and prospect. *Journal of Consulting and Clinical Psychology, 61*, 202–204.

Merleau-Ponty, M. (1962). *Phenomenology of perception*. London: Routledge & Kegan Paul.

Neimeyer, G. J. (1993). *Constructivist assessment: A casebook*. Newbury Park, CA: Sage.

Neimeyer, G. J., & Neimeyer, R. A. (1985). Relational trajectories: A personal construct contribution. *Journal of Social and Personal Relationships, 2*, 325–349.

Neimeyer, R. A. (1985). *The development of personal construct psychology*. Lincoln, NE: University of Nebraska Press.

Neimeyer, R. A. (1987). An orientation to personal construct therapy. In R. A. Neimeyer & G. J. Neimeyer (Eds.), *Personal construct therapy casebook* (pp. 3–19). New York: Springer.

Neimeyer, R. A. (1988). Integrative directions in personal construct therapy. *International Journal of Personal Construct Psychology, 1*, 283–298.

Neimeyer, R. A. (1993a). An appraisal of constructivist therapy. *Journal of Consulting and Clinical Psychology, 61*, 221–234.

Neimeyer, R. A. (1993b). Constructivism and the cognitive therapies: Some conceptual and strategic contrasts. *Journal of Cognitive Psychotherapy, 7*, 159–171.

Neimeyer, R. A. (1993c). Constructivism and the problem of psychotherapy integration. *Journal of Psychotherapy Integration, 3*, 133–157.

Neimeyer, R. A. (1993d). Constructivist approaches to the measurement of meaning. In G. J. Neimeyer (Ed.), *Constructivist assessment: A casebook* (pp. 58–103). Newbury Park, CA: Sage.

Neimeyer, R. A. (1995a). Constructivist psychotherapies: Features, foundations, and future directions. In R. A. Neimeyer & M. J. Mahoney (Eds.), *Constructivism in psychotherapy* (pp. 11–38). Washington, DC: American Psychological Association.

Neimeyer, R. A. (1995b). An invitation to constructivist psychotherapies. In R. A. Neimeyer & M. J. Mahoney (Eds.), *Constructivism in psychotherapy* (pp. 1–8). Washington, DC: American Psychological Association.

Neimeyer, R. A. (in press). Problems and prospects in constructivist psychotherapy. *Journal of Constructivist Psychology*.

Neimeyer, R. A., & Feixas, G. (1990). Constructivist contributions to psychotherapy integration. *Journal of Integrative and Eclectic Psychotherapy, 9,* 4–20.

Neimeyer, R. A., & Mahoney, M. J. (Eds.). (1995). *Constructivism in psychotherapy*. Washington, DC: American Psychological Association.

Neimeyer, R. A., & Neimeyer, G. J. (1987). *Personal construct therapy casebook*. New York: Springer.

Neimeyer, R. A., Neimeyer, G. J., Lyddon, W. J., & Hoshmand, L. T. (1994). The reality of social construction. *Contemporary Psychology, 39,* 458–463.

Noaparast, K. B. (1995). Toward a more realistic constructivism. In R. A. Neimeyer & G. J. Neimeyer (Eds.), *Advances in Personal Construct Psychology* (pp. 37–60). Greenwich, CT: JAI Press.

Polanyi, M. (1958). *Personal knowledge*. New York: HarperCollins.

Procter, H. G. (1987). Change in the family construct system. In R. A. Neimeyer & G. J. Neimeyer (Eds.), *Personal construct therapy casebook* (pp. 153–171). New York: Springer.

Rennie, D. L. (1992). Qualitative analysis of the client's experience of psychotherapy: The unfolding of reflexivity. In S. G. Toukmanian & D. L. Rennie (Eds.), *Psychotherapy process research: Paradigmatic and narrative approaches* (pp. 211–233). Newbury Park, CA: Sage.

Rennie, D. L. (1995). Strategic choices in a qualitative approach to psychotherapy process research. In L. T. Hoshmand & J. Martin (Eds.), *Research as praxis* (pp. 198–220). New York: Teachers College Press.

Rogers, C. R. (1951). *Client-centered therapy*. Boston: Houghton Mifflin.

Russell, R. L. (1991). Narrative in views of humanity, science and action: Lessons for cognitive therapy. *Journal of Cognitive Psychotherapy, 5,* 241–256.

Schön, D. A. (1983). *The reflective practitioner: How professionals think in action*. New York: Basic Books.

Simons, H. W. (1989). *Rhetoric in the human sciences*. Newbury Park, CA: Sage.

Spence, D. (1982). *Narrative truth and historical truth: Meaning and interpretation in psychoanalysis*. New York: W.W. Norton.

White, M., & Epston, D. (1990). *Narrative means to therapeutic ends*. New York: W.W. Norton.

14

Couples Therapy
Changing Conversations

Steven Friedman

Contrary to the commonsense view, change is seen to
happen within language: What we talk about and
how we talk about it makes a difference and it is these
differences that can be used to make a difference [to
the client].

Berg & de Shazer (1993, p. 7)

Therapy, from a postmodern, social constructionist perspective, is a collaborative conversational process, a structured dialogue that engenders new perspectives and new possibilities for action (Friedman, 1993; Gilligan & Price, 1993). The therapist acts as a consultant working to deconstruct totalizing descriptions of people's lives in ways that enable previously unnoticed options to emerge (White, 1991). As a facilitator of the therapeutic conversation, the therapist is in a position to open space for the client to notice and acknowledge positive steps taken toward a preferred outcome.

The language we use with our clients imposes *our* reality and *our* assumptions on the process. *Problem talk* (that is, questions such as: What is the problem? How long has this been a problem? What makes the problem worse?) can quickly immerse both client and

Note: Special thanks to Donna Haig Friedman for her thoughtful comments on the manuscript of this chapter.

therapist in a process of interminable exploration, easily mired in pathological thinking and a search for underlying structures and explanations.

If a conversation is seen as problem focused, the goal is seen as diagnosis or categorization (Miller, 1992). In contrast, a competency orientation assumes change is inevitable. The therapist's attention is devoted to amplifying and building on what is working and to finding exceptions to the client's complaint or predicament.

Amplifying What Works

Louise and Joanne had a sixteen-year relationship that had gone through many ups and downs. They arrived for a consultation with me in the hopes of achieving a better understanding of their relationship and improving their "communication." The following conversation took place about five minutes into the interview.

THERAPIST: How is it that through the difficulties that you may have experienced in your lives and relationship over time, that you have stayed together and maintained the relationship, which is not easy to do with any relationship these days over an extended period of time? What has allowed you to maintain this relationship in spite of the difficulties you've faced?

JOANNE: That is a great question! I need to write that question down so that I can remember to ask myself that again and again. I realize there must be something that has allowed us to get this far.

LOUISE: There was always that constancy of being there . . . even when we were apart for periods of time. We could always reconnect on vacations.

THERAPIST: What kept that going? Why didn't that connection wane after a period of time?

JOANNE: I couldn't image not having that connection.

THERAPIST: So it was a given that this is your partner?

LOUISE: Yes.

JOANNE: Louise has always been such an emotional support to me. I can say anything, and together we could work out what is good for my life and for us. We were concentrating on each other. Even with interruptions, our main intent was to spend time together. So even with the interruptions, I didn't become frustrated because she was always there.

THERAPIST: So you were able to get past those obstacles and keep the relationship alive. . . . Who would be least surprised that your relationship has been able to survive these obstacles?

JOANNE: Besides us?

THERAPIST: Yes.

JOANNE: No one.

THERAPIST: So there has not been a lot of support from outside: friends or a family member?

JOANNE: Right.

THERAPIST: So even in spite of not having support, this relationship has been able to survive.

THERAPIST: What is it that you know about yourself that would have allowed you to predict that this relationship would last as long as it has and your connection would continue to be there?

JOANNE: For me, it's connections. I'm a strong connecter. In the face of all odds, I keep my connections. I'm talented at it, I guess.

THERAPIST: You're dedicated. Once you make a commitment you follow through. And that's been something constant for you.

JOANNE: Since forever.

THERAPIST [*to Louise*]: And that's been something you've been aware of, Joanne's loyalty and commitment?

LOUISE: Yes, yes.

THERAPIST: And what is it about you, that you know about yourself, that would have helped you understand how this relationship would have lasted as it has?

LOUISE: I think I've been able to listen well. . . . Although there was a period that this wasn't happening, it's been getting better lately. [*Joanne agrees.*]

In this conversation, I worked unremittingly to keep the focus on ways this couple have managed to cope and keep their relationship alive, in spite of the difficulties they have experienced. My interest and curiosity was directed to what works in their relationship, rather than to what is not working. The clients and I engaged in a conversation that constructed a reality of loyalty, connection, and love.

Conversation as Generative of Possibilities

"[Imagine putting] a small drop of red ink into a beaker of water. . . . You do not end up with beaker of water plus a small drop of red ink. All the water becomes colored" (Postman, 1976, p. 234). Words and descriptions are similar to that drop of red ink; they have the power to saturate our thinking and color our perspectives. In just this way, our conversations with couples can serve to open options, create a context of possibilities, and generate a variety of alternative views and ideas that bring each partner into connection with the other in positive and hopeful ways.

Therapists are in a unique position to engage in conversations that build on client resources, amplify client successes, and utilize client strengths in ways that offer hope for change. In turn, that hope inspires a sense of empowerment and personal agency (Friedman & Fanger, 1991). At any moment in a therapy session, the clinician is faced with a choice about the direction of the interview. Depending on the direction the therapist chooses, the conversation can immerse both therapist and client in a whirlpool of problems and deficits or generate a sea of hopeful ideas and possibilities.

Solution-Focused Therapy in Action

The current chapter explores the usefulness of a solution-focused framework, the *possibility paradigm*, in working in a time-effective manner with couples. To elaborate on this framework, excerpts from a series of interviews with a couple are presented, along with my commentary. Prior to meeting with the couple, I knew only that they had considered separating after thirty-nine years of marriage.

Session 1

At the outset, several minutes of social conversation take place, mainly related to each partner's job. I learn that Janice is in a "people-oriented" job, while her husband, Murray, designs auto equipment. I then ask a fairly standard opening question that acknowledges, first, that there is something they want from this consultation; second, that they have co-responsibility for any changes that take place; and third, that our work together needs to be goal directed, toward a result useful to them.

THERAPIST: Maybe you can tell me a little bit about what you were hoping to accomplish by coming here—how our conversation could be useful to you?

JANICE: About a month ago, our marriage almost came to an end, and I asked for a separation. It became a very separate kind of thing, with very little in common and with an undertone that wasn't very healthy. I was feeling there is no hope in this at all.

After three days, he came to me and said, "I'll do anything to save this marriage." During those three days, I felt a lot of sadness and grieving that I didn't expect to feel. I finally made a decision after all these years, and I was very surprised how sad I was. I thought about this [decision to separate] for eight or nine years. I was feeling very good about this decision, but I was surprised by my sadness. When he came back, he agreed to go to marriage counseling, and I'm hoping for myself that we can get better communication skills and listening skills to put this [relationship] back together because it's worth trying.

THERAPIST: So it was a month ago when you made the decision to separate?

JANICE: About a month ago, this all came to a climax.

My antennae are always tuned to mention of difference or change. I am particularly curious about comments that point to "exceptions" (de Shazer, 1985, 1988), to the past problem-saturated picture of the relationship. Janice's comment suggests such a change. In the following segment, I ask about this change and then emphasize how important these changes are. Then I engage the couple in a conversation using *scaling questions* (Berg & de Shazer, 1993; Kowalski & Kral, 1989). Scaling questions include a numerical scale through which an individual can assess his or her place along some relevant dimension.

THERAPIST: And . . . since you decided not to go in the direction of separating . . . and I assume made the decision to try to reconcile things, what has improved over these few weeks?

JANICE: Everything . . . everything. I think we both worked very, very hard at making things work. More sensitivity . . . more "How was your day?" A better quality of the whole marriage.

THERAPIST: These changes that you've already made are very important. Tell me, at the point that you were saying, "This isn't going to work," if you looked at a scale from 0 to 10, where 10 was the most confidence you had in things working out and the marriage going on and 0 was no confidence, where were you at that point?

JANICE: Zero.

THERAPIST: So you were at zero. And how about you [to Murray]?

MURRAY: I didn't realize that it was that bad . . . that what I was doing was that hurtful to Janice. Because I was going on my merry way. I could best describe it as very self-centered. I'm a passive-aggressive person.

Murray has just defined himself in a "totalizing" manner. Since my therapeutic interest and curiosity are tuned to exploring competencies rather than perceived deficits or limitations, I redirect the conversation by pleading ignorance.

THERAPIST: I'm not sure what that means, but go on.

MURRAY: And as I was saying, I didn't think it was that bad. But there was an undertone that I could feel.

THERAPIST: So where would you have put yourself on this scale at that point before Janice came to you? Where would you be on that scale in terms of your confidence and good feeling about the marriage?

MURRAY: Probably a 7.

THERAPIST: So you were feeling relatively okay and going along in your own world in a way.

MURRAY: That is correct.

THERAPIST: And then at the time Janice told you she had made this decision, where were you?

MURRAY: I probably went down to a zero.

THERAPIST: So you dropped very quickly.

MURRAY: Yeah. Janice said, "Let's take a walk. I want to talk with you." And so we did, and she said she didn't think the marriage was working and she'd just rather terminate it. At that point, I said, "Well, fine if that's what you want." I was out practically every night and had backed off on a lot of things to keep the marriage going. [*Discusses his involvement in multiple organizations and how he was "ignoring" Janice.*]

THERAPIST: When you were at a 7, you were going along—

MURRAY: In my own self-centered way.

THERAPIST: What was it like to hear from Janice that she was ready to end the relationship?

In what follows, Murray again defines himself in a negative manner, and I again continue to shift the conversation in a positive direction.

MURRAY: It was devastating. I know I haven't been the easiest person to live with. . . . I am a recovering alcoholic and a very controlling person. For example, if Janice shuts the front door, I need to check it again or ask her if she did it.

THERAPIST: So you're a vigilant person who is tuned into lots of things, which of course can feel intrusive to the other. Where would you say you are in terms of your confidence in the relationship . . . at this point?

MURRAY: I'm unsure. I'd say a 7. Janice said the other day that she felt things were getting much better. I didn't feel that I was trying that much harder to be good. Evidently something is coming from someplace that's making me act better . . . do better. Truthfully, it isn't 100 percent conscious.

THERAPIST: But you're feeling back up to a 7 in terms of your confidence that things can work out?

MURRAY: Yes. I think so.

THERAPIST [to Janice]: And where are you right now on the scale?

JANICE: Probably a 7.

THERAPIST: Okay. Now that's a big jump from a 0 to a 7 in a relatively short period of time.

MURRAY: Yes.

Instead of thinking of ourselves as therapists as persons with privileged knowledge about how to create change, it is more helpful for us to view our clients as the experts. Therapy becomes a more collaborative process when we develop and nurture a sense of curiosity and inquisitiveness about our clients' lives and relationships (Anderson and Goolishian, 1988, 1992). In the segment that follows, I simply ask each partner to give me specifics about the steps he or she has taken to improve the relationship. Since change is ever present, I focus on these specifics to further solidify the idea that change is occurring. The opportunity to expound on these specifics allows the couple's previously unexpressed "noticings" to emerge and a sense of hope to be established.

THERAPIST: What I would be interested in hearing from each of you is what you've noticed, [to Janice] and it sounds like you have noticed a number of changes recently. What are those very small specific things that have helped your confidence go from a 0 to a 7?

JANICE: Little Post-It notes left for me in the morning . . . little love notes . . . a call during the day to say hello and remind me that he has to do things, whereas, before, he'd just come home and then go right out again . . . with no communication. A great deal of communication now . . . about his plans. Sharing a walk together that is peaceful with good conversation. More cognizant that some of this stuff is affecting me medically. My blood pressure had gone way way up during those weeks. Now he says, "Let's take your blood pressure. . . . A walk would be good for you" . . . [more] attention. Maybe seeing a movie I want to see . . . and he did it and enjoyed it in spite of himself. And we had a nice talk about the ending, talking about people's feelings and all that, which we usually don't do. We had our granddaughter visiting for five days, and Murray took two days off which was an unusual thing. I had to work one of the days, and he said, "That is okay because I will be here." I saw a bonding between them that I had never seen before. He showed a real sensitivity. . . . Also a little more latitude with money. That's always been a bone of contention between us. Much freer and more generous with money. There seems to be a "180" happening that seems so positive.

THERAPIST: That's quite a lot of things that you've noticed. [*To Murray.*] And you are saying that you weren't trying in a conscious way to make these things happen.

MURRAY: Truthfully, I can't put my finger on it. They were done unconsciously, and maybe it is better that I wasn't consciously trying to please her so much. But the whole thing came to a head last April when I was supposed to take Janice to the hospital for a test and I had three other things on my calendar and unfortunately she was put last. I asked her to take a cab there, and that's the thing that got the whole ball rolling downhill.

THERAPIST [*to Murray*]: I'm interested in hearing from you about the kinds of changes you've noticed over the last few weeks.

MURRAY: Well, Janice seems more grateful for any little things I do. I had forgotten about notes I leave on the table. But I've been waiting to come here to really start the process. I don't feel like I started it yet.

THERAPIST: It seems to me like you have started the process. Many times people do start the process before coming here, and that is why I'm so interested in the steps you've already taken that can be built on and further amplified to help these changes continue.

JANICE: Before this last month . . . after an altercation or something . . . there would be several days of trying to placate. But what's happening recently, I don't see as placating. This is something different. This is entirely different than the usual pattern of placating and patronizing.

THERAPIST [*continuing to focus on differences as a way to amplify change in a positive direction*]: How is this different?

JANICE: Well, I don't know quite how to explain it other than the placating was quite transparent: "Let me do this for you, let me do that for you." This [current behavior] was much more sensitive and paced in a different way. There wasn't the anxiety. . . . It was just kind of flowing.

THERAPIST: So this has felt more paced and flowing—

JANICE: And more natural. It wasn't staged.

MURRAY: That was, I think, what I was meaning when I said it wasn't a conscious effort on my part.

THERAPIST: The sensitivity has just flowed naturally.

MURRAY: My goal is to make Janice happy and to see our relationship be better than it's been in the past.

THERAPIST: It sounds to me like you got the wake-up call from Janice when she said, "This is it, the marriage is over." And you've responded. I want to get back to what we were discussing a few minutes ago, the changes you've noticed about yourself, about Janice, and about the two of you over these past few weeks.

MURRAY: When I hug her, there's not as much of a rigidity.

THERAPIST: Okay, so she's more responsive.

MURRAY: It feels more comfortable in bed with her now. I feel more welcome.

THERAPIST: Other things that you've noticed?

MURRAY: Just Janice saying that I'm doing better. . . . Is she talking about the same person that I am? I wasn't really trying that hard. I guess, I wasn't doing my usual placating thing.

THERAPIST: It sounds like you're doing something differently now that is a surprise to you. It's different than other ways you've related to Janice.

MURRAY: Yes. I'm acting like a real person.

THERAPIST: You're not putting on a facade.

MURRAY: Correct.

THERAPIST: It feels more authentic.

MURRAY: Yeah.

Murray also describes cutting back on his outside activities, and the couple have gone out to dinner several times and enjoyed themselves. By taking seriously the couple's request and keeping my attention on their goals for change, I keep the couple engaged in a respectful and collaborative conversation. Again, this is a request-based therapy that places priority on the client's preferred outcome. Success is measured in the client's satisfaction with the results achieved.

THERAPIST: What needs to happen now? You've described a lot of very important steps that each of you has taken to improve your relationship over a relatively brief period of time [and that have] increased, for both of you, your sense of confidence in what the relationship can be.

MURRAY: Janice is the one who was pressing for this consultation, and I'm sure she has thoughts about the situation.

THERAPIST: What is it that you'd like her to be talking about?

MURRAY: The reason why we've come. . . . Why we need help.

JANICE: I think we both need better listening skills, to communicate more before things get to a peak. I let things build up, and then I explode. I'd like to figure out how to be less explosive.

MURRAY: I would say Janice doesn't usually explode. She talks things out, and I feel inadequate when I'm talking with her. To defend myself, I sometimes go off on an anger bent. I feel the anger well up inside me very easily. Probably too easy all my life. Within two sentences, I can be arguing. I think it's a lack of my skills in talking. Or I feel a righteous anger, "How dare she intrude on my going out!" No matter what she said, I would give her a hard time. It takes a lot to get Janice going.

THERAPIST: Over these few weeks, have there been situations that have arisen around your communication?

JANICE: In four weeks, there's only been one situation.

We discuss this situation, which turns out to be a very minor misunderstanding.

MURRAY: We never have an intelligent argument. I think of Janice as my worst adversary, and I stop listening and start reacting angrily.

THERAPIST [to Murray]: Even though you know you can have an argument with someone and still be friends. That would be a good sign, I guess, if you could argue but still be friends rather than feel like enemies. I wanted to go back to that scale again. If you're at a 7 in your confidence about the relationship, what would have to happen [for you] to feel like an 8? What would move things a little further along from where you are now? What would you need to see more of that would further increase your sense of confidence?

In the following segment, Murray presents himself as the one who most needs to change. While not accepting his story of himself as the "cause" of the problem, I do accept his willingness to take action to make things better. In terms of Prochaska and Di-Clemente's change model (Prochaska, DiClemente, & Norcross, 1992), Murray seems to be in the stage of "preparation for action." He can also be viewed as a "customer for change" (Berg, 1989, p. 27). My goal, again, is to generate optimism about change, and I do this by assuming a hopeful, future-oriented stance. Since change is inevitable and ever present, *change talk* can be promoted by a focus on future expectations about continued change.

MURRAY: The first thought that comes into my head is that I have to change my attitude the most of either of us. I think, deep down, I'm the person who's the cause of most of the problem. So both my attitude and how I do things have to change.

THERAPIST: What would be an example of a change in your attitude?

MURRAY: If I do have to do something, at least plan it with her a little in advance and see if it fits with her needs and our plans. More of a negotiation. I need to grow up and not be childish about things . . . to have an adult mentality. Don't play games or use various ploys but just be a straightforward adult. Try to express my feelings as best I can. I feel like an underdog when I try to express my feelings to Janice, and then it escalates into something unpleasant . . . where I know I'll win.

THERAPIST: What about your thoughts on small changes that will increase your sense of confidence about the relationship?

JANICE: I'd say to have some prime time together. I also need more information about our financial situation. Murray is going to retire in a few years, and I would like to be brought up to date on our financial planning. I'd like to see the house improved. . . . It needs a lot of work. I'm happy about what he said about the control issue. That would make it a 10 for me, I think.

Toward the end of the session, I summarize the issues discussed and give the couple feedback. This feedback contains a compliment about steps already taken to improve the relationship; my understanding of the perspective, or "story," that each member of the couple expressed to me in the session; and an accentuation and amplification of the changes that have been identified that increase my optimism about the couple's ability to continue to improve their relationship.

THERAPIST: I'm very impressed with the steps you've been taking. It sounds like, in some ways, things were building up over a long period of time. You were going your separate ways. [To Janice.] You were feeling more of the burden about the relationship and getting more and more upset. [To Murray.] You were going along focusing more and more on external things and not being sensitive and tuned in to Janice and to things in the relationship. [To Janice.] And finally your misery level got to the point you thought it would be best to call it quits . . . [to Murray] and somehow that served as a wake-up call to you. . . . Your ears opened up . . . you started hearing in a different way and obviously responding in a different way and not in the old way of "she's upset, so I'll be nice to her" . . . the alcoholic mode of "I've been bad, so now I'll make it up to her and be especially good." This is different. A different side of you is coming out in the past few weeks. You were saying it feels almost unconscious that it's coming to the surface now and doesn't require that you force it in ways that you have in the past . . . the placating and

so on. The fact that the two of you have been able to move yourselves from the bottom up to a 7 makes me optimistic that you can
continue to work things out. It seems like the two of you are at a
new stage, developing a new foundation from which to build things
back again. That's not to say it isn't easy to fall back into old patterns. So you need to be vigilant about that.

JANICE: I was so doubtful that this was real. In my mind, I was
saying, "I'm being manipulated here." He was being so good, and
then I'd cancel the appointment here and we'd go back to the old
way. I had a lot of doubt that these changes were real. I said to
myself, "This is like a good dream." It's so good.

THERAPIST: You expected it to end after several days, and it didn't.

JANICE: Yes. Then my confidence went way up. He really means
this. It's not another sham.

Since Murray still appears to be a customer for change, I suggest
several things for him to do that may further improve his relationship with his wife. I end the interview on a positive note, telling
them they are building a new chapter in their relationship.

THERAPIST: What I'm wondering about is if, between now and
when we meet again, the two of you would be willing to sit down
and discuss some of the things we've been talking about here that
need attention: for example, the finances and maybe planning a
weekend together. [*To Murray.*] And for you to be aware of when
that child part is coming out and how you can be straight with Janice. And I'm sure there will be issues that will come up that may get
an argument going. I'm wondering if you can keep in your awareness that you're arguing with a friend . . . this is not an enemy or
someone who is trying to hurt you. You will need to argue in a different way than you have in the past.

MURRAY: Yes. I'll try.

THERAPIST: And Janice, also, I get the sense, is already arguing in a new way. She's asserting herself more actively. So the arguments will be different . . . an expression of differences and an opportunity to sit down, listen to one another, and come to some understandings. Again, I'm impressed with the steps you've taken and with the way you've been able to turn things significantly around. And now it's a question of building on these things you've already started to begin a new chapter in your relationship. So, if you're interested, we can set up another time.

After Murray and Janice confer, we set the next appointment in two and a half weeks.

Session 2

THERAPIST: How have things been going with the two of you?

JANICE: Strained at times, but I think we're both trying very hard.

THERAPIST: Okay. So you've noticed the effort but also some rough edges.

MURRAY: A person is trying hard, but when a feeling comes, it immediately comes to the forefront.

THERAPIST: You're more sensitive and aware of yourselves and each other right now?

MURRAY: Right. But I'm still holding to what I think I own . . . by that I mean the money . . . the ultimate control. It's difficult for me not to do.

THERAPIST: That pattern seems well entrenched at this point.

MURRAY: Yes.

THERAPIST: Has that been a source of tension, then?

MURRAY: No. But I'm aware that it could be.

JANICE: I asked him about the finances in regard to getting our kitchen remodeled . . . and his answer was the bank. I didn't know what bank he meant. I'm sure between the two of us we can certainly pay back the loan, but he got very upset and said, "I'm the only one working, and I would have to pay for it." That's not exactly true since I work a couple of days a week and have another job once in awhile. He's thinking with a 1940s mentality that this woman hasn't been working. It's just never, "She works, too."

THERAPIST: Somehow he sees himself as the sole responsible person in this.

MURRAY: Right.

THERAPIST [to Murray]: It feels like it's all on your shoulders.

MURRAY: It does. It's good that it's coming up at this time because, without this, it may have seemed like a smooth life we were having without any problems. And this is a good problem to be working on.

Murray and Janice are ready to focus in on a "problem" area. Rather than dive straight into this conflict, I redirect their attention to the positive changes they have been noticing since we met last. My goal is not to discount the problem or to sweep it under the rug. I merely want to create space for this discussion in a warm atmosphere, where the changes each partner has made can be identified and acknowledged. Later in the session, I will come back to this area of concern.

THERAPIST: Yes. It certainly touches on some of the issues we've discussed. Before we go too far, I would like to know . . . in terms of the changes you've been making since I saw you last . . . how things have developed further in a positive direction? I'd be interested in the changes you've made and how you've built on those.

MURRAY: Okay. I was going to go over money matters with Janice, and I haven't gotten to that yet. I don't think I'm holding back, but the time hasn't presented itself where I've had all the information together.

THERAPIST: Okay.

MURRAY: There was something else we were working on that we did good with, but I can't think of it now.

JANICE: A concrete thing that was positive was that Murray said, "Let's think about the kitchen.". . . And "let's go and see some ideas" was really nice to hear. Before we talked about finances, we had some fun talking about possibilities for the kitchen. Our tastes are pretty much in common. But it got very testy around the possible home equity loan, and there was a backsliding that was all the way back to zero as far as I was concerned. I got a little disheartened, because it started out very nicely. I think what we have to do is find some common way to discuss how we're going to do things. I don't feel badly that we haven't gone over the finances. Murray has been working on some projects at work that have kept him pretty late, and he's tired when he comes home. And I don't expect instant gratification for any of the concrete things I want to see.

THERAPIST: Okay.

JANICE: The nice one was that we went out and had a beautiful dinner. We dined . . . and it was lovely. We talked through it about some feelings and some interesting observations he had. He talked about having some feelings after noticing me sitting by myself in church on Sunday while he was helping the minister up front.

MURRAY: Well, with what we've been going through, there was the potential that you would be alone, and it didn't make me feel good to see you sitting alone at that time in church. It distressed me that you were alone.

JANICE: I thought that was a sensitive thing to say.

THERAPIST: Yes. [*To Murray.*] So you had a picture of Janice—

MURRAY: As a widowed or divorced person sitting alone. It wasn't that she was sad or anything.

THERAPIST: But it made you sad?

MURRAY: Yes. It made my heart . . . you know the feeling you sometimes have on the inside. . . . It's a physical thing . . . a feeling. So I told her about that at dinner.

JANICE: There was some very nice personal conversation that happened, and it was a very happy kind of meal. It was very relaxed. We had planned to do some awful errands at the shopping mall, and Murray said, "It's raining. . . . I don't feel like going there. . . . Let's just dine and relax and then go home." And there was no pressure or tension. It was fun.

THERAPIST: How long do you think you were sitting there?

MURRAY: Two or three hours.

JANICE: It was a candlelight dinner. We just don't do that very often.

MURRAY: It was a spur-of-the-moment kind of thing.

THERAPIST: How long has it been since you've done something like that?

JANICE: We haven't dined since our anniversary.

THERAPIST: What other positive things are going on?

JANICE: Murray has been working late recently, and he's been calling early in the day to let me know what time he'll be home. Before, he'd call late.

THERAPIST: So he's thinking about you.

JANICE: Yes. I would say a lot more positive things have been happening over the two weeks than negative. Each one is looking out for the other person. More awarenesses.

THERAPIST [*returning to the area of conflict raised at the beginning of the session*]: And it's important to keep that in mind in light of the strain that is going to exist as you make changes, and to keep in mind the positives and not let the strain pull you back to feeling you're at point zero . . . which can happen when your expectations are at a high level. I think it's part of the natural process that there will be some strain as you go through these changes and move forward. Now, in terms of the kitchen, what is it that you have to work out, and how do you want to work it out differently than you have in the past?

When we discuss the details of their plans and alternatives for remodeling their kitchen, the project serves, in an interesting way, as a springboard for discussion about their relationship. The couple agree not to move ahead too quickly on the project but to spend time planning to do it right. Janice says the important thing is that "he said let's do it, and that was a big, big plus." We talk about how Janice does not "pussyfoot" around any more and will not "walk on eggshells" with Murray. Janice says, "I don't think he likes that." Murray admits that he does not take easily to changes: "I like old, really." I normalize this feeling by telling them that most people get used to the familiar, so change can be a bit startling. Murray then describes having put together the original kitchen himself in his own perfectionist way and being attached to it. He says that there are areas that Janice will be expert on, like colors, and that he can be helpful about things like floor covering, areas in which he can systematically gather information about alternatives. I tell them that they seem to have a way of complementing one another in this project. We also talk about how finances affect the project, in light of Murray's concern about his impending retirement. In the following segment, we return specifically to their relationship, and then I ask a future-oriented question. The future provides a blank canvas on which to paint a new picture of the relationship.

THERAPIST: What are your ideas about how you'd like to work out this kitchen situation? Or would you prefer not to work together on it?

JANICE: I don't want it all in my lap. I want us to share responsibility for this. I'm worried that there could be major blowups on this one.

THERAPIST: You are imagining this?

JANICE: I guess I'm projecting, but it's pretty much the way it goes.

THERAPIST: Blowups of what kind?

JANICE: I don't know. Maybe some flooring that I picked out Murray is going to be critical of.

THERAPIST: He might comment in a critical way on your choices?

JANICE: Right. I'm very scared about doing this. [We're] trying to be compatible . . . [and] as far as colors, choices, taste, et cetera, we never have a problem with that. We're very fortunate. And as I said, I don't need "fancy" to be happy. But it's the getting-it-off-the-ground stuff that's hard, like deciding which contractors to get for what jobs.

THERAPIST [asks a future-oriented question]: So what do the two of you have to do to get the ball rolling on this thing?

MURRAY: We've got to sit down and make some decisions and keep going forward with our goals and just work together.

THERAPIST: What's your idea of how you'd like . . . your roles in working together [to be on this project]?

JANICE: A pleasant conversation in discussing things, not a closing down. I'm not as knowledgeable about some things, and he's got the practical sense about quality and construction and those things, while my eye would go to color and a warm look and that sort of thing. Mostly, we need to communicate. I need to listen better to what he's saying, and I want him to listen better to what I'm saying.

THERAPIST: And how would you know that you're listening better? What would you be doing?

JANICE: Sort of reiterating it.

THERAPIST: Listening rather than reacting.

JANICE: Yeah.

THERAPIST: And in terms of Murray's listening to you, what would you be looking for?

JANICE: Staying in the conversation rather than walking away.

THERAPIST [to Murray]: Do you have a sense that there may be situations when you feel like walking away in a huff?

MURRAY: Yes. But I worry that I don't know how to assert myself with Janice without going overboard. My communication skills with Janice end up with me not saying anything or trying to overpower her.

THERAPIST: So something in the middle is what you're looking for.

MURRAY [to Janice]: I've pulled that off a couple of times recently, where I haven't backed off, but I haven't tried to overpower you. I felt good about it. I can't think of specific instances, but I felt like I didn't win the argument, but I felt good that I got my point across. It was something that could have escalated in the past into something serious. There was one time I felt unbending about a situation, but I didn't go off the deep end or try to shout you down. I feel like I'm starting to learn how to argue correctly with you on a higher plane.

JANICE: That's promising.

THERAPIST: So there must have been some satisfaction. You clearly noticed that you were doing something differently.

MURRAY: Yes. Maybe it was a 30 percent improvement over the old way.

THERAPIST: So you were experimenting with a different way . . . from walking away or trying to impose your way on Janice.

MURRAY: Right.

THERAPIST: And you may have to try several different things to see what will be most comfortable. But it's a step in the right direction.

MURRAY: Yes.

. . . .

THERAPIST: You're really courageous to take this kitchen project on at this point, because it's an area that will really challenge the two of you. It's got the possibility of pulling you back into old ways that are not going to be very pleasant or to challenge you to develop some new ones which will lead to something much more satisfying.

A little later in the interview, we talk about the effect of making one change in the kitchen (replacing the sink) on the need to make other changes (replacing the floor tile and cabinets)—noting that this is a metaphor for the process the couple are experiencing. This leads to a conversation about the need for Murray and Janice to be flexible and open. We then discuss how some people have construction projects that go on for years while others get the work done efficiently, another metaphor for their relationship. They both say they want to see the work completed quickly with the least possible disruption to their lives. I comment that both of them want to see the changes happen efficiently at this point in their lives and that people can often think about things for years that can be taken care of relatively quickly.

THERAPIST: As I was listening to you, I was having some thoughts. As you know, there are different ways to remodel a kitchen, the slow way, where you replace a little of the old with the new, or the fast way, where you have somebody come in and do the work in three days. The two of you seem to be looking for some big changes. You don't want this to be a gradual process of a little of the old and some of the new. You want to be rid of the old. You want the new.

JANICE: Yes.

MURRAY: Yep. That's a great way of looking at it.

THERAPIST: And both of you seem committed to wanting a new relationship.

JANICE AND MURRAY [*together*]: Yeah.

We set an appointment for another session two weeks ahead.

Session 3

THERAPIST: So, I'm interested in hearing how the remodeling of your relationship is going.

MURRAY: Very good [except for one unpleasant episode].

THERAPIST: So there was one conflictual episode?

JANICE: That's a good word.

MURRAY: Yeah. And again it was over money.

Once again, in the following, my goal is not to reimmerse the couple in the problem but to have them begin to consider how they can get it to "dissolve."

THERAPIST: Instead of [your] telling me the details about the episode, I would be interested in hearing how you got past it, beyond it. How did you resolve it? What actions helped this conflict to dissolve?

MURRAY: Just a little bit of effort on my part. Nothing grand.

THERAPIST: Sometimes it is those small things that make a difference. So I'm interested in hearing what put that episode in the past.

MURRAY: That episode is still lying there ready to break out again probably.

THERAPIST: So it's somewhere in the background. So what do you think you need to do to get that to dissolve, so that it's not there lurking in the background?

MURRAY: I would say talk it out a bit and come to an understanding.

THERAPIST: Has that talking process started . . . ?

MURRAY: No. I think I'm probably trying to ignore it, hoping that it would go away. But I know that it's still there.

THERAPIST: What kind of talking about this will help it go more into the background?

MURRAY: Having a good conversation directly with Janice about it. But that's difficult for me.

THERAPIST: So what would be the best way to proceed to help this fade? Because it sounds to me that this is one episode over two weeks . . . and I'm wondering, other than that, how were things working?

JANICE: I think well. [*Murray agrees.*]

THERAPIST: How much did this incident pervade everything else?

JANICE: It just went underground like it never happened, and we just go on with our lives. I would like to give some details about this . . . since it is this one thing that keeps rearing its ugly head.

THERAPIST: Okay.

JANICE: The underlying thing, I think, is there's a basic resentment on Murray's part to my stopping formally working in 1992 and taking my social security. It's never been resolved, and it's been a sore spot with him.

Janice provides historical background about Murray's attitude toward money and his resentment over Janice's early retirement. They agree that this needs to be discussed and resolved. I engage them around this issue by encouraging them to have a conversation that is satisfying, right here in today's session.

THERAPIST: What I'm wondering about that might be useful for you is to have this conversation about what you've been discussing but to have it in the way that you would like it to go . . . in a way that would not be conflictual. . . . [You] would come out with some feeling that you've both been heard and that your ideas are out on the table with no hurt feelings. Do you think you can pick up the issue and continue the conversation and get it to some kind of closure?

JANICE: As we speak?

THERAPIST: Yes. Right now. The closure doesn't mean you have to make a decision. . . . [Just] replay this conversation so that it comes out in a more satisfying way.

Murray and Janice engage in a ten-minute conversational role-play in which each has an opportunity both to talk and to express his or her understanding of the other's position. After this conversation, Murray was comfortable agreeing to Janice's request that he not raise the issue of her early retirement again ("to throw it in her face") when they discuss money matters. They are making progress, and as a way to limit their expectations and normalize their setbacks, I define progress as something that is not necessarily smooth or without rough edges.

JANICE: I came in very discouraged about that conversation we had over the money. I came in with a heavy heart tonight, but with doing the role-playing, I can see there is another way to work things out intelligently and in a calm manner.

THERAPIST: I think you've both been working hard at this process and are making progress. Sometimes it may feel like two steps forward and one step back or that the progress is not fast enough, but you're both working very conscientiously at this, and I don't foresee an interminable process here. Maybe meeting two or three more times is about what will be required before you're able to go on your way. We might need a little booster session two or three months down the road. But you'll need to tell me how satisfied you are with the progress you are making. I do think you're moving in the right direction. So let's set something up.

We set an appointment for five weeks from now.

Session 4

THERAPIST: How have you been doing?

JANICE: I think very well.

MURRAY: I would agree.

THERAPIST: What has contributed to your thinking that things are going well?

MURRAY: Probably that there isn't any tension.

THERAPIST: What has replaced the tension?

MURRAY: I think just getting along with each other.

THERAPIST: Let's say a 0 would be that things are in the pits, maybe the way it was back in August [when Janice was talking about a separation] . . . and a 10 is that things are super wonderful. . . . [Where are you now]?

MURRAY: I'd say a 6.5, maybe a 7.

THERAPIST: And what would you have said three weeks ago?

MURRAY: Probably the same. But it's more steady. Not so many ups and downs. I can't think of any major conflicts that occurred.

THERAPIST [to Janice]: What's your sense of where things are?

JANICE: The Christmas season is always stressful and busy, but that kind of tension just wasn't present. It's probably the nicest Christmas season I've known in the forty years I've been married. [Things went well over the holidays: Murray sent me a beautiful card, and he put] an awful lot of thought into the presents he bought me. . . . In August, I would have given this marriage a zero chance of going. As a last-ditch effort, Murray said he would go for counseling, something he always resisted. Up until maybe five weeks ago, I would have said, "He just doesn't get it. This just isn't working. He still isn't hearing anything being said." Again, maybe I was at a 5, maybe 4.5. But he does get it. There are wonderful changes: his thoughtfulness, his communication with me. I had given up. I thought, "He's not going to get it." But he does, and I'm very hopeful.

THERAPIST: So where would you put yourself now?

JANICE: Maybe a 7.

THERAPIST: So you're both about at the same place. What would be involved in moving to a 7.5 or an 8? Or does it feel like a 7 is okay and acceptable to both of you?

MURRAY: I don't know what it would take. I'd say probably doing more of the same . . . being consistent would move it up to an 8.

JANICE: You asked about whether it could go beyond a 7. I was thinking, we've been married almost forty years, how much better can it get than a 7? Because life is life. Who could have expectations of a 10? And I was thinking, "This is a pretty damn good life."

MURRAY: I was also thinking how lucky we are. We're healthy. We're very fortunate. We're blessed.

JANICE: How much more can you have than a 7? That's pretty good.

THERAPIST [to Murray]: It sounds like you have been very responsive to feedback from Janice over this period. [To Janice.] At the beginning, it sounded like you were asking more of your husband [to Murray] than you were asking of your wife in terms of changes. In fact, you acknowledged that there were certain things that you needed to change about yourself. So you accepted that and have actively and successfully taken a number of very positive steps that Janice has noticed and appreciated. [To Janice.] And it's been nice that you've been noticing these changes and actively showing your appreciation. . . . [To Murray.] You were saying that doing more of what you've been doing will increase your confidence . . . and move things along that scale a little bit. Are there other things that you'd like to see going on between the two of you that would increase your confidence to a 7.5 or an 8? Or, as [Janice was] saying, [do you feel that] you've been married forty years, you have your health and feel grateful for what you do have, and that a 7 is just fine, without [your] setting new heights or raising expectations beyond what is realistic? And that is an individual decision, how people think about this. If what's happening now continues, knowing that there will always be some places where there will be some tension, some conflict, but overall there would be the sense of satisfaction that you've both been experiencing recently, would that be satisfying?

MURRAY: I think that if we continue on that way, it will snowball into something better and better.

THERAPIST: So things may naturally evolve into something better.

MURRAY: Yes.

JANICE: I'm very happy.

THERAPIST: It seems like you've really turned the corner.

MURRAY: I think we're really doing better.

JANICE: I even went to the doctor last week, and my blood pressure is normal, and I think that says a lot. The doctor commented that I seemed so much more relaxed.

THERAPIST: I certainly admire the work the two of you have done.

JANICE: It's been worth it.

MURRAY: I think so.

We set the next appointment for one month ahead.

Session 5

THERAPIST: At our last visit, we had discussed using this time for a reassessment of our work. Is that okay? Is there anything pressing that you wanted to bring up before we get into this?

MURRAY: Actually, no.

THERAPIST [to Janice]: Did you have something you wanted to bring up?

JANICE: Not that's pressing. It's been a very good month.

THERAPIST: So you've been able to continue the progress you've been making?

Murray and Janice agree that they have continued their progress. In my review of their progress, I begin to externalize (White & Epston, 1991) the relationship "patterns" they have developed, presenting the patterns as forces outside the couple that have been influencing them. These patterns, rather than the behavior of either member of the couple, have become the "problem." By working together, Murray and Janice are liberating themselves from the influence of these patterns and moving their relationship to a new level. I then begin to ask *unique account and redescription questions* (Epston & White, 1992), as a way to increase the couple's sense of personal agency.

THERAPIST: Let me go over some things as a way of review of what we've been doing. I also have some questions that I can ask you as a way of reviewing where we are. [*To Janice*.] When you first came in here . . . you had spoken about having come to a point, a few weeks earlier, where you were feeling like it wasn't going to work in the relationship and that this feeling had been building over a period of years. [*To Murray*.] At the same time, you were going on thinking things were okay while at the same time getting involved in outside activities and organizations, spending less time tuning-in to Janice and more time in external pursuits. And then Janice hit you with the wake-up call of, "I've had it. . . . It's not working." At that point, you realized very quickly that you weren't tuning-in . . . that something was very wrong. Over that few weeks, from the time you took a walk and had that conversation until you came for the first appointment, you were already starting to make some changes. [*To Janice*.] And initially you didn't trust that the changes you were seeing were real, since in the past you had seen Murray get into more of a placating position, where [he] would try to be nice after some episode, but then the old patterns would return. But this time, you began thinking this is not the same old style; it was more authentic, real, and you were feeling more confidence. Over a very long period, up until you confronted this situation head on, there was tension, withdrawal, and this overpowering kind of behavior that wasn't working. [*To both*.] And now you've been able to free yourselves from some of those old patterns. What I'm wondering is what you did to reduce the influence of those old patterns of withdrawal, overpoweringness, isolation, "tuned-outness" . . . so that those patterns would not be able to dominate your lives in the way they had in the past. What did each of you do that prevented those patterns from continuing to dominate your lives in the ways they had?

MURRAY: I think I was the biggest culprit in this thing. I was going around without consideration for Janice. Whatever I did, I did without getting Janice's approval, not consulting with her or anything. That was the way I sort of did things. And Janice took a back seat. I would make decisions for the two of us, and she would go along with it. I might say, "Let's go out to dinner tonight," and I wasn't really asking Janice.

THERAPIST: So it was this pattern that was in control. [*To Murray*.] You decided and [*to Janice*] you went along with his decision. This was something the two of you were caught up in, cooperating with this pattern rather than doing it differently.

MURRAY: That was the basis for all my dealings with Janice. What I do now is try to consider her a little bit. There's still a long way to go. Old habits die hard. It's hard to make changes when you've been brought up a certain way all of your life. When I grew up, I didn't have a choice about anything. All the choices until the time I got married and left the house were made for me.

THERAPIST: So that pattern was part of your past that you were bringing along with you.

MURRAY: Yes.

THERAPIST: That was baggage you were bringing with you.

MURRAY: Yes. I thought it was okay to yell at your wife, things like that. But then you do grow up and relearn things, too. I think I am making changes, and I will continue to try to make them.

THERAPIST: How does making the changes that you've made affect your picture of yourself as a person?

MURRAY: In the old days, it would have been a weakness, control the family, control my wife. I would have considered it a weakness that I wasn't strong enough to control my wife, but I can see that this is wrong. You have to consider the other person.

THERAPIST: In acting in some new ways that have been different from those old patterns, how has that affected how you think about yourself?

MURRAY: As I say, a little bit weaker.

THERAPIST: So, you're still carrying around those old rules, ideas from the past that say a real man is supposed to be in control of the household?

MURRAY: And not to cry . . . and stuff like that.

THERAPIST: What is the impact of thinking of yourself as weaker?

MURRAY: Actually, not bad. It feels good to know that you're considering another person . . . calling to let them know you'll be late.

THERAPIST: I imagine that these steps will change how you think about yourself. Particularly in the face of the strength of the old patterns, it's not surprising that you'd still have some of that old feeling that being considerate represents weakness rather than strength. . . .

MURRAY: Right.

THERAPIST: The steps you have taken, what do they tell you about what you want in your relationship with Janice?

MURRAY: To do things together, to have fun, to talk about things, to be more thoughtful, to comfort one another in bad times . . . support. Things like that.

THERAPIST: From the time that Janice talked to you—you took that walk and she told you how unhappy she was—what have you learned about her over this period of time that's given you some renewed confidence in the relationship and respect for her?

MURRAY: I respect her for how she handles her job. I admire her for that.

THERAPIST: What does that say about her that she's been willing to stick with you?

MURRAY: Yeah, right. She kept the family together, raised the children. I admire her for that. And putting up with what I've given her . . . my drinking and all.

THERAPIST: Janice, what's your sense. . . . What did you know about Murray, early on, that would have predicted for you that he would be able to take these positive steps, make these changes?

JANICE: Basically, he was a very good person. Before I married him, I knew this was a very upstanding gentleman, a good person, a hard worker, ambitious, someone who would provide for his family. In fact, through all the years of his drinking, he never missed a day of work. There was a very strong fiber, a very moral man. Knowing that he was a good person. He had a disease [alcoholism], and I understood it as a disease. But there was something underneath that was special and good.

THERAPIST: You saw through to who he was as a person.

JANICE: Basically a good person with a lot of that other stuff that got in the way.

THERAPIST: So you were able to keep that in mind, that through the hard times, you knew he was basically a good person.

JANICE: Yeah.

THERAPIST: You held on to that even in the face of the difficulties. That's not easy to do. What's your sense about the future?

JANICE: I feel very positive about the future. Earlier, as I said, I didn't think this had a snowball's chance in hell. [I thought] that he didn't get it. But yes, he does get it. And really, really good things have been happening. . . . Affection. This was never too forthcoming in the last few years. But now, an arm around me, a hug, a kiss. And he said something to me Sunday . . . this is hard [*begins to cry*] . . . that he was glad that I hung in all those years. And I had never heard that from him before. And it was very special. I don't know what brought it on.

THERAPIST: It just came out of the blue?

JANICE: He just came up behind me and said it. He never said that to me before. It's just very comfortable now. I can go over to him and give him a hug, or vice versa. It's slow, but it's coming. It's almost nightly now that we embrace, which to me is very positive. The first year [*of marriage*] was lovely, and I feel like there was always something there that went away because of this damn disease, but [I] feel some great strength that it could come back. Maybe not in that young-love intensity but like an easy chair . . . soft and comfortable.

THERAPIST: Did Murray's comment that he appreciated your sticking by him take you by surprise?

JANICE: It did, because those years are never discussed really.

MURRAY: It comes back to the weakness thing. To tell you that would make me in turn look weak.

THERAPIST: This is another example of how you didn't let the old patterns and scripts determine your behavior or dominate your life.

MURRAY: Yeah.

JANICE: I see the awarenesses now. Light has dawned on Marblehead. I guess it was always there, but what one considers a weakness, someone else might consider a strength. To me, it's very manly to be an honorable person, and I see great honesty in Murray now. He's able to verbalize some of these things.

THERAPIST: So you're seeing strength in what he might consider weakness.

JANICE: Yes.

MURRAY: That's good.

JANICE: I don't feel angry the way I felt angry. I just feel this inner peace. I've been able to let go of a lot of [anger]. The changes become contagious, and one becomes more affirmative to the other person.

THERAPIST: I certainly admire what the two of you have been able to do.

JANICE: It's work!

THERAPIST: Yes.

I met with Murray and Janice on five more occasions over a period of four months. Although experiencing a few "bumps" along the way (when one of the old patterns resurfaced and Janice felt "discouraged and worried"), this couple were able to build on the strengths of their relationship to establish a new and more comfortable complementarity.

Conclusion

The framework presented in this chapter exemplifies a collaborative, respectful, and competency-directed therapy. The therapist coconstructs and coauthors alternative narratives that open opportunities for change and growth. The approach discussed is representative of critical shifts that are now occurring more generally in the practice of psychotherapy (Amundson, Stewart & Valentine, 1993; Andersen, 1991; Anderson & Goolishian, 1988; de Shazer, 1991; Friedman, 1993; Gergen, 1985; Gilligan & Price, 1993; Hoffman, 1985, 1990; McNamee & Gergen, 1992; White & Epston, 1991). These current transformations in thinking emphasize the therapist's role as a coparticipant in a meaning-generating process that is both hopeful and empowering.

By way of summary, I outline these shifts and transformations below. The postmodern therapist

- Believes in a socially constructed reality.

- Emphasizes the reflexive nature of therapeutic relationships in which client and therapist co-construct meanings in dialogue or conversation.

- Moves away from hierarchical distinctions toward a more egalitarian offering of ideas and respect for differences.

- Maintains empathy and respect for the client's predicament and a belief in the power of therapeutic conversation to liberate suppressed, ignored, or previously unacknowledged voices or stories.

- Co-constructs goals and negotiates direction in therapy, placing the client back in the driver's seat, as an expert on his or her own predicaments and dilemmas.

- Searches for and amplifies client competencies, strengths, and resources and avoids being a detective of pathology or reifying rigid diagnostic distinctions.

- Avoids a vocabulary of deficit and dysfunction, replacing the jargon of pathology (and distance) with the language of the everyday.

- Is oriented toward the future and optimistic about change.

- Is sensitive to the methods and processes used in the therapeutic conversation.

We live a storied existence, and it is these stories that clients bring to therapy. Our dialogues with ourselves and with others come to define our views and determine our actions. Each member of a couple develops, over time, his or her own narrative for describing the ebb and flow of the relationship. The stories of each partner become interwoven and integrated into a multidimensional tapestry that gives coherence and meaning to the partners' lives together. A therapy of possibility invites clients to consider future options, to rewrite old stories, to develop alternative visions for new chapters to come, and in so doing, to experience a sense of personal agency or efficacy. The therapist serves as a facilitator or catalyst who, through the medium of conversation, enables suppressed voices to be heard. In this conversational process, clients are able to liberate themselves from problem-saturated narratives that have been constraining and limiting. They have a re-vision of their lives and relationships, seeing them in ways that emphasize new possibilities and offer hope for the future.

References

Amundson, J., Stewart, K., & Valentine, L. (1993). Temptations of power and certainty. *Journal of Marital and Family Therapy, 19,* 111–123.

Andersen, T. (Ed.). (1991). *The reflecting team: Dialogues and dialogues about the dialogues*. New York: W.W. Norton.

Anderson, H., & Goolishian, H. A. (1988). Human systems as linguistic systems: Preliminary and evolving ideas about the implications for clinical theory. *Family Process, 27,* 371–393.

Anderson, H., & Goolishian, H. A. (1992). The client is the expert: A not-knowing approach to therapy. In S. McNamee & K. J. Gergen (Eds.), *Therapy as social construction* (pp. 25–39). Newbury Park, CA: Sage.

Berg, I. K. (1989, January/February). Of visitors, complainants and customers. *The Family Therapy Networker,* p. 27.

Berg, I. K., & de Shazer, S. (1993). Making numbers talk: Language in therapy. In S. Friedman (Ed.), *The new language of change: Constructive collaboration in psychotherapy* (pp. 5–24). New York: Guilford Press.

de Shazer, S. (1985). *Keys to solution in brief therapy*. New York: W.W. Norton.

de Shazer, S. (1988). *Clues: Investigating solutions in brief therapy*. New York: W.W. Norton.

de Shazer, S. (1991). *Putting difference to work*. New York: W.W. Norton.

Epston, D., & White, M. (1992). *Experience, contradiction, narrative & imagination: Selected papers of David Epston & Michael White*. Adelaide: Dulwich Centre Press.

Friedman, S. (Ed.). (1993). *The new language of change: Constructive collaboration in psychotherapy*. New York: Guilford Press.

Friedman, S., & Fanger, M. T. (1991). *Expanding therapeutic possibilities: Getting results in brief psychotherapy*. New York: Lexington Books/Macmillan.

Gergen, K. J. (1985). The social constructionist movement in modern psychology. *American Psychologist, 40,* 266–275.

Gilligan, S., & Price, R. (Eds.). (1993). *Therapeutic conversations*. New York: W.W. Norton.

Hoffman, L. (1985). Beyond power and control: Toward a "second order" family systems therapy. *Family Systems Medicine, 3,* 381–396.

Hoffman, L. (1990). Constructing realities: An art of lenses. *Family Process, 29,* 1–12.

Kowalski, K., & Kral, R. (1989). The geometry of solution: Using the scaling technique. *Family Therapy Case Studies, 4,* 59–66.

McNamee, S., & Gergen, K. J. (Eds.). (1992). *Therapy as social construction*. Newbury Park, CA: Sage.

Miller, S. (1992). The symptoms of solution. *Journal of Strategic and Systemic Therapies, 11,* 1–11.

Postman, N. (1976). *Crazy talk, stupid talk*. New York: Delacorte.

Prochaska, J. O., DiClemente, C. C., & Norcross, J. C. (1992). In search of how people change. *American Psychologist, 47,* 1102–1114.

White, M. (1991). Deconstruction and therapy. In D. Epston & M. White, *Experience, contradiction, narrative & imagination: Selected papers of David Epston & Michael White* (pp. 109–152). Adelaide: Dulwich Centre Press. [Reprinted in S. Gilligan & R. Price (Eds.). (1993). *Therapeutic conversations* (pp. 22–61). New York: W.W. Norton.]

White, M., & Epston, D. (1991). *Narrative means to therapeutic ends.* New York: W.W. Norton.

• •

15

The Meaning of Relationship in Residential Treatment

A Developmental Perspective

Robert L. Selman, Steven Brion-Meisels, and Gregory G. Wilkins

The context for the research on developmental-relational social behavior presented in this chapter is the Brandywine Treatment Center (BTC) of the Devereux Foundation. The BTC serves over one hundred latency-aged and adolescent males who have a range of social, academic, emotional, cognitive, and behavioral problems. The center provides educational, clinical, medical, and residential services. One programmatic goal at Brandywine is to integrate various strands of social and emotional intervention, including individual psychotherapy, pair therapy, milieu approaches, psychoeducational efforts, and innovative programs that make use of the Brandywine Center's rural setting (for example, its vocational program, Companionable Zoo and Nature Program, horticultural program, and Outward Bound).

The Devereux-Brandywine approach is *relationship* oriented. Each effort includes a commitment to engage the youngsters in ways that positively affect their social skills. Therefore, efforts to evaluate the

Note: We wish to express our appreciation to Jonathan Fieldman and to Christopher McGlinn, both of whom worked on the construction and refinement of the Devereux dilemmas; to Kenneth Ferro, executive director of the Brandywine Treatment Center, for his steadfast support of our project; to Leonard Green of the Devereux Academy for his enthusiasm and continued support; and to Ronald Burd, president of the Devereux Foundation, for his vision of innovation and research across the residential centers of the foundation.

success or failure of treatment outcomes need to incorporate ways of assessing the efficacy of the relationship approach. The research we discuss here concerns an interview method of identifying individuals' levels of relationship functioning, both to evaluate each child's or adolescent's current status and to formulate the kinds of interventions likely to have an enduring positive effect on that person at this particular stage in his or her development. Before presenting our research, however, we offer portraits of three boys who were focal points of our research.

Three Conduct-Disordered Adolescents

At the Devereux-Brandywine dining hall, Lawrence, James, and Jerry walk in for the noon meal.

Lawrence

Lawrence is well dressed, in a pair of Guess jeans purchased during a home visit in suburban Philadelphia. He is maturing rapidly; we know this from his deep fluctuating voice and the stubble of a too-obvious mustache on his lip. Lawrence enters accompanied by an adult counselor; as on most days, he is assigned to eat with his "special," an assigned counselor. If left to his own devices, Lawrence is likely to meander throughout the dining hall, disrupting and agitating staff and peers alike with catholic impartiality. He is an isolated young man, who enjoys video games (especially Super Mario) and hangs on the periphery of peer groups. Even when in physical proximity of a counselor, he is boisterous and provocative. His conversation is likely to be highly sexualized and replete with complaints regarding the inequities of the world or the interminable faults of others. At any moment, he may lose control—with anger washing over him like a toxic tide. Of necessity, his counselors remain vigilant and prepared to act.

James

James enters soon after Lawrence. They are the same age (fourteen), but in no way are they bookends. James has just returned from a good home visit in a small mid-Atlantic coastal town. He is short and chunky. His bright eyes and large cheeks make us smile in return; he has the kind of smile that can win over an angry teacher or counselor even after an act of mischief. James loves to fish, most often with any peer who can be persuaded to join him. He is very involved with the animals in the school's Companionable Zoo and Nature Program (Katcher and Wilkins, 1993). Unlike Lawrence, James is oblivious to what he wears. As we walk past him, he is settled into lunch with a "zoo counselor," and they are having a lively conversation about the impending arrival of Vietnamese pigs. James has just made a positive transition to a program for older boys, but he also talks about several of the recurrent problems with which he struggles, particularly his penchant for merciless teasing of peers.

Jerry

Finally, we encounter Jerry entering the dining hall. Jerry is scheduled to leave Devereux, having attained his treatment objectives and concluded a successful transition to the high school program. He is starting to look like the young man he is becoming. His infectious smile, however, is still boyish. Jerry sits down to talk with a counselor from his previous program. In his inimitable style, he spins some yarns about roller-skating and a dance in the community the previous weekend. Girls, cars, and the promise of leaving are important to him these days. When we speak with his counselor, he reminds us that Jerry still carries a mean streak; he is quite capable of hurting his residence mates, especially the younger ones. Yet at the same time, he has become more helpful and responsive to the needs of others as his disenrollment approaches.

Comparative Background and Behavior

Each of these three boys confronts significant challenges in his movement toward adulthood. Each shares a somewhat similar history, but each has an individual set of ideas, feelings, and behavior patterns in construing and responding to his social world. Developing fundamental skills to navigate the social world is essential for these three boys if they are to progress along a psychologically adaptive path from childhood to adulthood. Each carries with him a history of emotional or physical neglect and abuse, cognitive deficits resulting from a range of genetic and environmental factors, and traumatic relationship experiences associated with loss, anger, and abandonment. In addition, each has often been deprived of the social experiences that other children take for granted—a safe and secure home that provides time to read, talk, observe, play, and learn. These boys are thrice victims, denied their birthright as a result of genetic, familial, and societal problems. However, they have many of the same needs as their peers: they seek love and care, friendship and trust, adults to emulate and admire, opportunities to learn, and encouragement and support when they make mistakes.

Lawrence

Lawrence relates to people through superficial and short-term attachments, which exist only to fulfill his immediate needs. He has developed a consistent but primitive approach to the social world: stay isolated, grab what you can when you can, make no interpersonal connections, strike before you are struck, and leave before you are kicked out. It is a pattern that has protected him and enabled him to survive a difficult psychosocial history with a limited repertoire of cognitive and social tools. A series of episodic aggressive behaviors has previously resulted in a brief psychiatric hospitalization. The improvement made during this period was temporary, however, and before long he had resumed his basic impulsive propensity to fight or flight as the primary strategy for his "social" survival.

James

James shares some similar history with Lawrence, having experienced four psychiatric hospitalizations. James had been physically abusive to his mother and had been medicated in attempts to suppress his rage reactions and facilitate his acquiring more adaptive methods of coping with powerful affects. His parents had reported his aggression at a young age—in his case, it was almost exclusively against authority figures. James's parents are divorced, and there is a history of alcoholism as well as bipolar disorder in his family. On his intake evaluation, his biopsychosocial information converged on a diagnosis that included such descriptors as "intermittent explosive disorder" and "fair psychosocial functioning"; he demonstrated, however, a high-average level of intellectual functioning. Yet his academic successes were limited, largely as a result of his diminished frustration tolerance, desultory efforts in classroom endeavors, and heightened impulsivity.

James's voluminous behavior incident reports, however, are quite different from Lawrence's. The frequency and qualitative descriptions of his inappropriate behaviors yield a portrait of an adolescent who is less physically violent, though equally aggressive, and whose behavior is substantially affected by the social context in which he finds himself.

Behavioral incident reports, furthermore, indicate that the quality of James's behavioral problems and the processing that he can do subsequent to their occurrence are quite different from the responses of Lawrence. James turns his aggression toward staff, particularly when they set limits for him; Lawrence directs his aggression primarily toward peers. James's aggression is often verbal; Lawrence's is predominantly physical. James's reports indicate no incidence of flight; Lawrence frequently flees or isolates himself in response to unmanageable interpersonal conflicts or the imposition of unpalatable demands. Most importantly, James is able to talk about his own behavior after the fact; Lawrence's communication skills are abysmally inadequate.

James has capacities that exceed Lawrence's at this point, although the boys are similar in age and have many parallels in their histories. James's behavioral levels and incident reports suggest a boy who is more reflective about his behavior, assumes the perspective of others to a greater extent, and exercises some limited self-control—at least when compared with Lawrence. Finally, Lawrence's behavior is more rigid than that of James: it varies less over time. However, it is also more consistently problematic, with higher levels of both physical aggression and isolation (both fight and flight). Lawrence's rare instances of program compliance are ephemeral, at best.

Jerry

Jerry is slightly older, approaching his fifteenth birthday. He came to the BTC with a long-standing history of provoking and engaging in physical fights with his peers. Like Lawrence, he exhibited high levels of self- and other-directed aggression: he brought a weapon to school, threatened to assault a police officer with a knife, and was referred to the Devereux Foundation months after he exposed himself and then tried to leap out of a school window, at age eleven. Jerry's intake assessments described him with such phrases as "impulse disorder" and "experiences a high degree of internal stress." He obtained high-average intelligence scores, though lower than those of James. The psychological evaluation completed at admission noted questions about gender identity, feelings of being "damaged and inadequate," and troubles with limited controls. Jerry's home life has also been chaotic. According to Jerry, women are "helpless" against his aggression and unavailable as resources for him. His father is suspected of abusive behavior toward Jerry during the time he was involved in Jerry's life. In these ways, Jerry is much like Lawrence and James. He combines aspects of both boys in his capacity for directing aggression against both adults and peers. Jerry is isolated, has few friends at the BTC, and gravitates toward relationships with adults as substitutes for peer relationships.

Jerry combines aspects of both James and Lawrence in his behavioral content and patterns. For example, Jerry's aggression seems more likely to be directed toward his adolescent peers; adults become the target when they intervene to protect the other adolescent. Jerry is like Lawrence in that both have few peer relationships. Instead they orient themselves toward adults, predictably with negative results. However, Jerry and James are similar to one another insofar as they both have a broader behavioral repertoire (or capacity) than Lawrence. Jerry continues to be described by a counselor as "the most unpredictable of the three." We believe this apparent unpredictability and the complexity of his response patterns (as compared to Lawrence's), in part, stem from his more expansive and complex set of social and cognitive abilities.

Although Jerry's aggression can be dangerous in some contexts, it has a focus that is not qualitatively different from that which is normative in adolescence—that is, it is directed primarily at adults who impose limits and is designed to test those limits (through theft, defiance, violating curfew, and smoking). Compared to Lawrence's aggression, Jerry's aggression is more often verbal. Finally, Jerry's *amplitude* (that is, the amount of variance between his best and worst behavior levels) is less marked or contrasted than is Lawrence's. Jerry has frequent outbursts (though less frequently than Lawrence does), but they are quickly diffused. He recovers more quickly than Lawrence in his behavior, as well, and somewhat more quickly in his ability to reflect upon and reconstitute the incident through analysis and synthesis.

The Theoretical Foundation

The behavioral and clinical labels common to these boys fall into categories that include impulsivity, aggression toward self and others, isolation, anger, dysregulated behavioral controls, and violations of the rights of others as well as of social norms and situation-specific rules. However, these behavioral labels mask significant differences in each boy's capacity for forming and maintaining friendships—a capacity that is important when structuring interventions that will facilitate these adolescents' social development and reduce the frequency and severity of their behavioral pathology.

In our research, we closely studied the thoughts and actions of these three boys through a developmental and relationship oriented lens (Selman & Schultz, 1990). Our pilot research project, carried out over six months, provides a perspective on the lives of these boys and our efforts to assist them. Our portraits, like all portraits, are partial. They are snapshots, frozen from a moving film of daily events. Ultimately, they must be seen in broader social, psychological, and cultural contexts.

The Developmental-Relational Orientation

Our focus, at this point, is on a combined developmental and relational approach that examines children's and adolescents' social behavior according to their *interpersonal negotiation strategies* (INS). This approach contributes to our understanding of children and adolescents who have severe social, emotional, and behavioral maladaptation and our understanding of interventions to take with them. It integrates a developmental view of these youngsters' social understanding (an analysis, by developmental levels, of the extent to which their capacity or willingness to coordinate their own and others' social perspectives influences their views on friendship and peer group relations) with an *interpersonal orientation* view of their social relationship behavior (an analysis of whether and in what ways their social negotiations are dominant or submissive in any given social interaction or social relationship). The interaction of the developmental framework with the relational framework produces information that helps us diagnose and understand the meaning and maturity of the strategies we observe children and adolescents using to negotiate meaningful problems involving other persons. As a developmental-relational lens focused on growth from immaturity to maturity, this approach complements the traditional disorder diagnosis, which focuses on behavioral excesses, performance deficits, and the alleviation of psychopathology.

Cognitive-behavioral and psychosocial treatments are frequently employed to address the cognitive deficits and behavioral disregulation of children and adolescents with disruptive behavior disorders

(Breen & Altepeter, 1990; Craighead, Craighead, Kazdin, & Mahoney, 1994). Although the empirical literature demonstrates the general short-term efficacy of such psychotherapeutic interventions, children's and adolescents' behavioral gains consequent to treatment are not generally maintained for reasonable periods. Just as importantly, the new skills acquired do not generalize sufficiently to new and salient contexts (Kendall & Braswell, 1985). These skills unequivocally lack staying power, due, at least in part, to the narrow focus that treats specific and socially decontextualized deficits in cognitive-behavioral domains within the individual child, rather than focusing directly on relational skills *between and among pairs or groups of children or adolescents*. We believe that more robust interventions must not only be built upon a psychological assessment of how children understand and make meaning of the social context within which they operate but must also focus on an assessment of children's and adolescents' social interactions and their real interpersonal relationship skills (that is, on how they actually put their social thought into social action).

Residential programs are uniquely suited to foster social development because their social setting can take advantage of the child's inherent desire to make friends no matter how much his or her approach has been warped by earlier interpersonal experiences. We believe that our preliminary research takes a modest step toward giving theoretical direction to the developmental and relational assessment of the actual social interactions of youths in residential treatment. Such assessment is achieved through studying both how children and adolescents in residential treatment understand interpersonal relationships and how they propose to deal directly with significant others in order to resolve the inevitable relationship conflicts of communal life.

Social Perspectives and Interpersonal Skills

The interpersonal negotiations strategies approach encompasses developmental and interpersonal analyses that explore and conceptualize the ways in which children and adolescents negotiate interpersonal problems. The cornerstone of the analyses is the individual's operative ability to differentiate and coordinate the social perspectives of self and others both cognitively and emotionally. The developmental framework within which social perspective coordination functions is delineated in greater detail in Selman's *The Growth of Interpersonal Understanding* (1980). Selman's approach was strongly influenced by the social philosophies and developmental psychological theories of Baldwin (1902), Mead (1934), Piaget (1932/1965), Werner (1948), and Kohlberg (1969).

More recently, we have proposed that the child's level of social perspective coordination has implications not only for how he or she *understands* interpersonal issues like fairness, friendship, or peer group formation but also for how he or she *behaves* in peer relations—as measured by how he or she deals with others around interpersonal issues. (This research is more fully described in *Making a Friend in Youth: Developmental Theory and Pair Therapy*, Selman & Schultz, 1990, which describes in considerable detail the developmental levels of social perspective coordination and their analogs across various developmental lines of social relationships.)

Three Domains of Social Development

Exhibit 15.1 describes the structural parallels across the three domains of social development that are the focus of our research: (1) the developing capacity to coordinate social perspectives, (2) the developing understanding of social and interpersonal relationships, and (3) the developing ability to negotiate interpersonal problems. We need to emphasize that our claim is not that children and adolescents function synchronously; they are not locked in step at the same developmental levels across all three lines of social functioning. Instead, we contend that the use of a developmental lens on a child's progress and position on *each* of the three domains improves the therapist's understanding of the nature of that child's social behavior, and hence his or her ability to formulate critical treatment interventions. For example, treatments for children and adolescents whose functioning is truncated or regressed across all three domains would be quite different from treatments for youngsters with, on the one hand, a sophisticated capacity to coordinate social perspectives and construe interpersonal relationships and, on the other hand, an immature or limited repertoire of interpersonal negotiation strategies. In fact, it is the lacunae or deficits in level of functioning across these three domains of social development that most clearly illuminate a child's interpersonal and social difficulties.

The Devereux Hypothetical Dilemmas and Interview Process

Our research addresses several key questions: first, how do clients understand the specific and particular interpersonal and institutional issues that are important in their own lives at Brandywine? What strategies do they propose for dealing with these issues? Second, what range of cognitive, emotional, and behavioral functioning is incorporated in the DSM-IV diagnostic category "conduct disorder" (American Psychiatric Association, 1994). (Conduct disorder is the diagnosis most often used to describe BTC clients.) How can therapists' understanding of these clients (and this category) be expanded in the service of enabling the psychosocial maturation of such clients into successful adults? Third, what are the implications of such analyses for assessment, treatment, and outcome research within residential treatment settings?

One method we often use in our research is a person-to-person interview. It begins with a discussion of a set of hypothetical dilemmas focused on the everyday interpersonal experiences of the participants in our research and then moves, as trust and rapport develop, to a discussion of the individual participant's *personal* experiences. Using this method requires the construction of hypothetical dilemmas that are contextually relevant and personally meaningful to the lives of the participants. (See the Appendix at the end of this chapter for our "Devereux Dilemmas," used at BTC.)

Exhibit 15.1. Levels of Social Perspective Coordination, Understanding of Friendship, and Interpersonal Negotiations Strategies.

Level 0

1. Undifferentiated, egocentric, and impulsive undifferentiated social perspectives. Very young children have a difficult time differentiating between their perspective and that of others and between the physical actions and psychological intentions of other people. "You are what you seem" might be one way to describe this perspective, and "you mean what you do," another way.

2. Egocentric understanding of friendships. At this level, concepts of friendship are often based on physical phenomena: my friend is the person who lives next to me or who sits next to me at lunch in day care or who has the same Ninja Turtles. This notion of friendship has real limitations: if my friend moves, he may no longer be considered my friend; if she won't get off the swing, she is no longer my friend (at least for the moment).

3. Impulsive and physical negotiation strategies. With this foundation, negotiation strategies are most often based on impulsive, physical responses, what might be called an impulsive fight or flight approach. Faced with a conflict, the child sees only two strategies available, both physical: fight, grab, hit (an aggressive or externalizing response), or flee, hide, withdraw (an internalizing response).

Level 1

1. First-person, one-way, and unilateral first-person social perspectives. At this level, the child differentiates intentional from unintentional actions and begins to appreciate and understand that other people in his or her life have individual, subjective, and covert psychological experiences different from his or her own. In other words, people become more than simply their physical surface characteristics: they have thoughts, feelings, and intentions, which are important factors, obstacles, and resources in forming friendships with them as well as in solving social problems.

2. One-way understanding of friendships. At this level, the child can recognize (differentiate) but not coordinate the different perspective of the other person. Therefore, friendships continue to be based on the perceived needs (undifferentiated from wants) of *either* the self or the other but not of *both* self and other: "He is my best friend because I do what he tells me to do." This new understanding of friendship is progress, but it will not sustain mature interpersonal relationships. This level characterizes many of the young people who are referred to institutions like Devereux.

3. Unilateral negotiation strategies. At this level, negotiations tend to focus on "command or obey" strategies. Available solutions are one-way and often win-lose. Children look to an authority figure to tell them what to do and how, and then they begin to resist that authority figure, as the conflict between two one-way solutions becomes inevitable. Again, this level represents progress over a simply physical approach, but it will not sustain long-term relationships.

Level 2

1. Second-person, two-way, and reciprocal second-person social perspectives. The key conceptual advance in perspective coordination at level 2 is the growing child's ability to mentally step outside himself or herself to take a self-reflective or second-person perspective on his or her own thoughts and actions. This ability allows, but does not ensure, the child or adolescent access to an understanding of the balancing of needs, thoughts, feelings, and intentions of self and others that opens the door to two-way relationships.

2. Two-way understanding of friendships. At this level, friendship takes on more aspects of reciprocity and sharing: "She is my best friend because we can trust each other to keep secrets." "He is my best friend because I know he'd back me in a fight just like I'd back him."

3. Reciprocal negotiation strategies. The key strategies at this level focus on trades and exchanges: "I'll let you use my Walkman if you let me have those new comic books for the weekend." These reciprocal strategies open the door for adequate interpersonal problem solving. Learning these strategies is often seen as the key achievement for

children and adolescents like those at Devereux, enabling them to
begin to function more successfully in peer settings.

Level 3

1. Third-person, mutual, and collaborative third-person social perspectives. At level 3, the child or adolescent can imaginatively step outside the relationship, to see it from a third-person point of view. This new perspective allows the child or adolescent to take into account the needs, ideas, and intentions of both parties simultaneously. Therefore, a new understanding about norms like fairness becomes possible.

2. Mutual understanding of friendships. At level 3, the central organizing principle children or adolescents use to think about friendships is the extent of mutual commitment within a relationship. At this collaborative level, individuals believe that both trust and jealousy are related to the ongoing and lasting bond of commitment between friends, a bond often perceived as exclusive to the peer dyad. It also goes beyond the time-limited specificity of self-interested reciprocity (level 2).

3. Collaborative negotiation strategies. At level 3, the child or adolescent begins to look for win-win solutions in which both parties can achieve success (or get what they want). This level of negotiation, though often a challenge even for adults, is present with surprising frequency in the solutions developed by well-functioning peer groups. Adults responsible for group settings (like classrooms or residences) often depend on the ability of adolescents to develop such mutual solutions. However, mutual solutions pose a substantial challenge for children and adolescents who have cognitive, social, or behavioral problems. Their deficits in this ability often cause them to be removed from social situations that might otherwise support their further social development.

What the Interview Responses Reveal

Discussion of each dilemma opens up a vista on the adolescent's view of the complex social and psychological world that exists in a residential setting. The interviews, therefore, can serve a multitude of purposes, depending on the kinds of analyses that are employed. For example, the interviews assist us in understanding the issues that are most conflictual and perturbing to each adolescent (the issues that rise to the surface in this kind of open-ended dialogue), and the pathological coloration of each adolescent's responses to the range of dilemmas presented. That is, the responses reveal the general frame each adolescent uses when attempting to understand the dilemmas and the contextual strategies he suggests for the hypothetical protagonists.

During the interview, we make specific inquiries to identify the level of the interpersonal negotiation strategies the youngster suggests. What and whose perspective(s) is he able to take? Does he understand the problem only from a physical point of view, characterized by either flight or fight (level 0); from a unilateral perspective, in which he either commands or obeys (level 1); from a second-person perspective, which includes trades, deals, exchanges, and reciprocity and hence involves his influence or accommodation (level 2); or from a third-person point of view, characterized by compromise or collaborative solutions (level 3)?

Through this approach, we examine the ways in which each adolescent is able to assume another person's perspective and coordinate it with his own regarding the issue at hand. Further, we seek to learn whether this ability remains constant across peer and adult contexts and how it is affected by an issue's emotional intensity.

An issue of equal importance is whether the adolescent's negotiating strategies for conflictual social situations are consistent across interpersonal and environmental contexts. Or does the adolescent tend to regress or change strategies when new situations (which may involve different kinds and intensities of affect) are presented?

Interpersonal Negotiating Strategies

As we have indicated, one line of questioning we pursue when discussing the dilemmas with adolescents focuses on the youngsters' repertoire of methods for relating harmoniously and reciprocally to others, that is, their interpersonal negotiation strategies (the third developmental domain for each level in Exhibit 15.1). After each dilemma was read to the adolescent being interviewed, the interviewer asked the following functional or problem-solving questions, designed to assess these strategies.

1. What is the problem? Why is it a problem?
2. What do you think each person feels about this problem?
3. What are all the ways he can solve this problem? What is the best way to solve the problem?
4. What might go wrong with this solution?
5. How would he know that his solution worked?

This set of questions allows us to classify the adolescent's strategy for interpersonal negotiation according to level and according to interpersonal orientation. That is, if the problem-solving strategy is essentially one in which the adolescent attempts to change the other person's actions or viewpoint, we call it an *other-transforming* strategy. If the strategy achieves a solution by changing the self's viewpoint or behavior, we call it a *self-transforming* strategy. These two orientations are akin to, but not identical to, the traditional two dimensions used for conceptualizing child psychopathology: externalizing and internalizing. Note, however, that higher-level strategies naturally use approaches that *integrate* these two polar orientations; that is, by using higher-level negotiations the individual moves toward functioning collaboratively, integrating the other person's and his or her own perspectives. It is rare, however, to see this higher level of social interaction among BTC adolescents, even in the relative safety of an interview about hypothetical situations.

Interpersonal Understanding

A second line of questions focuses on the adolescent's level of interpersonal understanding (the second social developmental component within each level). For example, we ask such questions as:

1. What does it mean to trust someone at Brandywine? How do you know if someone is trustworthy?

2. What makes a rule fair? What makes a staff member (or parent) fair?

3. What makes a good friend? How do kids become friends here? Can they still be friends if they are mad at each other?

4. What happens if one person wants to be really good friends and the other does not?

5. What is hard (or easy) about leaving a place like Brandywine? What do people in the community think of kids from here?

Examples of Developmental and Relational Analysis

This section considers Lawrence's, James's, and Jerry's responses to interview questions about Devereux dilemma 5, which is hypothesized to arise between a residential staff member (Phil) and an adolescent on his unit (Doug) who have formed an initial close attachment.

> Devereux dilemma 5: Doug really gets along with Phil, a new residential staff person. At first, Phil is very friendly to Doug. He talks to him and gives him good advice. But when Doug starts signing up for all of Phil's recs, Phil starts getting on his case and taking all his points. [*Recs* is the BTC term for recreational activities.

To take part in recs, adolescents must amass points that
are controlled and allocated by the counselors.]

As we consider the boys' responses to interview questions about
this dilemma, it is important to remember that unlike many forms
of psychological assessment, the INS interview approach does not
claim to be an exact predictor of *what* adolescents' would specifically do when faced with real-life dilemmas similar to those presented in the interview. Instead, this approach gives us a measure
of insight into *how* the adolescents generally understand the social
world and operate within it, how they frame interpersonal problems
and construct solutions. In other words, as we analyze the interviews
conducted with Lawrence, James, and Jerry about the problem faced
by Phil and Doug, we are not looking for surface evidence that
would predict or corroborate that what each boy proposes to do in
the hypothetical dilemma is exactly what he would actually do in
real life. But we do believe that this method of analysis goes beneath
the surface of inferred actions to produce an understanding of *how*
each boy operates interpersonally, that is, his developmental range
(for example, from acting impulsively to acting unilaterally) and
interpersonal orientation (for example, defer but not be subservient;
manipulate but not manhandle).

In fact, the three adolescents responded to the dilemma by suggesting, in one way or another, that Doug should implement active
strategies that on the surface all sound like the same strategy: "talk
to [the counselor]." However, our analysis is designed to clarify the
deeper developmental differences among different adolescents' fram-
ings of a problem and the level of maturity underlying what each
suggests; in other words, in this case, the analysis clarifies what each
boy *means* by "talk to" the other person.

Although each of these adolescents has the identical psychiatric
diagnosis (conduct disorder), the presentation of a standard set of
dilemmas and the subsequent interview process highlighted the differences among them, both interpersonally and developmentally.

An understanding of these developmental and relational differences has powerful implications for better assessments of these students by the staff and hence for treatment and outcome evaluation. The following sections examine some salient excerpts from the interviews in order to clarify how the process and analysis work.

Interview with Lawrence

INTERVIEWER: What's the problem [in the dilemma]?

LAWRENCE: Well, I wouldn't sign up for his recs anymore.

INTERVIEWER: How do you think Doug feels?

LAWRENCE: Pretty bad.

INTERVIEWER: Why do you think he feels bad?

LAWRENCE: He lost a good buddy.

INTERVIEWER: How do you think Phil feels, that's the residential staff person?

LAWRENCE: I don't know, I don't know—go on to the next question.

INTERVIEWER: What are all of the things you can think of for Doug to do.

LAWRENCE: Probably talk to him.

INTERVIEWER: What would he say?

LAWRENCE: I don't know—just talk to him. He could say, "Why the hell did you take all my points when I sign up for your recs?" Tell him, "Stay out of my way from now on."

INTERVIEWER: What do you think Phil would say back?

LAWRENCE: I don't know. I've never been in that situation.

INTERVIEWER: Is there anything else Doug could do?

LAWRENCE: Just don't hang out with him no more.

INTERVIEWER: Okay, why would he not hang out with him anymore?

LAWRENCE: 'Cause he's takin' all his points. Why should he?

Developmental-Relational Analysis of Lawrence

When the interviewer asks Lawrence about his understanding and perceptions of the problem, rather than defining the problem, Lawrence impulsively frames a retributive action response: "I wouldn't sign up for his recs anymore." In fact, he has a great deal of difficulty framing the problem in a way that is distinct from some impulsive and retributive action or solution, an indicator of an impulsive level of interpersonal negotiation. Lawrence also tells us of the difficulty he has taking another's social perspective. Each time he is asked how the counselor Phil might feel, he interprets the question concretely and literally ("I've never been in that situation!"), as if he cannot take that perspective, or he avoids the question by saying, "Go on," as if to say, because I am not and have never been a counselor, I cannot possibly tell you how a counselor might feel.

Without further probing, Lawrence generates a solution to the problem that might appear to involve communication: "Probably talk to him." But what he means by "talk," it turns out, is to accuse or refuse rather than to question. His tone, not clearly evident from the flat words of the written transcript, implies that the reason for the loss of points is arbitrary and without justification. He does not consider whether Doug played any part in Phil's actions. All Lawrence can focus on in the dilemma is the loss of Doug's points, and the only solution to the dilemma that he can envision is for Doug to retaliate and strike back: "Don't hang out with him no more." There is little to suggest a focus on the relationship per se. As noted in the review of his developmental history, Lawrence is not ignorant. He demonstrates a substantial amount of what one might label "street smarts," or more specifically, "Brandywine smarts." On the developmental part of the INS coding scheme, however, Lawrence would be classified as oscillating between levels 0 (impulsive) and 1 (unilateral). Interpersonally, he uses an other-transforming orientation.

Whereas the developmental analysis provides a way to *describe* the way Lawrence frames interpersonal problems and solutions, and is consistent with his behavior on the Brandywine campus, the *explanation* for the way Lawrence copes with the world must come from his early relationship history. If a child lives in a world where things are taken away arbitrarily, or where no one listens to him or explains the feelings or reasons that underlie their actions that affect him, then the child is very likely to feel as Lawrence does when confronted with an apparent rejection or restriction such as occurs in this dilemma. Rejection, like everything else is whimsical at best and more likely commonplace to Lawrence; one person's actions seem to have little to do with another's. Lawrence does not stop to think that Doug might be doing something that moves Phil toward a different stance. In this sense, Lawrence is interpersonally other-transforming as well as developmentally impulsive. As he identifies with Doug, the student, he assumes that the other, in this case Phil, the counselor, must change his behavior if he is to ever regain Doug's acceptance. Just as he does not reflect on the motives behind his own behavior, Lawrence does not reflect upon those behind Doug's behavior either.

Interview with James

INTERVIEWER: What do you think the problem is here?

JAMES: Um, they're getting mad at each other cause they're hangin' around too much, I guess. Like stickin' to each other too much.

INTERVIEWER: Okay, then why is that a problem?

JAMES: Because it's getting the staff frustrated.

INTERVIEWER: Okay, why is it a problem when a staff member and a kid stick too much together?

JAMES: They get too good of a relationship and when they get a good relationship . . . uh . . . um . . . maybe they don't want to get a good relationship 'cause the kid's about to leave and he'll miss him or something.

INTERVIEWER: Okay. So you're saying sometimes a kid can get too close to a staff person here?

JAMES: Right.

INTERVIEWER: Okay. Now, when you said they have too good of a relationship, how would you know a relationship had gotten too close between a staff person and a kid?

JAMES: Maybe Doug—the kid?—. . . maybe he's just realizing that he's bothering the staff and that he's probably going to have to start taking different recs and not taking his [Phil's] rec every time. It gives him a little chance to have time alone or hang around with the other kids or something.

INTERVIEWER: Okay. Um, what are all the things you can think of that Doug and Phil really can do to solve this problem?

JAMES: Maybe Doug could talk to him. Tell him he wouldn't take so many recs with Phil. And maybe, Phil, the staff, would kinda be like regular friends. He wouldn't work with him all the time. It's like, "Hi," every time he sees him, and they won't hang around with each other so much.

INTERVIEWER: Okay. So they're both just gonna back off a little.

JAMES: Right.

INTERVIEWER: Okay. Is there anything else you can think of they can do besides kinda backing off each other?

JAMES: Uh, maybe they can let the staff guy work on a different wing.

Developmental-Relational Analysis of James

James presents a much different picture, both in terms of the range of developmental levels and the interpersonal orientation of the strategies that he suggests. First, unlike Lawrence, James frames the problem of this dilemma in a unilateral rather than impulsive way. Second, he suggests (assumes) that the protagonist, Doug, is probably either bothering or antagonizing the counselor. James can take a second-person or reciprocal social perspective ("they're getting mad at each other"), but when he moves from understanding to action, his view of the interaction is limited to one perspective. From James's unilateral but largely self-transforming perspective, only the Brandywine Center student (Doug) can do wrong, not the staff.

Thematically, the way James views this problem is fairly consistent with the way he constructs relationship problems and offers solutions to them across all the Devereux dilemmas. He seems to be saying, if you get too close to someone, you are vulnerable to rejection, so it is safer and better to (unilaterally) keep your distance. More than that, and perhaps at a deeper and more personal level of meaning than he is aware of, James may feel that if you get too close to another person, the other person may find out how unlikable you are and reject you, so the safest thing in relationships is to keep your distance. In this dilemma, James suggests that Phil be transferred to another unit, and then Doug and Phil will see each other only intermittently.

For James, "talk" translates to "have a polite, but noninteractive exchange; do not reveal too much about how you feel or explore how the other feels about you." Neither of his solutions has the two participants really exploring the source of the problem in a reciprocal way, even though James gives clear evidence, certainly clearer evidence than Lawrence, that he is capable of taking a second-person perspective.

James's assumption that this inherently interpersonal problem really lies solely within Doug and that Doug should back off, suggests a level 1 strategy in a self-transforming interpersonal orientation. Although James is dissimilar from Lawrence in orientation, he has in common with Lawrence a view of the social world as a place where you can only be sure someone is listening to you if that person does what you desire, regardless of his or her own perspective or interests. You are either the teller or the listener; there are few two-way streets in James's world. Unlike Lawrence, however, who deals with his feelings of helplessness to get his way through externalizing his dissatisfaction and blaming the world around him, James staunchly believes that he must acquiesce to the demands, often perceived as whimsical, of the people with whom he feels a close attachment. If these people do not listen to him or do what he wants, it is because there is something wrong with or basically unlikable about himself.

Interview with Jerry

INTERVIEWER: What's the problem here?

JERRY: Maybe Phil's caught some anger from the supervisors because Doug's hanging around with Phil too much and Doug's not, like, . . . doing stuff with the kids instead of the staff.

INTERVIEWER: Now, why is that a problem?

JERRY: Maybe Phil was told, "You have to chill out with Doug or you get fired," or something.

INTERVIEWER: Okay. What are all the things you can think of that Doug can do to solve his problem with Phil?

JERRY: They should go sit down and talk about the things that are bothering each of them.

INTERVIEWER: So what should Doug do?

JERRY: Get, like, Phil—get Phil and just sit maybe in Phil's office and just talk.

INTERVIEWER: What would he say?

JERRY: "Why are you giving me all the minuses? Why are you ignoring me. Why are you getting mad at me?"

INTERVIEWER: How would that solve the problem?

JERRY: It might and it might not.

INTERVIEWER: Okay, how might it?

JERRY: Maybe Phil sees how hard he's been on Doug, and he lays off him just for a bit, and he acts like Doug's just like every other student.

INTERVIEWER: What else could Doug do?

JERRY: Tell the supervisors that Phil's being a little bit hard on him.

INTERVIEWER: How would that solve the problem?

JERRY: Maybe the supervisor can talk to Phil, tell him lay off Doug just a little bit.

INTERVIEWER: What do you think the best way for Doug to solve this problem is?

JERRY: Talking, sitting down with Phil and just talking about it.

INTERVIEWER: Why do you think that's the best way?

JERRY: Because if Doug went behind Phil's back to talk to the supervisor, the supervisor might get overreacted when he talks to Phil, and Phil might get fired or something.

INTERVIEWER: How would Doug and Phil feel if Doug pulled Phil aside and said, "Let's talk"?

JERRY: They might feel a little bit relieved that they were talking.

INTERVIEWER: Tell me how they might feel relieved, why they might feel relieved. Why might they feel relieved that Doug had suggested they talk?

JERRY: They got the stuff out in the open, and they talked about it instead of just Phil just taking all of Doug's points and Doug not making his level.

INTERVIEWER: Why is that a good thing to do?

JERRY: Why is it a good thing to do?

INTERVIEWER: Yeah, why is it a good thing to get all that out in the open?

JERRY: So you don't keep it bottled up and it all comes out at once, and instead of just talking about it, you flip out or something, and you get in more trouble than what you already were in.

Developmental-Relational Analysis of Jerry

Jerry has the most sophisticated level of interpersonal understanding of the three adolescents interviewed with the Devereux dilemmas. This is evident in his speculation that there are or may be some systemic issues behind the scenes of the stated problem ("Phil's caught some anger from the supervisors because Doug's hanging around with Phil too much, and Doug's not . . . doing stuff with the kids instead of the staff.") This is clear evidence of Jerry's capacity for taking a third-person perspective, as is his speculation that Phil may be perturbed because Doug's upset with him.

Perhaps what most differentiates Jerry from Lawrence and James is his response to what Doug should do: "Get Phil and just sit maybe in Phil's office and just talk. [Ask] 'Why are you giving me all the minuses? Why are you ignoring me? Why are you getting mad at me?'" Jerry's tone, unlike that of Lawrence or James, is neither accusatory nor assuming of self-blame; rather, it is full of dismay and puzzlement.

Jerry has enough perspective to realize that in this dilemma, Doug does not understand the basis of the change in Phil's behavior. Whereas Lawrence assumes that Doug's behavior has nothing to do with Phil's, and James assumes Doug's behavior has everything to do with Phil's, Jerry understands that they may or may not be related. We would classify Jerry as capable of at least level 2 interpersonal negotiations, and clearly, he is capable of using level 3 social perspective coordination in his interpersonal understanding. The puzzle that needs to be solved is why Jerry, who has more advanced developmental capabilities than the other two boys, regresses so dramatically at times to primitive relationship behavior. What Jerry needs is a form of treatment that will enable him to be the one to discover the solution to this puzzle.

Implications for Treatment Intervention

Therapists' ability to understand the personal issues, social perspectives, and interpersonal negotiation strategies of adolescents in a residential setting has important implications for treatment interventions and outcome evaluations. The information that therapists can gather and the interactions (dialogues) between staff member and client that they may initiate can be of assistance in many areas. A residential setting provides opportunities for both individual and group interventions. Continuing to look at the three adolescents we have introduced here, and drawing now on their responses to all the Devereux dilemmas, we examine some ways in which the INS analysis might be useful for residential counseling and group work. In the discussions that follow, the reader will come across additional comments made by the boys that were not included in the interview transcripts presented earlier.

Intervention Strategies for Lawrence

Lawrence was very concerned with issues of anger, disenfranchisement, aggression, unfairness, and privacy. His strategies were physical and impulsive—ranging from denial of problematic feelings to strategies that emphasized retribution: "I just wouldn't be in that situation." "Just sock him in the jaw. I wouldn't care." "Pee on his bed. He shouldn't be messing with me."

Given his pattern of low-level functioning across all three social developmental domains (social perspective coordination, interpersonal understanding, and interpersonal negotiation strategies), an intervention for Lawrence might focus on enabling him to move to a level 1 (unilateral) perspective with parallel interpersonal negotiation strategies. For example, individual counseling might assist Lawrence in learning to voice (rather than only act out) his feelings, including his fear or anger. The therapist might invite him to talk about his own feelings in a way that will enable him to bring some order to the psychological confusion that he experiences. In labeling and ordering his emotions, Lawrence would be preparing for the kind of reciprocal perspective and exchange that characterizes more mature interpersonal relationships. But if treatment expectations are set too high for Lawrence (for example, if an attempt is made to move him from impulsive to reciprocal ways of relating without initially moving through a unilateral phase), he will become confused, hearing calls for fairness or kindness as wimpy weakness on the part of the treatment representative.

Discipline and behavioral principles should also support Lawrence's move toward less impulsive behaviors, offering consistent consequences for antisocial behaviors and reinforcements for prosocial functioning. Even shouting, commanding, and ordering are, from this perspective, progress over hitting or running away. These behaviors might be tolerated in Lawrence and even supported as intermediary steps toward final goal attainment because they represent progress for him.

At its most essential level, treatment planning for Lawrence must be guided by the question, How much can Lawrence understand? Although his core capacity for coordinating perspectives is average for his age, that is, he does not have biologically based operational limitations in social perspective, Lawrence has yet to develop either his interpersonal understanding or his strategies for interpersonal negotiation to an adequate level, on a par with others of about his age. His low-low status in these areas implies, at least theoretically, that Lawrence will not develop higher-level relational strategies until his understanding is enhanced. The first step in his treatment may therefore be psychoeducational (social cognitive) improvement: for example, through small-group discussions (in the classroom or elsewhere) about basic social relationships, so as to increase his *interpersonal understanding*.

Intervention Strategies for James

James shows a broader range of interpersonal concerns and strategies than Lawrence does. For example, throughout his interview, he talked about feelings, through the use of descriptors such as "confusion," "trying to fit in," "feeling a little sad and a little happy," and "losing touch with friends." These words never came up in Lawrence's interview. Although James suggests some physical strategies, he more often uses unilateral strategies and demonstrates the capacity for coordinating perspectives at a higher level: "Just not be so angry with staff." "Bother them until they give you what you want." "Find someone to tell you right from wrong."

If Lawrence is low-low, James is best described in developmental-relational terms as high-low, that is, higher, normatively speaking, on interpersonal understanding, lower on putting it into practice. A cognitive-behavioral approach that fosters stronger links between his social thought and action is most likely the primary treatment of choice for James. A counseling program for James might therefore focus on strengthening and making more consistent his use of higher-level (reciprocal) interpersonal strategies. Through matching him with another boy for weekly pair counseling meetings, a therapist might give James opportunities to practice the higher-level *social negotiation strategies* of which he is capable and to do so in increasingly challenging and trans-situational social contexts, with increasingly more intensive emotions.

Intervention Strategies for Jerry

Jerry presents yet a third kind of pattern, one that demonstrates a sophisticated level of interpersonal awareness, and a more frequent use of level 2 and level 3 negotiation strategies: "No one's bed should get flipped." "He should give reasons—sit down and talk with staff." "After a time, they might start talking again." "Sometimes staff brings things into work and they take it out on the kids." "Phil needs some time for himself and to spend with other kids." "Doug can understand how Phil needs some time with other kids." "He shouldn't curse at someone he likes." However, Jerry is also capable of rapid decompensation in social relationships under certain circumstances.

Although Jerry has a good intellectual understanding of relationships, and the most consistently high-level social behavior of the three boys, he still lacks insight into the *personal meaning* of some of his own more regressive social interactions and relationships. Such regression happens particularly when interactions and relationships correspond to his unconscious conflicts associated with past highly negative relationship patterns. Jerry needs to be involved in insight-oriented treatment methods, in the context of a long-term psychotherapeutic relationship that allows trust to develop between him and a psychotherapist trained to help him focus on the meaning of his specific associations between current and past relational experiences. (Although Lawrence and James also could use this intensity of treatment eventually, it would be largely wasted at this point in their respective developmental pathways.)

A residential program for Jerry, therefore, can assume that he has the competence to use reciprocal and to some degree collaborative strategies. Counseling sessions should support the generalization and consistent use of this ability in, for example, new settings, affectively charged situations, and settings with people he might not yet know or trust. Discipline and reinforcement procedures should converge on Jerry's acquisition of collaborative behaviors. Counselors might expect him to function at higher behavioral levels more often, and shape their expectations contingently. They might also structure opportunities for him to assume leadership roles and tasks. Most importantly, Jerry's treatment needs to help him not only to practice maintaining high levels of developmental functioning under stress but also to explore in some depth the personal meaning of events leading to his regressive behavior and thus the reasons why he regresses.

Conclusion

Our research found that although each of the three boys studied carries a diagnosis of conduct disorder, each has a qualitatively different way of making meaning out of his social world, and this leads to a correspondingly different interpersonal negotiating strategy. This difference, in each case, has significant consequences for the boys' everyday relationships.

The data generated through our analyses and INS interviews refocused the view of each boy, for the purposes of understanding him and refining his treatment. Rather than look at the three adolescents' difficulties solely as functions of malfunctions or disorders within each boy that need to be "fixed" on an individual basis, much as one would fix a malfunctioning clock, we changed our lens so we could examine each boy in terms of how he relates in his current relationships with others, asking which relationships are working well or better than others and which are not. This interpersonal analysis helped us create for each boy a dynamic and individualized portrait that suggested different treatment interventions and, we are optimistic, different outcomes.

Appendix: The Devereux Dilemmas

Each of the eight dilemmas that follow is preceded by italicized words that identify the critical issues the dilemmas were designed to explore.

1. *Truth-trust/adult authority/loyalty; self-reflection.* Staff have told kids in Ken's dorm that they will be going on a trip this weekend. Ken has been looking forward to going on this trip all week. Suddenly, a staff person says to Ken, "You can't go because we think you flipped another kid's bed last night." Ken knows that he didn't do it.

2. *Friendship formation/conflict resolution; trust/loyalty.* Alan and Carl have been friends for a few months. They like to hang out together and do things like fishing at the pond. All of a sudden, Carl stops talking to Alan. He won't do anything with him anymore. The other day, Alan thought he heard Carl saying something nasty about him behind his back.

3. *Peer pressure; assertiveness; aggression/friendship/loyalty.* Ted has been hanging out with a group of kids who like to bully younger students. He doesn't like that but doesn't say anything about it. Last week, a new kid came to the center. Ted enjoys playing cards with this kid. Now the older kids have started to push Ted into hitting the new kid.

4. *Transition/independence; success; changing expectations; keeping friends; self-reflection; ambivalence.* Chris has been at Devereux for three years. At first, he hated the place, but now he has made some good friends and likes several staff members. Chris still has problems with his family. His father hits him when he's home. Now it's time to leave Devereux and return home.

5. *Staff/resident conflict resolution; loyalty/betrayal role models.* Doug really gets along with Phil, a new residential staff person. At first, Phil is very friendly to Doug. He talks to him and gives him good advice. But when Doug starts signing up for all of Phil's recs, Phil starts getting on his case and taking all his points.

6. *Self-reflection; being responsible; managing/communicating anger.* Bill returns from a bad home visit during which he had several fights with his parents. That day in school, he is having a rough time. He can't do his schoolwork and kids are picking

on him. Bill ends up swearing at a teacher he likes. The teacher wants to keep him after school, but Bill knows the soccer team is depending on him.

7. *Heterosexual relationships; trust.* Ken meets this girl, Janet, at a mall while home on a weekend visit. They get along pretty well. The next day, he takes her out to a movie. When Ken is home the following weekend, he calls Janet to ask her out. She replies that she is going to be busy all weekend with her girlfriends. However, the next day, Eddie, a friend of Ken's, tells him that he thinks he saw Janet out with another guy.

8. *Adult trust versus peer pressure.* Jim is home on a weekend visit. Things have been going really well. Jim has gotten along with his parents—there have been no fights, and they even went out for dinner tonight. Jim's parents said they really feel like they can trust him. His parents are going out, and they said they want him to stay home tonight. But Jim's friends have called to ask him to go out to a movie. Jim really wants to keep his parents' trust, but he also wants to keep his friends, especially since he's only home on weekends.

References

American Psychiatric Association. (1994). *Diagnostic and statistical manual of mental disorders* (4th ed.). Washington, DC: Author.

Baldwin, J. M. (1902). *Social and ethical interpretations in mental development: A study in social psychology.* New York: Macmillan.

Breen, M. J., & Altepeter, T. S. (1990). *Disruptive behavior disorders in children: Treatment-focused assessment.* New York: Guilford Press.

Craighead, L. W., Craighead, W. E., Kazdin, A. E., & Mahoney, M. J. (1994). *Cognitive and behavioral interventions: An empirical approach to mental health problems.* Needham Heights, MA: Allyn & Bacon.

Katcher, A., & Wilkins, G. G. (1993). Dialogue with animals: Its nature and culture. In S. R. Kellert & E. O. Wilson (Eds.), *The biophilia hypothesis* (pp. 173–197). Washington, DC: Island Press.

Kendall, P. C., & Braswell, L. (1985). *Cognitive-behavioral therapy for impulsive children.* New York: Guilford Press.

Kohlberg, L. (1969). Stage and sequence: The cognitive-developmental approach to socialization. In D. Goslin (Ed.), *Handbook of socialization theory and research* (pp. 347–480). Skokie, IL: Rand McNally.

Mead, G. H. (1934). *Mind, self, and society.* Chicago: University of Chicago Press.

Piaget, J. (1965). *The moral judgment of the child* (M. Gabain, Trans.). New York: Free Press. (Original work published 1932)

Selman, R. L. (1980). *The growth of interpersonal understanding: Developmental and clinical analyses.* San Diego, CA: Academic Press.

Selman, R. L., & Schultz, L. H. (1990). *Making a friend in youth: Developmental theory and pair therapy.* Chicago: University of Chicago Press.

Werner, H. (1948). *Comparative psychology of mental development* (rev. ed.). Madison, CT: International Universities Press.

Part VII

. . . .

An Integrating Framework

16

. . . .

Interweaving Themes and
Threads of Meaning-Making

Kevin T. Kuehlwein

I n writing this concluding chapter, I am faced with the daunting
task of relating and integrating the various visions of the preceding writers, who themselves have converged from different fields and
perspectives. Compared to the contributors in the last book Hugh
Rosen and I coedited, the contributors to this book were less likely
to be familiar with each others' work, coming as they do from such
disparate fields and schools of thought as social constructionism, psychoanalysis, experiential therapy, solution-focused therapy, personal
construct theory, and narrative theory. I therefore envision myself as
assembling a marvelous quilt from related but diverse panels never
before juxtaposed. Like any data we perceive, these panels do not
align themselves neatly into a single intuitive gestalt but rather await
my (and your) making sense of their first-order reality (see Chapter
Two) to form a coherent pattern. The quilt has continuity from one
panel to another but also displays creative contrasts across its length
and breadth, as befits a socially constructed phenomenon emanat-
ing from the work of many hands, minds, and hearts.

As I eagerly read through the chapter manuscripts for this book,
I kept note of some of the assorted images, metaphors, and narratives the chapter authors offered in support of their various unique
visions of what it means to be and practice as a meaning-making
psychotherapist. (Please note that in the following discussion, cita-
tions of contributors to this book refer to their chapters herein,

unless otherwise indicated.) Some of these authors and ideas relate easily and harmoniously to each other, whereas other authors disagree on their visions of the very terms meaning-making, constructivism, postmodernism, social constructionism, and narrative theory. The creative tensions inherent in this book, therefore, far from detracting from the goal Hugh Rosen and I had in creating it, are designed to provide the reader with the same excitement as the unexpected turns of a good story.

What I seek to do in this chapter, therefore, is to examine and highlight both certain harmonious as well as contrasting themes and threads running throughout this book, for it is in relating to each other that the various patterns and colors of the quilt (or of the beautiful carpet, as described in the Somerset Maugham novel cited by Rosen in Chapter One) will gain increased meaning. Also like a quilt, this book has given voices to a multiverse of individual points of view, including some that have traditionally been silenced or underprivileged in scholarly discourse (see Chapter Six). It has also offered creative metaphors and stories to spark new thinking and interventions to be used by the reader. In this way, the book itself mirrors postmodern and Buddhist (see Chapter Seven and Gergen, 1991) views of the self as multitudinous rather than unitary.

Personal Admission: Beckian Strands of Constructivism

Although I have also been trained in psychodynamic and Ericksonian therapy (and wrote my doctoral dissertation on the social construction of adulthood), some might consider my primary therapeutic orientation as a Beckian cognitive therapist heretical to the spirit of this book. Indeed, Beck's model (Beck, Rush, Shaw, & Emery, 1979) is an approach often criticized as modernist and anticonstructivistic (Neimeyer, 1993). I do not entirely disagree with certain points made by some constructivist critics of Beck's paradigm. The model does admittedly often seek to help clients better understand what can be taken as an objectively knowable, external reality. With its highlighting of *cognitive distortions*, which themselves presuppose a particular correct version of reality to a certain extent, the model can also focus the client on problem-laced narratives (compare Friedman, Chapter Fourteen), deemphasizing what the client is already adaptively doing to move toward his or her goals. At the same time, however, Beck's model, like many phenomena discussed in this book, does not neatly or entirely fit within the limits of rationalist positions. I therefore wish to suggest that there are strong constructivist threads running throughout Beckian cognitive therapy, elements often underappreciated by outsiders. Routine interventions such as looking at alternate ways of viewing a situation, asking clients for the personal meanings they attach to particular events, and restructuring meanings via creative, non-reality-based imagery exercises are all cognitive therapy approaches that are not particularly rationalist or realist. Common questions posed in the normal course of cognitive therapy treatment include the very open-ended, "What does that mean to you?" Other questions probe the client's understanding of the utility of his or her beliefs: "What are the advantages and disadvantages of that belief?" "What's another way of looking at the situation?" is also a common question on which Beckian therapists encourage clients to reflect. More recently applied questions include ones designed to help the client explore the necessary meaning-making conditions for adaptive change to occur: "What would you need to believe in order to act [a new way]?" When clients are restructuring traumatic memories (the accuracy of which cannot ever truly be known, as Russell and Wandrei point out in Chapter Eleven), we often help them develop more adaptive narratives, which serve as more "useful fictions" (see Watzlawick, Chapter Two) for clients than their current ways of making meaning of their past experiences. In this way, we do not hold to a particular view of reality or demand that clients perceive reality more "accurately" in order to make gains toward their therapy goals. Also interesting to me as I read the chapters was the way in which some of the interventions offered intersect with cognitive therapy interventions, albeit sometimes with different labels. Friedman, for example, is keenly aware of the negative effects of clients' using totalizing descriptions of themselves, much as Beck would note the pernicious effects of labeling oneself only on the basis of certain characteristics, omitting other facets of one's experience. Furthermore, Beck's emphasis on the collaborative relationship is also echoed by other chapter authors as they speak of therapist and client co-constructing reality. In rational-emotive behavioral therapy (Ellis, 1989), the therapist determines the reality the client must adhere to (that is, one without absolute "musts") and quite actively steers the often-reluctant client toward that reality. Beckian cognitive therapy, in contrast, helps the client to come to his or her own conclusions about his or her own current ways of meaning-making, by means of the therapist's Socratic questioning and behavioral experiments designed to test the adequacy of the client's ability to predict based on his or her current meaning-making structures.

Furthermore, many interventions described in the foregoing chapters have very close relatives in cognitive therapy approaches and thinking. Friedman, for example, notes the importance of staying away from problem-saturated talk, counseling therapists to focus instead on exceptions to the client's problem. This is similar in spirit to Beck's penchant for probing clients for evidence running counter to their negative automatic thoughts, especially when those thoughts are about personal inability to change. (One can still argue, of course, that Beckians have much to learn from solution-focused therapists about the relative *emphasis* to be placed on these positive exceptions.) I find Beckian similarities in Watson and Greenberg (Chapter Nine), also. In an example of exploring a client's problematic reaction to an event, they essentially elicit client thoughts and feelings, then examine the validity and usefulness of these phenomena and judge their applicability in the current situation. An observer would likely be hard pressed to distinguish such interventions from those of Beckian cognitive therapists, even though the theoretical foundations of the interventions may indeed differ markedly.

One of my favorite more constructivist techniques is to help the client better notice and grapple with some of the internal inconsistencies of his or her meaning-making system when aspects of it are not working well. By producing just the right amount of perturbation, the therapist can jolt the client into disembedding from particular problematic cognitive, emotional, and behavioral reactions. He or she steps outside them and is no longer bound by them. Essentially, I see a number of aspects (although by no means all aspects) of Beckian cognitive therapy that seem to be in harmony with the viewpoints in this book.

Individual Versus Relational Emphasis

The tendency in most of the chapters is to focus away from narrowly personal meaning-making approaches and toward interpersonal approaches, to see meaning as socially constructed: existing between rather than within persons. Certain chapter authors, however, display a more individualistic view of meaning-making than others. Watson and Greenberg, for example, speak of clients who symbolically externalize aspects of their experience so that they can better examine them, be less bound by them, and in that way move toward problem solving, but there is little suggestion that this process must be a particularly social one. Such movement often takes place as a result of the therapist's provoking such client reflexivity, but the key ingredient in change for Watson and Greenberg seems to be clients' ability to move dialectically between their inner experience and the symbolic representation of it in language and extract new meanings from this process. Carlsen (Chapter Twelve), likewise, speaks of the therapist joining in client metaphors, but does not emphasize an interpersonal stance extending much beyond the therapy room. Soldz (Chapter Ten) also focuses his attention primarily on clients' individualistic ways of constructing their realities. This is perhaps not surprising, given the intrapsychic emphasis historically found in psychoanalysis. However, Soldz also focuses to some extent on the interpersonal aspects of meaning-making, noting that his modern analytic approach sees exploration of the therapeutic relationship rather than insight as the agent of change in psychotherapy. This is very much in opposition to more traditional psychoanalytic views of the process of therapeutic change, but note that it is still a very narrow interpersonal meaning-making focus.

In contrast, the other psychoanalytic contributor to this book, Saari, focuses Chapter Five on the relationship factors in the creation of individuals' identities. She argues that identity is developed interpersonally and requires multiple experiences of hearing and using certain words linked with particular social contexts for the individual to make coherent sense out of his or her inner experience.

Selman, Brion-Meisels, and Wilkins (Chapter Fifteen) note the disappointingly evanescent results of teaching children and adolescents with conduct disorders when relationship skills are learned out of context, away from the social environment of peers. In keeping with their relationship-focused interventions, they suggest that clinicians will achieve better results in promoting children's and adolescents' increased meaning-making competency in the social arena when these skills are developed within the context of peer relationships.

McNamee (Chapter Four) chronicles the paradigmatic movement of our culture from romanticism to modernism (with its emphasis on rationality, control, and individualism) to postmodernism (with its notions of multiple truths, relativism, and relationality). She traces how our current vision of psychotherapy largely stems from modernist discourse, with its emphasis on fixing and controlling things, individuality, and internal factors, as opposed to relationality and external factors. Thus, the modernist view has the unfortunate result of locating problems within the individual, a view that leads people who experience problems to conceive of themselves as having personal deficits rather than difficult inter-actional situations. Nunley and Averill (Chapter Eight) cite a good example of the modernist view in the form of a 1930s *Ladies' Home Journal* article that places the blame for any marital difficulties squarely on the shoulders of the wife. Many readers of today coming across this advice would be appalled at such a unilateral construction of marital responsibility. Both McNamee and Lax (Chapter Seven) go beyond many contemporary authors in maintaining that our very notion of our selves as individuals emanates from our relatedness. By placing centrality on our relatedness, rather than our individuality, they stand much prior (modernist) psychology on its head. Lax notes, further, that Buddhism presents no bounded concept of self but sees the reflexivity between self and others as creating a sense of self. The focus on the relational in Buddhist thought merges the stances, often seen as separate in Western scientific thought, of observer and observed.

Neimeyer's self-disclosing observations (Chapter Thirteen) invite us as readers into his personal journey away from an individualistic meaning-making paradigm (traditional personal construct theory) to a point of view that attends more to the construction of meaning in the interpersonal sphere and the spaces between people, a journey that incorporates some of the connectedness underemphasized in Kelly's work but beginning to be explored in family construct psychology and social constructionist approaches. Neimeyer currently finds that these relational emphases enrich his understanding of both his clients' and his own experience. By sharing his tentative evolving constructions of how he works in therapy, he invites us to view his ongoing process of discovery at the "growing edge" of his experience.

Goldberger (Chapter Six) views the meaning-making process as very much influenced by families, cultures, and communities, all of which shape the various boundaries of our constructs. As we meet these novel perspectives outside of ourselves, she suggests, we construct our own narratives of those constructs most relevant to our experience. In Goldberger's exploration of women's ways of knowing, she also speaks of the epistemological stance of connected knowing, which involves an exploration from within the narrative context of another and contrasts with the positivistic stance of dispassionately examining the experience of another, regarding oneself as separate from it.

Psychoanalytic Tensions

Neimeyer notes his unease when psychoanalytic therapists and theorists refer to themselves as constructivists in spite of the apparent inconsistencies between many psychoanalytic notions and constructivism as he sees it. The two psychoanalytically oriented contributors, however, see these contrasts as less absolute. Saari, for example, draws on current developmental approaches in psychoanalytic theory that emphasize the significance of the relational and interactive experiences that precede linguistic competency in determining identity formation and meaning-making competence. One example given is the importance of affective attunement in parenting, whereby the parent, or outsider, can nurture the infant's early inner affective-cognitive experience by paralleling it in some fashion. These repeated experiences help the growing infant later to link certain affective-cognitive states to certain words used in the larger community, assisting the child in making better meaning from his or her ongoing internal experience. Soldz, for his part, acknowledges that his modern analytic background produces some interventions at odds with traditional psychoanalytic theory. Specifically, he relates how modern analysts often encourage the client to actively articulate certain problematic constructions, which the analyst does not judge. The more these constructions are allowed to emerge and differentiate without being challenged, he suggests, the more likely the client is to try out differing ways of making meaning of his or her experiences. It is the safety of the therapeutic environment that promotes the loosening of constructs (as Neimeyer might say). While admitting their differences, Soldz attempts to bridge the fields of constructivism and psychoanalysis via their shared focus on clients' meaning-making structures. He takes issue, however, with constructivism's sometimes extreme open-ended notion that life is an experience of continual growth and change, suggesting instead that research shows a surprising stability of personality tendencies from at least the age of thirty on. Another criticism he levels at constructivism generally is its almost complete omission of the importance of bodily experience, especially sexuality. Whether psychoanalytic and constructivist approaches will be able to successfully bridge these gaps remains unclear, but it is interesting that an increasing number of psychoanalytic theorists are reaching toward meaning-making approaches to enrich their understanding of the human experience (see, for example, Dorpat & Miller, 1992).

Unease Inherent in Meaning-Making Approaches

Many contributors to this book remark on the unease that can be felt by both client and therapist while working with meaning-making approaches. This unease can direct the client toward growth, as Watson and Greenberg observe, as the client seeks to resolve internal tensions such as perplexity and doubt. Indeed, the postmodern therapy session often leads the client away from certainty and toward a multiverse of options and viewpoints, without specifying one right one. Carlsen concurs with Neimeyer in suggesting that the activity of meaning-making can move us not only closer to but also further away from understanding. Meaning-making is both risky and rewarding—one reason, Carlsen maintains, why therapy is not always comfortable. I am reminded of O'Hanlon and Wilk's point that "one of the most important tasks in psychotherapy is the introduction of doubt" (1987, p. 32). This is very likely *not* what clients themselves have in mind as a therapeutic goal when they present for therapy, but it seems appropriate to me in that clients typically come to us with problems resulting largely from inadequacies of their meaning-making ability in certain contexts. One truth proffered by constructivists is that there are no ultimate truths. We as therapists, therefore, cannot reveal what "is" to our clients, no matter how much they seek to elicit this from us. Instead, we can assist them to discover and create what is most meaningful to them. Therapy with a constructivist orientation involves the acknowledgment that this is a world with no easy answers. McNamee, in fact, notes that psychotherapy from a meaning-making perspective helps the client and therapist better accept the indeterminacy of our constructed realities. In the clever postmodern musical *Into the Woods* (Sondheim and Lapine, 1987), this point is well illustrated. Practically all the characters at one point struggle with the nonlinearity of cause and effect as they try to resolve the very serious problem of why they are being threatened by a giant. In the song "Your Fault," they go around and around, each trying to affix culpability outside himself or herself. The audience, however, sees clearly what escapes the characters: each person's perspective about who is to blame is just as legitimate as the next person's, and there can be multiple starting points for any particular negative event. The one chosen, as the song says, will depend on the person doing the looking.

Some readers may wonder whether I am stating the obvious: that the change inherent in psychotherapy itself is uncomfortable for the client. That is not the point I seek to make here. Instead, I am suggesting that what may be distinctive in the meaning-making approaches offered in this book is that the sense of disequilibrium can be felt during the session as much by the *therapist* as by the client, for the therapist in meaning-making therapies locates himself or herself firmly within the psychotherapeutic context, rather than viewing it as though outside it. Neimeyer acknowledges this when he comments that the reflexive focus in constructivist therapy reminds him of his own presence in the therapy encounter. Lax makes a similar point in noting that postmodern therapy requires as much examination of the therapist's role as of the client.

A related question, one that also creates disequilibrium for the therapist, is that if all ways of looking at something are equally valid, then how are we to clarify what the constructs of constructivism and its relatives mean? Neimeyer, for example, observes that the difficulty of separating constructivist from nonconstructivist approaches is growing greater now that people from such theoretical camps as rational-emotive and critical realism have begun to self-label themselves constructivists. The larger issue, of course, is that the constructs discussed in this book have no universally agreed upon boundaries themselves, an idea unsettling to many. It is a bit ironic, after all, for therapists and theoreticians to talk about constructivism as the best *metatheory* while at the same time disavowing that there is any correct way to view human experience because, after all, all constructions are only constructions. Perhaps this is only one of the contradictions that weave themselves through our postmodern lives.

Picking up the thread of therapists' inevitable involvement in the stories their clients tell, Russell and Wandrei similarly point out that narrating implicates the listener as well as the narrator, marking the listener as someone affected by the ongoing story being spun, because telling a story does not involve the passive transfer of information verbatim from one repository to another (as one might transfer binary files unchanged from one computer to another). Narrative does not simply relate experience, in other words; rather, the very act of narration creates and changes the identities of the narrator and listener. I am reminded of how Michael J. Mahoney, in a few introductory remarks prior to a lecture, once spoke eloquently of the cumulative effects of hearing certain experiences from his clients and how these narratives now "populate" him, as Gergen (1991) might put it. So one aspect of the unease inherent in the meaning-making approaches is that we as therapists are active participants as meaning is woven by our clients. Other therapeutic approaches, most notably traditional psychoanalysis, have disavowed therapist participation to a greater or lesser extent, but an exciting if daunting aspect to the constructivist therapies is this very active collaboration of therapist and client in the meaning-making process.

Submerged Voices

A number of chapter authors pointed out the increasing attention paid to marginalized aspects of experience in meaning-making approaches. Lax observes that people's tendency in today's modern Western world is still to hold onto their current states of being, a tendency that leads them to privilege the culturally dominant discourses of their experiences. Only recently have postmodern approaches (themselves submerged by the larger cultural mores) begun to emerge and to air marginal beliefs and practices. Goldberger's work highlights the importance of contacting submerged voices in our culture by exploring marginality and difference. She suggests that when therapists do this with their clients, they help those clients question authority as well as outmoded assumptions and frameworks, giving rise to new ways of seeing and being in the world. Hugh Rosen and I were pleased in this book to offer a forum for certain traditionally submerged voices to present their ideas as well as to comment on the results of privileging certain messages over others. As a gay man whose cultural experience has often been misunderstood and underestimated, I, too, resonate with the notions expressed by Goldberger. Likewise, I have seen the incalculable damage done to members of various minority groups and positions because they have been silenced and their experience has been overassimilated into the dominant society's narratives. Like gestalt therapists' experiments with shifting figure and ground (Polster & Polster, 1973) in a person's experience, the highlighting of often-neglected aspects of the human experience while letting others recede assists individuals to appreciate multiversal ways of understanding their inner and outer worlds. Neimeyer speaks of *accentuating,* a similar process intervention that lifts some aspects of client experience to a higher awareness.

Soldz echoes Goldberger's power and authority concerns as he wonders whether the therapist or the client will direct the exploration of new meaning structures arising from therapy. The issue is that we as therapists risk imposing our therapeutic constructs on our clients, since client and therapist rarely have the same meaning-making structures. Constructivist approaches, at least, voice an awareness of this potential for abuse and such awareness can lessen its occurrence.

Emotion and Its Rules

Nunley and Averill focus on the various ways that all of us construct emotions, the rules and concepts we have that create our emotional experiences. They delineate common myths about emotions that locate these felt experiences as external and see them as all powerful. The authors suggest that such beliefs obscure for most people the extent to which they create their emotional experiences. Rosen provides a striking illustration of the extent to which emotions are socially constructed when he recalls the fate of Meursault in Camus's *The Stranger,* the story of a man convicted of murder not on the basis of direct evidence but on the strength of jurors' negative judgment of his failure to adhere to socially constructed norms for emotional experiences following the death of his mother. The notion that emotions are socially constructed gives people much more freedom in exploring creative affective responses to situations, as Nunley and Averill's cross-cultural research suggests, but we must be careful not to be creative in the wrong direction or in the wrong social context, lest we, like Meursault, be negatively judged for our creative responses.

Distancing Oneself from One's Thoughts

Metareflection on our own thoughts and thought processes is a key aspect in all progression, it seems to me. Theorists such as Beck

(Beck, Rush, Shaw, & Emery, 1979) and Kegan (1982) speak of the phenomenon in different ways, but both of them seek to generate experiences that lift clients out of their present views of situations so that other perspectives are possible, especially ones that enable clients to decenter from the problematic. Kegan (1982) speaks of the subject-to-object transformation in which that which one is (for example, impulses) becomes that which one has (for example, impulsivity), thereby establishing a critical measure of distance from which one can view the phenomenon differently. Watson and Greenberg note, in a similar vein, that symbolic representations of emotions and subsequent reflection on the representations permit clients to disembed themselves from feelings and actions, coming to possess problems rather than be possessed by them. Carlsen likewise maintains that transitions arising from active meaning-making liberate us from being embedded within our problems and enable us to step outside them. This liberation, of course, is not a one-time event but an ongoing process of development in which we move toward increasing differentiation, complexity, and order. As this occurs, we become transformed, suggests Carlsen. Rosen (1985) characterizes the new form of meaning-making at each developmental stage by comparing it to the butterfly that emerges from a chrysalis. It is not simply an improved version of a caterpillar but a fundamentally different creature. Other therapists (for example, Young, 1990) have taken a cue from gestalt therapists and have externalized internal voices still further by asking clients to experientially personify the internal voices in role-plays and/or by placing them in chairs, so that another facet of the client may dialogue with these other, as yet inchoate, facets of his or her experience and thereby come to a greater measure of understanding and integration of them. Clients who go through this exercise are subsequently often better able to differentiate their experiences by incorporating new insights and affects, once they have elaborated aspects of their inner world that for many years have been shut off due to the competing beliefs they contain about affective-cognitive processes.

Rosen gives the poignant parallel example of the brother of the executed murderer Gary Gilmore, who speaks of being stuck inside his own story and freed only by the telling of it. So, too, do many of our clients (and colleagues) have stories inside them that need to be liberated and shared (and modified by that sharing) before those individuals can integrate the stories back into their experience in a way that allows for personal growth beyond the experience.

New Views of Language

As I noted above, many contributors to this book highlight how meaning-making approaches encourage novel ways of viewing language. Efran and Greene (Chapter Three), for example, speak of *languaging,* emphasizing that our action of putting our experience into language is process-oriented and ongoing, as opposed to a static entity that somehow exists independently of us "languagers."

Similarly, Carlsen separates the word *meaning* into its component parts (mean + ing), highlighting its verb-ness and its process-oriented developmental roots.

Russell and Wandrei contrast the emerging expressivist view of language as creating worlds with the old positivist one of language as standing for a reality that exists prior to being spoken about. Interestingly, as mentioned earlier, they also reflect (consistently with the postmodern idea of boundaries as indistinct) that narrating implicates the listener as much as the narrator: that it changes the identity of both parties and that what we listen to as well as what we say tells a great deal about us. Far from agreeing with the modernist view of language as objective and denotative, these authors direct our attention to the phenomenon of *performative* sentences (for example, the exchange of wedding vows), which by their very utterance create particular events. Russell and Wandrei further maintain that the interpersonal act of languaging is what constructs us and our ideas of selves. Of course, the narrative tendency they speak of—our drive to construct a coherent story for the disembodied facts of our existence—is perhaps *the* hallmark of all of us as humans. (They also use the metaphor of threads that I, too, have employed here, speaking of stories as "the symbolic threads that hold together the meanings we orient to and exchange in our everyday lives.")

Saari also speaks of the unfortunate linguistic-affective phenomenon whereby individuals, through their socially cued use of appropriate emotion words at the appropriate times, may fool others (perhaps even themselves) into thinking they are having a particular emotional experience (for example, remorse) when they are, in fact, capable only of *discussing* that emotion owing to their poorly differentiated inner experience. That is why, in Saari's opinion, the repeated experiences in particular contexts of hearing and understanding certain emotion-based words is an important developmental occurrence for clients if they are to better link their own internal experiences to these words (compare also Watson and Greenberg). She views the individual's capacity to represent his or her inner experience through language as a necessary condition for psychological health, and this capacity results from the individual's involvement in social experience, including affective attunement with others. Such involvement permits the development of a very differentiated yet integrated idea of self.

Again, authors such as Friedman warn against therapy that becomes mired in problem-focused talk and thus leads to an emphasis on clients' difficulties rather than the clients' often common exceptions to these difficulties; the study of these exceptions is much more likely to lead to the accomplishment of a client's goals. Efran and Greene and also Watzlawick note the similar problems inherent in transposing vocabulary from medicine into the arena of mental health; this type of languaging may create rather than resolve difficulties because it transports presuppositions of maladaptation into the field of mental health. As Watzlawick points out, language creates certain realities in the field of mental health as well as more generally.

Neimeyer uses the intriguing metaphor of therapy as "sculpting conversational realities," referring to the co-construction that occurs between client and therapist as coequals in the process of meaning-making. In McNamee's view, therapy and language intersect in the very aim of psychotherapy, which is to offer conversational opportunities, a place to explore multiple ways of meaning-making, none of which will be dismissed summarily.

Watson and Greenberg note that language and other symbolic representations of inner experience allow clients to make better meaning of their worlds. Moreover, the way inner experience is translated into words provokes change in the experience itself, altering how the individual feels that experience and how he or she reacts to it behaviorally. Each different way of symbolizing the experience will emphasize some aspects of the event while submerging others.

There is an interesting paradox in postmodern therapy: language is simultaneously the problem (when the client uses it to define himself or herself and the problem in a particular way) and the route to the solution. Client and therapist co-construct the problem and its solution, but must to some extent use language to do so (O'Hanlon & Wilk, 1987). Often it is the problem construction itself that needs to be negotiated. O'Hanlon and Wilk (1987), for example, relate a humorous anecdote of a Jay Haley supervisee who was hopelessly mired with a family because of the insoluble way he had defined the problem (as a symbiotic enmeshment between two members of the family). Haley is reported to have remarked that he would never have let that be the problem.

Are Some Ways of Meaning-Making Better Than Others?

No one way of making meaning is correct in any absolute sense. Some theorists in the field (for example, Watzlawick) would likely even challenge the notion that some ways of constructing reality are better than others. Yet other theorists (for example, Carlsen) maintain that there are better ways of understanding: those that lead us all to higher human potential. Likewise, the cognitive-developmental constructivists (see Rosen and also Selman, Brion-Meisels, and Wilkins) suggest that there are clear advantages to having access to higher levels of meaning-making (even if one does not always use or *need* to use them). The capacity to make coherent meaning within a particular social context enables the individual to better negotiate his or her world, to better predict the reactions of others, and what he or she can accomplish toward his or her goals. It is with this awareness that some constructivists (following the lead of Piaget), have been doing research in the area of meaning-making.

Constructivism and Research

One of the criticisms made against constructivism and other meaning-making psychotherapy approaches by mainstream psychology has been their deemphasis on research. However, Russell and Wandrei argue that narrative theory, for example, does have important contributions to make in the arena of research. They maintain that one can determine much about a person's functioning by the various ways (for example, complexity, representation of subjectivity) he or she constructs narratives. Giving examples of ways in which evaluation of clients' narrative competencies already informs therapists' knowledge of how these clients are likely to negotiate problems in their lives, Russell and Wandrei note that, nevertheless, narrative theory is underutilized in research. Their observations about the value of narrative theory remind me of one of my first experiences of administering the Thematic Apperception Tests to a schizophrenic woman. In keeping with Maturana's notions that the perceptual system is essentially a closed system with its own structural properties, the output of which is undetermined by external events (see Efran and Greene), the client constructed ten narratives, all culminating in a lesbian rape scene, as I somewhat quizzically displayed each successive card and asked her to tell me what was going on in the picture. Clearly, she had a closed system capable of producing essentially one narrative from whatever stimulus (boy staring at a violin, for example) that I presented to her.

Russell and Wandrei also reveal some intriguing new research differentiating heroin from cocaine addicts on the basis of their disparate narrative tendencies: closing down versus opening up experience, respectively. This finding may assist us in better understanding and therefore matching therapeutic approaches to the various needs of clients who experience drug addiction.

Development of Meaning-Making Competency in Relationships

Selman, Brion-Meisels, and Wilkins highlight the importance of developing basic social skills to better negotiate within the social milieu. These skills include meaning-making skills in relationships and an associated behavioral repertoire (in contrast to mere stereotyped response). One skill is the ability to discuss and reflect on one's own behavior; this is a metacognitive skill. Another is social perspective taking, which enables one individual to take the point of view of another, even when it differs from his or her own. By discussing the importance of interpersonal negotiation strategies, Selman, Brion-Meisels, and Wilkins hope to give readers a framework for better understanding children's and adolescents' social behavior.

Neimeyer notes that constructions are valued for their utility more than validity and that it is their predictive power that is critical, one reason why perspective-taking competence is so important. The ability to predict another's internal and external reactions is key in creating adaptive social relations.

Nunley and Averill talk, also, of the importance of certain emotional competencies in rendering fuller lives for people. An individual with alexithymia (a poor ability to identify and label his or her emotional experience), for example, is likely to live a very constricted life and to have limited ability to cope with dysphoria.

Again, as Watson and Greenberg remark, the ability to describe and externalize one's internal experience is key to not being imprisoned in it. And as other authors comment, increased personal adaptability results when the individual acquires a more differentiated view of self and other (learning, for example, that he or she has options beyond fight or flight or that a person can be simultaneously loving and angry toward another).

What Selman, Brion-Meisels, and Wilkins do, we should note, is not to predict how the adolescent boys they studied would *actually behave* interpersonally but to understand better how each boy *frames* interpersonal dilemmas and goes about achieving resolutions to them. Such research gives therapists a sense of the interpersonal competency ranges of each boy.

In Selman, Brion-Meisels, and Wilkins's research, developmentally lower-level interpersonal stages of understanding are associated with certain self-schemas: helplessness when it comes to influencing the behavior of others, in one example. It is interesting to consider the effects of similar meaning-making processes in entire groups of individuals, as Goldberger does in noting the pernicious effects when certain voices are disqualified by the larger society.

It is clear that there are major advantages to individuals' having more differentiated schemes for understanding certain constructs in the interpersonal sphere achieved by relationships that are co-constructed and that there is room for negotiation of the boundaries and meanings generated by certain actions. Recall how Jerry, the most sophisticated seeming of the three adolescents discussed by Selman, Brion-Meisels, and Wilkins, is capable of viewing a hypothetical interpersonal dilemma at a systemic level, able to simultaneously coordinate the perspectives of all the characters in the dilemma: the boy, the counselor, and the counselor's supervisors. Selman, Brion-Meisels, and Wilkins would seem to agree with Watson and Greenberg about the need for individuals to verbalize their feelings to better understand and give order to them.

Meaning-Making Psychotherapies and Managed Care

Managed care companies typically view psychological problems as existing almost apart from the individual and his or her meaning-making structures, thus perpetuating to an enormous extent the modernist worldview delineated by McNamee. The paradigms of these companies often imply, if not outright claim, that psychological difficulties exist independently, fit neatly into categories, and are to be controlled by certain discoverable, easily implementable technologies that are procedure-specific. I have wondered how likely they are to appreciate and understand the utility of approaches that are not readily cast into a manual of techniques, have less empirical research supporting them (at least to date), and are somewhat harder to define than modernist approaches. Yet the therapists and theorists collected here have noted the inextricability of their clients' problems from a fabric woven from meaning-making. This meaning-making has created and maintained the problems and also impeded possible solutions. For an instructive analogy, I point to the failures of modernist discourse–driven medicine, which have recently forced increasing understandings of the rich interconnections between psychological, cultural, biological, and environmental factors in disease processes where once purely biological factors were studied (Garrett, 1994). The ultimate utility of meaning-making approaches is a question that remains to be answered, but I believe that managed care organizations will eventually adopt meaning-making as an overarching metatheory for all types of psychotherapy.

Conclusion

The meaning-making approaches delineated in the preceding chapters offer exciting new perspectives for psychotherapists of all schools and backgrounds. By providing a metatheory for making sense of phenomena of interest to all of us as therapists and theorists, the meaning-making paradigm can inform our work across our diverse schools. While many of the notions sketched out here will unsettle and challenge us, that perturbation can serve as a compelling impetus for us to explore and create further meanings, as we continue to weave a socially constructed, and exciting, tapestry of our ongoing experience. It is my hope that this book will serve as a foundation for further investigation of what it means to us and to our clients to be meaning-makers, open to multiverses of possibility and wonder.

References

Beck, A. T., Rush, A. J., Shaw, B. F., & Emery, G. (1979). *Cognitive therapy of depression*. New York: Guilford Press.

Dorpat, T. L., & Miller, M. L. (1992). *Clinical interaction and the analysis of meaning: A new psychoanalytic theory*. Hillsdale, NJ: Analytic Press.

Ellis, A. (1989). Rational-emotive therapy. In R. J. Corsini & D. Wedding (Eds.), *Current psychotherapies* (4th ed., pp. 197–238). Itasca, IL: Peacock.

Garrett, L. (1994). *The coming plague: Newly emerging diseases in a world out of balance*. New York: Farrar, Straus & Giroux.

Gergen, K. J. (1991). *The saturated self: Dilemmas of identity in contemporary life*. New York: Basic Books.

Kegan, R. (1982). *The evolving self*. Cambridge, MA: Harvard University Press.

Neimeyer, R. A. (1993). *Constructivist psychotherapy*. In K. T. Kuehlwein & H. Rosen (Eds.), *Cognitive therapies in action: Evolving innovative practice* (pp. 268–300). San Francisco: Jossey-Bass.

O'Hanlon, B., & Wilk, J. (1987). *Shifting contexts: The generation of effective psychotherapy*. New York: Guilford Press.

Polster, E., & Polster, M. (1973). *Gestalt therapy integrated*. New York: Brunner/Mazel.

Rosen, H. (1985). *Piagetian dimensions of clinical relevance*. New York: Columbia University Press.

Sondheim, S., & Lapine, J. (1987). *Into the woods*. New York: Theatre Communications Group.

Young, J. E. (1990). *Cognitive therapy for personality disorders: A schema-focused approach*. Sarasota, FL: Professional Resources Exchange.

Name Index

• •

Subject Index

• •